THE
WINERIES
OF BRITISH COLUMBIA

THE WINERIES
OF BRITISH COLUMBIA

COMPLETELY REVISED AND UPDATED

JOHN SCHREINER

whitecap

Edited by Elaine Jones; revised edition by Naomi Pauls
Proofread by Joan E. Templeton
Cover design by Mauve Pagé
Interior design by Margaret Lee / bamboosilk.com
Interior typesetting by Mauve Pagé
Maps by Eric Leinberger

Printed in Canada by Friesens

LIBRARY AND ARCHIVES CANADA CATALOGUING IN PUBLICATION

Schreiner, John, 1936–

    The wineries of British Columbia / John Schreiner. — Completely rev. and updated.
Includes index.

ISBN 978-1-55285-983-4

    1. Wineries—British Columbia—Guidebooks. 2. Wine and wine making—British Columbia. I. Title.

TP559.C3S36 2009   663'.2009711   C2008-905592-6

The publisher acknowledges the financial support of the Government of Canada through the Book Publishing Industry Development Program (BPIDP) and the Province of British Columbia through the Book Publishing Tax Credit.

09 10 11 12 13   5 4 3 2 1

FOR DR. BERNARD HOETER, A MAN OF MANY ACCOMPLISHMENTS: HONORARY consul of Guatemala in Western Canada from 1964 to 2003; secretary of the Society of Notaries Public of British Columbia from 1969 to 1986; a member of virtually every Vancouver wine society; and a widely published wine writer. Bernard was among the earliest champions of British Columbia wines with his 1971 thesis (for an oenology diploma) titled "Vines and Wines of Western Canada: The Story of British Columbia's Wine Industry." Succeeding generations of wine writers have been proud to walk in his erudite footsteps.

LIST OF WINERIES

INTRODUCTION: THE GOLD RUSH

I HAVE BEEN WRITING ABOUT BRITISH COLUMBIA WINES FOR MORE THAN 30 years, and there should be no more surprises. However, researching this third edition of *The Wineries of British Columbia* provided many surprises, including how dramatic the expansion of the industry has been. The readers of this book will discover many wineries they have never heard of before. This, along with significant changes among established wineries, is the major reason why it was imperative to write a third edition only six years after the second edition. The latter profiled 118 producers; this edition includes about 200.

There has been a ninefold increase in the area under vine in British Columbia since the 1988 pullout left a rump of about 566 hectares (1,400 acres) of vineyard. The 2008 vineyard census sponsored by the British Columbia Wine Institute found 3,626 hectares (9,000 acres) of vineyard. The census also projected that a further 600 hectares (1,500 acres) will be planted by 2010.

When the census was done in mid-2008, there were 144 licensed grape wineries and at least 20 proposed wineries, up from 90 licensed grape wineries in 2004. This does not include the burgeoning number of fruit wineries, cideries, meaderies, and Canada's only sake producer. The 200 producers, including those under active development, is an astonishing number: there were only 14 wineries in British Columbia in 1988. The prevailing view then was that some of those would fail after the free trade agreement ripped away the protected status of Canadian wine against imported wine. On the contrary, the industry's success has led to a gold rush that has driven up land prices, grape prices, and, ultimately, wine prices.

In 1988 no one would have believed that an Okanagan Shiraz would be judged the best Shiraz in an international competition in London in 2006, better than

Australian entries. Or that numerous Okanagan wines would consistently score best of class at rigorous national and international competitions. The BC wine industry today has won international respect. The proof is in the number of foreign-born winemakers who have chosen to make their careers here rather than in Australia, France, the United States, or Germany.

The watershed was the pullout after the 1988 harvest. Prior to that, there were 1,418 hectares (3,500 acres) under vine, primarily in the Okanagan and Similkameen Valleys. Eight of the 10 most widely planted varieties were hybrids. Okanagan Riesling, a grape of uncertain origin, accounted for almost a quarter of the total vine population but produced mediocre wine that could never compete on a world stage. To help the industry adjust to free trade, government paid growers to remove the hybrids. Government also removed the restrictions on importing vinifera vines from France.

Many old-time growers took the money and sold their vineyards, which remained fallow for the next five years. But when consumers perceived the big jump in the quality of BC wine being made from the vinifera that remained in the vineyards, a new generation of growers was encouraged to start replanting, this time with vinifera. One of the first was Sumac Ridge founder Harry McWatters. In 1993 he bought a fallow vineyard on Black Sage Road and put in the largest single block of vinifera (40 hectares/100 acres) that had ever been planted in Canada to that time. The Merlot from the first harvest in 1995 was the top red wine in a national competition a few years later. That was one of several medals for BC wines in the 1990s that began to validate the Okanagan as the best wine-growing terroir in Canada.

The other validation has been the growth of wine sales. The Vintners Quality Alliance was established in 1990, with a taste panel to screen wines and with a budget to help market them. In the 1991–92 fiscal year (ending in March), VQA wine sales were $6.8 million. In the 2007–08 fiscal year, VQA sales totalled $156.7 million. That figure understates total sales of British Columbia wine by at least $50 million because a significant number of wineries operate outside the VQA umbrella. Clearly a major industry has emerged, with impacts reaching far beyond the wine sales. Numerous support businesses have developed around the wine industry, including a barrel maker, several tank manufacturers, two operators of mobile bottling lines, operators of custom harvesting machines, many premium restaurants and resorts, and at least a dozen wine tour companies.

BC wines enjoy enviable customer loyalty, even as wine prices have risen. There is no serious restaurant in the province without a good BC wine list (unlike what one finds in Ontario). Some restaurants list *only* BC wines. Many wineries sell out each year, especially those with cult followings. In 2008 the Black Hills Estate Winery boasted that its 3,300-case release of its flagship Nota Bene sold out in 47 minutes. In some recent vintages, production has outstripped demand in British

Columbia. All this means is that, finally, there is enough wine to deal with the pent-up demand on the Prairies and beyond.

As satisfying as all this success is, it has spawned a gold rush mentality. Vineyard land in British Columbia, especially in the Okanagan where 84 percent of the plantings are, is now as costly as premium sites in California. Harry McWatters paid about $3,000 per acre for the Black Sage Road property in 1993. The Black Hills winery, based on a nearby vineyard, changed hands in 2007 at a price that put a value on the vineyard of $153,676 per acre. Land values like that have become a barrier to anyone but the wealthy entering the wine industry. They are also becoming an impediment to selling when owners want to retire. High land costs mean high grape costs, which, in turn, drive high wine prices. The average price of a VQA wine in 2008 was $18 a bottle, up from $13 a decade earlier. Icon wines, which admittedly are more expensive to make, sell for $50 a bottle and up. Other emerging New World wine regions have seen similar trends, of course.

The enthusiasm for wine has led to wineries opening in areas off the beaten path, from the Kootenays in southeastern British Columbia to the Gulf Islands. A few of the vintners have gone there in search of cheaper land. In most instances they like where they live, they like wine, and they see no reason why they need to live somewhere else to make wine. The northernmost winery on the Gulf Islands, SouthEnd Farm Vineyards on Quadra Island, is opening on the family farm where Ben McGuffie and his forebears have lived for 60 or 70 years.

While the Okanagan is almost fully planted, there is still room in the Similkameen Valley and in non-traditional regions where vineyards have sprung up over the past decade. Climate change, while impacting negatively on available irrigation water, may be opening new possibilities. In 2008 businessmen Ed and Jeff Collett started developing the first major vineyard on the South Thompson River east of Kamloops. Until now it had been thought that winter temperatures here were low enough to kill vinifera grapevines. Thirty years ago that was also thought to be true for the South Okanagan. Only time will tell whether the Collett brothers or the other vintners pioneering off the beaten path are opening new vineyard regions for an exciting wine industry.

One thing is certain: British Columbia wines, which were not much more than a risible notion a generation ago, have now won international respect.

ACES WINE GROUP

OPENING PROPOSED FOR 2009

> 1309 Smethurst Road, PO Box 40, Naramata, BC VOH 1NO
> www.aceswine.ca
> When to visit: Wine shop to be established in future

RECOMMENDED

POCKET KINGS

THE FIRST BOTTLE OF WINE THAT HOLGER CLAUSEN ACQUIRED, A 1982 Sumac Ridge Gewürztraminer, sits unopened on his mantel. He was 14 when he won it from his father in a chess game. Since then, poker has become his game of choice. The Aces Wine Group brings together his twin passions for wine and Texas hold'em poker in a unique approach to marketing wines.

Holger was born in Summerland in 1969. After growing up on an orchard, he studied natural resources science at the University College of the Cariboo. He hints that some of his student loan money was "invested" at the poker table. "I graduated cum laude in Texas hold'em poker," he says. "I spent a lot of money educating myself in poker, and it is paying off, there is no question." He spent a few years after school working in the forest industry before finding his way into the wine business.

"When I turned 21 and was legal to drink, I toured the Napa Valley," Holger says. "That's really when I fell in love with the industry. I have been there several times since." On the same trip, he also took in the casinos at Las Vegas. "The bright lights and the big city, that got me." In 2002 he conceived combining his two passions in a winery. The poker boom was just beginning in North America. Holger watched it develop, often as a tournament player himself, and nursed his idea until he believed the time was right.

Now the most popular form of poker, Texas hold'em (according to *Wikipedia*) was invented in Texas in the early 1900s. It was introduced to Las Vegas in 1967 by a group of Texan card players and soon became the main event when poker tournaments were inaugurated. After growing slowly, the popularity of the game exploded in the first decade of this century when television began covering the tournaments. The 2003 World Series of Poker was covered by a sports channel. The winner of the first prize, $2.5 million, was an amateur player with the improbable (but real) name of Chris Moneymaker. Since then the number of players of Texas hold'em, and the prize money, have both grown exponentially. Holger intends to capture this demographic with wines whose labels feature poker hands. The icewine, for example, has eights on the label because poker players refer to eights as snowmen.

Holger's entry into the wine business was more prosaic. In 1999 he purchased a French-made grape harvester (he now has two) and established a custom harvesting business in the Okanagan. In the off-season he worked with custom harvesters in Australia. Naturally, he also played poker there. "In Melbourne they have a great poker room in the Crown Casino," he says. "It is one of my favourite places to play."

In late 2007 a realtor asked Holger to assess the vineyard potential of a property in Osoyoos. Holger said he would prefer to have a vineyard on the Naramata Bench. Sure enough, the realtor had one there as well, but too expensive for Holger. Then Holger outlined his idea for Aces Wine Group and the realtor became the first of Holger's three partners. "That year I made about $36,000 in ring games, which is cash games, and I used that to start this project," he says.

The idea was to establish a successful wine brand first and invest in vineyards and a winery later. Holger began calling on wineries around the Okanagan, looking for good-quality bulk wine. In the summer of 2008 he was able to acquire about nine hundred cases of red wine (Bordeaux varieties and Syrah) that consulting winemaker Philip Soo had made the previous vintage for Black Sage Road grape grower Ron Fournier. Ron had planned a winery called Lavender Ridge but shelved the project when financing proved difficult. The wines were made for Ron at the Adora custom winery. The winemaker there, Jason Parkes, finished those wines and made the 2008 vintage for Aces. Holger intends to establish a small winery for Aces on a friend's vineyard near Naramata.

"We're building a market for our wine before we spend the money on land and buildings," Holger says. "We are not buying an existing vineyard." In addition to investing in wine inventory, Aces engaged Vancouver marketing whiz Bernie Hadley-Beauregard to develop labels that speak instantly to poker players.

"There are a lot of angles and spins that we can use," Holger believes. "What is true to the poker world is true in the wine world. Every year Mother Nature deals the vineyards and the winemakers a different hand. Poker players are dealt a different hand all the time as well."

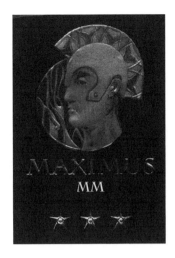

ADORA ESTATE WINERY

OPENED: 2003

16414 Highway 97, Summerland, BC V0H 1Z6
250.404.4200 | 1.866.404.9463 (toll free)
www.adorawines.com
When to visit: Open daily 11 am – 7 pm May through October

RECOMMENDED

CURRENT RANGE NOT TASTED

BY LETTING OTHER VINTNERS RENT SPACE AND WINEMAKING EQUIPMENT IN Adora's cellars, Reid Jenkins has likely launched more new wineries than anyone else in the Okanagan. Custom crushing was rare in the Okanagan before Adora opened. Shared winemaking is common in California and the logic is obvious: it allows winemakers to get established without sinking millions into ego-satisfying wineries of their own.

The model developed by Adora has worked so well that, in 2008, Reid, who had been turning away clients, began building an 1,100-square-metre (12,000-square-foot) facility more than double the size of his initial winery. He will end up with a better facility that includes an underground cellar, an efficient gravity-flow design, and a highway-frontage location just a few hundred yards from popular Sumac Ridge Estate Winery.

The original Adora was also beside the highway, on a speed-restricted curve south of Summerland. The plain Jane industrial structure was functional enough and continues as the winery for 8th Generation Vineyard. A business breakup between the initial partners in Adora, Reid and Kevin Golka, triggered the sale of the building to 8th Generation. Adora took up temporary quarters for the 2007 and 2008 vintages in a former packing house south of Oliver while the new Adora was being built on a former Summerland orchard, now a four-hectare (10-acre) vineyard with Viognier and Riesling and three varieties for sparkling wine.

The soft-spoken Reid was born in New Westminster in 1970. He became interested in the Okanagan in the mid-1990s when he owned a Vancouver company that created the websites for Sumac Ridge and Hawthorne Mountain Vineyards (see See Ya Later Ranch, page 368), some of the Okanagan wine industry's earliest websites. Hawthorne Mountain's winemaker at the time was Eric von Krosigk. Reid, Kevin, and Eric conceived the Adora project in 1999. When Eric left the group to join another winery, Tilman Hainle and then Jason Parkes, who also composes and plays rock music, took over as Adora's director of winemaking.

Typical of the wineries that have used Adora over the years is Calliope Vintners. It was started in 2001 by a foursome that included winemakers Ross and Cherie Mirko. Reluctant to take on the debt that would come with building a winery, the partners initially rented space at Thornhaven Estates winery, then moved to Adora when that facility opened. Calliope's wines were well received; the brand was wound up in 2005 only because the Mirkos moved to New Zealand, where both have family, to continue their wine careers.

Other clients have included wineries on Vancouver Island and the Gulf Islands, such as Pender Island's Morning Bay Vineyard & Estate Winery, that source some of their grapes in the Okanagan. While grapes can be shipped from the interior to the coast (and have been in the past), it is always best to make the wines close to the vineyard. Adora's winemakers craft the wines the clients desire and also guide distant winery owners, such as Morning Bay's Keith Watt, with on-site winemaking.

Adora's own production is about four thousand cases per year. With the winery's move in 2008, Adora also changed its winemaking philosophy. The initial releases, big reds and complex white blends, were deliberately aged longer than usual before being sold — two to four years. The style was contentious. Although some of Adora's fans bought wines by the case, others found the style out of step with current tastes. In the new winery Adora has made what Reid calls a fresh start by offering both young, fruit-forward wines as well as the sophisticated blends originally conceived.

Another carryover from the former winery was the insistence on using really good stemware in the tasting room. "There is nothing worse," Reid asserts, "than a dinky little glass that you can't get your nose into or swirl the wine in." Tasting with Reid is especially memorable because of his remarkably evocative wine vocabulary. Here is how he once described a Pinot Noir that had aged 28 months in French oak before release: "It is sort of dried strawberries, violets, little bit of cedar. It moves into raspberries, cassis, and currants and then finishes like espresso bean and candied cranberry."

ALDERLEA VINEYARDS

OPENED: 1998

1751 Stamps Road, Duncan, BC V9L 5W2
250.746.7122
When to visit: By appointment

RECOMMENDED

PINOT NOIR
CLARINET
FUSION
VIOGNIER
PINOT GRIS
HEARTH

"GOOFY STUFF." THAT IS HOW ROGER DOSMAN TALKS ABOUT GRAPE VARIETIES that have come and gone in Alderlea's 3.25-hectare (eight-acre) vineyard since he first planted it in 1994. To hear him, it sounds like patient trial and error. There was precious little guidance for growing grapes in Vancouver Island's marginal climate when Roger started. Weeding out the goofy stuff — varieties like Dunkelfelder and Agria — has made him a lot wiser and helped his peers avoid (if they sought his advice) planting oddball varieties in their own vineyards.

It also led Alderlea to commit a quarter of its vineyard to the varieties developed by Swiss plant breeder Valentin Blattner. Canada's first commercial Blattner wine was Alderlea's Fusion, released in 2008. The vines that yield Fusion are a cross of Cabernet Sauvignon and Maréchal Foch. The plants resist disease, ripen well within the island's restricted growing season, and produce a full-bodied red that tastes a lot like Cabernet Sauvignon — a *European* Cabernet, not a New World one, which, Roger believes, adds to the appeal of the Blattner variety wines. "That's what

I like about them," he says. "They are going to bring a different flavour profile to the industry." And Alderlea is on the leading edge.

It has been quite a journey for a man who was educated as a town planner. Born in Vancouver in 1948, he never practised as a planner because he took over his father's auto body repair shop in 1976, running it successfully for a dozen years. It was a way of making money, he said later, but not a way to make a living. In 1988 he and Nancy, his wife, began scouting for a career with a more appealing quality of life and not located in a big city. That they chose the wine industry speaks to Roger's penchant for contrary thinking. With the advent of free trade, the Canadian wine industry was being written off by many. Roger's view? "In fact," he said at the time with great foresight, "it's just begun."

After looking for property in the Okanagan and on the Sunshine Coast, the Dosmans bought on a quiet dead-end road just north of Duncan, the Cowichan Valley city originally called Alderlea. Trees were cleared from the south-facing slope, vines were ordered, and planting began in 1994. Initially the largest blocks were Bacchus, Siegerrebe, and Auxerrois, along with a trial plot with about 30 varieties. This vineyard has supported estate-grown wines ever since the winery opened in 1998. "My commitment is to use only estate-grown fruit," Roger says. "It always has been that and always will be. That's just me. Quite frankly, I think I make some very distinct wines."

Over the past decade he sorted out what works best for Alderlea and has discarded what he discovered were those "goofy varieties." They included Dunkelfelder, which, in addition to making mediocre but dark red wines, is one of several German vines — Bacchus is another — susceptible to mildew that is controlled with chemical sprays. No farmer likes to spray, and especially not if, as is the case at Alderlea, he and his family live among the vines. "I'd never plant them again in a hundred years," Roger says.

For a few years he had a brief fling with Agria, a Hungarian red variety yielding dark and gamey reds too coarse for Alderlea's style. Even worse, the vines grow in a wild tangle. Roger is a man of orderly, organized habits; the vines in his vineyard line up like cadets on parade. Agria was banished.

The same fate befell Auxerrois and Siegerrebe, but for different reasons. Both grow well on Vancouver Island. Siegerrebe is one of the first varieties to ripen. Unfortunately, the spicy aroma and flavour that make the wine so appealing also bring swarms of wasps into the vineyard, where they pierce the skins of the grapes to get at the juice. Damaged bunches rot and wasps hang around to feed on the other grapes as they ripen. During one very heavy infestation, Roger used a hand-held vacuum cleaner to suck wasps from the bunches. He decided it was more practical to replace Siegerrebe with later-ripening Gewürztraminer and to plant more Pinot Gris.

Auxerrois has never become fashionable even though it makes appealing white wines, both on its own and blended with Chardonnay. The wine never commands the price of, as an example, Alderlea's Viognier, a variety in high esteem among consumers. Wineries as small as Alderlea, which makes between 1,800 and 2,000 cases a year, will not support their owners by making inexpensive wines. "We have to average at least $20 a bottle, which we are doing now," Roger says. "That is just the long and the short of it. You have to make wine that you can sell for that price. If not, then you have got a problem."

Over the years, as he separated the performing vines from the non-performers, Roger has turned Alderlea primarily into a producer of reds. Very early in developing the vineyard, he planted Maréchal Foch. That French hybrid has proved one of the most reliable vines on Vancouver Island, easily managed in the vineyard and yielding rich, plummy reds. Alderlea created the name "Clarinet" for its Foch, to distance this well-made wine from the badly grown Foch wines of the 1980s. "It's a great wine," he believes. "This is the grape for Vancouver Island. If you learn how to grow it and how to make wine from it, it will knock your socks off."

Like many island wineries, Alderlea grows Pinot Noir, a variety in high demand, and has established a good reputation for its wine. "Everybody wants to do Pinot Noir," Roger notes. "Well, Pinot Noir is marginal here, unless you have the best grower in a very good location." Along with Venturi-Schulze Vineyards, Alderlea was one of the first island wineries to tent its Pinot Noir each spring, creating a minigreenhouse by covering the budding vines with plastic for a few weeks. He tested tenting in 2000 with his small Viognier block and, finding that it advanced the maturity of the fruit by about two weeks, went on to tent most of his Pinot Noir. The higher sugars and better flavours that result make a big difference in the final product.

The Blattner reds, however, seem capable of yielding interesting red wines without quite as much struggle as Pinot Noir. Roger is dedicating a quarter of his vineyard to these varieties, with confidence in their promise. But after a decade and a half of weeding out goofy varieties, he cautions: "I will tell you more in five years."

ANTELOPE RIDGE ESTATE WINERY

OPENED: 1994 (AS DOMAINE COMBRET)

32057 #13 Road, PO Box 1170, Oliver, BC V0H 1T0
250.498.6966 | 1.866.TERROIR (toll free)
www.anteloperidge.com
When to visit: By appointment

RECOMMENDED

EQUILIBRIUM
CABERNET FRANC
CABERNET SAUVIGNON
MERLOT
OLD VINES CHARDONNAY

IT IS RARE FOR AN OWNER TO CHANGE A WINERY'S NAME WITHOUT SELLING, BUT that is what Olivier Combret did in 2006. In 1992 when he and his parents arrived from France, where the Combrets had been making wine since 1638, they naturally attached the family name to their new Okanagan winery.

"Domaine Combret means the house or the estate of Combret, which is my family name," Olivier explains. But, he adds, "We have to remember that Canada is not a traditional wine country. The people have absolutely no clue as to what the word 'Domaine' means." Complicating his effort to secure a profile in the wine market, another French vintner had opened Domaine de Chaberton in the Fraser Valley about the same time. The two wineries were always getting inquiries meant for the other.

"In 2002 I said, 'That's it, we've got to do something here,'" Olivier recalls. "I decided to change the name." He trademarked several choices around the word "Antelope" before finally settling on Antelope Ridge. He also used the winery's relaunch to change the style of its reds. The Antelope Ridge reds have more power and richness than most previous Domaine Combret reds. Some, such as Equilibrium, are built in the classic French style to reach their peak development with cellar aging. He describes Equilibrium, a blend of red Bordeaux varieties, as a *vin de garde — garder* meaning "to keep." "Like any good Bordeaux, you are going to cellar this," he says. "People should not rush."

The Combrets chose the Okanagan over other New World wine regions because Olivier's father, Robert, already knew the amazing "Mediterranean valley" after having spent the summer of 1958 there while getting his master's degree in agriculture from the University of British Columbia. Olivier, who was born in 1971, began working with his father in the vineyards at the age of 12. Olivier was in his final year at the Montpellier wine school in 1991 when the family accepted an attractive unsolicited offer for their winery, Château Petit Sonnailler.

"We have fantastic climatic conditions eight years out of 10 in the Okanagan Valley," Olivier says. "The wineries that are going to make top wines in 10 years out of 10 will be those with the perfect sites. And there are not that many in BC." He believes their hillside property on the Golden Mile is one of those top sites. With exquisite contrarian timing, they arrived when the Okanagan was still depressed after two-thirds of the vineyards had been pulled out four years earlier. Virtually everything was on sale. The Combrets bought 31.5 hectares (78 acres) that included six hectares (15 acres) already producing Chardonnay, Riesling, and Cabernet Franc. They ordered vines from France, planting about half the area. The other half remained bare for 15 years until they sold it to Donald Triggs, the founder of Jackson-Triggs, who is developing a new winery next door to Antelope Ridge.

The Antelope Ridge winery, which Olivier designed shortly after graduating from wine school, was the Okanagan's first true gravity winery. It nestles into the hillside, allowing wines to flow gently by gravity throughout the process, from crushing the grapes at the winery's upper level to bottling the wine at the bottom level. It has more than enough capacity for the five thousand cases of wine currently produced here.

Initially the Combret Chardonnay and Riesling wines won the greatest acclaim. (Domaine Combret was the first Canadian winery to win a medal at the Chardonnay du Monde competition in Burgundy.) "My first vintage was 1993," Olivier recalls. "My first red wine vintage was 1994. White wine to me was faster to master. Red wines, I had to basically find what kind of process was going to work. It took a while and I made my mistakes. Let's face it, when I came here, I was 21 years old."

He found his feet fully with the bold Antelope Ridge wines. "My wines before were complex but you can say they were like rough diamonds," he says. "Now the diamonds are shaped."

ARROWLEAF CELLARS

OPENED: 2003

1574 Camp Road, Lake Country, BC V4V 1K1
250.766.2992
www.arrowleafcellars.com
When to visit: Open daily 10:30 am – 5:30 pm May 1 to November 15. Picnic facilities

RECOMMENDED

GEWÜRZTRAMINER
PINOT GRIS
BACCHUS
CHARDONNAY
PINOT NOIR
SOLSTICE CHARDONNAY
SOLSTICE RESERVE
THE SNOW TROPICS

IT IS TOUGH BEING A "BORN FARMER" LIKE JOSEF ZUPPIGER WHEN ONE LIVES in Switzerland, where farms are tiny but very expensive. Born in 1950 near Zurich, Josef rented his father's small dairy farm and orchard for 12 years. In 1986, after it was sold, he brought his wife, Margrit, and their five children to Alberta, where they purchased a farm with about 80 dairy cattle.

It transpired that their children were not born dairy farmers. "I wanted to stay in agriculture," Josef says. "We travelled once to British Columbia, saw the vineyards, and liked it." With son Manuel, who was born in 1976, also showing an interest in viticulture, the Zuppigers sold the dairy farm and bought a producing vineyard in 1997. Josef had no experience with grapes, but he did not think growing them would be difficult. "Because I was an orchardist in Switzerland, I had an idea how to do it," he says. "I knew how to prune trees. I also learned it from books and took a course, so I knew how to do it."

Initially Josef sold his grapes to Gray Monk, the patron of the vineyard's first owner. But he realized that he would not prosper and support a family as a grape grower with a vineyard only 6.5 hectares (16 acres) in size. He believes a grower needs a minimum of eight hectares (20 acres) to earn a living from selling grapes. "I would even say a bit more," he suggests. "But when we have a winery with that acreage, I am sure we can make a living here." Accordingly, Manuel was enrolled in the three-year winemaking program at Wädenswil, Switzerland's leading wine school.

Arrowleaf is located on well-travelled Camp Road, a short drive west of the village of Winfield. The winery, a practical building designed by the Zuppigers, is perched at the end of a steep driveway. From the veranda of the compact tasting room, there is an attractive view of Okanagan Lake. The vineyard dips sharply southwest, ideal for catching the sunlight that reflects from the lake. A deep gully on the south side of the vineyard, while serving as a local ecological reserve, also assures excellent air drainage. There is little risk that freezing air will pool among the vines. The lean soil, comprised of sand, gravel, and rocks, ensures that the growth is not too vigorous. As a result Josef's grapes ripen easily, achieving full varietal flavours.

The original owner had established the vineyard in 1986 with Gewürztraminer, later adding Bacchus, Pinot Gris, and Auxerrois. The Zuppigers added Merlot and Zweigelt for their major red wines. To Manuel's disappointment, there was no room in the vineyard for Pinot Noir, a variety he had come to appreciate when he was in school in Switzerland. What little planting room remained was filled with a few vines of Dunkelfelder, an inky German red useful for blending. There also is some Vidal, both for icewine and for a popular off-dry white called the Snow Tropics, made with lightly frozen grapes.

Once the winery was established, Arrowleaf dealt with the winemaker's desire for Pinot Noir by finding contract growers. These include three vineyards at nearby Carr's Landing, one near Westbank, and one near Oliver. These sources provide Manuel with a palate for flavours with which he makes a vividly expressive Pinot Noir. Like all of Arrowleaf's wines, it is very fairly priced.

Manuel Zuppiger acquired solid winemaking experience at Wädenswil, where students spend most of the year apprenticing in wineries, with periodic breaks to study theory. "It's more practical," his father suggests. "A lot of people go to university and don't find out what hands-on really means." Manuel worked the 2001 vintage in the Barossa Valley with Grant Burge, one of Australia's most awarded winemakers. In British Columbia, he also worked briefly at Tinhorn Creek before beginning to make Arrowleaf's wines in 2001. Burge wanted him back in Australia for the 2002 vintage but, with the new winery under development, he could not spare the time to go.

The vintages Arrowleaf has released since opening in the spring of 2003 show that Manuel had learned his art well. Both the Merlot and the Zweigelt, from estate-grown grapes, are ripe, juicy wines. The Merlot is lightly burnished with oak. "There is a lighter structure to the fruit flavours in the northern Okanagan, so we don't want to drown it with oak," he says. "We basically focus on the fruit and complement it with a bit of oak." The crisply fruity whites are all aged in stainless steel tanks. The one exception among the winery's whites is the Chardonnay, partially barrel-fermented. Like all of Arrowleaf's dry white wines, the aromas and flavours of the fruit come through with refreshing purity.

"Manuel prefers more dry wines but we kind of persuaded him to make some a little sweeter, maybe, just because the customers may prefer it," Josef says with a chuckle. The winemaker leaves a touch of sweetness in the Bacchus; in White Feather, a fruity blend based primarily in Auxerrois and Pinot Blanc; and in Red Feather, the winery's quaffable rosé. The other whites are dry, depending on the intensity of the fruit flavours to appeal to those who demand off-dry wines. The Gewürztraminer, made from the true Alsace clone of this variety, is remarkable for its intense aroma and flavour.

The winery, with its picnic area, might be at its most attractive in the spring, when the surrounding slopes blaze yellow with the so-called Okanagan sunflower. This is the inspiration for the Arrowleaf name. The plant is balsam root, a perennial with bright yellow flowers and large leaves in the shape of arrowheads.

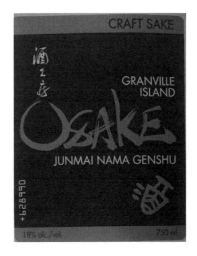

ARTISAN SAKEMAKER AT GRANVILLE ISLAND

OPENED: 2007

> 1339 Railspur Alley, Vancouver, BC V6H 4G9
> 604.685.7253
> www.artisansakemaker.com
> When to visit: Open 11:30 am – 6 pm Wednesday to Sunday

RECOMMENDED

> OSAKE JUNMAI NAMA GENSHU
> OSAKE JUNMAI NAMA
> OSAKE JUNMAI GINJO NAMA GENSHU
> OSAKE JUNMAI GINJO NAMA NIGORI GENSHU
> SPARKLING SAKE

LIKE A RESTAURANT WITH AN OPEN KITCHEN, MASA SHIROKI'S ENTIRE SAKE-making process is out in the open in this tiny Granville Island boutique. That is as it should be. This was Canada's first sake house when it opened in 2007. Even the minority who knew something about sake likely had never seen how this iconic Japanese rice wine is made. Masa, the soft-spoken, diminutive evangelist of sake, never tires of explaining the process.

He was born in Japan in 1950 into a family with "absolutely no connection" to sake production. Neither had Masa, for many years. After college he went to work in the Tokyo office of the Bank of Montreal, which transferred him to Montreal in 1974, even though he spoke no French. A capable banker, he was moved to the bank's main North Vancouver branch in 1976. A few years later he became an air cargo executive in Vancouver with Japan Airlines; then he set up his own import-export company, dealing in Japanese goods. Eventually he began running the Japan desk for the British Columbia Trade Development Corporation.

At this time Japan deregulated its beer industry, allowing small brewers to get into business. Masa helped Canadian makers of microbrewery equipment export to brewers in Japan. These included small sake producers, and Masa, following up on sales of the brewing equipment, got inside sake houses for the first time and started to develop his contacts in the industry.

In 2001 he established his own sake importing agency. "I wanted to do something that had a cultural base," he says. "I wanted to convey the true cultural sense of Japan." He settled on sake because, he says, tongue in cheek, "I don't do flower arrangements, I don't do tea ceremonies."

As an importer he began working closely with Japanese sake masters, absorbing both the passion and the art of sake. "I have been blessed with my contacts in Japan," he says. "Every time I go back there" — he still imports sake even though he now makes it here — "I go right onto the floor of the sake wineries and acquire training." When he had decided to make sake in Vancouver, it took him several years to negotiate a licence and to find his spot on Granville Island. This location makes his storefront accessible to the many consumers flocking to the bustling market every day. Equally important to him is the ambiance of Granville Island, a perfect fit for a craft sake maker.

Using polished rice imported from Japan, Masa bottled his first commercial sakes just before Christmas in 2006, a mere six hundred bottles. "I had no idea how much I should make," he admits. But when he opened the next month, sales were encouragingly brisk. He hurried to make additional batches. Unlike wine, it takes only two months from the start of fermentation to bottling a market-ready sake. Unable to keep up to demand, Masa jammed a second 1,000-litre (220-gallon) stainless steel fermentation tank into the storefront that serves as his sake house. In his first year he produced a total of seven thousand bottles, including his first sparkling sake, a hit during the 2007 holiday season. A bit surprised at how well he was doing, Masa started his second year in business by developing additional markets in Toronto and Montreal, with an eye to eventually tripling production.

Perhaps the secret of his Osake brand (which means "honourable sake") is its freshness. All of his products are unpasteurized or, as the labels say, *nama*. Restaurants and consumers are expected to keep the products refrigerated and to enjoy them young. Each batch of sake yields several styles of beverage. Some might consider the cream of each batch to be the clear Osake Junmai Genshu, with about 17 percent alcohol. This sake is rich in texture, with fruity aromas but a dry finish. Masa pairs it with strong cheese or red meat.

The equivalent of a white wine is achieved by adding water to reduce the alcohol a few degrees. This clear sake is Junmai, comparatively light and crisp. Masa pairs it with seafood. The third style, Junmai Nigori, is a deliberately cloudy beverage containing some of the rice lees, which contribute a creamy richness and a hint of sweetness.

Masa also makes, in small volume, a more complex grade of sake called Ginjo, which calls for highly milled rice and special yeast. Made in both clear and cloudy versions, this grade is sold in half bottles. With growing confidence in his craftsmanship, Masa might add a Daiginjo sake, made with even more highly milled rice. (Milling the polished rice allows more of the starch to be converted to alcohol during fermentation.) Ordinarily Daiginjo is the pinnacle of the sake maker's craft. Masa also has his eye on sparkling sake after having released several bottles of carbonated sake. "My goal ultimately would be a traditional-method sake, the same way Champagne is made," he says.

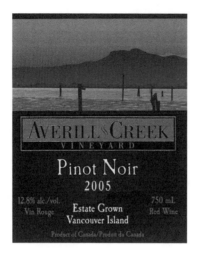

AVERILL CREEK VINEYARD

OPENED: 2006

> 6552 North Road, Duncan, BC V9L 6K9
> 250.709.9986
> www.averillcreek.ca
> When to visit: Open noon – 4 pm Thursday to Sunday plus holiday
>   Mondays during summer or by appointment

RECOMMENDED

PINOT NOIR
PINOT GRIS
PINOT GRIGIO
PREVOST

ANDY JOHNSTON'S HANDS TELL THE STORY. A COMPACT MAN WITH COILED-spring energy, he extends his vineyard-seasoned palms showing a farmer's callusing. They are no longer the hands of the doctor he was for 32 years before beginning his second career as a Vancouver Island wine grower. "That's why I am Andy, not Dr. Johnston," he says. "I knew a long time ago that I had only so much doctoring in me."

Born in Britain in 1947, he emigrated to Edmonton in 1973, three years after getting his medical degree. A general practitioner, Andy and a partner ultimately owned 24 walk-in medical clinics in Edmonton and Calgary. "To be a good doctor, you've got to be *one hundred percent* a doctor. You have got to be really committed to it. I knew I wasn't going to be, and there was a time coming when it was time for me to stop doing it. I planned an exit strategy, which is Averill Creek winery."

Andy is a serious wine connoisseur. He has been secretary of the Edmonton chapter of the Opimian Society (a national Canadian wine club), a member of the exclusive Commanderie de Bordeaux tasting group, and a collector of fine wines with a palate for 30-year-old clarets. He was also one of the investors in Hotel Villa Delia, Umberto Menghi's cooking school and winery in Tuscany. In 1998, when Andy disclosed his ambition to make wine, Menghi suggested he start by joining the team for Villa Delia's vintage that fall. "That was a great experience for me, in a small vineyard," Andy recalls. "That's where I discovered that I can do this."

Andy levered that vintage into a peripatetic wine apprenticeship. "I'm a kind of organized person," he suggests. "I didn't like sailing into this without any knowledge, so I spent the next four or five years working in vineyards and wineries around the world." One of the visitors to the Tuscan winery in 1998, noting the doctor's enthusiasm, helped him get a job in the next crush at a winery in Australia. There Andy worked with a French winemaker who found him a job the following vintage in a small Bordeaux château. Then, through a Vancouver doctor with shares in a New Zealand winery called Trinity Hill, Andy arranged to do several vintages in New Zealand. The winemaker who most influenced him was Larry McKenna, a partner at Escarpment Vineyard in Martinborough and one of New Zealand's leading proponents of Pinot Noir. "The way he makes wines made a big impression — the importance of not cutting corners and of doing everything right," says Andy, after doing a winemaking sabbatical there in 2004. Several Averill Creek vintages have been made by winemakers from New Zealand or trained in Australia. The 2008 vintage was made by Daniel Dragert, who was born in Saanichton in 1979 but did his graduate wine studies in New Zealand.

As obsessed with Pinot Noir as McKenna, Andy considered many options, including New Zealand, before settling on the Cowichan Valley for his vineyard. In 1999 he even came close to buying a property in Bordeaux with a producing vineyard and a character farmhouse. "My daughters vetoed that and said I was not allowed to leave Canada," Andy says and smiles. He concluded that the Okanagan might be too warm for Pinot Noir but believes that the Cowichan Valley, closer to the latitude of Dijon in Burgundy, has the soil and the sunshine to produce a fine Burgundian-style Pinot Noir.

There was another reason Andy chose the Cowichan Valley. "One of my hobbies and pleasures in life is sailing. So for me, then, it was Vancouver Island." In the fall of 2000, armed with soil maps of the Cowichan Valley, he began scouting properties. In February 2001 he came across contiguous treed properties, each about 18 hectares (45 acres), on the south-facing slope of Mount Prevost, north of Duncan. Andy bought the upper half. (A vineyard on the lower half is owned by Godfrey-Brownell Vineyards.)

Planting began at Averill Creek in 2002. (The name derives from a salmon-spawning creek that cuts through the eastern corner of the vineyard.) By the time Andy finished planting four years later, the 11-hectare (27-acre) vineyard was two-thirds committed to Pinot Noir and Pinot Gris, with modest plantings of Gewürztraminer and, perhaps his only mistake, some Merlot, which was later pulled out because it ripens poorly here. The vineyard includes three hectares (7½ acres) that are divided equally between Maréchal Foch and a disease-resistant Cabernet Foch cross developed by Swiss plant breeder Valentin Blattner and pioneered commercially by Roger Dosman at nearby Alderlea Vineyards. Both varieties reliably provide Vancouver Island vineyards with quality grapes even in cool, wet years.

The natural slope of Mount Prevost dictated the winery design, which Andy calls "Italian rustic." The building flows down the contour, so that Andy can use gravity to move the wines. "The way I've planned it, the Pinot Noir will not be pumped ever, from the time it is crushed to the time it goes in the bottle," Andy says. All wines benefit from gentle handling but none more so than Pinot Noir.

The winery is designed to process a maximum of 90 tonnes (100 tons) of grapes, producing about five thousand cases of wine per year. A significant amount of this is sold at the winery, which features a Tuscan-style patio and a glass-fronted tasting room with a breathtaking view over the Cowichan Valley and well beyond. "I can see the planes landing at Sydney," says the sharp-eyed Andy, referring to Victoria International Airport on the distant Saanich Peninsula.

BEAUFORT VINEYARD & ESTATE WINERY

OPENED: 2008

5854 Pickering Road, Courtenay, BC V9J 1T4
250.338.1357
www.beaufortwines.ca
When to visit: Open 11 am – 5 pm Friday through Sunday May to September,
    11 am – 4 pm Canadian Thanksgiving weekend, and most December weekends
    before Christmas

RECOMMENDED

ORTEGA
PINOT GRIS
BLACK FORTIFIED WINE

JEFF AND SUSAN VANDERMOLEN LIKELY ARE THE ONLY VINTNERS IN BRITISH Columbia publishing their winery's latitude and longitude (49°45'76" N, 125°00'76" W). They are making the point that their Beaufort Vineyard, the first winery in the Comox Valley on Vancouver Island, is one of the northernmost and westernmost in the province. But given the growing conditions near Courtenay, they believe nothing stops them from growing good grapes in their mid-island site. They launched their vineyard in 2007, planting 7,500 vines in three hectares (7½ acres), perhaps a fifth of their vineyard's potential size.

To get their compact tasting room open in 2008, they purchased grapes both from Vancouver Island and from the Okanagan, with Susan making the wines. They intend to achieve an ultimate production of about three thousand cases per year, half coming from their own vines and the remainder from purchased fruit. Susan also makes a fortified dessert wine called Black, with a twist on the usual approach to blackberry wine by blending in 10 percent blackcurrant.

Susan was born in Chemainus in 1958 and has a chemical engineering degree from the University of British Columbia. Jeff, born in Burlington in 1959, is a University of Calgary graduate and an accomplished amateur blues musician (guitar, mandolin, harmonica, and accordion). The couple pursued careers in the oil industry in Canada, the United States, and Britain. The oil patch enabled them to travel, going as far afield as Hungary, Portugal, and Chile. "We always targeted wine," Susan says. In 1991 they found themselves at a Loire château during harvest. "There we were, picking grapes with the peasant farmers," she remembers. "At the end of the week, we were invited to the caves of some of the local farmers. It was such a wonderful experience. What a dream it became to grow grapes."

When they exited the fast lane in 2005, they chose the quiet and scenic Comox Valley and set out to pioneer a new wine region. To find suitable property, they distributed 2,100 brochures in the valley and looked at about a hundred possible sites. They purchased a 34-hectare (84-acre) farm about 10 minutes north of Courtenay. Just over half was cleared, including a southwestern slope suitable for vineyard.

Joining wine industry associations on Vancouver Island, they visited vineyards and picked the brains of established producers. As a result, they planted the vineyard intelligently and planned their winery well. With the exception of test blocks of Merlot (soon replaced with Schönburger), Gamay, Pinot Gris, and Gewürztraminer, they put in early-ripening vines already proven elsewhere on the island: Maréchal Foch, Léon Millot, the Cabernet Foch Swiss hybrid, Ortega, and Siegerrebe.

"We are two-thirds planted with red wine grapes," Jeff says. "With red wines, you have to develop inventory. From the time you pick to the time you sell is a year and a half, whereas with white wines it is eight months. From an economic point of view, it does not make a lot of sense to have all the red wine grapes, but we prefer red wine and we are going to do a port. At the end of the day, it is all about us."

The winery's intimate tasting room, adjoining both their kitchen and a veranda overlooking the vines, keeps them close to their visitors. This gregarious couple is inclined to keep it that way even after they relocate the winery to larger quarters on the farm.

Beaufort's most striking feature is the Vineyard Guardian. The Vandermolens have erected a four-metre (13-foot) replica of an Easter Island Moai (or statue), a striking figure with a long face and prominent nose. On Easter Island, these statues were crafted from stone and represented deified ancestors. The Vandermolens became intrigued with the culture when visiting Easter Island during a trip to Chile.

When they cut down several large trees on their property, they recalled that a Courtenay chainsaw artist, Stan Skuse, was adept at carving Moai images. "It turns out he is also a tree faller," Jeff says. "We had him take down the few trees we needed to and then turn a portion of one of the trees into our Moai." The Vineyard Guardian, looming over the vines, now casts an eye on the Comox Valley's wine-growing future.

BEAUMONT FAMILY ESTATE WINERY

OPENED: 2008

2775 Boucherie Road, Kelowna, BC V4T 2G4
250.769.6776
www.beaumontwines.ca
When to visit: To be established

RECOMMENDED

PINOT NOIR
GAMAY NOIR
PINOT GRIS

ALEX LUBCHYNSKI'S THREE VINEYARDS WERE, AS HE SAYS, "CERTIFIED ORGANIC from day one." That is a decision that certainly endears him to his neighbours, for the vineyards are all in the Lakeview Heights district of Westbank, surrounded by suburban homes. Alex and his wife, Louise, had a young family when they moved into Lakeview Heights in 1995, and that influenced their decision to do agriculture without pesticides or herbicides.

"We knew the kids would have to help us," Louise says. "They were small but they had to learn everything." Now the winemaker at Beaumont, daughter Alana, who was born in 1987, learned to drive tractor when she was eight, which is not unusual in farming families. "We did not want the kids to be near the chemicals," Louise says.

Both Louise and Alex grew up on farms in Alberta. Alex was born in 1954 at Newbrook, a village about 100 kilometres (62 miles) north of Edmonton, where his parents and grandparents had farmed. Louise was born in Beaumont, a town just south of Edmonton, so named — beautiful mountain — by its French-speaking founders, including her forebears. Since Lakeview Heights has fine views of Okanagan mountains, it was a natural for the Lubchynski family to adopt the name of Louise's hometown for their vineyards and winery.

Before coming to the Okanagan in 1990, the couple farmed near Beaumont. Alex is also musically talented (as is Alana and her brother, Scott). In his free time, Alex, a guitar player and a singer, teamed up with other musicians to form week-end bands, the most enduring of which was a group called the Twilighters. In the Okanagan, where he started building houses before buying land, he put his musical career aside. Several of his vintage guitars are to be displayed in the winery.

Five years in construction convinced him that he wanted to return to farming. Impressed by the burgeoning wine industry, he bought a cherry orchard, the first of the three five-hectare (12-acre) parcels the family now owns in Lakeview Heights. Alex consulted a nearby winery for grapevine suggestions but finally listened to his "gut instinct," which, fortunately for him, was sound. He planted Gewürztraminer, "which we always liked to drink," along with Pinot Blanc, Pinot Noir, Pinot Gris, and Gamay. He put similar varieties into the two other nearby properties, purchased in 1999 and 2000. In fact, one is planted entirely to two clones of Pinot Noir. "It is our favourite grape to grow," Louise says. In one vintage, an entire five-hectare (12-acre) block of Pinot Noir was turned into icewine by Summerhill Pyramid Winery, one of several wineries that have bought grapes from the Lubchynski family.

The family began to consider launching its own winery in part after a disagree-ment with Summerhill but primarily because Alana expressed an interest. "I have always done the work in the vineyard," she says, admitting that "it was kind of rep-etitious." She had done a year of business studies at Okanagan University College when a meeting with the winemaker at Tantalus opened her eyes to a new career path. "I thought this is a different side of the industry that I could see myself doing," she says. She switched to the college's wine industry courses. She also buttressed her practical skills by doing vintages at two small Okanagan wineries and working in a Kelowna wine store. In early 2008 she went to Australia to work the crush at Poole's Rock, a large winery in the Hunter Valley where she worked 14-hour days, with assignments ranging from the crush pad to the laboratory. It just whetted her appetite to get additional experience at other wineries, either in the southern hemi-sphere or in California.

She believes she learned a good deal in Australia about "the diversity in winemaking, with different equipment. I also learned just how important lab work is. Thirty samples a day. Monitoring the wines every second day." Although the vivacious, auburn-haired winemaker is clearly a quick study, for its first vintage in 2007 Beaumont also retained consultant Christine Leroux, whose 15 or so years of experience made her an ideal mentor for Alana. In that debut vintage, produced at nearby Rollingdale Winery, Beaumont made about one thousand cases in total. "Our main source of income is definitely through selling the grapes," Alex explains.

"That is where we started and where we will continue. Our wine, we want to make it very exclusive."

Ultimately, Beaumont intends to build its wine shop at the foot of one vineyard that fronts on Boucherie Road. That will make it the first one that travellers from Kelowna reach when they head out to visit the winery cluster on the slopes of Mount Boucherie. In keeping with the organic philosophy, the Lubchynskis plan to tap the architectural talents of a family member to design an innovative "green" winery.

BLACK HILLS ESTATE WINERY

OPENED: 2001

> 30880 – 71st Street (Black Sage Road), RR1, Site 52, Comp 22, Oliver, BC V0H 1T0
> 250.498.0666
> www.blackhillswinery.com
> When to visit: By appointment

RECOMMENDED

> NOTA BENE
> CARMENÈRE
> ALIBI
> CHARDONNAY
> SEQUENTIA

MANY OF THE 265 INDIVIDUALS WHO BECAME SHAREHOLDERS OF BLACK HILLS in 2007 wear pride of winery ownership on their sleeves. They own the strongest cult brand among BC wineries. Benefits of ownership include a case of Nota Bene (each vintage) and a place at the head of the line to buy two more cases each. This full-bodied red is so coveted that a recent 3,300-case vintage was sold in 47 minutes!

How does such a legend develop? In 1996 two couples — Bob and Senka Tennant and Peter and Susan McCarrell — moved from Vancouver to a 14-hectare (35-acre) derelict vineyard property on Black Sage Road, south of Oliver, and planted grapes. Three years later, they started making wine in a metal-clad hut on the property formerly used to assemble demolition derby cars. The disconnect between this scruffy facility and the seven awesome vintages of Nota Bene produced therein only added to the cult status of Black Hills. In 2006 a purpose-built winery replaced the shed, which was torn down.

However, Black Hills was sold in 2007 when the McCarrells, the older couple in the partnership, began thinking about retirement. Wine growing was already a second career for all of them (Peter was a carpenter, Susan a legal secretary, Bob a general contractor). Croatian-born Senka Tennant, formerly a retailer with a degree in botany, became the winemaker. For her first vintages of Nota Bene in 1999 and 2000, she was mentored (mostly by telephone) by a winemaker in Washington State named Rusty Figgins. Having lived in Croatia until she was 15, she also had a wine culture heritage to fall back on. "I have a picture of my grandfather drinking wine," she said once.

Nota Bene is a full-flavoured blend with about 50 percent Cabernet Sauvignon, supported by Merlot and Cabernet Franc — a Bordeaux blend that many wineries like to call "Meritage." It is probable that the distinctive proprietary name for the wine — Latin for "take notice" — contributed to the success of Black Hills. The winery assigned catchy names to its next two wines, both blends of Sauvignon Blanc and Sémillon. Several other wineries also use Meritage for these blends because the grapes are white Bordeaux varieties. Black Hills, however, calls its dry table wine Alibi. Its dessert wine is Sequentia. The winery only used varietal names on its labels when it released Canada's first Carmenère (from the 2005 vintage) and then the winery's first Chardonnay.

With its focused portfolio, Black Hills produced a very strong brand in half a decade. "We always tried to produce a bottle and a package that can sit on any restaurant table in the country and be accepted alongside other world wines," Bob Tennant said as the winery was changing hands. "We are on top of our game and that is perhaps a good time to move on to something else."

The speed at which Black Hills was sold surprised the partners. When they set out to plumb its value in the fall of 2007, they expected to wait as long as two years to find a buyer. Within a week they had several offers and accepted an $11 million offer from Vinequest Wine Partners Limited Partnership. It represents a group of investors in Alberta and British Columbia, including Jason Priestley, a British Columbia–born Hollywood actor.

To ensure continuity, the new owners kept Senka as the consulting winemaker through the 2007 vintage, supporting Graham Pierce, the new winemaker. He came into the wine business in 1996 as the chef at Summerhill Pyramid Winery. Five years later he moved into winemaking at the new Mt. Boucherie Estate Winery at Westbank and remained there until joining Black Hills in the spring of 2008.

Black Hills now produces about five thousand cases per year, all from grapes in its 10.5-hectare (26-acre) vineyard. With demand for the wines clearly ahead of supply, the new owners intend to acquire at least as much additional vineyard and to raise production to eight thousand cases, still a modest volume for such a hot brand. The founding partners, now all in their 50s, recognized as well that the winery needed to grow. "We kind of thought if we were 30, it would be nice to take it to the next level," Bob says. "But we are not and there is no changing that."

BLACK SHEEP WINERY

OPENED: 2009

9503 12th Avenue, Osoyoos BC V0H 1V1
250.495.3245
www.blacksheepwinery.ca
When to visit: To be established

INITIALLY, WINEMAKER STEVE WYSE, WHO WAS BORN IN 1967, WANTED TO BE an airline pilot but he was unlucky enough to get his pilot's licence just when Air Canada was laying off pilots. He tried selling real estate for a couple of years but did not find it fulfilling. In 1992 he moved to Whistler with Michelle Young, his wife, to do what Steve calls "a little soul searching." They both worked as mountain guides, and Michelle, a Hong Kong–born hotel manager, ran one of the resort's restaurants.

He was drawn to the wine industry after his parents, Jim and Midge Wyse, began developing the Burrowing Owl Vineyard on Black Sage Road (see page 52) in the early 1990s. Steve and Michelle moved to the Okanagan and Steve worked with vineyard manager Richard Cleave, who was planting major new south Okanagan vineyards. When construction of the Burrowing Owl winery began in 1997, Steve became one of the project managers and then the cellar master under Bill Dyer, Burrowing Owl's first winemaker. Finally, Steve had found his career.

Bill is a highly regarded winemaking consultant who looks after clients from his base in the Napa Valley. He was on hand at Burrowing Owl during all the critical times of the winemaking year, with Steve responsible for the wines when he was not there. Steve equipped himself for the task by taking Brock University winemaking correspondence courses as well as the winery assistant course from Okanagan University College. As a team, Bill and Steve produced exciting wines that achieved an immediate cult following and a reputation for quality that has endured. When

Bill left Burrowing Owl in the summer of 2004, Steve took over as winemaker for the next three vintages. (Bill subsequently re-emerged in the Okanagan as Church & State's consulting winemaker.)

Given his towering reputation, Bill Dyer was believed to be a hard act to follow. The Wyse family began picking up critical comments that Burrowing Owl wines were losing the edge. There was no serious foundation for this suggestion. "I know that I was making wines that were no different than when Bill was there," Steve says. "If anything, I think I brought in a couple of little things that may have improved the overall quality of the wine. If you look at the record, it shows that we started getting more medals as time went on, not less, as some people were saying." But rather than let the unfair perception undermine the winery, Steve decided to leave, replacing himself with a Burrowing Owl winemaker from outside the family.

"It was time for me to spread my wings and find my own identity," Steve says. "I kind of always have been the black sheep of the family anyways." Hence the name of his own winery with its cheeky note of defiance. "It's fun to stir up a little bit of controversy here and there, without it being too serious," Steve says. "It's all in good fun."

In the summer of 2008, after having taken a year off from the wine industry, he and Michelle purchased a farm on Highway 97 south of Osoyoos, almost at the United States border. Anxious to get started again, they scrambled to convert an industrial building, part of which had been used for fruit cold storage, into a winery. They were too late to buy good white grapes but were able to make 60 barrels of Syrah and 50 barrels of Merlot with purchased grapes. Meanwhile, the fruit trees were pulled out, with vines ordered to plant four hectares (10 acres) in 2009, primarily to Malbec, Zinfandel, and Viognier. "We did not want to make varietals that had already been done over and over again," Steve says.

Black Sheep expects to release its first wines late in 2009, followed by a fuller range including some whites the following summer. The style of the wines should definitely be familiar. "I am very proud of what I achieved at Burrowing Owl," Steve says. "Essentially, I have taken all of the tricks of the trade that I developed and learned there and simply brought them over to my winery. It gives people another choice if they like the Burrowing Owl brand and the style of winemaking. But maybe the costs won't be so high."

BLACK WIDOW WINERY

OPENED: 2006

1630 Naramata Road, Penticton, BC V2A 8T7
250.487.2347
www.blackwidowwinery.com
When to visit: Consult website and by appointment

RECOMMENDED

MERLOT/CABERNET SAUVIGNON
GEWÜRZTRAMINER
PINOT GRIS
OASIS
VINTAGE ONE
DESSERT SCHÖNBURGER

BLACK WIDOW'S WINERY IS AS MODERN AS ANY IN THE OKANAGAN, WELL equipped for modern winemaking and draped down a slope for gravity-flow production. It comes as a surprise that winemaker and co-owner Dick Lancaster once crushed grapes by foot.

Not at Black Widow, let me be quick to add, but years ago when he was getting his feet wet as a home winemaker in Vancouver. He had purchased Maréchal Foch grapes from the Okanagan and, without proper winemaking equipment, he just stomped the grapes. "That was quite a horrible wine," he recalls. He has come a long way, as one discovers on tasting Black Widow's wines.

Dick has spent a lifetime mastering an astonishing array of skills. Born in 1953, he grew up in Montreal and got his initial interest in wines from his father, Graham, a manager of food services for Air Canada. Before leaving Montreal in 1970, he took his first stab at winemaking with grapes from wild native vines. "From that point forward I was experimenting," he says. In the mid-1970s, he spent a summer in European wine regions and briefly sought a job with a Vancouver wine importer.

After the foot stomping episode, he joined a winemaking club and soon was winning awards. He also developed a professional interest in the business by writing a paper on starting a BC winery while completing a master's degree in business administration in the mid-1980s.

That is but one of his many degrees and professional qualifications, starting with a master's degree in biology. He worked as an ecologist after graduation but concluded that he needed a doctorate to make a lucrative career of it. While he was in university, he worked as a car salesman. He liked it and discovered he could make more money than as a biologist. A car leasing company made him a district manager, leading him to better his qualifications with the business degree. Then one of his leasing companies hired Dick as a finance executive; to handle that job better, he trained as a certified management accountant, graduating near the top of his class in 1989. That led to a controller's job with a major lumber company and then, from 1992 through 2007, as vice-president of Imasco Minerals, a producer of industrial minerals. That is Imasco stucco on the sage-hued exterior of the Black Widow winery.

In the summer of 2000 Dick and Shona, his wife, began looking for a summer getaway and found the Naramata Road vineyard that the winery now anchors. At three hectares (7½ acres), it was bigger than they were looking for but, with producing vines and a panoramic view of Naramata Bench and the lake, it was too good to turn down. "Classic upselling," Dick says of the realtor.

"And as soon as we got a vineyard, the goal was to set up a winery, but in a cautious way," he recounts. "Our first objective was to learn about grape growing. We wanted to establish a reputation for as high a quality grape as we could grow." The vineyard already had Gewürztraminer, Pinot Gris, and Schönburger when the Lancasters bought it. In 2001 they added Merlot and a bit of Cabernet Sauvignon, selling grapes to Kettle Valley Winery until launching Black Widow. Dick's wines are reminiscent of the wines Kettle Valley made. "We like wines that have some real flavour and character to them, and that comes from really ripe grapes," he says. Targeted production is 1,200 cases per year.

The winery is named after the indigenous spider so shy it is seldom seen, but which has venom 15 times more poisonous than that of a rattlesnake. The bites — only females bite — are rarely fatal, although children and the elderly can have life-threatening reactions.

BLACKWOOD LANE VINEYARDS & WINERY

OPENED: 2007

25180 8th Avenue, Langley, BC V4W 2G8
604.856.5787
www.blackwoodlanewinery.com
When to visit: Consult website

RECOMMENDED

ALLIÁNCE
CABERNET FRANC
MERLOT
VICUÑA RIOJA

WINEMAKER CHARLES HERROLD, ONE OF THE FOUNDERS OF BLACKWOOD LANE, owns a well-informed palate and a rich wine vocabulary. That taste for fine wine (and cognac) began, he asserts surprisingly, when he played bass guitar in a rock band. "I ultimately retired from music in 1987, but I had developed an appreciation for fine wine and good dining," he says — relating his biography during a rather good lunch in one of his favourite White Rock restaurants.

Born in Iowa in 1959, he was headed for college on a music scholarship when he dropped out to play in rock bands, first in the United States and then in Canada after coming to Winnipeg in 1981. "I had always loved Canadian music," he says. Alas, he was not fully informed about Canadian musicians. He turned down a chance to play with Bryan Adams because he did not know who the singer was.

Charles quit music to establish a company in Richmond that specialized in residential construction, from solariums and roofing to custom-designed housing. He continues in the business, mostly working in Hawaii. It has progressed from a way to make a living to a way to buy new barrels for his winemaking.

He was introduced to winemaking about 20 years ago when he won a kit at an Italian cultural festival. The wine was mediocre but the process interested him and he started buying grapes, first from California and, since 1997, from the Okanagan. With several friends he formed a winemaking club in White Rock, where he lives on a street called Blackwood Lane. Charles took to the hobby with such enthusiasm that his basement was soon jammed with wine.

Then he met Carlos Lee, at the time the owner of a White Rock restaurant and now a partner in Blackwood Lane. Born in Korea in 1961, the son of a diplomat, Carlos grew up in Peru, which explains his Spanish given name. He has had a career as a successful inventor (for example, automobile parts). Carlos also has a well-informed palate and once entertained ideas of a winery with a friend at university, Marc Castel. Carlos agreed to team up with Charles; a year after the winery opened, Marc also invested in Blackwood Lane.

The partners decided to base the winery in Langley, on a property near the border with room for about one hectare (2½ acres) of vines and a view of Mount Baker. Even though most of the grapes come from the Okanagan, the partners believe it is advantageous to locate close to their major markets — the consumers and restaurants of greater Vancouver. An existing house has been renovated for the winery but long-term plans call for three cellars and a domed tasting room to be built into the side of a hill. The terrain also allowed for the development of an amphitheatre where winery concerts are held.

A man with an amiably persuasive personality, Charles has courted some of the South Okanagan's best growers to secure top-quality grapes. Sam Baptiste, the manager of Inkameep Vineyards, became a close friend, providing Charles with choice fruit, most notably Cabernet Sauvignon from a block in the Inkameep Vineyards called U2. That U2 Cabernet Sauvignon forms the fleshy spine of Alliànce, the winery's big Bordeaux red and a wine that defines Blackwood Lane's style. Charles lets the grapes macerate on the skins for up to 42 days, extracting as much flavour and colour as possible. After fermentation the wine spends 25 months aging in barrels before being bottled.

At the Langley property, Pinot Noir, Pinot Gris, and Gewürztraminer have been planted. As well, Charles was quick to pick up interesting varieties from other Fraser Valley vineyards. In 2006 he was offered Siegerrebe from a struggling little vineyard. He made a crisply dry white in the style of Alsace, a big hit with his restaurant clients. Blackwood Lane then got involved with the grower to improve the vineyard and grow better grapes in 2007. To his distress, Charles discovered a disadvantage of being too close to a big urban centre. Just as the grapes were ready to be picked, thieves entered the vineyard at night and, right under the nose of the grower's penned-up Rottweiler, made off with four tons.

"I was quite furious about it for a day and a half," Charles says.

BLASTED CHURCH VINEYARDS

OPENED: 2000 (AS PRPICH HILLS WINERY)

378 Parsons Road, Okanagan Falls, BC V0H 1R0
250.497.1125 | 1.8.SPELLBOUND (toll free)
www.blastedchurch.com
When to visit: Open daily 10 am – 5 pm in summer and fall; by appointment at other
   times

RECOMMENDED

REVERED SERIES WINES
SAUVIGNON BLANC
CHARDONNAY MUSQUÉ
PINOT GRIS
CABERNET MERLOT
SYRAH
GEWÜRZTRAMINER
HATFIELD'S FUSE
THE DAM FLOOD
MALBEC SYRAH

YOU WOULD NEVER GUESS THAT LIVELY CHRIS AND EVELYN CAMPBELL USED TO
be accountants. Before they bought this winery in 2002, she had her own accounting
practice in Vancouver and he handled administrative work for a brokerage firm.
Wanting to run a business of their own, they settled on an Okanagan winery. They
knew a bit about wine, having started their careers in the hotel business; the lifestyle
appealed; and to be frank about it, the business plan also appealed to them. "The
numbers were the reality of it," says Evelyn. "We did not just want to come to the
beautiful vineyard."

The undulating 17-hectare (42-acre) property is, in fact, a beautiful vineyard that
has attracted many professional photographers. It is north of Okanagan Falls, on a

plateau above twisty Eastside Road, with a red-roofed winery standing in sharp relief against the green vines. The view from the log cabin tasting room takes in Skaha Lake, with the village of Kaleden directly across the lake from Blasted Church.

The Campbells bought a two-year-old winery from a Croatian-born grape grower, Dan Prpich, who was retiring. He had called it Prpich Hills. The Campbells, needing a new name and new labels, turned to Bernie Hadley-Beauregard, a clever Vancouver marketing consultant. "I told him we had to do something very, very different," Evelyn recalls. "The more outrageous, the better." They canvassed a number of ideas, settling on Blasted Church because of the solid local story behind it. There is a century-old wooden church in Okanagan Falls that originally was in Fairview, the long-vanished mining community near Oliver. In 1929, when the church was dismantled to move it, the crew loosened the nails from the sturdy timbers by exploding dynamite inside the building.

Inspired by the story, Bernie created a colourful family of caricature wine labels. (A popular blend of Chasselas, Optima, and Gewürztraminer is named Hatfield's Fuse for Harley Hatfield, the foreman of the crew that dismantled the church.) The whimsical and arresting labels gave Blasted Church a profile overnight. This has powered the winery toward its goal of making 20,000 cases of wine annually with their own grapes and grapes contracted from independents that the Campbells call "Devout Church Growers."

One of their biggest challenges has been coping with unintended turnover among their winemakers. They started with Frank Supernak, a Nanaimo native who previously was Hester Creek's winemaker. Tragically, he died in an accident in November 2002 in another winery. The vintage was completed for Blasted Church by volunteers from other wineries, notably from Quails' Gate. Blasted Church acknowledged these Good Samaritan winemakers by putting them on the label of the 2002 Pinot Noir.

The winemaker who took over for the 2003 vintage had to return to South Africa when he could not get immigration clearance. Their third winemaker did the 2004 vintage but quit suddenly the following summer, to be succeeded by former Calona Vineyards winemaker Kelly Moss. She made two vintages but returned to her Ontario hometown in 2006 to raise her young family. She was succeeded by winemaker number five, Richard Kanazawa, who seems to be a keeper. Remarkably, in spite of the turnover, the wines have shown consistent improvement. The winery won a Lieutenant Governor's Award of Excellence for its 2006 Syrah.

Richard, who was born in 1972 in Langley, is in the wine industry because he started as a delivery man for Domaine de Chaberton after a brief career playing professional rugby in Japan. His eight years at Chaberton supported studies in food technology at the British Columbia Institute of Technology, preparing himself, he hoped, for a winemaker's job. "I had a lot of experience at Domaine but I couldn't get a cellar-hand job in British Columbia if my life depended on it," he recounted later. "I thought if I can't get a job here, going overseas was my best opportunity."

In 2002 he went to Australia, taking courses at Charles Sturt University and working at several wineries. The Simon Gilbert winery recognized his potential. "They said I was being wasted in the cellar, so I moved up to the lab." He returned to Canada in 2004 with winemaking experience on his resumé, joining Red Rooster for two vintages. His debut 2006 Malbec at Red Rooster also won a Lieutenant Governor's Award of Excellence (although by then he was in charge of winemaking for Blasted Church).

For all his Australian training, he has kept some Old World winemaking tricks up his sleeve. In 2007 a portion of Blasted Church's estate-grown Pinot Noir grapes started their fermentation as whole berries with stems in the big bins in which they were shipped from the vineyard. Once ferment was established, the grapes were crushed by foot before being pressed, in the age-old manner of Burgundy. The resulting wine was much more expressive and complex than the previous vintage.

"It is nice to be working at a winery where you have your own vineyard, which I haven't had previously," he says. (Red Rooster purchases most of its grapes.) Blasted Church gets most of its grapes from its 16.5-hectare (41-acre) vineyard or from nearby growers on the same benchland high above Skaha Lake. Dan Prpich had planted at least 14 varieties, some of which now disappear into either Hatfield's Fuse (white) or The Dam Flood (red). The latter label commemorates another of Harley Hatfield's adventures, the construction of a local dam in 1935 that failed the following year. Significant recent changes in the vineyard have been the replacement of Optima with Sauvignon Blanc and the planting of more Syrah.

Since 2004 Blasted Church has released all wines, including reserve wines under the Revered Series label, in bottles sealed with screw caps in order to avoid cork-tainted wines, one of the industry's big headaches. There is another advantage as well. "It eliminates the grief when you can't find a corkscrew," Evelyn Campbell explains.

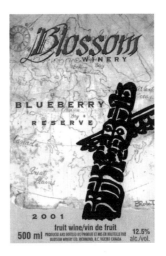

LULU ISLAND WINERY

OPENING PROPOSED FOR 2009

16880 Westminster Highway,
Richmond, BC V6V 1A8

BLOSSOM WINERY

OPENED: 2001

5491 Minoru Boulevard,
Richmond, BC V6X 2B1
604.232.9839
www.blossomwinery.com
When to visit: Open daily
11 am – 6 pm

RECOMMENDED

ICEWINE
BLUEBERRY WINE
RASPBERRY WINE
SELECT LATE HARVEST RIESLING
TWO LEFT FEET MERITAGE

WHENEVER THE CANADIAN WINE INDUSTRY MOUNTS AN ICEWINE SEMINAR in China, there is a good chance that John Chang will be one of the speakers. Immigrants who came from Taiwan in 1999, John and Allison Lu, his wife, speak the language, know the culture, and export both fruit wine and icewine from British Columbia to Asia. In 2006 Blossom Winery was named one of the province's top 24 exporters, as measured by how rapidly sales have grown.

That represents quite an achievement since Blossom opened in 2001, located improbably in a strip mall in Richmond. "We lost money in the first two years," Allison remembers. Business turned around in the third year, and by 2009 they opened Lulu Island, their second winery, at 16880 Westminster Highway in a $3.5 million Spanish-style building backing onto 2.4 hectares (six acres) of vineyard. With Blossom they focus on wine exports. Lulu Island is set up to receive winery visits with four tasting rooms, including three staffed and decorated specifically for

Chinese, Japanese, and Korean visitors. The vineyard was planted in 2007 mostly with Muscat grapes. John figures that people who come to wineries expect to see vineyards. Blossom has two large tasting rooms but only a furniture store for a neighbour.

Over a cup of green tea, John explains (through a translator) that one needs to understand Blossom against the culture in which he grew up. Life was very hard in rural China, including Taiwan, and people worked seven days a week from dawn to dusk. Alcoholic beverages served to rejuvenate the weary. "The people believed that drinking alcohol was better for your health," John says. "For instance, if you worked a hard day, and you came home and had some wine, it replenished your body."

Aside from nourishing the body, wines were socially important. In a society with no money for luxuries, wines were made at home. His grandmother, Soo Gao Chang, made wines in their home, and he became interested in wine by watching her. John was born in 1955. Before coming to Canada he built a business as an electrical equipment dealer in Taiwan. As a young adult he had taken up his grand-mother's craft of making wines, even to the point of planting a few grapevines. He began to dream of having a winery of his own, not very practical in Taiwan, where the single winery at the time was state-owned. But Canada provided him with the opportunity.

In Richmond, John and Allison discovered flavoursome raspberries and blue-berries, fruits not well known in Taiwan. John set out to capture those flavours in berry wines. He made a number of trial lots of fruit wines in small containers, then retained a veteran winemaker, Ron Taylor, to help Blossom scale up to commercial volumes. Ron had made wine at Andrés for 25 years but not fruit wines. As it turned out, John and Ron learned from each other, with John acquiring the necessary skills by the time Ron moved on to coach several other fruit wineries.

The style of Blossom's wines has been informed both by John's memories of his grandmother's wines and by his perception of the Asian wine palate. "Sweeter wines sell better in Asia," John says. "Chinese people are the only people who are afraid of 'sour' things." The reference is to cuisine with an acidic bite. "The Japanese and the people of Thailand or Malaysia all have sour foods in their diets. Chinese people don't. In China and Taiwan, there is very little demand for dry white wine. For sweet white wine, there is no problem. That's why icewine seems to do so well in China and Taiwan."

Blossom now makes as much as 30,000 litres (8,000 gallons) of icewine a year. John buys grapes from five vineyards in the Okanagan and Similkameen valleys. Blossom has its own press in the interior, since icewine grapes must be crushed while frozen, although the juice comes back to Richmond for fermentation. John believes (as do many of his peers) that Riesling is the best grape for icewine, but he blends it with Chardonnay icewine to soften the acidity to the taste of his Asian cus-tomers. He also makes red icewine, blending Merlot and Pinot Noir. While icewine is the priority, Blossom sets aside some grapes to make a Meritage red called Two Left Feet. This is also exported to Asia.

The Lulu Island Winery is strategically located near busy highways and with good access from the airport, to benefit from the same tour traffic — as many as 80 buses per month — that kept Blossom's tasting room busy. Once Lulu Island is well established, John might just relocate Blossom to the Okanagan.

John and Allison bought the Lulu Island property, a six-hectare (15-acre) former nursery site, in late 2005 and planted vines in 2007. They got a shock when applying for a permit to build the 2,044-square-metre (22,000-square-foot) winery: Richmond wanted a $200,000 development fee. They argued that the winery is on agricultural land and the fee did not apply, a battle that lasted six months. The Canadian Federation of Independent Business came to their aid, arranging a meeting with the mayor at which the fee was dropped.

BLUE GROUSE ESTATE WINERY

OPENED: 1993

> 4365 Blue Grouse Road, Duncan, BC V9L 6M3
> 250.743.3834
> www.bluegrousevineyards.com
> When to visit: Open 11 am – 5 pm Wednesday to Sunday

RECOMMENDED

> BLACK MUSCAT
> PINOT GRIS
> PINOT NOIR
> ORTEGA

WHEN HANS KILTZ MOVED BLUE GROUSE'S WINEMAKING FROM THE BASEMENT of the family home to a commodious new winery in 2000, he ensured that the new building included a superbly equipped laboratory. "I like laboratories," he says.

That is to be expected. "I had laboratories all my life," he says. Born in Berlin in 1938, Hans has four scientific degrees: one in veterinarian medicine, one in tropical veterinarian medicine, one in fish pathology, and a doctorate in microbiology. As an employee of the United Nations Food and Agricultural Organization, he worked both in Asia and Africa, once managing a laboratory with 42 employees. Drawn repeatedly to Africa, where he first began working in 1965, Hans returned reluctantly to Germany about two decades later when his two children had reached high school age. That lasted about a year.

"If you are used to life in Africa, you cannot easily get back to a European lifestyle," Hans says, explaining how a much-travelled man with his credentials ended up growing grapes on Vancouver Island. "The other problem, of course, is when you are 50, you won't get a job anymore. You are on your own." So in 1988, intending to apply one of his degrees to fish farming, he came to Vancouver Island. As it happened, British Columbia's aquaculture industry went into a slump.

However, the farm that Hans and his family purchased had been an experimental vineyard that had fallen into neglect when the previous owner experienced financial difficulty. Hans, who had winemaking relatives in Germany, started making wine for personal consumption. When the rules changed in British Columbia to allow small farm wineries, Hans turned his hobby into a business, getting a licence late in 1992 and opening the tasting room the following April. In 2008, when he reached 70 and decided to retire, Hans put Blue Grouse up for sale.

"My scientific degrees helped me to do this," Hans says. "It is not much different, winemaking and veterinarian medicine. Both are half science and half art. When you do operations, you have to imagine things because the animal doesn't talk to tell you where the pain is. It's a sort of art, you know."

The 12.5-hectare (31-acre) Blue Grouse property has an excellent southwestern exposure. The vines get adequate sun, ripening without having to be tented. "Why should I tent?" Hans asked during a 2003 conversation. "I have been growing grapes here now for 14 years and I have never had a problem ripening them. I refuse to tent. If I cannot grow good grapes without all this extra investment, then I would say I am on the wrong spot here. I think then I should have a greenhouse to grow grapes."

Hans and his Philippines-born wife, Evangeline, maintain commendable discipline and order in the vineyard, growing varieties most suitable for Vancouver Island. These include Ortega, Pinot Gris, Siegerrebe, Bacchus, and Müller-Thurgau. The primary red is Pinot Noir, matured to produce a rich and expressive wine.

The winery neither grows grapes suited to the Okanagan nor buys any from there. Hans is opposed to making wine on Vancouver Island with Okanagan grapes. "It is against our philosophy," he says. "We were one of the first ones trying to establish an identity for Vancouver Island wine." He worries that the identity of island wines will be lost among all the wines being made from grapes grown elsewhere.

The flagship whites at Blue Grouse, which makes a total of three thousand cases per year, include a Pinot Gris that is remarkable for its ripe flavours and for sturdy alcohol approaching 15 percent. Its alcohol content high for Vancouver Island (unless the grapes are tented), this wine is the result of meticulous grape growing, including low yields. Blue Grouse also has established a reputation for its Ortega, a variety with an array of flavours running from grapefruit to Muscat that arguably is the signature variety for Vancouver Island.

Blue Grouse also has an exclusive wine Hans calls Black Muscat. The variety has been developed from a few vines, perhaps of Hungarian origin, that were in the vineyard when Hans bought the property. "I gave the grapes to a home winemaker, a friend of mine, and he made a wonderful wine from it," Hans recalls. Now Hans produces about 800 litres (175 gallons) annually of this aromatic dry red, a wine aged in American oak barrels and unique in British Columbia.

BLUE HERON FRUIT WINERY

OPENED: 2004

18539 Dewdney Trunk Road, Pitt Meadows, BC V3Y 2R9
604.465.5563
www.blueheronwinery.ca
When to visit: Open daily 10 am – 6 pm

RECOMMENDED

CRANBERRY RESERVE
BLUEBERRY RESERVE

AT 84, GEORGE FLYNN GAVE NEW MEANING TO THE TERM "ESTATE WINERY." As he was completing the wine shop at the end of 2003, he explained that "it adds value to the estate" to establish a winery on the cranberry and blueberry farm he has owned since 1946. The first fruit winery in the Vancouver area that is north of the Fraser River, it was inspired by the success of the Fort Wine Company across the river at Fort Langley.

Born in Moosomin, Saskatchewan, in 1919, George recounts that he made it to British Columbia "with difficulty" by moving from job to job during the Depression. When the war began, he enlisted in an army engineering regiment and was posted to Britain in 1941, where he saw action when the Allies invaded Europe. "I did swim ashore on D-Day," he says in his laconic style. "More or less had to. The boat had been blown up." Discharged as a lance sergeant, he returned to British Columbia.

The eight-hectare (20-acre) property he bought on Dewdney Trunk Road was then in a largely rural area of the Fraser Valley. George eventually planted blueberries but earned a living in marine construction, applying the engineering skills he had acquired in the army. He still reflects on the irony of building docks and bridges after having once blown them up on another continent. "A lot of loud noises," he remembers.

After retiring from construction in the mid-1980s, he devoted himself to the several cranberry bogs that he owned. With cranberry prices strong at the time, he removed some blueberry bushes to make room for cranberries on his Dewdney Trunk Road farm. In doing so, he was flying against conventional wisdom that said cranberries cannot be grown on ordinary farm soil. George concedes it took a few years to establish his new cranberry bog, but he did succeed.

"Up until the end of the 20th century, there was nothing but money from cranberries — until everybody in the country started planting them," George says. The collapse in cranberry prices (there has been a recovery) was the catalyst behind his decision to research and then build a fruit winery. This was, of course, the same impetus behind the development of the Fort winery, which opened in 2001. George arranged to have The Fort produce the initial wines for Blue Heron Fruit Winery (named for the abundant heron population in the area). "I have never made wine in my life," George says. The products with which the winery opened included wines from blueberries, cranberries, raspberries, peaches, and apricots.

To develop the winery, George dipped into the expertise within his family. One son, a union business manager, steered the winery application through the regulators. Another, an engineer, designed the building, a simple and efficient structure with cedar siding and a veranda on the front, not unlike the period architecture around Fort Langley. A daughter, an accountant, helped set up the business systems. In 2006 George's son Richard, who had retired early from an engineering job, agreed to take over making Blue Heron's wines.

The production, 1,100 cases in 2007, is driven by demand, which should be brisk. Once a remote rural road, Dewdney Trunk is a thoroughfare bustling with traffic created by urban sprawl on the north side of the Fraser River. Flynn Farms, the parent of Blue Heron, operates a long-established farm market each season for its cranberries and blueberries. "We've sold blueberries here for 35 years," George says, adding proudly: "Anybody can sell a blueberry, but for repeat customers, you must have quality. We have customers that have been coming for years and years."

Since 2004 those customers have been given another reason to return to Flynn Farms.

BLUE MOON ESTATE WINERY

OPENING PROPOSED FOR 2009

4905 Darcy Road, Courtenay, BC V9J 1RS
250.338.9765
www.bluemoonwinery.ca
When to visit: To be established

THE FIRST FRUIT WINERY IN THE COMOX VALLEY, BLUE MOON FLOWS FROM A lifestyle decision that George Ehrler and Marla Limousin made in 1999 when they moved to the West Coast after many years in the Arctic. "We were pretty tired of winter," says Marla, a landscape architect and community planner who first went to the North in 1980. On October 15, 1980, to be precise. "It is funny how you remember the day you arrived in the Arctic and the day you left the Arctic," she says. George, an engineer, arrived in the North on June 19, 1989. They met there, married, and in 1998 set up their own consulting company, Ehrler Limousin & Associates. They continue to work in the North from their current base on a Courtenay blueberry farm, on assignments ranging from project management and community development to parks and community planning.

Cold weather aside, they moved to British Columbia primarily to get their two school-age boys into better educational institutions. They lived a couple of years on Saltspring Island until they found a 2.4-hectare (six-acre) organic farm just 10 minutes outside Courtenay. "We wanted that lifestyle of growing our own food, and having our kids know where food came from," Marla says. "And that work ethic of the farm."

George, whose heritage is Swiss, was born in Edmonton in 1958, while Marla was born in France and grew up in Ontario. Both have wine culture in the blood. Marla, after all, bears the name of the famous French forest that provides oak for premium wine barrels. Her family were not vineyard owners but certainly were familiar with wines and how to make them. "Grandma would get what she could and start fermenting it," she recalls. George's family travelled to the Okanagan most summers to pick cherries for homemade wine; and George absorbed winemaking skills and a desire to make wine.

"George has always wanted to make wine," Marla recounts. "He researches and drinks wine and has played with making wine. He'd always wanted a vineyard." Once they took over the blueberry farm, they realized they could also make fruit wines, encouraged by some test batches made with the help of a friend who was an experienced fruit winemaker.

The farm, known as Nature's Way Farm, has been growing blueberries since 1988. Surrounded with shade trees and berry bushes, the property has a remarkable spiritual serenity about it. "When we bought it, we felt that," Marla agrees. The farm had about a hectare (2½ acres) of mature blueberry plants growing on ideal peaty soil. They have planted more and now have five different varieties among their 2,700 plants. They credit the soil — what Marla calls the "blueberry terroir" — for their bountiful yields of berries. They have had no difficulty selling all the berries they can grow either at the farm gate or, along with their other produce, at local farmers' markets. Vancouver Island's biggest grocery chain also purchases their berries.

The farm has established a loyal and substantial clientele for its berries (customers start pre-ordering in January). Several years ago, not long after taking over the farm, George and Marla decided to send Christmas cards to their best customers. "We sent a thousand cards!" Marla recalls. "So we thought, 'We have an established market,' and we'd been talking about wine for a couple of years." With a solid client base, they moved ahead to develop the winery, alertly snapping up the winery equipment that came available when the Marshwood winery on Quadra Island closed in 2007. By the following summer they had converted one of the farm buildings into a spacious and attractive winery.

The debut wines are primarily dessert-style, but George is working on dry table wines made from fruit, including an oak-aged blackberry wine. Because they are cautious but perhaps also because their northern consulting keeps them busy, they started by making only the minimum volume of wine required for their licences, some 4,500 litres (1,000 gallons), that is, 500 cases, a year. Naturally, as consultants, they have a business plan that plots future growth. "If we get to 19,000 litres [about 2,100 cases] in five years, that is the target," Marla says. "If we are there, we are pretty happy."

Blue Moon, along with Jeff and Susan Vandermolen's Beaufort winery (grape wines), which also opened in 2008, opened a new wine region in the Comox Valley. Along with the other artisanal food producers in the valley (cheese, beer, and whisky), there is emerging what Marla calls the "critical mass" to draw wine tourists into the valley. She plans further developments of Blue Moon, adding cooking classes and wine pairings with local chefs.

BLUE MOUNTAIN VINEYARD & CELLARS

OPENED: 1992

2385 Allendale Road
RR1, Site 3, Comp 4, Okanagan Falls, BC V0H 1R0
250.497.8244
www.bluemountainwinery.com
When to visit: By appointment

RECOMMENDED

PINOT NOIR (BOTH STRIPE AND CREAM LABEL)
CHARDONNAY
PINOT GRIS
BRUT
SPARKLING ROSÉ
PINOT BLANC
GAMAY

BLUE MOUNTAIN'S SPINDLY FRENCH-MADE VINEYARD TRACTOR RESEMBLES A
moon buggy and is quite unlike any other vineyard tractor in the Okanagan. But
then, the dense new vineyard that Blue Mountain planted in 2007 and 2008 is also
unique in the Okanagan, double the usual planting density. One has to go to France
— say, to Domaine de la Romanée-Conti — to find the model. Blue Mountain may
make wine in the New World, but its benchmarks are the best of the Old.

The pattern was set in the 1980s when Ian and Jane Mavety switched their
vineyard from hybrid grapes to European varieties and started thinking about a
winery. "Jane and I actually packed our bags and went to Europe," Ian recounts.
There they discovered a taste for dry wines. They were out of step with their peers
back home who were planting German white varieties and making sweet wines.
Ian and Jane preferred the wines of Burgundy and, figuring their terroir was

Burgundian, imported the appropriate Burgundy varieties from France. They went to California for a consulting winemaker, hiring one who was born and trained in France. Later their son, Matt, studied winemaking in New Zealand but brought back Old World ideas, notably biodynamic viticulture and other sustainable farming concepts widely practised by top French estates. All of these influences have made Blue Mountain an island of original winemaking in the Okanagan.

Born in Vancouver in 1948, Ian Mavety armed himself to be a windburned farmer with a university degree in agriculture. In 1971, in partnership with a friend, he bought a rundown fruit farm 10 minutes south of Okanagan Falls, gradually converting the hay meadows and derelict cherry orchards to the hybrid grape varieties then planted widely in the Okanagan. They were not ideal wine varieties, but the grape growers of the day prospered. "Maréchal Foch financed this property," Ian once quipped. Like most other growers, he took the government-funded incentive to pull out hybrids in 1988 and replant with vinifera (something he had started to do on his own a few years earlier anyway).

Unlike their partner, who went into another business altogether, Ian and Jane wanted to keep farming. But they recognized that they had to open their own winery. "We just had to control the product from beginning to end and have some control over our own destiny," Ian says.

They developed Blue Mountain's vineyard, now 31.5 hectares (78 acres), with Pinot Noir and its relatives. "Pinot Gris, Pinot Blanc, and Pinot Noir all come from the very same parent," Ian notes. "Chardonnay comes from a different parent but basically requires the same conditions." Gamay, also a grape of Burgundy, was planted to give the winery a second red. Sauvignon Blanc, which thrives next to Burgundy in Sancerre, was added in the 2007 vineyard extension.

The architecture of the new plantings is radical compared with other Okanagan vineyards, or even compared to older sections of Blue Mountain's farm. The vines are planted surprisingly close to each other, a practice that tricks the vines into producing fewer grapes but grapes with more flavour. The vines are trained to posts and wires reaching no higher than the waist, in contrast to the shoulder-high rows of virtually every other vineyard. The balloon-tired moon buggy tractor lightly straddles these low-slung rows, with the operator looking onto the vines from above when tilling the soil. The tractor does not compact the soil and the weeds are eliminated mechanically, a sound organic practice.

The anchor in the vineyard has always been Pinot Noir, with six different clones grown for table wine and two more for sparkling wine. "I planted it because I was told I couldn't grow it," says Ian, whose stubborn independence is legendary. "I'm serious. I was told by a German winemaker that I couldn't grow it. But I knew that I liked the wine and that I couldn't afford it, so it was going to have to be made." Clonal diversity in the vineyard gives Ian and Matt, no longer relying on a consulting winemaker, more options when they put together complex blends in the winery.

The winery now makes about twelve thousand cases per year, including several sparkling wines. The understated wines display finesse and delicacy, with the ability to age. Beginning with the vintage of 2001, Blue Mountain — bucking an almost universal trend to higher-alcohol table wines — has moderated the alcohol level of its wines by picking the grapes when, as Ian says, they are ripe, not over-ripe. "The key," Matt argues, "is making wines that are suitable for food, that can be consumed without being heavy, because there is balance between the acid and the fruit — and the flavours are there." The labelling system is the essence of clarity. Reserve wines, which are the best cellar selections and get the longest barrel and bottle aging, have striped labels while the regular wines have cream labels.

The public perception is that Blue Mountain's wines are hard to get, although checking the winery's website may produce surprises. Blue Mountain wines are released to only a few select wine stores. Most are sold directly to its extensive mailing list and to restaurants.

The winery's tasting room is not open for drop-in visitors. As a family winery, Blue Mountain lacks the staff to look after casual visitors and insists on appointments, quite firmly. A telling wisecrack made the rounds of Okanagan wineries in the fall of 2003, the forest fire year, in which one fire swept right up to Blue Mountain's picturesque vineyard but was stopped at the fence. The fire did not go any farther, the joke went, because it did not have an appointment.

BONAPARTE BEND WINERY

OPENED: 1999

2520 Cariboo Highway, Cache Creek, BC V0K 1H0
250.457.6667
www.bbwinery.com
When to visit: Open daily 10 am – 5 pm April through September (closing at 4 pm
    Sundays and holidays) and 10 am – 5 pm Monday to Friday October through March
Restaurant: Bistro lunches

RECOMMENDED

RASPBERRY
RHUBARB
CRANBERRY

THE ONLY WINERY IN BRITISH COLUMBIA'S VAST RANCHING INTERIOR,
Bonaparte Bend was conceived on a beach in Hawaii. JoAnn and Gary Armstrong
were passing their Christmas vacation walking the beach in 1998, mulling ideas for
a business at their 65-hectare (160-acre) Cache Creek ranch. For some reason JoAnn
remembered a fruit wine that had been brought as a hostess gift to a seasonal party
at their home. "I turned to my husband," she recalls, "and said, 'When I get home
I am going to do a business plan on fruit wineries, because that is something we
might do.' That's what started it."

   Born in Idaho, JoAnn grew up on the legendary Gang Ranch, which her father
was managing. Located near Clinton, this was once the world's largest ranch (about
400,000 hectares, or 1 million acres), although it has since been broken up among
several owners, including a Saudi sheik. Gary Armstrong, born in Montana, is a veterinarian whose clients once included the Gang Ranch, where he met JoAnn. When
they married in 1974 he had interests in five veterinarian hospitals in the interior. He
wound up those interests after the couple moved to Cache Creek in 1980, where he

worked until selling his veterinary practice in 2006. JoAnn, trained in accounting, has looked after the numbers at their various businesses.

Eminently practical, JoAnn approached the Bonaparte Bend venture from a business viewpoint. "Neither one of our families were partakers of the wine industry," she says. It is not that they are teetotallers; the Armstrongs enjoyed wines when they encountered them in social settings. "But it is not something that we purchased or served at home a lot." That has changed little since the winery opened. "We usually have half a glass once or twice a week before dinner," she says. "I guess that's because we are getting up and going back out to work after dinner."

Having decided on that Hawaiian beach that a winery was a good idea, the Armstrongs applied their professional skills. "I did my business plan in February and March, and started building our building May 1, 1999," JoAnn remembers. The winery is an attractive structure just beside the highway, large enough to house the processing facility, a gift shop, and a small restaurant. She could have taken a cheaper shortcut but chose not to.

"I have cattle barns down here," she says of the Bonaparte Ranch, which the Armstrongs purchased in 1993. Overlooking the Bonaparte River, the property is a hobby ranch compared to the vast spread on which she grew up. But the pleasant acreage has been a ranch since 1862. "I could have started the winery in a barn but I didn't think that was the right facility. It was not the image I wanted to portray right off the bat. We decided we were going to do it the right way, right from the start."

They also contacted a consulting winemaker from the Okanagan who, unfortunately for the Armstrongs, bowed out after two long drives to Cache Creek and a few emails. "Then when I contacted a couple of other winemakers," she says, "they never did come to meet us or see our facility. It was just obvious that they weren't really interested."

So the Armstrongs did it themselves, with JoAnn poring over winemaking texts and Gary dipping into his veterinarian's invaluable knowledge of chemistry. "We were advised to make smaller batches, test batches," JoAnn says. She does not know whether it was courage or foolhardiness, but they plunged ahead with commercial lots, often as large as 1,400 litres (300 gallons) at a time. "I really wanted to get started," she says. "We had the building. We had the investment. People in the area were asking us what was going on. If we had taken the time to do a bunch of test batches, that would have put us behind another six or seven months. I thought if I was going through the effort, I wanted to be able to have a product for sale. I wanted to get started right away."

In no time they had a dozen or so different products, including wines from apricots, apples, blueberries, blackcurrants, blackberries, cranberries, raspberries, rhubarb, chokecherries, and honey. A blueberry-blackcurrant wine came about when JoAnn blended them to save the cost of separate labels. It has stayed in the line because it succeeded. "All our customers have their own favourites," she says.

Jamie Armstrong, her daughter who now manages the wine shop and bistro, has noted the strong loyalty that Bonaparte Bend's clients show for anything that is produced locally. Some of the winery's fruit is grown on a two-hectare (five-acre) orchard on the ranch and the rest is purchased.

Bonaparte Bend sells most of its wines at the wine shop and in the bistro, which is another example of JoAnn's commercial savvy. When she was writing the business plan, she concluded that it would not be economic to staff a tasting room without another activity also generating revenue. The object here is to serve fresh seasonal food in an informal setting. The bistro also lets the winery show off the many applications of its fruit wines. "We put a little bit of the raspberry wine in our raspberry cheesecake sauce," she reveals.

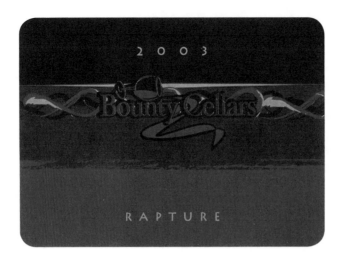

BOUNTY CELLARS

OPENED: 2005

7 – 364 Lougheed Road, Kelowna, BC V1X 7R8
250.765.9200 | 1.866.465.9463 (toll free)
www.bountycellars.com
When to visit: No wine shop

RECOMMENDED

RAPTURE
MERLOT

NOT MANY WINERIES WILL FILL ORDERS FOR CUSTOM-LABELLED WINES, because designing labels for short runs is considered a nuisance. But Ron Pennington, the nimble marketer who runs Bounty Cellars, saw this as an opportunity. He found a short-run labelling machine in the United States, hired graphic designers, and turned Bounty Cellars into the go-to winery for corporate clients needing personalized labels. More than three hundred private label designs were created during Bounty's first three years in business. "We do it better than anyone else," he believes.

This is an unusual niche. Other wineries will make custom-labelled wines on demand, typically asking for minimum quantity orders. At another Okanagan winery, the minimum order is one thousand cases. Bounty will do two cases at a time. "You wouldn't be our best customer," Ron admits. These cases add up. In 2007, when the winery produced 4,200 cases of wine in total, the private label niche accounted for about 60 percent of the revenues. Many of the clients are familiar names: Canron, the company that built the Vancouver Convention Centre; the Calgary Airport Authority; and the Mount Royal College Alumni are examples. It means you are just as likely to find a Bounty wine at a private reception as in a wine store — even at the occasional wedding. "We don't do a lot of weddings," Ron says. "They are very high-maintenance."

As Ron tells the story, the idea for Bounty Cellars arose when he took Alan Marks, then the winemaker for Summerhill, on a tour of his offices in a commercial mall not far from Kelowna's airport. Alan observed that the sprawling two-level building would be suitable for a commercial winery. Ron agreed, hired a consulting winemaker, and launched Bounty Cellars in 2005, with projected first-year sales of three thousand cases. The model, Ron says, is a French *négociant*. Bounty buys wine from other producers — both VQA wines and wine imported primarily from Washington State — and also ferments some of its own wine. This flexibility is permitted under the commercial licence.

Todd Moore, the consulting winemaker, is responsible for making the wines and for blending and polishing, if necessary, the purchased wines. The business plan calls for the production of premium wines commanding between $15 and $25 a bottle. "We don't dabble in the $9 market," Ron says.

Born in Medicine Hat in 1962, Ron, who has a degree in chemistry, got his marketing acumen during a long career with Canada Safeway. In 2001 he and his wife moved to the Okanagan for family reasons and quickly fell in love with the valley. He started a marketing company, then partnered with an Internet company and soon had a client list that included wineries. He also launched the Okanagan Wine Club, a wine-of-the-month club selling over the Internet. His partner is Wade Rains, a pharmacist with a rising passion for wine who is taking winemaking courses from the University of California at Davis.

In its initial years Bounty has continued to operate from its industrial park quarters. As practical as this location is for business, longer-term plans call for the development of a facility with a more public face. "We would like to have a destination for people to come to and try our products," Ron says. "That is a little bit more of the romance side of the business."

BURROWING OWL ESTATE WINERY

OPENED: 1998

> 100 Burrowing Owl Place, Oliver, BC V0H 1T0
> 250.498.0620 | 1.877.498.0620 (toll free)
> www.bovwine.ca
> When to visit: Open daily 10 am – 5 pm Easter through October or by appointment
> Restaurant: The Sonora Room. Closed during winter
> Accommodation: The Guest House (10 rooms)

RECOMMENDED

> SYRAH
> MERLOT
> MERITAGE
> CABERNET FRANC
> CHARDONNAY
> PINOT GRIS

THE BURROWING OWL VINEYARD IS RATTLESNAKE-FRIENDLY. THE FARM workers do not kill any diamondbacks they encounter; they have the vineyard manager move the snakes back to the surrounding desert. And in spring, when meadowlarks nest among the vines, the nests remain undisturbed until the eggs have hatched. These are but two examples of the green conscience informing decisions at the Burrowing Owl winery. It began with naming the winery for an endangered bird and setting up programs to protect wildlife, funded in part from the winery's modest tasting fees.

These green practices are not just marketing, winery founder Jim Wyse says. His environmental values run deep. Burrowing Owl was the first winery in the Okanagan to install solar panels, in 2006. With those and the geothermal heating and cooling system buried under the winery parking lot, Burrowing Owl gets much of its hot water and its cooling liquids from natural sources. Right from the start, the winery's extensive barrel cellars were buried five metres (16 feet) so that the ambient earth temperature provides the perfect cellar environment without artificial cooling.

Even the lighting at Burrowing Owl is designed so that the winery does not contribute to light pollution. "I am a bit of an astronomer," Jim says. "I love it up there when the stars are out. You can buy lights that are dark sky–approved. They shine down and they don't shine up. Those are the ones we picked."

Born in Toronto in 1938, Jim is a civil engineer with a business administration degree who came to Vancouver in 1968 as a management consultant, establishing a real estate development company five years later. Wine touring in Europe ignited his wine interest. In 1991, while working on a project in Vernon, he began looking for vineyard property. Two years later a realtor steered him to Black Sage Road. Sprawling vineyards had flourished here for 25 years until 1988, when most of the vines — mediocre hybrid varieties then — were pulled out. Believing this to be a prime site on which to grow big red wines, Jim first bought 40 hectares (100 acres), then added adjoining land until Burrowing Owl controlled 116.5 hectares (288 acres). "Our original big leap of faith was to get into the Bordeaux reds," Jim says. Sixty percent of the initial plantings were primarily Merlot, Cabernet Sauvignon, and Cabernet Franc, followed by Chardonnay, Pinot Gris, Syrah, and even small plantings of the Italian varietals, Sangiovese and Barbera.

He began by selling the grapes to Calona Vineyards but established a winery when he saw Calona winning awards with wines made from Burrowing Owl grapes. Jim struck a joint venture in 1997 with Cascadia Brands, Calona's parent at the time. Cascadia put up the money for the winery in exchange for 50 percent of the joint venture and the majority of the grapes from the vineyard. Cascadia also launched Sandhill Wines, capitalizing on Burrowing Owl's success with a label featuring a likeness of the owl also found on Burrowing Owl's label.

Many consumers confused the wineries for years, even after the joint venture was unwound in 2002, leaving Cascadia with two-thirds of the vineyard (including the Italian varietals). The Wyse family got the remaining third plus the winery. The Burrowing Owl vineyard today, including 10 hectares (25 acres) purchased from a neighbour a few years ago, totals 55 hectares (136 acres). After Andrew Peller Ltd. bought Calona and Sandhill in 2005, Sandhill's portion of the Burrowing Owl vineyard was renamed the Sandhill Vineyard and the owl was dropped from the labels. The distinction between two superb wineries will not be fully resolved until Sandhill builds a long-planned winery in its own vineyard.

Burrowing Owl's cult reputation was built on a succession of superb vintages made by a skilled team. Jim retained grower extraordinaire Richard Cleave to farm the vineyard and Bill Dyer of California — a "top-notch, world-class winemaker," Jim says — to make the wine. Jim's son, Steve, mentored in the cellar with the

Californian and took over for a few years after Bill left in 2004. Jeff Del Nin, a Canadian with Barossa winemaking experience, joined as winemaker in 2006. Alain Sutre, a leading Bordeaux wine consultant, has also been retained from time to time. This team has developed an unmistakeable style for its wines. "Our wines have never been accused of being thin," Jim says. The reds are fleshy and ripe. The barrel-fermented Chardonnay shows lush fruit. The Pinot Gris, crisp and fresh, defines the best that the Okanagan does with this variety.

The Wyse family — Jim's other son, Chris, took over management in 2007 — have turned the 30,000-case Burrowing Owl into perhaps the leading destination winery in the South Okanagan, with self-guided tours, a year-round restaurant run by a top chef, and a luxurious country inn. Most important, however, are the winery's green values, including sustainable agriculture in the sensitive black sage ecosystem. "We may never get to be truly organic, but we want to make sure we are not doing permanent damage," Jim says.

CALONA VINEYARDS

OPENED: 1932

1125 Richter Street, Kelowna, BC V1Y 2K6
250.762.9144 | 1.888.246.4472 (toll free)
www.calonavineyards.ca
When to visit: Open daily 9 am – 6 pm June through December, 9 am – 5 pm January
through May

RECOMMENDED

PRIVATE RESERVE EHRENFELSER ICEWINE
ARTIST SERIES PINOT BLANC
ARTIST SERIES PINOT GRIS
ARTIST SERIES PINOT NOIR
ARTIST SERIES UNOAKED CHARDONNAY
ARTIST SERIES CABERNET MERLOT
ARTIST SERIES SOVEREIGN OPAL

CAP CAPOZZI'S GRANDSON GREG TOOK OFFENCE ONCE WHEN HIS TEACHER told him he was not spelling "Kelowna" correctly. The next day he brought a bottle of "Calona" wine to class to support his spelling. And another Capozzi story joined the rich and legendary history of Calona Vineyards, the oldest continuously operating winery in British Columbia.

Originally called Domestic Wines and Byproducts, the winery shed that awkward name after a province-wide competition yielded the phonetic spelling that, years later, confused young Greg Capozzi. The winery was started by Giuseppe Ghezzi, an Italian entrepreneur (he had run a silk factory in Italy and a farm colony in Manitoba), who arrived in the Okanagan in 1931 with the know-how for making wines from cull apples. Short of cash, he got the support of Kelowna's business leaders, notably grocer Pasquale (Cap) Capozzi and hardware merchant W.A.C. Bennett, the future premier and then president of the city's chamber of commerce.

They raised the money, provided management, and, with Ghezzi's son Carlo as winemaker, got the Okanagan's first winery off the ground. The winery began making grape wines in 1936. Calona's early success was assured when it began producing St. John sacramental wine for the Catholic Church in Canada on the initiative of a Kelowna priest, Monsignor W. B. McKenzie.

Calona began selling other wines nationally (from a new Quebec winery as well as from the Kelowna plant) after 1960 under the management of Cap's hard-charging sons, Joe, Tom, and Herb. Cleverly, they patterned Calona's wines on the successful jug wines made by another Italian family they admired, the Gallo brothers in California. They even asked Gallo to invest in Calona. When that did not happen, they sold the winery in 1971 to a Montreal food conglomerate.

The 1970s was the decade in which Calona made its millionth bottle of wine. It had a national home run when, in 1977, it released Schloss Laderheim, an off-dry white then made from Okanagan Riesling grapes. It became Canada's best-selling domestic white within a few years. Three decades later the brand still endures.

Today's Calona still operates from the same sprawling winery in downtown Kelowna that the Capozzi brothers ran. The jug wine image, however, was laid to rest after the winemaking team headed by Howard Soon began producing the Artist Series of VQA wines. Born in Vancouver in 1952, Soon trained as a biochemist, joined Calona's quality control laboratory in 1980, and was quickly promoted to winemaker. His talents became evident once he began working with the vinifera grapes that were planted on Black Sage Road and elsewhere in the Okanagan in the 1990s. In 1999 an Artist Series Chardonnay won a gold medal at the Chardonnay du Monde competition in France. Two years later, an Artist Series Pinot Gris was best of show in the Los Angeles County Fair Wine Competition.

Calona drew attention to these fine new wines by commissioning original art for the labels, one of the first Okanagan wineries to do so. The first artist on a Calona label was Robb Dunfield, a Vancouver quadriplegic painter who holds the brush in his mouth. His first painting appeared on the winery's 1987 Rougeon, a red made with a hybrid variety no longer grown in the Okanagan. Today Dunfield's oils appear on the winery's unique Sovereign Opal, a spicy white made with the only commercial wine grape developed in the Okanagan. For the other labels the winery calls annually for submissions from BC artists.

In 2005 Calona was acquired by Andrew Peller Ltd., the national wine company formerly called Andrés Wines that was founded in 1961 in the Vancouver suburb of Port Moody. The latter winery was closed and Peller winemaking moved to the Kelowna winery, since there is capacity to spare on the three-hectare (7½-acre) property. Howard Soon, already the winemaker for Sandhill, also became Peller's senior winemaker in British Columbia. Kay Dickieson, a food science graduate from the University of Guelph, moved in 2008 from Peller in Ontario to become Calona's winemaker.

CAMELOT VINEYARDS

OPENED: 2009

> 3489 East Kelowna Road, Kelowna, BC V1W 4H1
> 250.862.8873
> www.camelotvineyards.ca
> When to visit: Open 10 am – 5 pm Thursday through Monday and by appointment

RECOMMENDED

CURRENT RANGE NOT TASTED

THE VENERABLE VINE GROWING WILD AGAINST THE VINEYARD FENCE HERE IS all that remains of the hectare (about 2½ acres) of Maréchal Foch that R.J. Young planted here in 1974. Unable to find a market for the grapes, he replaced the vines a few years later with apple trees. After R.J.'s death in 1996 his son, Robert, took over the property and continued growing apples until 2006. "I should have done grapes then," Robert says, looking back on 1996. The apple trees, which had produced as much as 2,700 kilograms (6,000 pounds) per year, came out after his accountant flagged apple growing as a losing proposition. In the spring of 2007 Robert and Denise Brass, his wife, planted two hectares (five acres) of Pinot Gris, Pinot Noir, Gewürztraminer, and Riesling.

Born in Quesnel in 1961, Robert came to the Okanagan when his father, a salesman of building supplies, arranged to take over a sales route in the interior. Although he grew up on an orchard, Robert's first love was aviation. In 1988 he started his career as a flight attendant with Air B.C., transferring the following year to Air Canada. Denise, who was born in Yorkshire and retains that country's melodic accent, became an Air Canada flight attendant in 1992. They met three years later when they were working the same flight. They continue working for the airline, generally arranging their schedules to work on the same flights to Europe and back once a week. That leaves time to run the vineyard and the winery.

They were nudged into the wine industry because apple growing had become unviable. "We decided we can only eat so many apples but we sure can drink a lot of wine," Denise says and laughs. "Initially we were going to grow the grapes and sell them, and Rob was going to build his dream woodworking shop. As we talked to other vintners, they said there is not a lot of money in selling grapes but there is a substantial amount in selling wine. That would carry us through to a nice little retirement."

They took a basic winemaking course but recognized that they should work with an experienced winemaker. Then they learned that Kelowna-born winemaker Ann Sperling and Peter Gamble, her winemaker husband, were looking for a winery in which to make the debut vintage for Sperling Vineyards Winery (which had not yet licensed its own winery). It was a remarkable fit, since Camelot is only a few kilometres from the Sperling family's vineyard. Bob and Denise signed Ann and Peter to a three-year winemaking contract and also let them make the first Sperling vintage in their winery.

"We were just lucky," Bob says. Ann is a member of the legendary Casoro family, which has grown grapes in the Kelowna area since 1925. Born in 1962, she started her winemaking career in 1984 with Andrés after getting a food sciences degree. She was the winemaker at CedarCreek from 1991 through 1995. Moving to Ontario, where she married winemaking consultant Peter Gamble, Ann consulted widely, worked at Malivoire Wine Company and, more recently, for Southbrook Vineyards (Canada's first vineyard with biodynamic certification). Bert and Velma Sperling, her parents, have an 18-hectare (45-acre) vineyard in East Kelowna, not far from Camelot. The Sperling family has considered establishing its own winery for several years.

Ann had plenty of incentive to re-engage with the Okanagan. Both she and Peter helped make Camelot's wines in 2008. She made Pinot Gris with grapes that Camelot purchased from the Sperling vineyard; and Chardonnay and Merlot from a small vineyard on the lakeshore in the nearby Mission district. Production totalled 400 cases, a modest start on Robert and Denise's ultimate target: 2,500 cases to 3,000 cases per year. At first the wines will be available primarily in the tasting room.

The winery's name is handed down from Robert's father. When the family lived in West Vancouver, R.J. carved "Camelot" onto a sign that he posted on his property. After R.J.'s death, Robert found the sign in the attic of the family's Kelowna home, and he posted it again as a working name for the orchard. Now as the winery name, Camelot has inspired a medieval theme. Robert fashioned a round table for the wine shop. "Knights of the Round Table," he explains. Denise, searching the Internet for artifacts, found a full-sized replica suit of armour in Germany. "We have swords and shields too," Robert says.

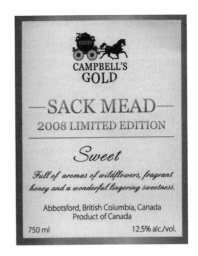

CAMPBELL'S GOLD HONEY FARM & MEADERY

OPENED: 2007

2595 Lefeuvre Road (280th Street), Abbotsford, BC V4X 1L5
604.856.2125
www.bchoney.com
When to visit: Open Saturday 10 am – 5 pm year-round. Also open noon – 6 pm
    Tuesday to Friday and Sunday June through December; 2 pm – 6 pm Tuesday to
    Friday January through May

RECOMMENDED

SACK MEAD
MELOMEL

BEFORE RETIRING IN 2004 TO BECOME A FULL-TIME BEEKEEPER, MIKE
Campbell spent 36 years teaching in Abbotsford schools. He has never stopped
teaching. Now his classroom is the red country barn that serves as the meadery
and retail store for Campbell's Gold Honey Farm. Mike knows just about everything
about bees, and he will share his knowledge with anyone who shows the slightest
interest. Coupled with tastings of honey and mead, Mike's lessons make Campbell's
Gold one of the most educational tasting rooms in the Fraser Valley. In fact, the
events staged here — and there is something new almost every month — include
an annual symposium for beekeepers.

Born in Vancouver in 1946 and raised on an Abbotsford dairy farm, Mike began
making wine in university. He became interested in mead in the 1960s. A friend with
honeybees near Peace River sold him surplus honey. Mike used a recipe from a 19th-
century medical book (a doctor's tonic honey wine) and liked the result well enough
to continue making mead.

He was introduced to bees in the mid-1990s by a member of his church who so upset her neighbours with a hive in an urban setting that she had to move it to the Campbell farm. One hive became 2 hives and then 10 hives. Mike and Judy, his wife, took a beekeeping course as they began keeping hives in 1997. They quickly found a profitable sideline when local blueberry farmers started hiring their hives to pollinate the plants. Soon they were deploying hives to raspberry fields and cranberry bogs under contract with the berry growers. "I started beekeeping as a hobby," says Mike. "It kept on growing like topsy. Now I have a few hundred hives. I think probably I'll stop around four hundred hives."

They are among the largest of the numerous beekeepers in the Fraser Valley. Without bees to pollinate the flowers, the valley would not have a substantial commercial production of fruit and berry crops. "Each blueberry flower needs to be visited at least four times," Mike says. "And there are seven million flowers per acre."

The Campbells have lived on this Abbotsford farm since 1987. When they decided to begin retailing various honey products, they first thought of using the buildings already there. "We were going to renovate the old barn that was on site but we ended up starting right from scratch," Mike says. The building that houses the meadery, the honey processing facility, and the retail store was designed deliberately to look like a country barn. Behind the façade, however, are many green design features, including a geothermal heating system. Early adopters of green technology, the Campbells also installed solar panels on the roof to heat their swimming pool.

The products in the store are an astonishing display of what bees can produce. The honey selections reflect the seasonal flowers and the sites where the hives are deployed, from orchards and berry farms to forested mountainsides. The Campbells make wax candles and, being teachers, pass on their skills with candle-making workshops each fall. They produce personal care products, including hand creams, honey lotions, and soap. There are healing products because a substance called propolis — the coating the bees put on the honey combs — has remarkable healing powers.

The meads, just another extension of the bounty from Mike's hives, include traditional honey wine and *melomel* meads — the term for meads blended with fruit juice. To get a feel for what his customers prefer, Mike launched with a light mead (7 percent alcohol), a "regular" mead at 10 percent alcohol, and a sack mead at 12 percent. The initial *melomel* meads included blackberry, blueberry, and elderberry. Mike also plans to produce fruit wines to complement the meads.

He started tentatively, making small lots to test the market and releasing his first meads on Valentine's Day in 2008. The demand caught him off guard. Even after limiting how much each customer could buy, he sold out his first batches before the next was ready. "If I had my druthers, I would hold onto it for four or five years," Mike says. "It ages well."

60   THE WINERIES OF BRITISH COLUMBIA

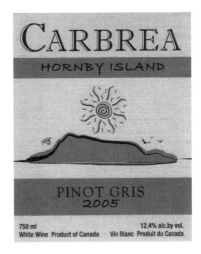

CARBREA VINEYARD & WINERY

OPENED: 2006

1885 Central Road, Hornby Island, BC V0R 1Z0
250.335.3120
www.carbreavineyard.com
When to visit: Open noon – 6 pm Wednesday through Sunday or by appointment.
   Picnic facilities
Accommodation: One-bedroom vineyard cottage

RECOMMENDED

PINOT NOIR
BLACKBERRY DESSERT WINE

WITH A POPULATION OF NINE HUNDRED, HORNBY ISLAND DESCRIBES ITSELF as a tightly knit community and "a well-kept secret to thousands of visitors." Only two short ferry rides and the traverse of Denman Island from Vancouver Island, Hornby is popular each summer with tourists, some of whom spend their vacation at the island's best-known resort, the Sea Breeze Lodge. Both the lodge and Carbrea Vineyard are operated by Stephen and Susan Bishop.

Both are long-time island residents, examples of Hornby's tightly knit community. Born in Edmonton in 1964, Stephen came to the island in 1972 when his parents purchased Sea Breeze Lodge. Susan, who is from Prince George, came to the island with her farming family in 1976, coming to know the Bishops while working at the resort. For some years the couple lived in Vancouver, where Stephen ran a small mining exploration company. He was so firmly rooted to the island that he called the company Hornby Exploration. In 1992 he and Susan moved back to take over the lodge.

Hornby Island gets its flavour, at least to some degree, from what islanders call the "counterculture" people who began moving here in the 1970s. Before that it had been a hard-scrabble farming community for one hundred years, as evidenced by the derelict orchards. Before that it was a fishing and trading outpost, given its current name about 1850 by the Hudson's Bay Company. The name remembers Rear Admiral Phipps Hornby, a one-time junior officer under Lord Nelson who commanded the Royal Navy station on Vancouver Island. History buffs exploring island landmarks with a gazetteer in hand will find a remarkable number of place names drawn from naval ranks.

Today Hornby Island is richly populated with artists and musicians who organize an annual festival that is the highlight of the summer. This is an ideal social milieu for a winery. Carbrea, which opened in 2006, was the island's first vineyard-based winery. Two years later another islander, Larry Pierce, planted a 1.2-hectare (three-acre) vineyard for his Little Tribune Farm and Winery.

"I've always had a passion for wine," Stephen says. That passion flourished once he took control of the wine list in the Sea Breeze dining room and dealt with the guests, many of them wine consumers. One in particular encouraged him to start a winery. In 2001 the Bishops, who had been living at the lodge but wanted more privacy, moved to a four-hectare (10-acre) property in the centre of the island. The following spring they began planting what ultimately became a three-hectare (7½-acre) vineyard. The varieties planted include Pinot Gris, Pinot Noir, Gewürztraminer, Agria, and Maréchal Foch. They picked a small harvest in 2005, although — in a story familiar to all with isolated vineyards — they lost Agria and Gewürztraminer to birds.

The name for the winery, which opened its tasting room in the spring of 2006, is fashioned from the names of their young daughters, Carlyn and Breanna. The first wines in the tasting room were produced from Okanagan grapes and under the tutelage of Stephen's mentor, Saanich winemaker Ken Winchester. The long-term plan is for Carbrea to produce primarily estate-grown wines, selling the entire production directly from the winery.

To Stephen's chagrin, no Carbrea wines are available in the Sea Breeze dining room. This is due to an antique prohibition against owners of licensed premises from selling their own products in those premises, unless located at the winery. This is the so-called "tied house" rule created in different circumstances a century ago. He has argued with politicians that the rule is particularly damaging to Carbrea, which cannot even hold winemaker dinners on Hornby, since the only white-tablecloth restaurant is the Sea Breeze dining room. His entreaties and letters seem not to have moved the regulators.

CASSINI CELLARS

OPENED: 2009

32056 Highway 97, Oliver, BC V0H 1T0
250.483.4370
When to visit: To be established

RECOMMENDED

CHARDONNAY
MERLOT
SHIRAZ
PINOT NOIR

WHEN ADRIAN CAPENEATA PLANTED THE WINERY'S TWO-HECTARE (FIVE-ACRE) vineyard in 2007, he chose primarily Cabernet Franc and Merlot, with just a few rows of Pinot Gris. "I believe in red wine," he booms. That appetite seems entirely in character for this forceful one-time restaurant manager from Romania.

He was born in 1960 into a family that had an 18-hectare (45-acre) vineyard but no opportunity to develop a winery because the state ordered the grapes to be sold to the public co-operative. Adrian went to work in a restaurant, soon becoming a manager. In 1990, after the collapse of Communism, he emigrated to Canada looking for better opportunities. He started in Montreal, polishing the French and English he had learned in school and working at up to three jobs at a time, including car sales. He worked in restaurants in the morning before going to car auctions to buy vehicles to repair and resell.

He credits his time in restaurants for kindling a love of wine. "I had a chance to discover food and wine going together," he reflects. "I discovered the taste and the romance of wine."

In 1993 he moved to Vancouver and to an entirely different career, selling equipment to fitness clubs. Within a year he had formed his own company to distribute, build, and service fitness equipment. During a vacation, Adrian and his wife, Alina, a realtor, became enchanted with the Okanagan. He then found time to refurbish and resell houses in Osoyoos, and juggled that with working for a Vancouver company supplying film studios. "I have that entrepreneur thing," he says and shrugs. "I see something and I'll go for it."

In late 2006 he bought an organic lavender farm south of Oliver with a strategic highway frontage. He had also established a commercial construction business, but it was something he put aside when he concluded that the winery needed "150 percent" of his time. "I like the vineyards," he says. "I see myself walking the dog in that vineyard in a few years. It's a kind of retirement business." Only someone used to tackling so many jobs at once would think of a winery like that.

Removing the lavender to make room for vines was also a show of entrepreneurship. Adrian first considered burning the plants until he discovered how much affection people had for the farm, which had operated for some years. As he recounts the story: "Everybody said, 'Oh, what a shame, what a pity. Nice, old beautiful plants, they will go now.' I realized these people loved them. Well, I thought, I'll sell them. So I put an ad in the newspaper. The first day that we advertised, we had 20 people in the parking lot waiting for me. We managed to sell six thousand plants." He kept enough to landscape the winery site because, he says, "I do want people to remember the old lavender farm."

He was similarly gung-ho in sourcing grape plants — "the old-fashioned way," Adrian says. "In the first week of February [2007], when people started pruning their vineyards, I took cuttings and put them in soil with the right fertilizer and temperature." Once the cuttings had developed new roots, they were planted. Meanwhile, a 600-square-metre (6,450-square-foot) Tuscan-style winery rose on the site, grapes were purchased, and he got consultant Philip Soo to make wines for 2007 with these grapes.

Ask Adrian what he spent on the handsome winery and he will only say: "A lot." That includes, by his estimate, $400,000 in sweat equity because, as a former builder, he was able to pitch in during construction. He put the reinforcing bars in place, poured some of the concrete himself, put the wire around the building for the stucco, and put much of the stonework in place. "I wanted to build this big, and properly," he says. "I am sure people want to see a nice building." The winery's name, Cassini, is the surname of his Italian grandfather.

Of all the wineries along the Golden Mile, Cassini, with its location right on the highway, is the most visible. For that reason, the tasting room is one of the largest, with a 10-metre (33-foot) bar long enough that 25 visitors can be served at once. Windows on two walls give guests a view of the barrel cellar and the tank cellar. "You'll be able to see the magic," Adrian promises. "You see what is going on and how the wine is made."

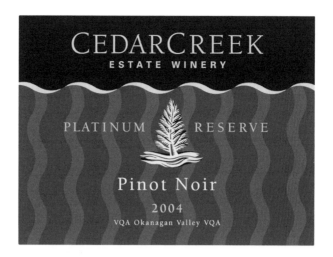

CEDARCREEK ESTATE WINERY

OPENED: 1980 (AS UNIACKE WINES)

> 5445 Lakeshore Road, Kelowna, BC V1W 4S5
> 250.764.8866 | 1.800.730.9463 (toll free)
> www.cedarcreek.bc.ca
> When to visit: Open daily 10 am – 6 pm May through October and 11 am – 5 pm
>   November through April
> Restaurant: Vineyard Terrace open daily 11:30 am – 3:30 pm mid-June
>   to mid-September

RECOMMENDED

> PINOT NOIR (ALL LABELS)
> CHARDONNAY (ALL LABELS)
> PLATINUM MERITAGE
> PLATINUM MERLOT
> PINOT GRIS
> EHRENFELSER

BEFORE HE CAME TO CEDARCREEK IN 2000, AMERICAN-BORN TOM DIBELLO made wine in California, Washington State, and Australia. "I love making wine here more than any place I have ever been," he says, launching into accolades for the Okanagan's potential. He makes them very well and CedarCreek has the awards to prove it, including winery of the year twice in the Canadian Wine Awards competition.

CedarCreek's story reflects the progress that turned the Okanagan into a top-drawer wine region in just three decades. One of the original estate wineries, CedarCreek was launched as Uniacke Wines in 1980 by David Mitchell, a geologist who, as his wife said at the time, "didn't even know how to start a tractor." Although hybrid grape varieties dominated Okanagan vineyards, David made the gutsy decision to plant noble varieties as well, including Merlot and Pinot Noir, now flagship varietals at CedarCreek.

In November 1986 the winery, which had been struggling, was purchased by Ross Fitzpatrick, a businessman with strong Okanagan roots (his father had managed fruit packing houses). While succeeding in business in Alberta and in the United States — in oil, aircraft parts, and gold mining — Ross pined for an Okanagan orchard and was attracted by Uniacke's apple trees. After taking over and renaming the winery, which is conveniently across the road from his imposing white Mediterranean house on the lakefront, Ross gradually replaced the orchard with vines, part of a $1.6 million investment to upgrade the winery.

The investment paid off with better wines, notably with Kelowna-born Ann Sperling as the winemaker from 1991 to 1995. Her 1992 Merlot was so well made that judges at a subsequent competition, on their own initiative, awarded it the only platinum medal ever given in the history of the Okanagan Wine Festival. Today the top CedarCreek wines are released under the Platinum Reserve label.

Gordon Fitzpatrick, Ross's son, took over as CedarCreek's president in 1996 when his father's political activities increased. (Ross was a member of the Canadian Senate for a decade until reaching the mandatory retirement age of 75 in 2008.) Gordon was a wine industry novice. Born in 1960 and a university economics graduate, he had previously worked in his father's mining company. The 1996 vintage, his first full year in the winery, was the worst in the Okanagan in a generation: cold, wet, and a month late. CedarCreek picked late-ripening Riesling in a snowstorm. "It was a scary harvest," Gordon remembers.

Gordon soon began correcting the shortcomings holding CedarCreek back. First he searched for an experienced winemaker. "I knew if we wanted to be the best, we had to surround ourselves with the best." He found Kevin Willenborg, a California-trained winemaker who arrived in the Okanagan for the 1998 vintage after 14 years with the Louis M. Martini winery. The winemaker talked Gordon into engaging a top-flight vineyard consultant from California. That has resulted in a dramatic jump in the quality of the grapes CedarCreek grows, which carried through to the wines.

CedarCreek has established vineyards in diverse areas of the Okanagan. The original 20-hectare (50-acre) vineyard at the winery now grows primarily Pinot Noir, Merlot, Pinot Gris, Chardonnay, Riesling, Gewürztraminer, and Ehrenfelser. The 16-hectare (40-acre) Greata Ranch vineyard, purchased in 1994 and now anchoring a proposed luxury housing development on Okanagan Lake's western shore south of Peachland, grows mainly Pinot Noir, Chardonnay, Pinot Blanc, and Gewürztraminer. The winery's big Bordeaux reds and its Syrah are grown on two Osoyoos Lake Bench properties — the 10-hectare (25-acre) Desert Ridge Vineyard, developed since 2002, and the 14-hectare (35-acre) Haynes Creek Vineyard, where planting began in 2008.

Tom DiBello took over as winemaker in 2000 when Kevin returned to the United States. Born in 1957 in New York, Tom grew up in California's Newport Beach, acquiring a lifelong love of surfing. After vacillating between medicine and business, he qualified as a winemaker at the University of California. His first job in 1983 was at Napa's respected Stag's Leap Wine Cellars, where he became director of cellar operations before leaving on a winemaking odyssey through several countries and states. Gordon lured him away from a Washington winery. CedarCreek's aging winery was rebuilt; by 2002 Tom had state-of-the-art winemaking tools to match the well-grown grapes.

No doubt the envy of his peers, Tom gets to buy some of the most expensive French oak barrels found in any Okanagan winery, from such high-end coopers as Dargaud & Jaeglé. "I am slowly changing the oak in this winery to [barrels imparting] much more finesse," he asserts. A few years ago he was able to buy D&J barrels made from the Napoleon Tree, a mammoth French oak tree that, according to legend, thrived for 350 years before being cut down because Napoleon's artillery avoided shelling the forest it grew in. Tom used these barrels in 2008 to age the wines for a super-premium Meritage.

For all the reputation he has earned with Pinot Noir, Chardonnay, and the big Bordeaux reds, Tom gets a special place in Okanagan wine history for elevating the profile of Ehrenfelser. The aromatic German white was planted in various Okanagan vineyards about 30 years ago (1978 in the case of the vineyard that grows most of CedarCreek's Ehrenfelser). Tom makes a uniquely expressive table wine that he calls "a big fruity monster." One of the most modestly priced of CedarCreek wines, it is always a tasting room favourite, so much so that the winery planted more on its home vineyard a few years ago.

CELISTA VINEYARDS

OPENING PROPOSED FOR 2009/10

2319 Beguelin Road, Celista, BC V0E 1L0
250.955.8600
When to visit: To be established

CELISTA VINEYARDS TAKES ITS NAME FROM THE COMMUNITY OF THE SAME name on the north shore of Shuswap Lake. Jake and Margaret Ootes (pronounced *O-tis*, like the elevator company) began planting vines in 2002, gradually expanding the vineyard as they gained experience in an agricultural career almost entirely new to them. After six years they had reached only two hectares (five acres) of grapes, about a third of the ultimate target. "I have to learn this game of growing grapes before I tackle the rest of the project," Jake said in 2008. "We're getting there."

Born in Holland in 1942, Jake came to Canada with his parents when he was eight and grew up in Renfrew, Ontario. After working as a journalist, he became a public information officer in Ottawa with the Department of Northern Affairs. In 1967 he moved to Yellowknife as an executive assistant to Stuart Hodgson, the commissioner of the Northwest Territories. Three years later he took charge of public affairs and communications for the territorial government. In 1975 he bought a small newspaper in Fort Saskatchewan (near Edmonton). He spent the next eight years building this into a trio of successful community papers that were then acquired by a large publisher. Returning to Yellowknife, he launched an in-flight magazine for a northern airline.

"Then I decided I would go into politics," Jake says. He was elected to the territorial legislature in 1995. During his two four-year terms in government he also served as the Minister of Education, retiring from politics in 2003. He and Margaret, the former owner of a Yellowknife art gallery, then moved to the rural property at Celista that Margaret had acquired several years earlier.

The 65-hectare (160-acre) farm overlooking the lake was at the time used primarily to grow hay and pasture animals. "This property was a bit of a wasteland," Jake remembers. "We thought we should plant grapes and get into wine." To decide what varieties to plant, he took advice from those already growing vines in the Shuswap district. "I am approaching it in steps," Jake said in 2004. "Because I am new to this industry, I want to make sure that what I do in the growing end is done properly."

He planted varieties that were already succeeding in other Shuswap vineyards. These include Maréchal Foch, Ortega, Madeleine Sylvaner, Madeleine Angevine, Gewürztraminer, and a small quantity of St. Laurent. The latter, a red variety popular in Austria, has shown itself susceptible to frost but the others all settled in on his vineyard. By the 2007 vintage he sold the first small crop of grapes from his plants.

Jake's plan was to start keeping some grapes for Celista's first wines beginning with the 2008 vintage, employing a consulting winemaker. Han Nevrkla, the founder of Larch Hills Winery, was available, having sold Larch Hills in 2005 to retire to nearby Salmon Arm. "I have never made wine," Jake says. Obviously that is a skill this many-talented man could acquire, but his priority is to master the art of growing good grapes. "First things first," he cautions. "Perfect the grapes, then move on to the winery."

THE CELLARS AT THE RISE

OPENING PROPOSED FOR 2009/10

364 Cordon Lane, Vernon, BC V1H 1Z9
250.542.5111 | 1.866.400.8488 (toll free)
www.therise.ca
When to visit: To be established

RECOMMENDED
_____

PINOT NOIR
RIESLING ICEWINE

THE TUSCAN-STYLE WINERY PLANNED FOR THE CELLARS AT THE RISE IS an anchor for the most northern of the Okanagan's wine villages. Indeed, the Okanagan Valley begins here. In their publicity material, the developers point out that boaters starting here, at the top end of Okanagan Lake, have 135 kilometres (84 miles) of clear sailing all the way to Penticton. It is a clever way of underlining a defining feature for this wine region.

The lake moderates the climate for the high-elevation vineyard at the Rise, almost 400 metres (1,300 feet) above the lake. This is one of the two reasons why good wine grapes can be matured this far north. The other is the steep southwestern pitch of the vineyard, which means that the vines are bathed in sun during the growing season. The vines have been planted on one side of a promontory that gets its name because it rises so dramatically above the valley. Once a ranch, this 297-hectare (734-acre) plateau just west of Vernon was acquired in 1989 for a resort and residential project by developer Leona Snider. Her firm, Okanagan Hills Development Corporation, had to sit on the property through a recession before starting to develop the resort in 2005. Some of the houses are to be located among the vines.

A hard-driving, earthy businesswoman, Leona was born in 1951 in Athabasca, Alberta. She moved to the Yukon in her 20s to start an accounting and management company. Then in 1976 she partnered with a trucker to form Yukon Drilling and Blasting Ltd. "My first job was on the Alaska Highway," she remembers. The business moved to British Columbia three years later. When the construction business softened in the late 1980s, she moved into real estate development, starting with a project in Whistler and then acquiring the Vernon property. She first tried to develop the property in 1992 but was frustrated when the housing market crashed and when governments blocked development. It was a decade before pro-development politicians came to power and Leona could proceed with the Rise. A professionally designed golf course, one of the resort's anchors, opened in 2008.

The winery project was launched with the planting of 2.4 hectares (six acres) of Pinot Noir and Riesling vines in 2005. Three years later, another five hectares (12½ acres) were planted with more Pinot Noir and Riesling as well as almost two hectares (five acres) of Gewürztraminer. Vineyard manager Jason Ranelli has blocked out a final two blocks, totalling another 2.4 hectares (six acres), and is considering planting Pinot Gris, along with a few rows each of Kerner and Muscat.

Working initially with winemaker Tilman Hainle, Leona considered building a 35,000-case winery that, for the most part, would be dug into the hillside. Ultimately the developer chose a more conservative design with just the barrel cellars underground. Glen Ragsdale Underground Associates, a builder of wine caves in Napa, has been consulted in the design. With a budget approaching $10 million, the Cellars at the Rise will still be one of the Okanagan's grander wineries when it goes ahead.

Before Tilman left this project to devote himself to his Working Horse Winery, he produced several vintages for the Rise with purchased grapes, starting in 2005. The winery had 4,600 cases of wine in its inventory in 2008, including Pinot Noir, Merlot, Riesling, and two vintages of icewine. The intent was to launch the winery with a well-stocked wine shop. However, direct sales prior to opening may cut into this cache of wine. "We have a huge database of people waiting for our wines," Jason said in the summer of 2008.

CHALET ESTATE WINERY

OPENED: 2001

> 11195 Chalet Road, North Saanich, BC V8L 5M1
> 250.656.2552
> www.chaletestatewinery.ca
> When to visit: Open 11 am – 5 pm Tuesday through Sunday. Closed Monday

RECOMMENDED

ORTEGA
BACCHUS
GEWÜRZTRAMINER
ORANGE MUSCAT
SYRAH
CABERNET MERLOT

PETER ELLMAN, TRAINED AS A CHEF, SPENT FOUR YEARS RUNNING A FINE French restaurant in Baton Rouge, Louisiana, until an economic downtown in 1984 had him considering other opportunities. In the restaurant he had met many wine salespeople, and he remembered that they "always looked tanned and relaxed." So he took a job selling California wines, beginning the long road that brought him and Jane, his wife, to taking over Chalet Estate Winery in the spring of 2008.

Chalet had been established by Michael Betts, a former British submarine officer, and Linda Plimley. In the 1980s they had purchased a pastoral forested property at the top end of the Saanich Peninsula, across the road from the storied Deep Cove Chalet restaurant. They considered growing walnuts or farming trout but, inspired by other new vineyards on the peninsula, planted grapevines in 1998. At first Michael, who had planted Ortega, Bacchus, and later Pinot Gris in a 1.2-hectare (three-acre) vineyard, thought of selling grapes to home winemakers. "Then I suddenly realized that it would be foolish to spend all this money and hard work just to grow grapes," he says. "So the next stage was establishing a winery."

Michael was not someone who shied away from learning a new career, having previously built boats and experimental aircraft. To learn winemaking he struck up a mentorship with Nanaimo-born Frank Supernak, a legendary Okanagan wine-maker. Sadly, Frank died accidentally late in 2002, but not before he passed on his winemaking skills. When the winery changed hands in 2008, Michael in turn agreed to mentor Peter through several vintages. "My background is truly marketing," Peter says. "But I have a cornucopia of winemakers that would help me."

Peter was born in Fish Creek, Wisconsin, on a peninsula remarkably similar to the Saanich Peninsula. A diploma from chefs school led first to jobs on luxury yachts and then to the Baton Rouge restaurant before he became a wine salesman, first for a big distributor, then for a group of California wine boutiques. Next Peter became a vice-president of marketing for a Napa winery called Folie à Deux as it emerged from bankruptcy. "We brought it from 3,000 cases to 38,000 cases in three years," he says.

By the time Folie à Deux was taken over by a larger group in 2005, Peter was in Edmonton, helping Jane, his wife, run a family-owned manufacturer of oil drilling equipment. She had spent 16 years as a general manager with the Marriott hotel chain. Unsettled by the 2001 terrorist attack on the World Trade Center in New York, they agreed to manage the Edmonton company when Jane's father decided to retire. Peter put his marketing skills to work and sales rose tenfold. "I made the phone ring," says Peter. "That's what I do." But, as Jane says, their heart was not in selling drilling rig mats.

They had wanted a winery of their own for about 10 years and looked as far afield as New Zealand. Bolstered by earnings from oil field equipment sales, they began looking at Okanagan wineries and were close to a deal on an Oliver-area vineyard when Jane, in an Internet search, spotted that Chalet was available. "We didn't know about island wineries," she says. They were utterly charmed by the Saanich Peninsula. "We knew immediately that this was where we wanted to spend the rest of our lives, it is so fantastic."

One of their objectives is to make what Peter calls "big dog red wines." That is hardly probable with the varieties that grow on the Saanich Peninsula, as Peter accepted when a visiting California winemaking friend told him: "You can't make big dog reds with chihuahuas." But what you can do, as Peter and Jane soon appreciated, was make those wines from purchased Okanagan grapes. Some of the best wines Michael Betts made for Chalet, such as Syrah, had been made with Okanagan grapes. Peter moved quickly to nail down Chalet's Okanagan grape suppliers and add a few more. As well, he continues to buy Saanich grapes, including Pinot Noir, to supplement the winery's small vineyard.

In the 2007 vintage, Chalet produced only 1,800 cases. Peter intends to increase production to about 8,500 cases over five years. "Market-driven is how we are operating at this place, with expansion being slow and steady," he says. There is a good chance that Chalet's reinvigorated tasting room will sell much of that wine. Peter has dug into his fund of recipes to prepare such Southern comfort food as Louisiana barbecued ribs on weekends, while Jane is running the wine shop with Marriott polish. "I told the managers that you can't train 'friendly,' " she recalls. "You have to hire friendly; they have to be that type of person. It is the same thing here."

CHANDRA ESTATE WINERY

OPENED: 2008

33264 5A Road, Oliver, BC V0H 1T0
250.498.1165 | 1.866.777.4081 (toll free)
www.chandrawinery.com
When to visit: Open daily 10 am – 6 pm April 1 to October 31 and by appointment

RECOMMENDED

PINOT GRIS
ISIS (BLAUFRÄNKISCH)
HALO (MERLOT)
RED FUSION

AFTER BUYING A VINEYARD EARLY IN 2005, DAVE DHILLON TELEPHONED THE news to his oldest daughter, Summer, who is an independent public relations executive in the Fraser Valley. Her astonished response: "I said, 'Dad, you're a suit man! You've been in the corrections service your whole life. What are you doing, becoming a farmer?' " But within a few years Dave had his entire urbanized family involved with him in this winery.

Born in India in 1939 and trained to be a teacher, Dave came to British Columbia in 1965 by way of Kenya and California. He planned to teach here as well but, finding that the intended post had been filled, he looked for something else and came across an advertisement for an officer in a BC penitentiary. "To be honest, I did not know what penitentiary meant," he recalls. "I thought that is a big thing, to become an officer." The recruiter soon disabused him of that notion but, impressed with Dave's qualifications, directed him to a more appropriate job, as a teacher in the federal penitentiary in Prince Albert, Saskatchewan. He arrived there in February 1966 when "it was 51 below with the wind chill."

In spite of that daunting start, Dave spent the next 30 years in the corrections service, advancing eventually to be the regional director in western Canada. In order to return to British Columbia he took a series of warden positions, surprising in view of his gentle nature and courtly manners. In the final two years before retiring in 1996, he was warden of a new minimum-security jail at Ferndale.

When he had had enough of the usual retirement pursuits (travelling), Dave went looking for something more challenging and found viticulture. A friend, Karnail Singh Sidhu, was a vineyard manager and organic grower in the Okanagan. (He opened Kalala winery at Westbank in 2008.) The two men partnered in businesses related to vineyards. Grape growing suited Dave's idea of a challenge, and he bought a four-hectare (10-acre) orchard and vineyard south of Oliver. The fruit trees came out and the entire property, except for a winery site, was fully planted by 2007. The primary varieties, which are grown organically, are Merlot, Pinot Noir, Blaufränkisch, Pinot Gris, and Chardonnay. Kalala's winemakers make the wine here, with the initial vintage being 2006.

Dave traces an interest in wine to a former colleague in corrections, who talked about wine all the time. "The whole field of the wine industry is very challenging," Dave says. "That's the kind of thing I like. I thought it can't be any more complex than inmate behaviour."

As mentioned, Dave soon involved his family in his winery project. Daughter Summer, who was born in 1971 and has a commerce degree, worked for a decade in BC liquor stores before launching her own public relations firm. "I personally would very much like to be a sommelier," she says. "We've grown up drinking wine. That's why I am so interested in the vineyard." With sister Kiren, who was born in 1975, she developed the winery's marketing plans. Their brother, Jess, who was born in 1977 and sells medical equipment, takes an interest in the vineyard.

The winery, based on an organic vineyard, was going to be called Ecovitis until Dave's family got involved. They thought the name sounded too much like a detergent and suggested Chandra, the Hindi word for moon. The name's echo of eastern mysticism reflects the Dhillon family's culture. Dave believes it also suits the vineyard's organic practices. "People used to plant and harvest according to the moon," he notes. "The moon played a great part in agriculture."

Chandra, with lunar names on the labels of its wines, opened its tasting room in 2009 in a portable building on the vineyard. The family's 10-year plan calls for the construction of an attractive winery encompassing both a restaurant and wine country accommodation. However, the Dhillons are in no rush to build. "Especially since the three of us are taking it over, we want to move a little slower," Summer said in 2008. "We're all learning to work together."

CHASE & WARREN ESTATE WINERY

OPENED: 2003

6253 Drinkwater Road, Port Alberni, BC V9Y 8H9
250.724.4909
www.chaseandwarren.ca
When to visit: Open daily 11 am – 5 pm in summer or by appointment

RECOMMENDED

PINOT NOIR
ORANIENSTEINER
BACCHUS
PINOT GRIS

CHASE & WARREN IS THE WINERY FOR STEAM TRAIN BUFFS. ITS VINEYARD is one of the stops for the Alberni Pacific Railway on its 35-minute run from the 1912 Canadian Pacific station in downtown Port Alberni to McLean's Mill, a national historic site with a steam-powered sawmill. A popular locally operated tourist excursion, the train is pulled by a restored 1929 Baldwin locomotive that was built for use in the region's logging industry. Vaughan Chase and Ron Crema, the partners behind Chase & Warren, shrewdly built a vineyard station where the railroad passes near the winery.

Chase & Warren is Canada's most western vineyard-based winery, with its vineyard a mere 10 minutes from downtown Port Alberni, a forestry and fishing community of 26,000 that has been redeveloping itself as a tourist and service centre. Vaughan has owned this acreage since 1979. When he decided to plant vines, one government expert he consulted warned him that the climate might be too challenging. Vaughan followed his own instincts. He had grown up in the Alberni Valley. He knew that the summers are every bit as hot as those of the Cowichan Valley where the majority of Vancouver Island vineyards are located. Of course, it rains heavily in the Alberni Valley, mostly in the winter. The trick is to get the grapes ripe and picked by October 15, but, with the valley's mild early spring, this can be done successfully. Vaughan has been doing it now for several years.

Vaughan left Port Alberni after high school, kicking around in various jobs in Alberta and elsewhere in British Columbia. After marrying, he and his wife, Joanne, lived in Victoria for three years until drawn back to Port Alberni by its affordability. "I went to work in the pulp mill for three years," he says. "It drove me crazy so I went back to university and got my teaching degree." Both he and his wife are teachers.

The vineyard was inspired after Vaughan planted a few vines of Gewürztraminer about 1991 and made a good wine. Then the slope just below his home was cleared of timber to generate cash for the needs of the Chase family. Vaughan and Ron, his brother-in-law, had no trouble envisaging a vineyard on that bare slope.

Grape growing is not new in the Alberni Valley, where many home gardeners have arbours, primarily of table grapes. But Vaughan had to go farther afield to research and acquire wine grapes. Conscious that he was pioneering, he tested about 40 varieties. The vines and the advice came from several sources, including the late John Harper's nursery at Cobble Hill in the Cowichan Valley. "A grand old man," Vaughan remembers Harper. "If it hadn't been for him, I don't think we'd be where we are."

Developing the vineyard had its challenges, as can be seen from an album of photographs displayed occasionally in the Chase & Warren tasting room. Vaughan applied many loads of lime to balance the acidity of what formerly had been the floor of a forest. To take away the winter rains, drainage was put into trenches dug 1.5 metres (five feet) deep. He began planting the vineyard in 1996. All of this work, along with modest winery building, was done on a shoestring, financed by his teacher's salary. Unable to afford bird netting in 2002, Vaughan lost much of the crop to birds. Anxious to get some revenue before the next vintage was ripe, Vaughan got the winery open in July 2003. Only about 150 cases of wine were on hand for the opening, but that was enough to get cash into the till and gain local notice.

The initial two-hectare (five-acre) vineyard's major varieties are Pinot Noir, Gewürztraminer, Chardonnay, Bacchus, and Pinot Gris. Since opening the winery, Vaughan has begun to extend the vineyard to a full 10 hectares (25 acres), and has consulted a landscape architect for site improvements.

Chase & Warren's wines, available primarily on Vancouver Island, are tailored sensibly to what Vaughan perceives as the tastes in his local market: "The original idea was that I would focus on the German varieties, Pinot Gris and Gewürztraminer, because they would suit the seafood that we have in the area." Several of the white blends were based on such aromatic Germanic varietals as Siegerrebe, Bacchus, and Oraniensteiner that he also had planted. Obviously it was a good call, because the wines sell out quickly. "We sold out of Bacchus on the opening weekend," he recalls. "We didn't have a lot of it, about 10 cases. The same with Müller-Thurgau. The reason we sold out of it was because the wines had oodles of varietal flavour." He attributes that to growing low quantities of grapes on each vine, enabling the vines to deliver vivid cool-climate flavours.

His personal palate is tuned to dry wines but, at this time, that is not where his local market is. "Most people don't like rippingly dry wines," he says. "Having done trials with friends, off-dry styles [of wines] are probably going to predominate. We have to sell the wine, and to do that, it has to be acceptable. As times goes on, and as I get more experienced, and as people's palates in our area become more educated, perhaps I'll go to more straight-up dry wines."

CHERRY POINT VINEYARDS

OPENED: 1994

> 840 Cherry Point Road, RR3, Cobble Hill, BC V0R 1L0
> 250.743.1272
> www.cherrypointvineyards.com
> When to visit: Open daily 10 am – 5 pm
> Restaurant: Bistro for brunch and lunch

RECOMMENDED

> ORTEGA
> FORTÉ BLANC
> SOLERA
> FORTÉ BRUT
> COWICHAN BLACKBERRY DESSERT WINE
> BÊTE NOIRE
> PINOT GRIS

SINCE 2004, THE COWICHAN INDIAN BAND HAS OWNED CHERRY POINT Vineyards, culminating a relationship begun several years earlier when winery founders Wayne and Helena Ulrich let band members sell wild blackberries each summer in the winery's parking lot. At first Helena used unsold berries for blackberry pies. Then Wayne and his winemaker began toying with blackberry wine, until finally creating the port-style dessert wine that has become Cherry Point's signature wine and has been emulated by several other island wineries. When the Ulrichs retired, the band took over the winery. They were following in the footsteps of the Osoyoos Indian Band, whose Nk'Mip Cellars was North America's first Aboriginal-owned winery.

The Quw'utsun', to use the band's proper name, is one of the largest First Nations bands in western Canada, with about 3,500 members living in the Cowichan

Valley. The band owns about 2,400 hectares (6,000 acres), much of it in small parcels throughout the valley. The band has a number of businesses, ranging from forestry to tourism. Noting the growth of the island's wine industry, the band's Khowutzun Development Corporation in 2001 took a hard look at planting vineyards. While identifying about 120 hectares (300 acres) of suitable land, they recognized that buying a going concern like Cherry Point gave them a considerable advantage. Cherry Point makes about nine thousand cases of wine, including its remarkably successful Cowichan Blackberry Dessert Wine (formerly called port).

No one seems to have commercialized blackberry wines before 2001, when Cherry Point was encouraged to do so after making a tasty trial batch of port-style wine. Putting out the word that it was buying berries, Cherry Point received 2,300 kilograms (5,000 pounds) by late summer. Because it is not a wine that needs much aging, the winery began pouring tasting samples within weeks and found that almost everyone who sampled it added their names to the list for when the wine was released. By Christmas the wine was being sold. It sold so quickly that Cherry Point tripled its blackberry purchases in 2003, then increased them again and again. In some recent vintages the quantity of blackberries processed each season has settled at around 12,000 kilograms (26,000 pounds).

Winemaker Simon Spencer has worked at Cherry Point from just before the 2003 blackberry vintage, mastering the challenge of processing a large volume of fruit with a small press. "That first year was pretty wretched," he recalls. Born in South Africa in 1981, he grew up in Britain, where his family is in the horse racing business. Interested in wine, he enrolled at Plumpton College, an agricultural college in East Sussex with a wine course. By the time he graduated in 2002, he had worked at an English winery, which specializes in sparkling wine, as well as in the south of France. When he came to the Okanagan for a summer job, planning to eventually head to Australia, Cherry Point needed a winemaker urgently and gave him a full-time post.

The popularity of the blackberry wine almost overshadows Cherry Point's track record for table wines. The vineyard was planted in 1990 on property that formerly was a mink farm. Over the years it has been expanded to 10 hectares (25 acres), with the major varieties being Pinot Noir, Pinot Gris, Ortega, and Gewürztraminer. With sufficient grapes from its estate and from other island vineyards, Cherry Point has stopped using Okanagan grapes for some of its wines.

The Ulrichs, Cherry Point's original owners, made a significant contribution to island viticulture in 1992 when they took over grape trials that the provincial government was abandoning. The 32 varieties in the test plot, including table grapes, had been imported from Europe. Wayne Ulrich considered the star to be a variety called Agria. The grape is a vinifera cross created in 1965 by Hungarian plant breeder József Csizmazia, although the legend recounted on the winery's website is far more colourful. Because the variety not only is red-skinned but also has very dark red juice, the winery has linked it to a Hungarian wine called Bull's Blood. As the story goes, when the outnumbered Hungarians were battling Turkish invaders in the 16th century, the soldiers refreshed themselves with Bull's Blood. The dark wine trickling onto their beards made them look so terrifying that the Turks fled.

The first Agria wines from Cherry Point were rough and sturdy, reflecting the considerable tannin in the skins. The winery had some success at taming the savage personality by blending it with Point Noir. Simon, the winemaker, saw Agria as a personal nemesis. "This is probably the most challenging variety to make," he said. "I hated Agria." While making 340 cases in 2003, he changed the winemaking technique so that the wine, still bold in taste and dark in colour, is far less gamey. Because of its earlier history, it was hard to sell it with the varietal name on the label. Cleverly, Simon created a proprietary name for the wine, Bête Noir, and commissioned a colourful series of label designs. Beginning in 2006 he began blending some Maréchal Foch into the wine, increasing the volume to about 400 cases and, in his view, making a more complex wine.

Another proprietary name, Forté, was coined for another premium series. The white is made with Pinot Blanc and the red is made with a French hybrid called Castel. More recently Cherry Point's first sparkling wine was released as Forté Brut. This is an effective way of dressing up varietals that might otherwise sell slowly, regardless of the wine's solid quality. Not that the winery has abandoned varietals: it continues to make excellent examples of Pinot Noir, Pinot Gris, Gewürztraminer, and Ortega.

CHURCH & STATE WINES

OPENED: 2002 (AS VICTORIA ESTATE WINERY)

SAANICH WINERY
1445 Benvenuto Avenue, Brentwood Bay, BC V8M 1J5
250.652.2671

OKANAGAN WINERY
31078 – 97th Street, Oliver, BC V0H 1T0
www.churchandstatewines.com
When to visit: Consult website

RECOMMENDED

QUINTESSENTIAL
SYRAH
MERITAGE
COYOTE BOWL MERLOT
PINOT NOIR
CHARDONNAY

WHEN KIM PULLEN TOOK OVER THE FAILING VICTORIA ESTATE WINERY IN 2004, the wines were so poor that a Victoria vinegar producer offered to buy some. Kim refused the offer, dumping 16,500 cases of wine instead and relaunching as Church & State Wines. "I thought to myself, as I was getting into this business, that I can just hear someone say, 'I have vinegar at home that came from *that* place,' " Kim says. Four years later the vastly improved Church & State wines were winning double gold awards at the major wine competitions in San Francisco and London.

Turning a venture around is nothing new for Kim. In the early 1990s when he was practising as a tax lawyer, he helped a fish farming company raise financing, only to be caught unawares when the directors told him the business was about to go into bankruptcy. Rather than let that happen, Kim took it over. Over a period of seven or eight years he was so successful that the company, Pacific National, grew to four hundred employees with sales of $25 million. He sold it to a Norwegian company, rewarding himself with a long cycling vacation in Australia. Kim has started several other businesses and is still the owner of a large marina in Sidney, not far from the Saanich winery.

There was no wine in his background other than a consumer's interest. "Mainly I just drink wine," he says. "I didn't drink beer, didn't drink a lot of spirits." He was born in Victoria into a military family and had a peripatetic upbringing as his father moved "from army camp to army camp" in Canada and Europe.

He was not long back in Canada from his Australian sabbatical when he was persuaded to take over Victoria Estate, the largest winery on Vancouver Island. "I knew that, over time, I could make this into something," he recalls. "Great building, great location." The winery, financed as a tax shelter, had opened in the spring of 2002 with a week-long party. That set the tone: the winery, just half an hour north of Victoria, was to be a compelling destination among the Saanich Peninsula's tourist attractions. However, the winery did not always make friends. The government once threatened to remove its licence after it sold wine not only in the winery's restaurant area (perfectly legal) but also in the adjoining tasting bar (not legal). Local vineyard owners, planting on the encouragement of the winery's promoters, were outraged at the lowball prices offered for their grapes. Restaurants were turned off by the inconsistent wines.

The decision to dump about $2 million worth of finished wine was triggered after Kim sent nine wines to the VQA tasting panel and all failed. To start Church & State with a clean slate, he hired a storied consulting winemaker, Bill Dyer of California. Bill had started consulting after 20 years as winemaker for Sterling Vineyards in the Napa Valley. His first client in British Columbia was Burrowing Owl winery, where he made the wine from 1997 through 2003. His distinctive wine styles won a cult following for Burrowing Owl's products that endured after he left. After a two-year absence from British Columbia, Bill joined the Church & State team, impressed that Kim was buying and planting vineyards a short distance from Burrowing Owl's Black Sage Bench vineyard.

Kim is planning a new winery in the Okanagan for Church & State, located just off Black Sage Road, on the vineyard he calls Coyote Bowl. Construction of a tasting room and boutique winery was put on hold in 2008 when Kim was able to lease a former fruit packing house nearby. Because the location almost fronts on Highway 97, a Church & State wine shop was established here in 2009. Ultimately, Kim still intends to erect a winery on the vineyard, in a building designed to make a statement.

In early 2008 he came close to selling the Saanich winery to a would-be winery owner from Alberta. When the financing fell through, Kim took the building off the market. It continues as an important sales outlet for Church & State wines, with an excellent location for weddings and other functions. The surrounding six-hectare (15-acre) vineyard is planted to Pinot Noir and Pinot Gris, grapes that are dedicated to sparkling wine. The cellar master at Saanich, Jim Faulkner, worked previously at Summerhill, a sparkling wine producer in the Okanagan. And Dawnine Dyer, Bill's wife, was the long-time winemaker at Napa sparkling wine producer Domaine Chandon.

Church & State now owns or controls 49 hectares (121 acres) in total, almost all in the South Okanagan. Two-thirds is planted to red varieties, including the five Bordeaux reds that go into Church & State's top blend, a premium wine called Quintessential. Kim relates how the winery staff struggled for 18 months to name the wine, with a 2008 release date looming. He went home from work one day and told his 14-year-old daughter about his frustrating search for a name that would imply five varietals. "She suggested Quintessential, like within 10 seconds," Kim marvels.

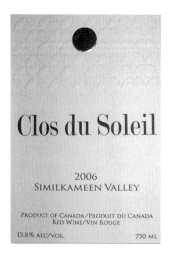

CLOS DU SOLEIL WINERY

OPENED: 2008

2568 Upper Bench Road, Keremeos, BC V0X 1N4
250.499.2831
www.closdusoleil.ca
When to visit: To be established

RECOMMENDED

CLOS DU SOLEIL WHITE (SAUVIGNON BLANC)
CLOS DU SOLEIL RED (MERITAGE)

WHEN HE WAS IN THE CANADIAN NAVY, CLOS DU SOLEIL SENIOR PARTNER Spencer Massie organized port appreciation nights for fellow officers. "It is not part of the normal curriculum," he says with a laugh. "I did it on my own. I thought it was important for our young officers to tell the difference between a tawny and a vintage port, and what it takes to create a good bottle of wine." He already knew the difference. When he was in charge of the ship's stores, he ensured that the supplies included good wine.

The son of an air traffic controller, Spencer was born in 1961 in Alert Bay, a tiny community on Cormorant Island on the BC coast. His father's numerous transfers, including a stint in Kenya, sparked an abiding taste for travel. His teen responsibility for getting dinner started (he was the oldest of four and his parents worked) fostered his interest in food. The wine part came naturally. In 1984, when he took a vacation after five years in the navy, he did a walking tour of French vineyards.

Spencer went to high school in Kelowna (winemaker Ann Sperling was a classmate) and joined the navy in 1979 as an officer trainee. "I became a captain of a ship and spent 15 years at sea," he says. "It was a good run, a great adventure, a great place to grow up." He retired in 2000 with the rank of lieutenant commander.

Spencer's last four years in the navy included a posting to San Diego. That provided many chances for him and Bonnie Henry, his wife (a physician), to spend time in California wine country, and not just to taste. "We are both runners," he says. "The Napa Marathon was part of our normal circuit." In 2002 they took part in perhaps the world's most famous wine run, the Marathon du Médoc, an event marking its 25th anniversary in 2009. "It's an event only the French would host," Spencer says. "What's unique about this marathon is that there are wine tastings along the way. The route goes through all the châteaux. It is a legitimate marathon but it is just a great experience. They say the more times you run it, the slower you get."

Spencer had also earned a master of business administration degree by the time he left the navy. He and Bonnie moved to Toronto, where she worked for a hospital. He helped set up two businesses (boat building and catering), then became a senior hospital administrator. In 2005 Bonnie's career took her to Vancouver and Spencer resumed business consulting there through his company, the Sixpence Group Ltd.

He had started "sniffing around" the Okanagan, as he puts it, for a way to get into the wine industry when he tasted a bottle of Josephine, the flagship red blend from Herder Vineyards, then met Lawrence and Sharon Herder at a Vancouver tasting of their wines. "When it came time to scope a few vineyards, I thought Lawrence makes great wines," Spencer recalls. "Maybe he is ready for another project." It turned out that he was.

By early 2007 Spencer (in partnership with three other professional couples) had acquired a four-hectare (10-acre) orchard on the Similkameen Valley's Upper Bench Road and enlisted the Herders in the Clos du Soleil project. That summer they planted all but a quarter hectare to red and white Bordeaux varieties. "I love everything classic French," Spencer says. "My family roots go back to Normandy. I really enjoy cooking and I do it in the classic French style. So a Bordeaux project is something I was excited about." The wineries' initial vintages — just 100 cases each of Sauvignon Blanc and Red Meritage in 2006 and 500 cases of each in 2007 — were made with purchased grapes, and that will remain so until the vineyard is in full production.

When the Herders completed their task in getting Clos du Soleil started in 2009, Spencer and his partners engaged Ann Sperling as the consulting winemaker. He and Ann were high school classmates in Kelowna, and lost touch with each other as their career paths diverged. However, when Spencer was living in Toronto in 2002, he read an article about Ann, who was then a rising star with the Malivoire winery in Ontario's wine country. The next time Spencer and Bonnie took a tasting weekend to that wine region, he looked up his former classmate. While still based in Ontario, Ann is now involved in launching family-owned Sperling Vineyards Winery in Kelowna and thus is available to help her school chum with Clos du Soleil.

COLUMBIA GARDENS VINEYARD & WINERY

OPENED: 2001

> 9340 Station Road, RR1, Site 11, Comp 61, Trail, BC V1R 4W6
> 250.367.7493
> www.cgwinery.com
> When to visit: Open daily 11 am – 5 pm May through October and by appointment.
>   Picnic facilities

RECOMMENDED

> MARÉCHAL FOCH PRIVATE RESERVE
> PINOT GRIS
> GEWÜRZTRAMINER
> GARDEN GOLD
> PINOT NOIR LATE HARVEST

THE SHADED PATIO AT THE COLUMBIA GARDENS WINERY, WHERE YOU CAN HAVE a glass of wine and relax beside 2.4 hectares (six acres) of vines, comes as a surprise to any tourist who has just driven past the hulking smelter at Trail. The winery is a verdant sanctuary, away from Trail's industrial heart, a pleasant 16-kilometre (10-mile) drive down Highway 22A toward the American border.

Columbia Gardens opened its log cabin tasting room in 2001. At the time it was the first winery in the Kootenays, two hours east of the Okanagan and well off the beaten path for wine tourists. The pioneering of Tom Bryden (who died in 2007) and Lawrence Wallace, his son-in-law, has borne fruit. Two neighbours have since planted vines. An hour's drive to the east in Creston, the second winery in the Kootenays, Skimmerhorn, opened in 2007, with a third and possibly a fourth under development. An entirely new wine region is being opened up.

The Bryden family have lived on this 20-hectare (50-acre) farm in the Columbia Valley since the 1930s, growing a range of products from vegetables to hay while

Tom worked in Trail as a purchasing manager. The fertile area referred to as Columbia Gardens is on a bench with a good southwestern exposure, overlooking the swift-flowing Columbia. The valley is hot enough for grapes, with mountains on both flanks of the river sheltering it from cold winds.

Except for one large dairy farm, whose corn crop draws the birds away from Columbia Gardens grapes, the bench consists largely of hobby farms (and now two other small vineyards). In the early 1990s, as Tom tired of growing hay, his son-in-law began researching the climate with grape growing in mind. They prepared thoroughly, seeking advice from Okanagan vineyard and winery professionals, spending time at the Summerland research station, and taking industry short courses. Their research on weather patterns over the years convinced them that the Columbia Valley, while not the Okanagan, was suitable for a wide range of grape varieties.

"Lawrence started experimental plots with some grape varieties to see which ones would do well in this climate and geographical region," Tom told me shortly after the winery opened. "Then we started phasing in plantings and over the next three or four years, we ended up with a six-acre vineyard. It's kind of grown from a bit of a hobby, to see how the varieties would do, to a commercial operation."

The reds in the vineyard are Maréchal Foch and Pinot Noir. The white varieties are Gewürztraminer, Auxerrois, and Chardonnay. As well there are small plantings of Kerner, Siegerrebe, and Schönburger; with their vivid aromas and flavours, the latter two varieties are good as single varietal wines as well as for lifting flavours in blended wines.

The white varieties struggled a little more than the reds before becoming established in the vineyard. The main problem was the soil's fertility. The vineyard stretching northward from the patio had been planted on a former hayfield. The vines responded to the rich soil with vigorous growth, putting more energy into foliage than into the grapes. They were brought into balance by limiting water and by planting grass between the rows to take up excess nutrients. Now that the vines have matured, they are easier to manage. Lawrence has found that especially so with the white varieties. "I always felt that reds would be easier to make and would be our signature wines," he said. "That hasn't been the case." Columbia Gardens's signature wine, in fact, has turned out to be an off-dry white called Garden Gold, a tasty blend of Auxerrois, Chardonnay, and Gewürztraminer.

A plumbing and heating contractor by trade, Lawrence is a winemaker by avocation. He makes his wines with the winery's own grapes as well as with purchased fruit. For a few years the winery was buying grapes from Skimmerhorn to produce a fine Pinot Gris. In most vintages, production consists of two or three reds, a rosé, as many as half a dozen whites, and a dessert wine or two. In the winery's early years, he set out to make a Pinot Noir icewine but happened to pick a winter that did not get cold enough. So he made a luscious late-harvest Pinot Noir, one of the winery's most popular wines. From the start Columbia Gardens has submitted its wines for tasting by the VQA panel. The VQA sticker on the bottles quietly makes the point that good wine can be made in the Kootenays.

The quiet charm of the Columbia Gardens wine shop, where Tom's son, Kevin, often resides, surprises first-time visitors, who do not expect a tasting room with sophisticated décor this far off the wine touring route. The shop is a comfortably appointed log house with a patio deck for wine tasting and picnic lunches in fine weather. The smokestacks of Trail are a world away.

CONSTANTIN & VASILICA WINERY

OPENED: 1998 (AS COLUMBIA VALLEY CLASSICS WINERY)

1385 Frost Road, Lindell Beach, BC V2R 4X8
604.858.5222
When to visit: Open daily 10 am – 7 pm April through September, 10 am – 4 pm
    Wednesday to Sunday October through March

RECOMMENDED
_____

CURRENT RANGE NOT TASTED

CONSTANTIN AND VASILICA NEMTANU, WHO BOUGHT THIS FARM AND WINERY IN 2004, smuggled themselves into Canada in 1992 — in a shipping container. It is an astonishing story.

Both are from Romania. Vasilica was born in 1968 into a family of 16. She combined work and schooling to earn a university degree in agronomy before marrying Constantin. He had been working in Holland, returned to Romania for a wife, and found Vasilica. In the turmoil surrounding the collapse of Romania's Communist government, they made their way to Belgium. There they arranged to stow away on a container before it was loaded onto a ship bound for Canada. They had one child and Vasilica was six months pregnant.

They barely survived the 13-day voyage. She remembers that they ran out of water five days before the ship arrived in Montreal. They were rescued after she banged on the wall of the container. "August 8, 1992," she says. "I will never forget. The police opened the container and gave us water and food. They got a translator because I did not speak French, I only spoke Romanian." Within months, however, they had been cleared to remain in Canada.

Perhaps the authorities sensed this was an exceptionally hard-working couple. Before long the pair had taken over the mortgage on a modest house and turned it into a rental property. One fixer-upper led to another as they scrabbled to establish themselves. "I fixed and I painted," she remembers. "I had three children at the time. I give the food to my children, put them in their room. Then I paint and I fix."

Although Constantin did the bigger jobs, Vasilica seldom avoided them. When a triplex they owned needed plumbing replaced and the tradesman's quote was a prohibitive $5,000, she rented the tools and did the job herself for $500. By the time they left Montreal, they had owned and run seven rental properties.

"I am making a future for my children," says Vasilica, now the mother of five. "I work hard. I want my children to go to school and to university. This is number one, to make good at school. It is good for their futures." Her second priority is to ensure a sound spiritual life for her family. "If you are not close to God, you do not know what direction you are going in your life."

In part that explains the family's decision to leave the city for the countryside. They chose British Columbia for the climate, after enduring a dozen Montreal winters, finding a 16-hectare (40-acre) nut and berry farm at the south end of Cultus Lake in the eastern Fraser Valley. It just so happened that the farm had a winery attached to it, called Columbia Valley Classics.

British Columbia's first modern-era fruit winery, it had been opened by John Stuyt, a Dutch-born horticulturist, who ran it for six years before falling ill with cancer. John did not have a winery in mind when he bought the farm in 1989. He just believed that the Columbia Valley is a superior place for growing berries and nuts. He came upon the scenic valley during a Sunday afternoon drive and bought the farm five days later. He planted hazelnut trees on half the property. On the rest he planted raspberries, blueberries, currants, gooseberries, saskatoon berries, and eventually a modest vineyard. After making jams, jellies, and other confections, he recruited a winemaker called Dominic Rivard. A Quebec native, Dominic mastered the art of fruit wines here and went on to an international career that has included wine projects in China and, currently, Thailand.

Vasilica recruited consultant Ron Taylor to make the wines for her. The former winemaker at Andrés Wines in Port Moody, Ron has become one the leading fruit wine consultants in British Columbia. "Thank God for Mr. Ron," says Vasilica, recognizing that she needed help to master the wine business. Given her career so far, it seems just a matter of time before wine will be as easy for her as, say, fixing plumbing.

The wine portfolio has changed little from the one originally created by Dominic. It includes a dry white currant wine made from a rarely grown variety called White Pearl, which John Stuyt sourced in Holland. One of the most popular wines is a blend of raspberry and red currant, called Velvet Royal. The fortified wines include a hazelnut liqueur, one of the many products from the farm's 7.5 hectares (18 acres) of hazelnut trees.

CROWSNEST VINEYARDS

OPENED: 1995

2035 Surprise Drive, Cawston, BC V0X 1C0
250.499.5129
www.crowsnestvineyards.com
When to visit: Open daily 10 am – 5 pm
Accommodation: Landgasthof (Country Inn) and Restaurant

RECOMMENDED

CHARDONNAY FAMILY RESERVE STAHLTANK
RIESLING FAMILY RESERVE
BARCELLO CANYON CHARDONNAY STAHLTANK

SINCE CROWSNEST VINEYARDS OPENED ITS QUAINTLY EUROPEAN COUNTRY inn in 2007, Sascha Heinecke has, from time to time, worn a white chef's apron while attending the wine shop. It is the apron he ties on early each morning to bake sourdough bread for the winery restaurant. The bread is as popular as Crowsnest's wine, with a repeat clientele. Sascha, who has a German diploma in hotel management, says with a laugh, "I never thought I would be running a kitchen, but it's a lot of fun."

The ambiance of Crowsnest, where the restaurant specializes in Bavarian comfort food, is how the Heinecke family — parents Olaf and Sabine, Sascha, and his winemaking sister, Ann — maintains its German roots. Olaf, a native of Leipzig in the former East Germany, traces his interest in wine growing to the house in Germany's Baden-Württemberg wine region where he settled his family after escaping from East Germany in 1982. Like other homes in the subdivision, it had three or four rows of vines. The grapes went to the local co-operative in return for cash or wine. "That's how it started," he says.

In West Germany, he became a successful property developer until he sold his company. "Part of the contract was that I couldn't work in the development business for the next five years," he says. "Then we started travelling." During a vacation to British Columbia, he was surprised to find vineyards. "I never thought there were grapes here, just polar bears and Eskimos." He and Sabine moved to the Okanagan in 1995. After running Penticton-area vineyards for three years with the intent to open a winery, they decided that an existing winery was a faster way into the business.

Crowsnest, which they bought in the fall of 1998, was opened in 1995 by Hugh and Andrea McDonald. Then only the second winery in the Similkameen Valley, it struggled to sell five hundred cases per year to the few wine tourists visiting the valley. Subsequently Olaf wondered whether it had perhaps been a "cuckoo idea" to buy a winery here rather than start from scratch on the Naramata Bench. But he has never been one to waste much time looking back. He and his family directed all of their considerable energies into making Crowsnest the largest Similkameen winery, raising the annual production from about five hundred to six thousand cases.

Olaf mustered his entire family for the business. Neither Sascha, born in 1978, nor Ann originally planned to follow their parents to Canada but responded to the summons. Ann, who is three years younger than her brother, has a winemaking diploma from Weinsberg. Beginning with the 1999 vintage, the winery retained consultant Todd Moore to work with her for several years. Today the cellar is her territory.

Crowsnest is primarily a white wine producer. That reflects the major varieties in the 5.5-hectare (13½-acre) vineyard: Auxerrois, Chardonnay, Riesling, Pinot Gris, and Gewürztraminer. The primary red varieties are Merlot and Pinot Noir. However, Sascha suggests that since Crowsnest can always buy red varieties from the Okanagan, the vineyard will continue to grow mostly white varieties. The site, he says, is "great for whites." Even though the growing days are hot, the temperature drops sharply at night as the cooling winds stream down the valley from Manning Park. And the cool evenings preserve the vivid flavours and acidity so important for the fruit-forward style of Crowsnest's white wines. The unoaked Stahltank Chardonnay — Stahltank means "steel tank" — and the Rieslings are crisp and fresh.

Ann has solved the challenge of selling Auxerrois, an excellent Alsace variety with peach flavours that has seldom won a consumer foothold among all the varietals made in British Columbia. She blends the variety into Barcello Canyon Cuvée 3, an easy drinking wine that is two-thirds Auxerrois, with Pinot Gris and Chardonnay making up the rest of the blend.

In recent years the Barcello Canyon has begun to replace Crowsnest on the labels. Originally it was designed to be the premium label, a role now assumed by the Crowsnest Family Reserve label. The name Barcello Canyon comes from the mountain pass between Oliver in the Okanagan and Cawston in the Similkameen Valley, passable in summer over a dirt road.

As soon as the family took over Crowsnest, Sabine Heinecke opened a well-received restaurant offering stick-to-the-ribs German cuisine (bratwurst, schnitzel, meat loaf). The restaurant now occupies part of the Landgasthof, as the Heinecke family calls its country inn. The seven rooms in the inn, with furniture imported from Germany, provide much-needed wine country lodging for the Similkameen Valley. Sascha, when he is not baking his loaves of sourdough, is busy finding local products for his kitchen. He takes advantage of the large number of organic farms in the Similkameen to use organic produce. "You can't get any more local than this," he says proudly of the produce coming into the kitchen.

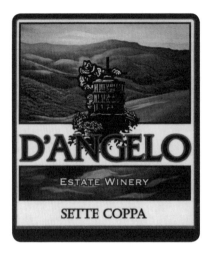

D'ANGELO ESTATE WINERY

OPENED: 2006

947 Lochore Road, Penticton, BC V2A 8V1
250.493.1364 | 1.866.329.6421 (toll free)
www.dangelowinery.com
When to visit: Open 10 am – 6 pm Monday through Saturday and 11 am – 5 pm Sunday
    May through October; and by appointment
Restaurant: Bistro
Accommodation: Vineyard View Bed & Breakfast (chalet and three suites)

RECOMMENDED

SETTE COPPA
TEMPRANILLO
TEMPRANILLO -8

SAL D'ANGELO GREW UP IN CANADA IN AN IMMIGRANT HOME WHERE HIS FAMILY made wine routinely each fall. "I grew up with the smell of fermenting grapes," he says. He became a science teacher but began to plant grapes in 1983 in his Windsor-area property, opening a winery six years later. He also began vacationing regularly on the Naramata Bench, attracted to the idea of growing grapes on sites more scenic than his flat Ontario vineyard, in a climate more suitable for grapes.

Since 2002 he has acquired an entire peninsula on the eastern bluffs above Lake Okanagan, only minutes north of Penticton. About three hectares (7½ acres) has currently been planted, but ultimately Sal expects to be growing three times that area. Not afraid to be original, Sal had the first Okanagan planting of Tempranillo, the leading red variety in Spain. He also planted red Bordeaux varieties and some Pinot Noir and intends to add Viognier, Sauvignon Blanc, and Chenin Blanc. The initial winery is in a metal-clad barn on the property, but Sal intends to have a three-level gravity-flow winery designed for a corner of the property that commands a view across Sal's entire peninsula.

Salvatore D'Angelo, to use his full given name, was born in 1953 in Abruzzi, a wine-growing province on Italy's Adriatic coast. He came to Canada three years later with his parents. Recalling his father's rustic wines, he says wine "is part of our culture. I, being the oldest son, had the responsibility every night to go down to the wine cellar and take out a carafe of wine for the evening meal." Eventually he and his father made wine together, soon arguing about techniques when Sal began applying modern winemaking practices. "It took me a long time to convince him," Sal says. "But in the last year we made wine together, he made six barrels of fabulous wine."

With opportunities limited in the Canadian wine industry at the time, Sal became an electrician and then a technical teacher (industrial robotics). Meanwhile he planted a small vineyard about 20 minutes outside Windsor, opening his Ontario winery in 1989. "I taught school and ran the vineyard and the winery as well for nine years," he says. "I left teaching in 1992. I took a two-year leave of absence and never went back."

He calculates that he was working 16-hour days while finding time to be a martial arts instructor. His superb fitness was the critical difference in his recovery from Guillain-Barré syndrome, an illness that leaves some of its victims in wheelchairs for life. It is a neurological condition that starts with paralysis in the feet and, over a few weeks, ascends toward the chest. Severe cases of paralysis interfere with breathing, sometimes fatally.

"I got stricken in 1993 and I was paralyzed from the neck down for three and a half years," says Sal, who had to be resuscitated once when he stopped breathing. He made what his doctors consider a complete recovery, as the paralysis receded gradually over five years. His illness began a week before the 1993 vintage. Sal stubbornly declined a wheelchair, figuring he would recover faster by forcing himself to walk.

The extent to which he refused to give in to a potentially lethal ailment is remarkable. On his last day in hospital, a technician spent a morning testing the conductivity of Sal's nervous system. "The technician put me on this cot and we started chatting," Sal recalls. "And after about three and a half hours — it was a four-hour test — he looked at me and said that most people that get on that cot were so depressed they had to be sent to a psychologist. 'And *you* want to keep selling!' I had snagged his wine order for their annual dinner in Windsor the next month. I got an $1,100 order from him by noon."

While recovering he always felt better in the Okanagan's dry climate, starting to vacation here in 1985. But only in 2002, after extensively exploring the region's back roads, did he purchase two adjoining orchards and begin converting the

11 hectares (27 acres) to grapes. "I should have bought back in 1989," he says wistfully, "when all the vineyards were for sale."

A former Ontario grape-growing king, Sal benefited from his experience to buy vineyard property with desirable qualities. It is a good frost-free site high on a peninsula with the lake on two sides and a dry creek bed on the third. And like all of the Naramata Bench, it has postcard-perfect views over Okanagan Lake.

The location, just beyond Munson Mountain, is strategic for wine touring. There are five wineries nearby, one reason why Sal converted a large house to a bed and breakfast. Guests can walk to all the nearby wineries and end the day by hiking the scenic Kettle Valley Trail, which runs just beside this vineyard.

DEEP CREEK WINE ESTATE & HAINLE VINEYARDS

OPENED: 1988 (AS HAINLE VINEYARDS)

5355 Trepanier Bench Road, Peachland, BC V0H 1X2
250.767.2525
www.hainle.com
When to visit: Open daily 10 am – 5 pm May through October
Restaurant: Vineyard Restaurant and Cookery School

RECOMMENDED

ZWEIGELT
PINOT NOIR
ICEWINE

DEEP CREEK WINE ESTATE PROPRIETOR WALTER HUBER HAS A $1 MILLION
icewine in the winery's cellar. Actually, the wine resides in a bank vault because
this is one of the very few bottles (if not the last) of the 1978 Hainle Icewine, the first
commercial vintage of a Canadian icewine. He used to have two but the other was
stolen from Walter's vehicle in 2007 the night before a wine show. Whether the wine
is really worth that much could only be settled in an auction — but Walter is unlikely
to part with this piece of wine history.

The bottle is a link to an earlier period. Walter bought this winery in 2002 from
the founding family, who had operated it as Hainle Vineyards. Family patriarch
Walter Hainle emigrated from Germany with his family in the early 1970s, initially to
Vancouver. He began buying Okanagan grapes to make wine at home. In 1974, con-
fronted with frozen grapes, he dipped into his knowledge of German winemaking
to make icewine, a style of wine then unknown in Canada. Within a few years the
Hainle family moved to Peachland, planted a vineyard, and, with a winery in mind,

sent their son, Tilman, back to Germany to train as a winemaker. Meanwhile Walter kept making icewine. As a result, when the family opened its winery in 1988, Hainle Vineyards had several vintages of icewine for sale, including the 1978, which was a Canadian first.

Now renamed Deep Creek, the winery reserves the Hainle name for the icewines made every year, except in mild winters or when bear or deer get into the vineyard at harvest. The 2003 25th Anniversary Icewine has sold in the tasting room for $188 for a 200-millilitre bottle. Rare bottles from the early 1980s, unavailable at any other Canadian winery, are priced up to $1,000 each.

Bold wine pricing came into the winery with Walter Huber, an entrepreneurial German resort operator who planted what he called the Deep Creek Vineyard in 2000 on a hillside overlooking Peachland. He was planning his own winery when he was able to buy the nearby Hainle winery from the family. The continuity of Hainle's singular wine style was assured because Tilman stayed on as winemaker for several years while launching his career as a consulting winemaker. He mentored his successor, Jason Parkes. The leader of a "spacepunk" rock band from Kitimat called Glasshead, Jason came into the wine industry by getting vineyard work with Walter because music was not paying the bills. Jason still maintains Glasshead but, to quote Walter, "he's a real fanatic about winemaking now."

The son of a successful car dealer, Walter was born in Munich in 1959. He was a management trainee with Mercedes-Benz when his family invested in a fishing lodge near Dryden, Ontario, and sent him to run it in 1980. Although he has had property in the Okanagan since 1991, he continues to operate the lodge. Not only that: noting that there are vineyards in nearby Minnesota, Walter has begun to toy with planting vines at his lodge. He speculates that, with a good winter-hardy rootstock, Riesling vines might survive the Ontario winters and allow him to produce icewine there.

Walter claims a substantial wine history for his family. On the winery's website he proclaims his adherence to something called the Wine Purity Law of 1856. This is a self-proclaimed standard said to have been created by the Huber family when they still lived in Germany, and adopted by Walter in the Okanagan in 2006. It is obviously inspired by Bavaria's famous Beer Purity Law of 1516, which, to this day, beneficially limits German beers to only natural ingredients. The Deep Creek wines, Walter notes, are made "without any chemicals or additives." He even wonders whether it might be feasible to list all of a wine's food values on the back label, assuming there is room enough and that the regulators let him.

When Walter bought the winery his intent was to triple its production, with a target of 12,000 to 15,000 cases per year. But after hitting 10,000 cases and discovering the marketing headaches of producing at that scale, Walter has shifted gears. He turned the winery into a boutique that makes perhaps 1,500 cases of estate-grown wine annually, producing small lots of premium-priced wines — between $80 and

$140 a bottle for Pinot Noir and $100 to $160 for Zweigelt. These highly concen-trated wines are from vines that are permitted to carry only a quarter to a third of the average for Okanagan vineyards. Limiting production like that makes the wines inherently expensive to begin with. Walter calculates that collectors and restaurants will pay his prices and give him a better living than volume production. However, he remains sufficiently down to earth that the winery continues to purchase grapes and produce more modestly priced wines for the tasting room.

"Zweigelt is by far my favourite wine," Walter says. "There is nothing that even comes close." He refers to a hearty red variety common in Austria. Now grown in the Deep Creek Vineyard (along with Pinot Noir), it is in the winery's portfolio almost by chance. When Walter took over the Hainle winery in the spring of 2002, there was little wine in inventory. He looked around for wines to buy. On the outskirts of Penticton, another German immigrant, Klaus Stadler, had planted Zweigelt in 1999 for a winery he called Benchland. Because Stadler had just opened the winery, he had more Zweigelt than he could sell, especially with that unfamiliar name on the label. Walter bought some inventory and renamed it Z. "It flew off the shelf in our place," he says. That inspired idea created a whole family of wines — Z2, Z3, and a Gewürztraminer-Riesling blend called G2 — that eliminate tongue twister names on labels.

There's a footnote to the story. Stadler sold his winery in 2005 (it is now Stonehill; see Holman Lang Wineries, page 186) and returned to Germany to import gourmet mushrooms. "He says it's a much better business than the wine business," Walter reports.

DEOL ESTATE WINERY

OPENED: 2008

> 6645 Somenos Road, Duncan, BC V9L 5Z3
> 250.746.3967
> www.deolestatewinery.com
> When to visit: Call for hours

RECOMMENDED

BLANC DE NOIR

THE DEOL FAMILY IS THE CLASSIC HARD-WORKING IMMIGRANT FAMILY. SURGIT Deol, the scion of the family, was born in 1930, and he still sets the pace for pruning in the winery's 9.3-hectare (23-acre) vineyard. Before bringing his family to Canada in 1980 from the Punjab, he ran a family farm. The crops included grain, corn, cotton, sugar cane, and rice, supplemented by livestock. The Deols collected the property taxes in their village and remitted them to the government. On the side, Surgit taught school.

"We always worked hard," says Gary, his son, who was born in 1961. "If you don't work, life is not good." It is a philosophy he shares with his older brother, Gurdip, who was born in 1956. They added to their workloads in 2008 by turning a red dairy barn on their farm north of Duncan into a winery. If the wines sell well, Gary says, they might plant another five hectares (12 acres) of vines.

When the family immigrated, they came first to Duncan and made a hard-scrabble living, doing such things as picking salal berries and harvesting holly. In 1982 they moved to Oliver and bought a small orchard but also laboured in vineyards, including Covert Farms (see Dunham & Froese Estate Winery, page 118) and the Shannon Pacific Vineyard on Black Sage Road (see Desert Hills Estate Winery, page 104). Gary spent a decade working with Lanny Martiniuk, the South

Okanagan's foremost propagator of grapes and now, with his family, owner of Stoneboat Vineyards.

When the fierce Okanagan sun caused some health concerns for the family, the Deols moved back to the Cowichan Valley in 1999. Now experienced grape growers, they planted vines the following year on what had formerly been a dairy farm. While waiting for the vines to produce marketable fruit, they grew a host of vegetables that they sold from their farm market. Several grape harvests were sold to other wineries in the valley before the Deols opened their own winery to add a little more value to the farm's production.

The vineyard is planted primarily with Gamay and Maréchal Foch, with small plots of Pinot Gris and Pinot Noir along with a little bit of Chardonnay, Orange Muscat, and early-ripening Schönburger. If more grapes are planted here, the vines are likely to include the Blattner hybrids now popular on Vancouver Island.

Daniel Cosman, who made the first vintage for Deol, was born in 1971 and grew up on a livestock and maple syrup farm in Quebec's eastern townships. His interest in fermentation began when, at 14, he began making both apple cider and mead in the basement of the family home. At the time he had no intention of making wine professionally and not much interest in remaining in agriculture. Instead he got a degree in international development and went to work in the Third World — in Africa and later in South and Central America. He returned to Canada when he realized, he says, "that agriculture was a whole lot less depressing than the corruption and poverty you find in the real world."

His first wine job in 2003 was in the cellar at the Fort Wine Company in Langley, where he mentored with Derrick Power, the winemaker at the time. From there he was recruited to work at the Godfrey-Brownell winery in the Cowichan Valley. That was where he met Gary Deol, who was doing some vineyard management there. Daniel, a partner in a grape propagation company, left the Deol winery in the fall of 2008 to concentrate on his own business.

The 2007 vintage on Vancouver Island was a challenging one, with a long cool summer that delayed the ripening. However, the Deols pulled off a reasonable vintage by cropping the vines lightly. The Gamay was turned into a tart rosé; the Pinot Noir, too light to be a good red, was produced as a crisp white wine. The Chardonnay was frozen after being picked and was turned into a cryo-extracted icewine, modelled on similar wines made in Oregon. The winery's big red was made from its Maréchal Foch, fermented on Pinot Noir skins to added character. In total Daniel produced about 1,600 cases, a volume that is a solid start for a new winery.

The winery's tasting room, with a commanding view of the vineyard, is in a century-old farmhouse that has been attractively restored. The ambiance is friendly, with no pretentions, reflecting the personalities of the owners.

DESERT HILLS ESTATE WINERY

OPENED: 2003

> 30480 – 71st Street (Black Sage Road), RR1, Site 52, Comp 11, Oliver, BC VOH 1T0
> 250.498.1040
> www.deserthills.ca
> When to visit: Open daily 10 am – 6 pm April through October, 10 am – 5 pm
>   November through March

RECOMMENDED

MIRAGE
SYRAH
GAMAY
MERLOT
PINOT GRIS
UNOAKED CHARDONNAY

BORN IN PUNJAB IN 1964, RANDY AND JESSE TOOR ARE THE ONLY TWINS running a winery in British Columbia. Their Desert Hills winery and vineyard is a family operation that includes their mother, Sukhminder, who patrols the impeccably managed vines with a small tractor. "She pretty well has a name for every plant," Randy suggests. Their younger brother, Dave, works away from the farm but takes time out to help.

Sponsored by a sister who already lived in Canada, the Toor family immigrated from India in 1982 after the death of their father, who had been in the farming and trucking businesses. They divided their time between Winnipeg, where a cousin lived, and the Okanagan, where the sister lived. The Toor brothers got their first taste of vineyard life as teenagers, spending several summers working on the former Shannon Pacific Vineyard across Black Sage Road from where they now live. Once one of the largest vineyards in the South Okanagan, most of Shannon Pacific's vines were pulled out after the 1988 harvest, and the property was replanted in the 1990s by new owners, with premium vinifera grapes.

The Toor family moved to their Black Sage Road property in 1988. It was an apple orchard that was struggling because the apples did not grow well on the sandy soil. The Toors tried other tree fruits, but when the vineyards across the road were replanted, the Toors decided to switch their 10 hectares (25 acres) to grapes if they could find a winery to buy the fruit. At the suggestion of Richard Cleave, a neighbour and veteran vineyard manager, the Toors approached the Domaine de Chaberton winery in Langley.

It was an inspired suggestion. Domaine de Chaberton, which grew only white grapes in its Langley vineyard, was desperate for premium red grapes after much-ballyhooed health claims created unexpected demand for red wines. The Toor brothers wanted to grow primarily reds. The winery agreed to help the Toors develop a vineyard in return for a grape supply contract. The brothers began removing the apple trees in 1995 and, within a few years, had planted the entire gentle west-facing slope with vines. "They [the Toors] grow very good grapes, which I was surprised to see, because they had never grown grapes before," marvels their winemaker, Elias Phiniotis.

Except for a small plot of Pinot Gris, the vineyard is dedicated to reds: Syrah, Merlot, Cabernet Sauvignon, Gamay, a little bit of Malbec, and Zinfandel. Domaine de Chaberton was able to augment its range of wines with award-winning reds with grapes from the Toor vineyard, beginning in 2000.

The brothers hired Cyprus-born Elias, Domaine de Chaberton's winemaker, as their winemaker as well when they launched Desert Hills. "It was a little dream, to start a small winery," Randy says. "We love the industry. We love the taste of wine." Desert Hills was launched with about 1,000 cases of wine. The intent was to remain small for some time, perhaps about 1,500 cases a year.

The outcome has been surprisingly different. With consumers and restaurants embracing Desert Hill wines, production in an expanded winery has risen to ten thousand cases annually. In 2005 the Toor family bought a nearby Black Sage Road property, a mature six-hectare (15-acre) vineyard planted mostly with Cabernet Sauvignon and Merlot, plus a little Petit Verdot. Then they acquired a three-hectare (7½-acre) property near Osoyoos, planting Cabernet Franc, Malbec, Viognier, and Syrah.

Although Desert Hills makes good whites, the thrust here is big reds. The winery's bold Bordeaux blend, called Mirage, now includes all five of the major Bordeaux red varieties. Perhaps the biggest red grown here is Syrah, which, in the Desert Hills terroir, produces wines distinctive for flavours of cloves and pepper. This Syrah produced wines that won the Lieutenant Governor's Award of Excellence for Domaine de Chaberton in 2006 and for Desert Hills in 2007.

The brothers have continued to grasp new opportunities. In 2008 they acquired (with a partner) a seven-hectare (17-acre) vineyard near the north end of Black Sage Road. The previous owner had cleared the property and planted vines that died because irrigation was not hooked up in time. With irrigation now in place, the Toors planted Syrah and Cabernet Sauvignon.

They are also thinking about opening a boutique winery on one of their Black Sage Road properties, perhaps two thousand cases per year. Time will tell whether they keep the second winery small.

2006 GEWÜRZTRAMINER
WOO WOO VINES

DIRTY LAUNDRY VINEYARD

OPENED: 1995 (AS SCHERZINGER VINEYARDS)

7311 Fiske Street, Summerland, BC V0H 1Z2
250.494.8815
www.dirtylaundry.ca
When to visit: Open daily 10 am – 5 pm April through October and by appointment.
   Picnic patio

RECOMMENDED

GEWÜRZTRAMINER THREAD BARE VINES
GEWÜRZTRAMINER WOO WOO VINES
GEWÜRZTRAMINER MADAM'S VINES
HUSH ROSÉ
PINOT NOIR

LAWYER BOB CAMPBELL'S EARLIEST CONNECTION WITH WINEMAKING WAS WHAT his grandmother made in her basement in Trail, where Bob was born in 1950. His connection with Summerland also far predates 2006, when, with five partners, he bought Dirty Laundry Vineyard. Since 1977, two years after he set up his law practice in Fort McMurray, Bob has had a second home on the Summerland lakefront.

In the 1980s he and a friend once talked about developing an Okanagan winery. Busy with a booming law office and running an Alberta motel chain, Bob kept that dream in the back of his mind until 2005. That spring he began converting a Summerland orchard to vines. Just as he started making winery plans, he learned that Dirty Laundry was for sale — because, ironically, it had become too successful after a daring image change the year before.

The winery had operated for a decade as Scherzinger Vineyards, after Edgar Scherzinger, a Bavarian woodcarver turned vintner. In 1978 Edgar planted

Gewürztraminer and Pinot Noir in this secluded vineyard, selling grapes primarily to Sumac Ridge until he opened his own winery.

Edgar retired in 2001, selling the winery to close friends Ron and Cher Watkins. Respecting that friendship, they retained the winery's original name for the next four years. Finally Ron got fed up explaining why the winery had a German name when he did not. To find a new name, he turned to Bernie Hadley-Beauregard, the Vancouver marketing whiz who had previously scored a home run by helping transform Prpich Hills Winery (also named for its founder) into Blasted Church.

Bernie dug into Summerland history to find a notorious Chinese laundry that, according to local lore, operated in the community around the turn of the 20th century. The owner, a former railway labourer, augmented the business by running a gambling den and a brothel. The business, of course, came to be called the Dirty Laundry, or so legend has it. In mid-2005 Ron and Cher adopted the name to replace Scherzinger. They also replaced the kitschy Scherzinger labels with pristine white labels featuring curvaceously naughty female figures.

The impact was immediate. Sales cleaned out the wine shop in a matter of weeks while, for the first time ever, restaurants began clamouring for product. Dirty Laundry's jammed winery, the size of a two-car garage if both cars were Volkswagens, was at capacity, making about two thousand cases per year. Faced with expanding or selling, Ron and Cher — she is a banker — took the financially prudent route and sold the winery to Bob Campbell and his well-heeled partners (all Alberta business people) just before the 2006 crush.

Bob had recognized a good thing as soon as they told him the Dirty Laundry story. "I thought it was an exciting story. I was very impressed by the marketing they had done and the success they had experienced," he recalls. "I saw an exciting business opportunity. Their shortfall was they weren't producing enough wine."

By the 2007 vintage Dirty Laundry's production, with the help of purchased grapes, tripled to 6,000 cases. Two buildings were erected in a hurry for winemaking and storage, pedestrian in design but functional. Nearby is the shaded picnic patio with attractive views over the vineyard and what remains of the Kettle Valley Railway. This expansion was just the first step in building Dirty Laundry to 18,000 cases, eventually with a second winery on a less secluded vineyard site on Giant's Head Road. Bob and his partners now have six Summerland vineyards, totalling more than 14 hectares (35 acres) of grapes. The primary varieties are Gewürztraminer, of course, and Pinot Gris, Sauvignon Blanc, Riesling, Viognier, and Pinot Noir.

Dirty Laundry also buys grapes from growers in the South Okanagan and the Similkameen Valley, emphasizing the big red varieties that mature better there than in the cooler Summerland vineyards. The objective is to raise the profile of Dirty Laundry's red wines as well. Naturally this involves the same cheeky marketing that propels the sale of the white wines. The winery's Bordeaux blend is called — what else? — Bordello.

DIVINO ESTATE WINERY

OPENED: 1983

1500 Freeman Road, Cobble Hill, BC V0R 1L0
250.743.2311
www.divinowine.ca
When to visit: Open 1 pm – 5 pm Friday and Saturday

RECOMMENDED

PINOT NOIR
PINOT GRIGIO

JOE BUSNARDO, THE VOLATILE OWNER OF DIVINO ESTATE WINERY, ONCE SAID in an interview that he does not even like making wine. The trouble is, when Joe says something outrageous like that, one never knows whether he means what he says or is just being ornery. He is, without question, the most independent-minded individual in British Columbia's wine industry. Sumac Ridge founder Harry McWatters, who can be just as strong-willed, once said of Joe: "If you were swimming down the river, you know Joe would be swimming up. And if the river changed directions, so would Joe."

Joe's determination has come in handy when he has locked horns with regulators. In 1996 he sold his original winery in the Okanagan and moved to a property south of Duncan, on Vancouver Island. "And to fight the system, I brought my licence here," Joe says. Fight he did: the Liquor Control and Licensing Branch tried to suspend his licence until he was producing wine from the newly planted Duncan property. Joe was able to get that ruling overturned by the Liquor Appeal Board.

If Joe were the kind of man who goes along to get along, he would never have planted premium vinifera grapes in the Okanagan in 1968, against all advice. He was born in 1934 in Treviso, not far from Venice, raised on a farm where his father grew a variety of produce. Joe, who studied at an agricultural college, "never liked any plants but grapes," he says. He emigrated to Canada in 1954 and, a few years later, his father ripped out the vines, planting mulberry bushes to raise silkworms.

Meanwhile Joe scraped together the money in 1967 to buy 27.5 hectares (68 acres) of raw land in the Okanagan Valley, south of Oliver. Within a few years he had as many as 128 different varieties of vines growing here in what was probably the biggest private trial planting of vinifera in the valley. Some of the cuttings came from California and some came from Italy, where a friend had a state-subsidized experimental vineyard. The friend thought Joe was mad to try the same thing in Canada without a subsidy.

Commercial wineries refused to pay him a premium for his vinifera. "I said, 'Look, grow your own grapes,'" he huffs. "I'll keep experimenting on the farm and let the birds eat it." He got a job as a heavy equipment operator, leaving the vineyard to its own devices until 1979. The previous winter a severe early freeze had devastated vineyards, killing even winter-hardy hybrid varieties. A good quantity of Joe's vinifera survived, however, and he took up grape growing again. This time he would become his own customer by opening one of the early estate wineries.

Self-trained, Joe approached winemaking in the tradition of the old country. "I'm making wine the primitive way, the way my father made wine," he has said. "I just throw in the grapes and hope for the best." And he made a lot of varieties and blends. "I make 25 wines," he once said. "I have wine for everybody. If a person says he does not like *any* of my wines, he had better stop drinking." His experimentation included varieties never before grown in the Okanagan. For example, he planted a big block of Garganega, the Italian white grape found in Soave wine. He grew other Italian whites no one else had, including Malvasia and Trebbiano. Hester Creek, which now owns that vineyard, has had great success with Trebbiano.

Over the years Joe narrowed his vineyard cohort down to about a dozen mainstream varieties, including Chardonnay, Pinot Blanc, Cabernet Franc, and Merlot. His wine production outpaced the sales and Divino became one of the few wineries able to offer mature wines, both at the winery and through several winery-owned retail stores. Visitors to his Vancouver Island tasting room are still able to taste and buy some of his older-vintage Okanagan wines.

Joe began entertaining offers for his superbly situated Okanagan vineyard in 1995. At the time he was buying a farm overlooking the busy Island Highway at Cobble Hill in the Cowichan Valley, heart of Vancouver Island's small wine region. He explained the move to Alan Daniels, a reporter for the *Vancouver Sun*: "I am tired of here. It is too hot. The place is too big. I am getting out."

Only Joe would consider the move to Cobble Hill as gearing down. With vines brought from his Okanagan vineyard, he has planted almost 12 hectares (30 acres). As always he has not paid much attention to what varieties are already being grown in the Cowichan Valley, choosing instead to learn for himself which varieties work and which do not. His beloved Garganega is not happy on the island, so he has replaced it, along with some other plantings. "But I am used to that," he says and shrugs. "In Oliver some grapes I planted and replanted eight times in 30 years. To come up with a varietal here will take me at least another five years."

Joe began making small quantities of wine in 1999 from the Cobble Hill vineyard. In 2001 he released his first two Vancouver Island wines, blends called Bay Rosso and Bay Bianco. "The wine here tastes completely different," he says. "We have to allow that, because in every country and in every area, there is a specific wine. Let's accept it."

DOMAINE DE CHABERTON ESTATE WINERY

OPENED: 1991

1064 - 216th Street, Langley, BC V2Z 1R3
604.530.1736 | 1.888.332.9463 (toll free)
www.domainedechaberton.com
When to visit: Open 10 am - 6 pm Monday to Saturday, 11 am - 6 pm on Sunday
Restaurant: Bacchus Bistro (604.530.9694) open 11:30 am - 3 pm Wednesday through
    Sunday and from 5:30 pm Friday and Saturday

RECOMMENDED

CANOE COVE WINES, INCLUDING SHIRAZ AND CHARDONNAY
SYRAH
MERITAGE
BACCHUS
MADELEINE SYLVANER
GEWÜRZTRAMINER
NORTH BLUFF PINK
NORTH BLUFF WHITE

THERE IS AN OLD SAYING THAT YOU ARE UNLIKELY TO MAKE GOOD WINE
unless you also drink good wine. Hong Kong businessman Anthony Cheng, who
owns this winery with Vancouver lawyer Eugene Kwan, maintains serious wine
cellars in several cities around the world and lists the legendary 1982 vintage of
Penfolds Grange as one of his favourite wines. Anthony brings his educated palate
to the blending of Domaine de Chaberton wines. It is hardly a coincidence, then,
that one of the first reds he helped blend, the 2003 Canoe Cove Syrah, won an
Award of Excellence in the annual competition run by British Columbia's lieutenant-
governor.

When the partners bought the winery late in 2004, Anthony had already
considered buying a villa in Provence. Eugene, on the other hand, had never even

toured a winery. He was the long-time Vancouver legal advisor for Anthony's West Coast real estate investments. Eugene was born in Shanghai in 1946. His family left China after the Communists took over, and he grew up in Victoria and Vancouver. After graduating from the law school at the University of British Columbia, Eugene practised in a wide range of legal disciplines. He met Anthony about 25 years ago when he began advising him on commercial real estate purchases in Vancouver. Ultimately they became fast friends, with some of Anthony's taste for fine wines rubbing off on Eugene.

Buying the winery was a matter of serendipity. The two had an afternoon free after negotiating another property deal. Anthony asked casually if there might be a country property an hour or so from Vancouver. Eugene telephoned a friend who happened to be consulting to Domaine de Chaberton and learned that the winery was for sale. The partners made a quick trip to the Langley winery. After looking at the property and at the financial statements, Eugene concluded that "as a business, it had a lot of potential." He called Anthony, saying, "I think I'll buy it and I want a partner and I need someone who knows something about wines." Anthony first scoffed at the notion of drinking $20 wines (most of Domaine de Chaberton's wines were priced around that range) but finally agreed. He now takes considerable pride in BC wines.

Domaine de Chaberton, now with 18.7 hectares (46¼ acres) of vineyard, pioneered commercial wine growing in the Fraser Valley. The founders were Claude and Inge Violet, who had come to Canada from France in 1979. Claude's family had been in the wine and spirits business for generations. One of Claude's ancestors created an enormously successful digestive drink called Byrrh. Claude's father merged the business with that of two competitors, a deal that left the Violet family more than comfortable.

He chose the Fraser Valley rather than the Okanagan because of its milder maritime climate (the hard winter of 1978–79 had just devastated Okanagan vineyards). He bought a farm south of Langley, almost on the US border, and bulldozed the soil into a gentle south-facing slope for the vineyard. He started planting in 1982 with Bacchus vines imported from a nursery in Germany, a variety bred a decade earlier to mature in cool climates. That variety remains the winery's flagship white; indeed, Eugene and Anthony have extended the Bacchus planting substantially in recent years after some of their growers in the North Okanagan switched to other varieties.

From the start, the Domaine de Chaberton vineyard has been growing cool-climate white varieties almost exclusively. The varieties, such as Madeleine Sylvaner, Madeleine Angevine, and Ortega, were a good choice viticulturally. But when Domaine de Chaberton opened in 1992, its portfolio of white wines was out of step with the market. The previous year's publicity about the so-called French Paradox — red wine drinkers in France supposedly had less heart disease in spite of eating high-fat cuisine — set off a frenzied demand for red wines. But there were almost no red grapes available for purchase in the Okanagan. The Violets finally resolved their problem by sponsoring orchardists on Black Sage Road, Randy and Jesse Toor, to switch to red grapes from apples in 1997. By the 2000 vintage, Domaine de Chaberton was getting Merlot, Cabernet Sauvignon, Gamay Noir, and Syrah. Elias Phiniotis, their winemaker (and the man who had linked them with the Toors), soon was making award-winning reds.

Anthony and Eugene have retained the labels and wine styles they took over from the Violets, including the Domaine de Chaberton name. This was the name of the Violet family farm in southwestern France. At the same time, Anthony's Grange-tuned palate has influenced the development of a different style — more New World than Old World — under the new Canoe Cove label.

DRAGONFLY HILL VINEYARD

OPENED: 2008

6130 Old West Saanich Road, Victoria, BC V9E 2G8
250.652.3782
www.dragonflyhillvineyard.com
When to visit: By appointment

RECOMMENDED

ORTEGA/AUXERROIS
CHARDONNAY

PLANTED IN 1993, DRAGONFLY HILL VINEYARD WAS THE FIRST COMMERCIAL vineyard on the Saanich Peninsula. This is a property with history. When stage-coaches travelled on picturesque Old West Saanich Road, there was a roadhouse here where passengers could get refreshments. In a closing of the circle, this became a place of refreshment again when Carol Wallace opened her tiny winery in 2008.

Born in 1959, Carol grew up in a Niagara Falls neighbourhood populated with Italian home vintners. Her father, a Scot, was drawn into the hobby, and he soon had his daughter involved. "My job was to start the siphon," she remembers. The second push to put her on the road to wine growing came in 1993 when her step-father, Wilf Middaugh, a former grape grower in Ontario, advised her to plant vines on the Saanich farm she had just acquired.

"A lot of people had berry farms," Carol recalls. "I wanted to grow something that was not prickly and that did not make me crawl on my knees to pick." After reading a government report on Cowichan Valley grape trials, she decided to plant Ortega, Auxerrois, and Schönburger. A clerk of the Citizenship Court in Victoria, she pored over reference books on viticulture until she was confused. Then, sensibly, she sought advice from Dennis Zanatta, the Italian immigrant who had begun grow-ing grapes in the Cowichan Valley in 1970. The government trials, in fact, had taken place on his vineyard (see Vigneti Zanatta Winery & Vineyards, page 439).

"I finally phoned him and said, 'I don't know what to do,' " she admits. "He said: 'Do it the way you would like to see it, the way that makes you happy, so you are happy in the vineyard. Don't worry about the books.' " So she laid out the vineyard and trained the vines in an unorthodox manner around the size of her tractor and her desire to work comfortably. She adopted organic practices, although the use of treated wooden vineyard posts has denied her organic certification.

The vineyard, less than a hectare (2½ acres) in size, has rows three metres (10 feet) apart, perhaps the widest spacing on the island. Giving the vines plenty of sunlight and good air movement resolves some challenges of island viticulture. Yet that was not the original reason for the spacing. "You base everything on the tractor," Carol explains. Her John Deere needs that much clearance between the rows, espe-cially when transporting the big sprayer. She once was asked how she would spend her share of winnings if she won the lottery. She said she would fly to Switzerland and buy the best small tractor she could.

Carol did not set out to open a winery, intending only to sell grapes. The Victoria Estate Winery (now Church & State Wines, page 83), when under devel-opment in 2000, promised to buy fruit from Carol and other new growers on the Saanich Peninsula. When it came time to do business, the price offered for the grapes was unacceptably low and the growers scrambled for other markets. Carol considered joining with the three partners behind the Starling Lane Winery, just a short distance away on Old West Saanich. Inclined to be independent, however, she started selling her grapes to other island wineries.

Salt Spring Vineyards, one of the buyers, made vineyard-designated wines from her grapes. "That's when I realized I was doing a pretty good job as a grape grower," she says. She got a further boost when the newly opened Brentwood Lodge began featuring Salt Spring's Dragonfly Hill Ortega in 2004. "Everybody was encouraging me," she says. With Salt Spring winemaker Paul Troop also making her wine, Carol began planning her own winery in 2005. Delayed by two surgeries to remove kidney stones, she opened three years later. "I tend to plod along steadily and slowly," she says, laughing gently. She worked her way up to five hundred cases per year, more or less the total capacity of her modest winery, a converted tractor garage too small for a tasting room.

"I'm not a huge red wine drinker," she says, even though she grew up with her father's red wine on the table all the time. While she planned a winery making whites only, she was struck at how often she was asked what red wines Dragonfly Hill would offer. So in 2005 she found one grape grower near Oliver to supply Merlot and Cabernet Sauvignon and another to sell her Chardonnay, all varieties not suited to the vineyards on the cool Saanich Peninsula.

"I was surprised that the Merlot Cabernet sold out first," she marvels. "I priced it the highest, $24.90 a bottle, and it was just, whizz, gone. Everybody wanted a whole case, everybody was reserving it. There were only 45 cases." She continued to buy those grapes in succeeding vintages. At the same time she added small plantings of red varieties in her vineyard — a selection of Swiss plant breeder Valentin Blattner's hybrids and some St. Laurent vines.

Dragonfly Hill's bucolic charm is heightened by the sheep that Carol keeps; after harvest they are allowed to graze in the vineyard. The winery's name is inspired by the dragonflies in the nearby ponds. The insects are featured on the winery's labels, which, Carol says, were designed for her by a Victoria tattoo artist. The script on the labels is Carol's own penmanship. "It's really personal," she says.

DUNHAM & FROESE ESTATE WINERY

OPENED: 2006

> 38614 107th Street (Seacrest Road), Oliver, BC V0H 1T0
> 250.498.9463
> www.dunhamfroese.ca
> When to visit: Open 10 am – 5 pm in May during spring wine festival, July 1 to October
> 31, and by appointment

RECOMMENDED

> AMICITIA (RED AND WHITE)
> MERLOT
> PINOT NOIR
> PINOT BLANC

THE FLAGSHIP WINES AT DUNHAM & FROESE ARE BLENDS MARKETED UNDER the Amicitia label, Latin for "friends." It is apt branding. This winery was conceived when two entrepreneurial friends, Shelly Covert and Crystal Froese, concluded that the project would be a great way to tap their skills and those of their spouses as well. Shelly is trained in accounting and administration, Crystal in marketing and promotion. Gene Covert manages a legendary organic farm near Oliver where he grows grapes (among other things), and Kirby Froese is a winemaker. "We're kind of the perfect foursome," Crystal suggests.

On the plateau just south of McIntyre Bluff, Covert Farms was established in 1961 by George Covert of California, a partner in a tomato packing company. As the family history puts it, he "tired of the rat race in California" and moved to the Okanagan. He had purchased a square mile of excellent farmland on a plateau flanking McIntyre Bluff. The farm very quickly became one of the Okanagan's major growers of tomatoes, onions, tree fruits, and grapes.

George's 73-hectare (180-acre) vineyard, planted to labrusca and hybrid grapes, was one of the five largest in the valley. In the late 1970s George even tested one of the valley's first mechanical harvesters. He abandoned the idea of using it because the machine, like many grape harvesters of that era, caused far too much damage to both the vines and the grapes. In any event, George had a traditional bent in agriculture: in the 1980s he reintroduced horses to replace some of the farm's tractors. All the vines except for six hectares (15 acres) of table grapes were pulled out after the 1988 vintage.

Wine grapes were planted again on the property in 2005 when the "perfect foursome" decided to launch a winery and when Andrew Peller Ltd. contracted to put in a separate 121-hectare (300-acre) vineyard, planted in 2007 and 2008. But Covert Farms has never kept all its eggs in one basket. The farm continues to produce apples, onions, and tomatoes, among numerous other fruits and vegetables, selling much of it at Pancho's Country Market, the farm market that Covert Farms opened in 2002. The farm also celebrates its tomatoes with an annual tomato festival on the first weekend of September, perhaps the best non-wine festival in the South Okanagan.

Gene Covert, who was born in 1971, is George's grandson. He is practical and down to earth, a family trait that guided his choice of a physical geography degree at the University of British Columbia. "When I looked at going into agriculture at UBC, it was too regionally specific," he explains. "There was the dairy program and the Fraser Valley stuff, but it does not adapt to what's happening in the Okanagan. So I figured, maybe if I don't go into agriculture, I have a degree I can use. But it is useful in agriculture. Everything I need to know about farming here, I have a whole family to teach me." He returned to the farm as operations manager and took over as general manager in 2004 after the sudden death of his father, Mike.

Shelly, an Edmonton-born teacher, conceived Pancho's Country Market. It is now the farm's principal retail outlet for a growing volume of organic produce. Gene is directing the gradual conversion of the property to organic standards, including the vineyards. That is why there are steel posts in the Peller vineyard — the vines that visitors drive by when they come to Dunham & Froese. Treated wood posts are not permitted in organic vineyards. "Our intent is that between 2008 and 2010, the entire property will be certified organic," Gene says. For Dunham & Froese, Gene has planted nine hectares (22¼ acres) of wine grapes, including the five Bordeaux reds, Zinfandel, Syrah, Pinot Blanc, Sémillon, and Sauvignon Blanc.

The winery's name draws on the families of both founders. Dunham is the maiden name of Gene's maternal grandmother. Crystal and Kirby bring Froese to the partnership. Both are Moose Jaw natives. She operates her own marketing and event management firm; one of her long-term clients has been the Festival of the Tomato. Born in 1970, Kirby Froese started his wine interest as a server at the Banff

Springs Hotel and as manager of a private wine store. From there he started wine-making at Sumac Ridge, a job that opened opportunities for him around the world.

He has made wine in Australia, in Chile, and in California. In the Okanagan, besides Sumac Ridge, he has worked at Hawthorne Mountain Vineyards (see See Ya Later Ranch, page 368), Red Rooster, and Hester Creek. While he likes to joke that he "can't hold a job," he has acquired an enviable amount of experience.

The partners have husbanded their resources carefully, establishing the winery and tasting room in existing buildings close to Pancho's on Covert Farms. "The infrastructure for a winery basically existed when this was conceived," Kirby says. "We didn't borrow any money to get into this and we want to stay in the black while we do this."

The winery launched with five hundred cases from its initial 2005 vintage, doubling that in 2007. The focus has been on Merlot, Pinot Noir, Pinot Blanc, and rosé. As the Covert Farms plantings come into production, leaving Dunham & Froese self-sufficient in grapes, production will be raised to about five thousand cases per year. At that point the perfect foursome will need to decide whether to coast or to ramp up production to ten thousand cases.

EAST KELOWNA CIDER COMPANY

OPENED: 2003

> 2960 McCulloch Road, Kelowna, BC V1W 4A5
> 250.860.8118
> When to visit: Open 9 am – 2 pm Tuesday through Thursday and by appointment

RECOMMENDED

ROSS HARD APPLE CIDER

FEW WORK AS HARD AS DAVID AND THERESSA ROSS, THE OWNERS OF THIS cider company. David, who was born in Kelowna in 1969, is a logger and often away in the bush during the week. That leaves Theressa, with a work ethic developed while growing up on a Sicamous, BC, dairy farm, to look after their two young children and manage the cider company with the occasional help of a relative or two. Between them the Rosses run their own apple orchard in the rural setting of East Kelowna. "I am out here four days a week, eight hours a day," Theressa says from the rustic tasting room in a corner of the cidery's warehouse. "I would be here seven days a week if I didn't have the orchard to manage too."

Somehow they found time to push through the change in provincial regulations permitting them to make hard cider (as alcoholic cider is called) from dessert apples. When they started working on their plans in 1995, existing rules for apple cider from an orchard-based cidery had been created around Merridale Estate Cidery on Vancouver Island. Merridale grows authentic European cider apples; therefore, the regulations specified that land-based cider companies — as opposed to commercially licensed producers — could use only cider apples. Even if David or Theressa liked the bite of English cider, their orchard grows only dessert apples. Over a period of three or four years, this determined couple pushed and prodded until the government broadened the regulations. "We actually wrote the stipulations to becoming a land-based fruit winery or cidery," Theressa says with quiet pride.

The East Kelowna Cider Company sits in the middle of an apple orchard that had been eight hectares (20 acres) in size when acquired in 1942 by David's grandfather, Charles. A photograph of him in the orchard is reproduced on the label of the cider. The orchard later was divided equally between David's father and his uncle, with David and Theressa buying the latter half in 2002.

The sparkling hard cider is David's dream. "Dave loves to create things," Theressa explains. "Ever since he was 12 he has been concocting mixtures of moonshine and that kind of stuff, just for the pure enjoyment of doing it." The motive today involves diversifying the farm. "But even if the fruit price was good, he would probably still be opening a cidery." He has created the proprietary blends for the cider, a quaffable beverage with a moderate six percent alcohol content that appeals both to traditional beer drinkers and to wine lovers.

Theressa's specialty is the carbonated soft, or non-alcoholic, cider that the farm has produced since 1997 and sold under the Ross label. Both the soft and the hard ciders are based on apple varieties grown in their orchard, including Red Delicious, Golden Delicious, McIntosh, Fuji, and Spartan. "Cider apples are very bitter, or tart," Theressa explains. "When you taste that in the apples, you are going to taste that in the beverage as well. That's just our type of cider. My thing is, if you can eat the apple and it tastes good, why would it not make a good drink?"

The Rosses have combined ingenuity and scrounging to create their production facilities. The original equipment to get the juice from the crushed apples consisted of household washing machines. "We have six of them," Theressa says. A petite woman given to easy silvery laughter, she has mastered the art of moving nimbly when apples are being processed. The apples are pulped, a box at a time, in a hand-fed manual crusher. She pours the buckets of pulp into the nylon sacks that are placed inside each machine, where the high-speed spinner separates the juice.

"You start with number one spinner and by the time you get to number six, number one is done. That is probably about two minutes. Then you take the pulp out and dump it. The spinners are all back to back. I have put plastic eavestroughing behind them, and the juice flows down that into a holding tank and then into our big tanks to be settled." Subsequently, she upgraded capacity by adding a large juice separator acquired from a commercial fruit processor. "Our equipment is old-fashioned but it works," she says with a laugh.

She spares herself much of the taxing work of crushing apples for juice by having a commercial processor do the job in the autumn when the apples are picked. Her equipment is pressed into service at other times when more juice is needed. The ability to store apples gives her the flexibility to match cider production against seasonal patterns of demand. Currently much of the orchard's crop still is sold to a large packing house. Premium apples head to fresh markets and the culls are returned for making cider. In time, perhaps, the cidery will need all of the orchard's production.

EAUVIVRE WINERY & VINEYARDS

OPENED: 2009

716 Lowe Drive, Cawston, BC V0X 1C2
250.499.2655
www.eauvivrewinery.ca
When to visit: To be established

RECOMMENDED

CURRENT RANGE NOT TASTED

IT NEVER OCCURRED TO DALE WRIGHT AND JERI ESTIN THAT THEY WOULD BE in the wine business some day when they made their first wines in Saskatchewan — crabapple champagne followed by a chokecherry wine labelled Bordeaux (the only labels Dale could find). "Neither Jeri nor I really sat down and said, 'Let's become winemakers,' " Dale says. "That wasn't on our list of things that we were planning on doing." How the couple came to open their own winery in the former home of the Herder Winery at Cawston is a simple but charming tale.

Born in 1949, Dale grew up on a farm in Rouleau, a community not far from Regina. After getting a geology degree at the University of Saskatchewan, he pursued a career in the oil industry. Elad Geological Consulting Ltd., the Regina firm that he set up in 1984, specializes in drilling horizontal oil wells. This technology places the production holes along the oil-bearing horizons rather than just punching through them, dramatically increasing the productivity of Saskatchewan's oil fields. Jeri, his wife, has an education degree and long career as a college-level teacher and counsellor. "I am not an official psychologist but I have had many jobs working in the counselling field," she says. "Teacher therapy has been a big one."

Their dabbling in country wines led Dale to wine kits. Then they began coming to BC wine country after Trina, their daughter, moved to the Similkameen Valley.

"We really like wine, we appreciate wine for what it is and what a wonderful thing it can be," Dale says. "We got to know all the wineries around here. We would tour around the valleys and go home with half the truck full of wine for the winter until we could come back in the spring." Soon their Regina wine cellar was stocked almost exclusively with BC wines.

Their favourites included the wines that Lawrence Herder was making. In the spring of 2007, when they were spending a week with their daughter and a new grandson, they discovered that the Herder Winery was for sale because the Herders had moved to their current site on Upper Bench Road. "We had lots of time to think about it," Dale says. "I just categorically said, 'No, that's not possible.' We even bought wine from him in that time, and got in our truck and went home."

Dale and Jeri had been looking for an Okanagan retirement property but found real estate prices excessive. It struck them that the Herder property was much better value since it included a three-year-old house and a potential business around the winery building and the one-hectare (2½-acre) vineyard. They were just mulling this over when they received an email from the Herder Winery, announcing a wine release. That triggered negotiations with Lawrence and Sharon Herder, with Dale and Jeri acquiring the property just before the 2007 crush. "Before you knew it, we became Sharon and Lawrence's apprentices," Dale says and chuckles.

To make the big leap from crabapple champagne to a commercial winery, they engaged Lawrence as their winemaker and viticultural advisor for at least three vintages. "His teaching skills are exquisite," says Jeri, who knows a bit about teaching. "He can't stop teaching and helping other people succeed in this business."

Half the vineyard was growing young Gewürztraminer. The other half was fallow after Lawrence had removed unsuccessful Syrah and Cabernet Sauvignon plantings. Dale and Jeri planted Pinot Noir in 2008, meanwhile relying on grapes purchased from Okanagan and Similkameen growers for the winery's initial vintages (800 cases in 2007, 1,500 cases in 2008). When Jeri opened the tasting room in the spring of 2009, the winery offered Gewürztraminer, Chardonnay, Pinot Noir, and Cabernet Franc. The wines are tailored by Lawrence to their palates; they prefer wines to show fruit while keeping the oak subdued.

The winery's name is their handiwork. "We thought it would indicate something vague, the ungraspable," Jeri says poetically. Not as much a romantic, Dale explains that "it is just a slang term for *water of life*."

ECHO VALLEY VINEYARDS

OPENED: 2003

4651 Waters Road, PO Box 816, Duncan, BC V9L 3Y2
250.748.1470
www.echovalley-vineyards.com
When to visit: Open 1 pm – 5 pm Wednesday through Sunday in summer, weekend
    afternoons in spring and fall, by appointment in winter

RECOMMENDED

PINOT GRIS
SYLVANER
GAMAY NOIR
PINOT NOIR

THE WINES OF FRANCE AND SWITZERLAND SERVE AS THE BENCHMARKS for Albert and Edward Brennink, the father and son operators of Echo Valley. A European palate comes naturally to the Brenninks, who opened their winery in the spring of 2003. Both were born in Holland — Albert in 1924 and Edward in 1958 — and lived in Switzerland. "We lived at the Lake of Geneva for 18 years, so we know the wine region there," the elder Brennink says. This is where he formed his appreciation of wine. "Exactly. There is no wine in Holland. It is only imported."

He also developed a taste for Chasselas, Switzerland's major white wine grape, which perhaps will one day be the leading white in the Echo Valley vineyard. Previously the only source of Chasselas on Vancouver Island was Blue Grouse vineyards. When Blue Grouse pulled out its 20-year-old Chasselas vines in 2002, the Brenninks transplanted a number around the border of Echo Valley's test vineyard and later harvested cuttings for a larger planting. "I decided that before I started," Albert says. "That's the famous white wine in Switzerland and I'm just fond of it."

Albert Brennink practised as an architect in Europe until retiring to bring his family to Canada in 1979. He specialized in reconstructing churches and schools, repairing the extensive wartime damage those buildings had suffered in Holland and Germany. He kept his office in Holland, commuting regularly to Switzerland, where the family had established a home for health reasons. (Mrs. Brennink had a chronic bronchial condition that resolved itself in the crisp mountain air of Switzerland.) When emigrating to North America, the family purchased a farm on Vancouver Island, attracted by the mild climate.

The 65-hectare (160-acre) farm, now about 15 minutes south of Duncan, was an early island homestead. The original cook shack, held together with forged nails, still survives. Located at the very end of Waters Road, the farm feels remote only because it nestles privately in its own valley below the Koksilah Ridge, surrounded by forest. Albert Brennink spent two decades pursuing other agricultural avenues before settling on grapes. For a time his sheep produced wool for the island's coveted Cowichan sweaters. When cheaper New Zealand wool took that business away, he raised hardy Highland cattle, successfully exporting breeding stock to Europe until beef markets there were devastated by mad cow disease. In 1999 the Brenninks began clearing 10 hectares (25 acres) of second-growth forest to prepare for a vineyard, inspired by the success of grapes at nearby Vigneti Zanatta.

Edward Brennink, lean and almost as tall as his towering father, has followed an eclectic career path in Canada. After studying hotel management for a year, he worked at hotels in the BC interior and in the resorts of Banff and Jasper. But with a taste for farming, he and his wife operated a successful Keremeos orchard and fruit stand for several years. After selling that, the versatile young Brennink became a driving instructor in North Vancouver. He returned to the farm when his father set the vineyard plans in motion.

The Brenninks moved cautiously, getting advice on suitable grape varieties from other Cowichan Valley wineries. Soon a test vineyard fanned out across the slope below Albert's home. Twenty varieties — 10 red, 10 white — grew here, including long shots such as Cabernet Sauvignon and Syrah, as well as Ortega and Siegerrebe, proven ripeners on Vancouver Island.

The vineyard itself, a short walk away through the bucolic valley, is being planted over several years, beginning in 2003, with white varieties on flat valley bottom and reds on the warm south-facing slope. The soil, the toe of a glacial moraine, is lean and rocky, with little topsoil. It is suitable for grapevines but, Edward suggests, not much else. "The only other thing we could do here is grow broom grass or Christmas trees."

As a further example of their caution, the Brenninks had a consultant make wines in 2001 from Okanagan grapes and then skipped the 2002 vintage altogether. The object was to find out how much demand there was before getting in too deeply. Tasting room traffic increased; they did not skip a vintage again until 2008 when, with Albert wanting to return to Europe, the winery was offered for sale. No transaction had yet occurred as this book went to press.

8TH GENERATION VINEYARD

OPENED: 2007

6807 Highway 97, Summerland, BC V0H 1Z9
250.494.1783
www.8thgenerationvineyard.com
When to visit: Open daily 10 am – 6 pm May through October and by appointment

RECOMMENDED

RIESLING
PINOT GRIS
CHARDONNAY
ROSÉ

THE EXPLANATION BEHIND THIS WINERY'S NAME IS SIMPLE. "WE ARE IN THE grape-growing business for eight generations," explains the still youthful Bernd Schales. "The first one was Christian Schales and he grew grapes in 1783 in Dalsheim, which is a town in the Rheinhessen." Bernd is the first of his family to make wine outside of Germany. If he and Stefanie, his wife, realize the dreams tied up in this winery, their three young children, Johanna, Philipp, and Helena, the ninth generation, will succeed them in the time-honoured tradition of the family.

There were perhaps too many family members already working at Weingut Schales in Flörsheim-Dalsheim to keep the ambitious Bernd in Germany. Born in 1972, Bernd worked one vintage at a New Zealand winery after graduating from Weinsberg before settling down for a few years at the family winery. It is a large winery for Germany, run by his father and two uncles. He was assigned an important role in the 60-hectare (148-acre) vineyard. When he found that too narrow, he went to a winery in South Africa before striking out on his own.

"We wanted to do something by ourselves," he says, referring to himself and Stefanie. She also comes from a grape-growing family but had been pursuing a drafting career in an architect's office. They ruled out going to South America, turned down job offers in New York's wine industry, and were about to settle in the Niagara wine region of Ontario in 2001 when they were advised to check out the Okanagan as well.

The following summer, with three-month-old Johanna and a rented camper, they explored Okanagan vineyards for four weeks. "It wasn't really a holiday," Bernd admits. With immigration papers in order, they returned in early May 2003. Within 10 days they had snapped up a producing vineyard near Okanagan Falls just as it came on the market. The eighth generation of the Schales family was back in business, selling grapes (Riesling, Chardonnay, Pinot Gris, and Merlot) to Okanagan wineries.

The four-hectare (10-acre) property came with a rambling house at the top of a slope, with a breathtaking view across the valley. (Because of this, the original builder of the home in the 1980s named the vineyard Vaseux View.) Stefanie got out her drafting tools and began designing an addition to the house that, in the European tradition, would place a winery under the same roof as the living quarters. Bernd began making commercial volumes of Merlot in 2005 and Riesling and Chardonnay in 2006, anticipating the winery in 2008. There was a moment of crisis when they could not find a contractor who would complete the winery before the 2007 harvest.

Luckily for them, the Adora winery building near Summerland was put up for sale in the summer of 2007 — although they hesitated a bit at the size of the deal. "For me, it was a harder decision to buy this than it was to immigrate into Canada," Stefanie admits. Soon they were working more hours than ever before. They began managing the 2.4-hectare (six-acre) Adora vineyard (Pinot Noir, Pinot Meunier, and Syrah) even before completing the paperwork for the purchase. That was on top of farming their Okanagan Falls vineyard and, under contract, farming a nearby three hectares (7½ acres).

In August they moved into the former Adora building, which then was totally empty. With the first grapes due in a month, Bernd scrambled to order tanks, winemaking supplies, and equipment. Fortunately he had one vital piece of equipment, his grandfather's wine press, which had been included in a container of household effects when they immigrated. "We never thought that we would use it and it actually did a pretty good job," Stefanie says. Because the press is small, Bernd found himself working around the clock several times to get grapes crushed promptly.

It was a roller coaster of a year that turned out well. The purchase allowed Bernd and Stefanie, who make only estate-grown wines, to boost the red wine side of their portfolio for a more balanced offering. The wines are shown off in a tasting room decorated to underline that eight generations stand behind the winery, including old family photographs. There is even a framed copy of a letter written in 1811 by an earlier-generation Schales, a soldier in one of Napoleon's armies in Spain, who tells his family how much he misses the vineyard and the wines.

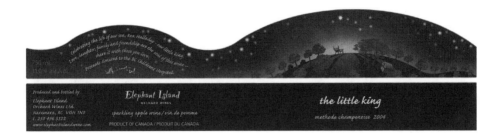

ELEPHANT ISLAND ORCHARD WINES

OPENED: 2001

2730 Aikins Loop, RR1, Site 5, Comp 18, Naramata, BC V0H 1N0
250.496.5522
www.elephantislandwine.com
When to visit: Open daily 10:30 am – 5:30 pm May through October and by
    appointment. Picnic patio
Accommodation: The Tree House (rental suite above wine shop)

RECOMMENDED

FUJI ICE
STELLAPORT
THE LITTLE PRINCE
PINK ELEPHANT
CRAB APPLE
FRAMBOISE
APRICOT DESSERT
PEAR

AT A TIME WHEN A GROWING NUMBER OF WINERIES CHARGE FOR TASTINGS, Elephant Island still offers free samples. As the winery once explained on its website: "As most people have had limited (or unpleasant!) experience with fruit wine, we relish the opportunity to make you a believer." Rarely do visitors leave here without discovering, perhaps to their surprise, how seriously good the wines are. To begin with, many are dry, made with food in mind. And if visitors are not sure how to serve these fruit wines, owners Miranda and Del Halladay, who opened the winery in 2001, suggest not only creative food pairings but also exceptional fruit-wine cocktails.

Both the wines and the winery's unusual name express the dreams of Miranda Halladay's grandparents, Catharine and Paul Wisnicki. The property on which the wine shop and orchard are located was purchased as an investment three decades ago by Catharine Wisnicki, now a retired architect. Her husband scoffed that it was a white elephant and said the house she designed for it was fashioned just for the eye. *Elephant eye–land* was born, to become Elephant Island.

Prior to his death in 1992, Paul Wisnicki, a home fruit winemaker, had begun a business plan for a cottage distillery in the Okanagan. Completing the plan led the Halladays to conclude that a distillery would not be viable — but that a fruit winery might be. They registered Elephant Island in 1999 and set out to prepare themselves for a business in which neither had any background. Miranda, born in Powell River in 1973, is a geologist. Del, born in Victoria in 1972, went to Loyola College in Maryland on a lacrosse scholarship. He earned a marketing degree and a spot on a professional American lacrosse team. Playing lacrosse, from which he retired in 2007, provided a "good part-time job" during the winter months as the winery became established.

They acquired cellar experience working at the nearby Red Rooster winery while Del took winemaking courses at Okanagan University College from Christine Leroux, a Bordeaux-trained winemaker who subsequently agreed to make the Elephant Island wines. An Ontarian who grew up in Quebec, she studied oenology at the University of Bordeaux and worked subsequently in Bordeaux, Australia, California, and at Inniskillin Okanagan Vineyards for two years. Since 1998 she has been one of the Okanagan's busiest consulting winemakers. "She's introduced quality winemaking practices," Del says. "What we're doing now compared to what we were doing in our research and development is completely different."

Del's own research focused the winemaking choices, including ascertaining the best fruit varieties. "For instance, for our apple wine, I tested over 30 varieties of apple and made wine and blends until we settled on our apple blend, with three varieties," he says. This wine is based on Granny Smith and Golden Delicious apples and an unidentified crabapple, all of which combine in a light, crisp wine that, he has found, goes well with shellfish.

The other fruits assessed at Elephant Island were pears, cherries, blackcurrants, crabapples, and apricots. Encouraged by their initial success, the Halladays subsequently added wines made from raspberry, blackberry, and quince. A century ago there were quince orchards in the Okanagan Valley until the bulbous, pear-shaped fruit was replaced by more popular tree fruits. Del's test lots of quince wine in 2002 were made with fruit scrounged from old trees now growing wild. The wine, a dry, aromatic white, was so successful that Elephant Island has planted just over half a hectare (1½ acres) of quince trees.

"We tried several varieties of apricot before we settled on the Goldrich," Del says. The variety, which matures to a high sugar content, has become obscure because its acidic skin makes it unappealing on the fresh market. However, that combination of sugar and acid is ideal for making a lively dessert wine. Although sweet wines are in the minority in the tasting room, they are made with a creativity that sets them apart. The winery has made an icewine-style apple wine using Fuji apples that were picked when frozen.

The winery's wood-aged Stella cherry port and its Cassis (made from blackcurrants) employ classic port wine techniques, where fermentation is arrested by adding grain spirit. Importantly, no water is added to the fruit juices at fermentation, with the exception of blackcurrant (whose citric acidity can only be defanged with water). "I know that it's a pretty common practice with fruit wine production to use water," Del says. "What better way to dilute flavours and dilute wine? We're doing everything we can to use the pure fruit and that's it."

Elephant Island "legitimizes" its products — as Miranda puts it — by following the same authentic standards that govern grape wines, including icewine rules. The two sparkling wines are traditionally fermented in the bottles. The solera method of making Stellaport compares to how sherry is crafted. "Certainly our goal has always been to put ourselves in the same category as the high-quality grape wines," Miranda says.

The Halladays have worked out many food matches with their wines, publishing recipes on their website and, one day perhaps, in a cookbook that Miranda has been working on. The innovative cocktails have been created for them by Chris Mason Stearns, a Vancouver restaurateur and photographer with a passion for mixology. (This book's cover photograph is by him.) "Loving wine," the Halladays suggest, "does not mean forgoing beverages of other sorts."

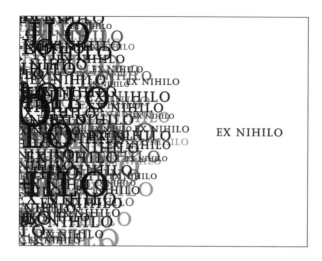

EX NIHILO

EX NIHILO VINEYARDS

OPENED: 2008

1525 Camp Road, Lake Country, BC V4V 1K1
250.766.5522
www.exnihilovineyards.com
When to visit: To be established

RECOMMENDED

RIESLING
MERLOT
ICEWINE

DEPENDING ON THE TRANSLATION FROM LATIN, EX NIHILO MEANS "CREATION" or "out of nothing." It is also the name of a sculpture in the Washington National Cathedral done by Frederick Hart, a major American artist. A few years after Hart's death in 1999, Jeff and Decoa Harder were transfixed by a model of the work in a San Francisco gallery. They subsequently adopted the name for their winery.

Like so many Okanagan vintners, they came to wine from other careers. Born near Edmonton in 1964, Jeff grew up on a farm and made his living initially as a fabricator of glass fibre products. In 1999 he was one of the founders of Svfara Marine, a Canadian maker of boats used in water sports. Decoa, who was born in 1973 in Innisfail, Alberta, came to the Okanagan as a ski instructor and then got a business diploma at Okanagan University College, specializing in marketing. She spent several years in radio sales and event management. However, a promotional job with Vincor Canada while she was in college gave her a taste of the wine industry. In 1998 she joined Quails' Gate, the first of a series of wine industry marketing posts she has had since then.

The major wine influence in Jeff's life was his younger brother, James, who rose through the ranks at Vincor to become national marketing manager for Vincor's Inniskillin winery. Ultimately James moved to California, buying a vineyard in the Napa Valley and establishing his own wine company.

Jeff's first experience in beverage alcohols involved apple cider. In the late 1990s he teamed up with Kelowna apple grower Chris Turton to set up Canada Ciders Ltd., a company making apple ciders for sale by the keg through pubs. Their Rock Creek Draft Cider subsequently became a brand distributed by the Big Rock Brewery in Calgary. By that time Jeff and Decoa had their sights set on a winery of their own. In 2003 they bought a four-hectare (10-acre) orchard just uphill from Arrowleaf Cellars, with a fine view of Okanagan Lake to the west. With the couple building a new home and Jeff extracting himself from the boat business, they did not plant vines (Pinot Noir, Pinot Gris, and Riesling) until 2007.

Meanwhile Decoa arranged to work for Arrowleaf to get vineyard experience. And beginning in 2005, they began contracting grapes from the Gidda brothers, owners of Mt. Boucherie vineyards. They arranged to have Mt. Boucherie's winemakers produce the debut Ex Nihilo wines, starting with one hundred cases of 2005 Merlot and five hundred cases of 2006 Riesling. Ex Nihilo has begun developing its own winery, with the help of consulting winemaker Alan Marks.

When Ex Nihilo opened, however, it achieved instant notice because Jeff and Decoa had pulled off a strategic link with the Rolling Stones, one of the most durable of rock bands. They got the idea in California in 2004 where Jeff's brother, James, took them to a Rolling Stones dinner. There they were served a wine (a Cabernet Sauvignon) in a bottle etched with the band's widely recognized logo. "I looked at my brother and [said], 'Why didn't we think of this?' " Jeff remembers.

Making celebrity-labelled wines is a comparatively recent trend, popularized by sports figures such as golfers Greg Norman and Mike Weir and hockey legend Wayne Gretzky, and by entertainers such as Madonna, Barbra Streisand, and Céline Dion. Jeff figured he could play in the same league with the California wineries that make these wines, even with a start-up winery, because Canada's ability to make world-class icewine gave him "a foot in the door." He locked up just over two hundred cases of 2004 Pinot Noir icewine that Mt. Boucherie had made. Then he tracked down Hollywood agent Martin Erlichman, whose company, Celebrity Cellars, negotiates many of the wine agreements with entertainers. It took three years of persistence until Ex Nihilo completed an agreement to release the icewine under a label inspired by a 1968 Rolling Stones song, "Sympathy for the Devil."

Pricing the label at $125 for a half bottle, Ex Nihilo quickly sold 2,664 individually numbered bottles of the icewine to collectors across Canada, quite possibly the start of a long relationship with the wine-loving band. More recently, Ex Nihilo has developed a Napa Valley red blend that is marketed under another brand, Satisfaction, based on another Rolling Stones song. "The sky is the limit," Jeff says, referring to the potential for celebrity wines.

FAIRVIEW CELLARS

OPENED: 2000

13147 – 334th Avenue (Old Golf Course Road), Oliver, BC V0H 1T0
250.498.2211
www.fairviewcellars.ca
When to visit: When wine is available, open 1 pm – 5 pm Tuesday to Saturday May
      to October, excluding August, or by appointment

RECOMMENDED

THE BEAR (MERITAGE)
MADCAP RED
CABERNET FRANC
CABERNET SAUVIGNON
CABERNET/SYRAH

IN FAIRVIEW'S WELL-GROOMED 2.4-HECTARE (SIX-ACRE) VINEYARD, BILL
Eggert grows four clones of Cabernet Sauvignon and two clones each of Merlot and
Cabernet Franc. Ask him to identify those clones, or to describe how he tends his
vines, and you get a surprise. He won't tell you. "A lot of winemakers will keep their
blending close to their vests," he says by way of explanation. "I am not a winemaker,
I am a grape grower. My wine is made in the vineyard and it is the vineyard secrets
I keep to myself, not the winemaking secrets."

He also instructs his vineyard help not to share his secrets. It would probably not be that hard to figure out how Bill grows the fruit for Fairview's bold reds.
Between 1998 and 2002, he developed and taught a viticulture course at Okanagan
University College. It would be a simple matter to ask his students — the owners
of such successful wineries as Orofino, Noble Ridge, Le Vieux Pin, and Van Westen
Vineyards — what their sometimes crusty professor taught them. But to the cult that
buys Fairview wines, the wines in each bottle are all the intelligence they require.

The wines, bold and honest, express Bill's personality. A muscular man with unruly black hair, Bill was born in Ottawa in 1957 and raised in northern Ontario, where his father was a mining engineer. An uncle had a vineyard near Beamsville, south of Hamilton. A few summers there fired his love of grapes as well as his taste for the wine that was always on his uncle's table. (He came from an open-minded family: his father told him that if he was allowed to taste Communion wine in church, he could also have it at home.) Bill got an agriculture degree at Guelph and worked in the vineyard until he failed to convince his uncle to replace the hybrids with vinifera grapes. He moved west to the Okanagan in 1983.

He spent a year at Covert Farms, a large commercial farm and vineyard (see Dunham & Froese Estate Winery, page 118). He went back to Ontario in 1984, spending a year and a half with a winery before returning to the Okanagan. He worked in vineyards when he could and at construction jobs when he could not, until purchasing his own property in 1989.

A wedge of a plateau overlooking the first tee at the Fairview Mountain Golf Course, it then had a few cherry trees and a trickle of irrigation water. Bill began planting in 1993 while improving the water supply, starting with Cabernet Sauvignon, Merlot, and a few Cabernet Franc vines that arrived by chance with his order. The quality of his first harvest in 1995 confirmed his view that his southeast-facing slope on the Golden Mile side of the valley suits the Bordeaux reds he planted. First, the heat units are comparable to those of vineyards in Bordeaux. Second, he believes that vines prefer the gentle morning sun over the blistering afternoon sun.

"The way I explain it," Bill says, "is, when does a person do his best work? In the morning, when the sun is shining but it is still cool. It is the same with grapes. By the middle of the afternoon, it is so smoking hot that the grapes have all shut down."

Until 2006, when he first bought Sauvignon Blanc grapes, he made only red wines. "I have some of the best land for supporting reds, and I honestly didn't want to waste any of my land on whites," he says. One of his most popular blends, now called Madcap Red, employs all three of the Bordeaux reds he grows. Recently he added a row of Syrah, making room for this big red by pulling out Vidal that had been planted for icewine. Bill changed his mind about making icewine after being chilled to the bone while helping nearby Willow Hill vineyards pick its icewine grapes.

Since opening Fairview in the spring of 2000, Bill has welcomed visitors in a small rustic tasting room or at a weather-beaten picnic bench in front of the winery. Deliberately, he has not erected a winery sign on the highway. At times a driveway barrier announces that the winery is closed, although a tap on the car horn might summon Bill from his vineyard or his well-equipped cellar. Most of the wines — he makes only 2,500 cases per year — are sold directly to individuals on Fairview's mailing list. There is not much left over for the tasting room.

Bill's longer-term plans include building a larger tasting room and a conference centre at the winery, making enhancements in the cellar, and adding Pinot Noir to his repertoire. In 2008 he made wine with purchased Pinot Noir as he prepared to plant the variety in 2009 on land he purchased just south of Vaseux Lake. "I figured I better get some experience with the grape," he says, explaining why he made his first Pinot Noir. "I don't know if I will release this wine or hold it until I have some from my own grapes."

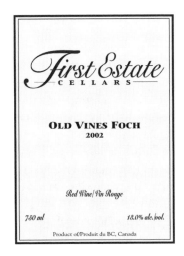

OLD VINES FOCH
2002

Red Wine/Vin Rouge

750 ml   13.0% alc./vol.

Product of/Produit du BC, Canada

FIRST ESTATE CELLARS

OPENED: 1979 (AS CHATEAU JONN DE TREPANIER)

5078 Cousins Road, Peachland, BC V0H 1X2
250.767.2299
www.firstestatecellars.com
When to visit: Open daily 9 am – 5 pm in spring and summer

RECOMMENDED

CURRENT RANGE NOT TASTED

THIS IS A WINERY WITH THE LIVES OF A CAT. THE ORIGINAL ESTATE WINERY IN the Okanagan, it has opened, closed, and reopened under a succession of owners and a variety of names. Frank Silvestri, the most recent owner setting out to revive the winery, is a Calgary trucking company owner with roots in Italy.

The winery was launched in 1979 as Chateau Jonn de Trepanier by a colourful character named Marion Jonn. Born in Bulgaria, he claimed a family tree going back to Roman Legionnaires. In 1972 he bought 14 hectares (35 acres) on the side of the mountain above Peachland and planted grapes. At first, he sold grapes primarily to home winemakers, for he was a keen amateur winemaker himself. However, it was not long before he was scaling up production for a winery. A risk-taker, he took most of his 1977 vintage over to what is now the Mission Hill winery and produced about 55,000 litres (12,000 gallons) of wines from Okanagan Riesling, Rougeon, and Maréchal Foch. When British Columbia's estate winery regulations were announced in April 1978, he built his own winery and, the next summer, it became the first of the vineyard-based wineries to open, with an adequate wine inventory.

The winery was open only a few months when, just prior to the 1979 vintage, John sold it to Bob Claremont, the ex-winemaker from Calona Wines. Chateau Jonn de Trepanier was then renamed Claremont Estate Winery. Because there was a surplus of red wine in the Okanagan, Bob removed some Rougeon and Foch to make room for more white varieties. Marion was already growing Okanagan Riesling, Gewürztraminer, and Muscat. Bob added Johannisberg Riesling, along with small plantings of other premium vinifera grapes, including the Okanagan's first Sauvignon Blanc. Unfortunately, the vineyard lies at a high elevation and the tender Sauvignon Blanc only survived for several vintages.

Bob had other problems as well. He had not been well enough financed when he bought the winery and, in 1986, it went into receivership. He returned to Ontario, picking up his winemaking career there until 1994, when a heart attack claimed his life at 51.

The winery resurfaced as Chateau Ste. Claire, named after an order of nuns by Goldie Smitlener, the new owner. A native of Croatia, she purchased the winery in order to move her young family away from the Vancouver area, where she had run a restaurant. She was an unusual winery owner in that she did not drink; wine just did not agree with her. But she certainly was familiar with the culture, having grown up among vineyards near Zagreb. "The lifestyle, it never gets out of your blood," she said. Shrewd in business, she did well in flipping vineyard property in the South Okanagan in the early 1990s.

However, the winery itself drifted indecisively for a few years and the vineyard deteriorated. In 1998 Gary Strachan and partner Nancy Johnson took over, renaming the property First Estate Cellars because it had been the Okanagan's original estate winery. Gary, a native of Toronto, had been a research scientist for many years at the federal agricultural experimental station in Summerland and subsequently had become one of the Okanagan's busiest winery consultants. But like Bob, he was not well enough financed to complete his plans for the vineyard. The winery slipped into receivership and reverted to Goldie Smitlener in 2000.

The Silvestri family bought the property a year later and have been busy ever since at rejuvenating the seven-hectare (17¼-acre) vineyard (now growing Foch, Gamay, Pinot Noir, Pinot Gris, and Gewürztraminer). While nine thousand vines were replaced, the mature Foch survived neglect in the vineyard, enabling the winery to debut with an oak-aged Old Vines Foch. Alferino Silvestri, who looked after the vineyard until his death in 2007, brought his family to Canada in 1952 from Bologna. One of his Canadian careers involved training racehorses. His son, Frank, named his trucking company Remwan after one of those horses.

Frank Silvestri, who was born in Bologna in 1948, harboured the ambition to own a winery for some time. In fact, he had come close to buying First Estate a decade earlier but could not come to terms with the hard-bargaining Goldie Smitlener. "Back in Italy, everybody makes wine," he says. When Frank, still busy with his trucking company, reopened the winery, his parents managed it for him. His mother, Fleana, brought a charming Italian gusto to the cozy tasting room. "In Italy," she asserts, "nobody drinks water."

FORBIDDEN FRUIT WINERY

OPENED: 2005

620 Sumac Road, RR1, Site 33, Comp 9, Cawston, BC VOX 1CO
250.499.2649
www.forbiddenfruitwines.com
When to visit: Open daily 10 am – 6 pm April to October and by appointment
Accommodation: Harvest Moon Retreat Guest House

RECOMMENDED

IMPEARFECTION
CRUSHED INNOCENCE
POMME DESIREE
CERISE D'EVE CHERRY PORT
ICE LADY MISTELLE

FORBIDDEN FRUIT WINERY IS TUCKED AWAY AT THE SOUTH END OF THE Similkameen Valley, on a secluded farm where Steve Venables and Kim Brind'Amour also operate a restful guest house and a small art gallery. The 59-hectare (146-acre) property was virgin land with sagebrush on it in 1977 when Steve bought it. Much remains a nature preserve; the nine-hectare (22½-acre) orchard is farmed organically.

Steve was born in Victoria in 1952, the son of a forensic pathologist. His father, to pursue professional opportunities, took the family to the United States and eventually retired as a coroner in Indiana. "After my second year of college, I came back to discover my roots in British Columbia and wound up right here in the Similkameen Valley," Steve recounts. "That was in 1972." A farmer by avocation, he worked in orchards until buying this farm. Kim joined him in the venture in 1981. The former owner of a health food store in Keremeos, she was born in Hull, Quebec, in 1963. She became interested in farm products because her father once was a truck gardener.

Today nearly half the farmers in the Similkameen grow products organically. Among the first to do so, Steve and Kim adopted organic practices from the start, motivated to safeguard the health of their family and of the environment. "It made no sense to come in and take a beautiful raw piece of land and start putting chemicals on it," Steve says. "Why would anyone do that? Everything grew extremely well without all the extras." Kim adds: "We all agree that organic food tastes better, because of the minerals that are still left in the soil." They grow more than 60 varieties of fruits, including 25 varieties of apples, 12 varieties of peaches, four varieties of Asian pears, and six varieties of cherries, along with plums and apricots.

It was a good living. "We rode the wave of getting top dollar for our organic fruit," Kim says. But as more and more Similkameen farmers followed their lead, rising quantities of organic fruit allowed retailers to be more selective. The buyers began rejecting organic fruit with a less than perfect appearance, even though the eating quality was as high as ever. The winery was born as a way of adding value to this fruit.

"There really was no longer a market for number two product," Steve explains. "This winery was just a perfect opportunity. We can take care of all our own [seconds] and help other growers out by taking their seconds. Second does not mean a half-rotten cull. It is just not a perfect fruit."

Besides, Steve and Kim were already wine lovers. "My father was a distributor for Hiram Walker's distillery in Ottawa," Kim says. "We grew up with the big dinners, the five-, six-course dinners. As we sat at the table, Mom and Dad would serve us wine with our meals. It started there."

To help them make their first several vintages, they retained consultant Dominic Rivard. Born in Quebec in 1971, he had already made the wines to launch several other BC fruit wineries, including the Fort Wine Company. He was consulting both in Asia and with Alberta fruit wineries when he agreed to work with Forbidden Fruit as well. He can maintain a globe-trotting consulting business because fruit wines are made with frozen fruit, allowing the winemaker to schedule vintages when convenient for him.

Employment of a professional paid off, allowing Forbidden Fruit to win a significant number of major awards and to grow its production quickly, from just over 500 cases in 2005 to 1,800 cases two years later. In style the wines run the gamut from dry to dessert. All of them have catchy, even provocative, labels, such as Plumiscuous Plum Mistelle, a fortified red plum dessert wine. (Mistelle is a fruit wine term for a fortified wine.) The dry pear wine is called Pearsuasion and the delicately spicy wine made from Asian pears is called Impearfection. A wine from white peaches is called Crushed Innocence, continuing the allusion in the winery's name to the Garden of Eden and its forbidden fruit. These names reflect Kim's artistic imagination. She is an accomplished artist and sells her canvasses in the wine shop.

Committed environmentalists, Kim and Steve have also planted 1.2 hectares (three acres) of organic grapes for what they call their Earth Series Wines. "When Kim and I decided to produce several grape wines for the 'discerning' customers, we also wanted to do something special that took our organic and sustainable lifestyle and production practices to a new level," Steve says. Some of the proceeds from these wines — so far, a Cabernet Sauvignon and a Sauvignon Blanc — go to groups like the David Suzuki Foundation that address biodiversity and sustainability issues.

THE FORT WINE COMPANY

OPENED: 2001

> 26151 84th Avenue, Fort Langley, BC V1M 3M6
> 604.857.1101
> www.thefortwineco.com
> When to visit: Open noon – 6 pm Monday to Thursday,
>   11 am – 6 pm Friday through Sunday
> Restaurant: Trapper's Bistro

RECOMMENDED
***

> MIGHTY FRASER RED CRANBERRIES
> VALLEY GIRL BLUEBERRIES
> GHOST BOGS WHITE CRANBERRIES
> PICK ME STRAWBERRIES

IN 1999, THE YEAR AFTER WADE AND ERINN BAUCK INVESTED IN A CRANBERRY farm just east of Fort Langley, the price of cranberries dropped from 85 cents a pound to 18 cents. Rather than wait out the market oversupply of berries, Wade set up the Fort Wine Company. Within two years of opening in the summer of 2001, the Fort was British Columbia's largest fruit winery.

Wade has juggled managing the winery with a long career working as a tow-boat captain. In 2007 the winery, which was then owned by the Baucks and a partner, was put on the market. Wade and Erinn had moved into Vancouver to be near a specialized school a family member needed, and the commute to Fort Langley was onerous. When none of the offers for the business were acceptable, Wade acquired his partner's interest and appointed new management.

"I am glad it worked out the way it did," Wade says now. "I was able to take a year off and move into Vancouver, and have the general manager here run things. It made me realize that I did not want to stop completely."

Wade grew up in Ladner, the son of a towboat captain. When Wade finished high school, he became a deckhand on a tugboat. After a few years crewing on tugs, he went to navigation school and qualified to captain towboats. Since 1984 he has been a master with the Seaspan fleet of tugs, based primarily at the Roberts Banks superport south of Vancouver.

"Tugboating allowed for a good deal of time off, so I thought I'd give cranberry farming a try," Wade said in a 2006 interview with *Mariner Life*, a trade journal. In 1988 he and George Flynn, one of his best friends, began looking for suitable property. George, who would later launch the Blue Heron Fruit Winery in Pitt Meadows, had retired from a marine construction company to grow blueberries and cranberries and talked Wade into farming as well. "Cranberries had always been the most profitable legal crop in North America," Wade told the trade journal. He farmed a small bog for a decade and had switched to the larger farm near Fort Langley when dropping cranberry prices triggered the winery decision. As it happens, the cranberry market eventually recovered and Wade expanded his bog by a quarter in 2008, to 3.6 hectares (nine acres).

The style of the fruit wines at the Fort has been remarkably consistent, given that there has been a succession of winemakers in the compact cellar behind the wine shop. The template style was created by Dominic Rivard, a Gaspé-born winemaker. Now working in Thailand, Dominic was the launch winemaker when Columbia Valley Classics Winery (now Constantin & Vasilica) began in 1997 at Cultus Lake. He got the Fort going a few years later and the Fort, in turn, made wines initially for both Blue Heron and the Wellbrook fruit winery in Delta. When Dominic left the Fort, his protegé, Derrick Power, took over for several years, and he in turn was succeeded in 2006 by Richard Roseweir, an engineer from South Africa and an excellent winemaker.

When Wade reorganized the Fort two years later, he replaced the full-time winemaker with consultant Mark Simpson. A 1982 graduate in microbiology from the University of British Columbia, Mark began working as a brewmaster, first with Molson Breweries and then, for nine years, with the Granville Island brewery. Subsequently he went on to set up his own consulting firm and to teach at the British Columbia Institute of Technology's food technology department.

Wade says that Mark took over the winemaking so "seamlessly" that consumers will not have seen style changes in their favourite fruit wines. The cranberry wine remains tangy and true to the flavour of a berry now much in favour because of its claimed health benefits. This wine as well as a white cranberry wine and a blueberry wine are top sellers. The fortified wines continue to be sweet, a style developed by Dominic because consumers expect berry wines to taste like the berries, which, in their fresh state, contain natural sugar.

Wade's restructuring of the Fort's business included new labels. Historically the wines had sober labels, making a connection to the nearby Fort Langley, a national heritage site. Architecturally, Wade's winery is a period design similar to the nearby fort. But when he brought in a label designer, Wade was persuaded to accept edgy labels inspired by fruit packing case labels from the 1920s.

"We think it is fun and something that catches people's eyes," Wade says. "We are finding that older people can remember the nostalgia, and younger people appreciate the artwork. So it captures both those demographics."

FOXTROT VINEYARDS

OPENED: 2007

2333 Gammon Road, Naramata, BC V0H 1N0
250.496.5082
www.foxtrotwine.com
When to visit: By appointment

RECOMMENDED

PINOT NOIR

THERE IS A CHARMING STORY BEHIND THE LABEL ON ONE OF THE OKANAGAN'S
most elegant Pinot Noirs. During one harvest some years ago, the pickers were
surprised by a big black bear helping itself to succulent grapes right in the vineyard.
Bears are to be expected, of course, because they live on the forest-covered
mountains bordering much of the wine country.

This bear was as surprised at encountering the pickers as they were to meet it.
The animal rose to its hind legs and shuffled as though it were dancing before wan-
dering off into the nearby bush. It returned several more times over the next few
days. Because of its characteristic shuffle, the pickers dubbed it "Fred" after Fred
Astaire, the master of a dance step called the foxtrot. In turn, that became the name
of the vineyard. The Allander family, current owners of the property, recounted the
story to Vancouver marketing consultant Bernie Hadley-Beauregard, whom they
had hired to design their label. It inspired him to create the memorable image of a
bear with a Victrola under one limb, dancing with a picker tall enough to look the
animal in the eye.

No doubt the Allander family itself suggested that lanky figure. They are lean
Swedes with courtly manners, tall enough to look comfortably over the tops of
the Pinot Noir vines. They have come recently to wine growing after significant

accomplishments in business and athletics. They have set themselves the highest bar possible — to produce primarily Pinot Noir and to release nothing but the best. "It has to be at this high end," Torsten Allander says of the wine's quality. "We can never compete at the low end." In 2008 the winery added a Chardonnay, made with purchased grapes.

Torsten is an engineer who came to Canada from Sweden in 1974, followed four years later by Elisabeth, his wife (who goes by the name Kiki). Their children, Gustav and Anna-Marie, were born in Canada. Anna-Marie has graduated in business while Gustav, after briefly studying engineering, has taken up winemaking.

For many years the Allanders lived in West Vancouver. Torsten worked as a consultant to the pulp and paper industry. Passionate about sports, he also was a founding member of the West Vancouver Track and Field Club. On subsequently moving to the Okanagan, he became president of the Penticton Athletics Track and Field Club and was honoured by his sports peers in 2006 as the executive of the year. Like everything the Allanders do, the club has been a family affair. Gustav and Anna-Marie both competed in and coached track and field.

The 1.4-hectare (3½-acre) Foxtrot vineyard had been planted entirely to Pinot Noir in the mid-1990s. In 2002, when Torsten was retiring from his consulting practice, he and his wife — previous owners of a Gulf Islands vacation property — bought the vineyard and its comfortable home as a country retreat. "Kiki and I decided we did not want to live alone on an island," Torsten explains. The vineyard is on the hillside high above Naramata Road and backs up onto the Kettle Valley hiking trail. Like so many Naramata Bench properties, it has enchanting views across vineyards, orchards, and Okanagan Lake.

For several years, as they acquired the skills to run the vineyard, the couple sold the grapes. "The first year we worked very hard," Torsten says. "But we liked it." In short order, Foxtrot became an exquisitely well-groomed property. Cropped at less than two tons an acre, it produced exceptional grapes. Possessed of an educated palate for fine wines, Torsten started to think about making his own fine wine.

Rather than plunging in with both feet, he arranged to have the first vintages, starting with 2004, made at the nearby Lake Breeze Vineyards. Torsten contributed winery equipment and barrels to the venture and tapped the skills of Lake Breeze winemaker Garron Elmes. "I wanted to convince myself, before I had invested a lot of money in a winery, that we can produce a top wine that can compete on a world level." The benchmark against which the barrels of Foxtrot Pinot Noir were measured included wines from both Oregon and Burgundy.

Relying on Garron to make the first vintage bought some time for Gustav as well. After starting engineering studies in Sweden, he changed his mind and came home, intending to become a pilot. While waiting to get into flight school, he began working in various wineries, including a year in the Lake Breeze vineyard. "Then I decided to become a winemaker," Gustav says. "I just got pulled in."

For the 2008 crush, they built a cellar of their own, buried between the house and the vineyard and connected to the house with a tunnel. The first cellar has a capacity of about 1,000 cases — more than enough, since Foxtrot made 394 cases in 2004, 440 cases in 2005, and about 480 cases in 2006. Since Torsten is actively looking for other Pinot Noir growers for Foxtrot, the cellar is designed so that it can be doubled and then tripled as production and sales grow.

The response to Foxtrot's early vintages was everything that a winemaker could hope for. Restaurants in Vancouver and Whistler, along with some private collectors, snapped up the wine. It was priced at about $50, with Torsten benchmarking it against top Oregon Pinot Noirs. The restaurant exposure generated many other inquiries, including one from a New York wine buyer who tasted the wine twice in Vancouver restaurants and wanted 50 cases. "Fifty percent of all private emails I get are from Americans who want to buy my wine," Torsten said with surprise. Foxtrot may well be hard to get in its home market.

GABRIOLA ISLAND WINERY

black & blue
FORTIFIED

handcrafted
using
the finest
blackberries
& blueberries

Produit Du/ Product of Canada
17%   www.gabriolawinery.com   375ml

GABRIOLA ISLAND WINERY

OPENED: 2007

575 Balsam Street, Gabriola Island, BC V0R 1X1
250.244.1648
www.gabriolawinery.com
When to visit: Open noon – 5 pm Wednesday through Sunday and by appointment
  in winter

RECOMMENDED

PINOT GRIS
ABSINTHE AUTHENTICA
BLACK & BLUE FORTIFIED

DURING FIVE YEARS AS A MANAGEMENT CONSULTANT IN SEATTLE WITH Deloitte & Touche, Fenix Theuerkorn learned all about coping with uncertainty. He dipped into those coping skills when launching the first winery on Gabriola Island.

There was, for example, his difficulty with the island's deer population. He and his wife, Chris, a former Chicago advertising executive, stepped off the fast lane in 2003, moving to Gabriola, a short drive and a 20-minute ferry ride from downtown Nanaimo. They bought a forested 18.5-hectare (46-acre) property and cleared enough for a vineyard, planting 1.2 hectares (three acres) of Pinot Noir and Pinot Gris in 2005. Their first property fence, at two metres (6½ feet), was not high enough to keep the deer out. Another half a metre (about two feet) of wire worked — until falling trees broke the fence. The deer ate the young vines down to their roots. Two guard dogs were effective, but the sight of dogs chasing deer upset the neighbours. Finally, Fenix built a high fence just around the vineyard in which, in 2008, he replaced the original vines with two of the Swiss-developed Blattner red hybrids that are showing such promise on island vineyards. "That's our vineyard woes," Fenix says philosophically. "We are taking it as an opportunity to improve our vineyard."

Born in Calgary in 1963, Fenix — his given name is Frank but Fenix is a nickname that stuck — acquired his appreciation for wine from his German parents. Fascinated as well by technology, he got a master's degree at Simon Fraser University in managing information systems, joined the World Future Society, wrote a book on management, and became a consultant. But when he found himself working hundred-hour weeks in Seattle, he and Chris made the lifestyle move to pastoral Gabriola Island with their two children. Subsequently, Fenix joined the faculty of management at Malaspina College (now Vancouver Island University) in Nanaimo, where the flexibility of his teaching schedule allows him to make wine on Gabriola.

He and Chris had been making wine at home for about 10 years and were interested enough that they considered starting a winery in Washington State before returning to Canada in 2003. On Gabriola he scaled up his production in 2005 with purchased grapes. It was a learning experience and he had the courage to dump a batch that, as a knowledgeable consumer, he knew was not up to snuff. He signed up for extension courses in winemaking from the University of California, filling in the gaps in his knowledge. He was satisfied with the three hundred cases he made in 2006 and has since increased that to about one thousand cases. While he waits for his vineyard to become established, Fenix buys Merlot from the Okanagan and other varieties, mostly white, from Vancouver Island vineyards. His port-style wine is made from the wild blackberries on his property and purchased blueberries.

In 2008 Fenix installed a handmade Portuguese copper still, augmenting his winery licence with a distillery licence. Gabriola Island Winery, he says, is planned to be a niche producer, drawing visitors to a destination where the "opulent" pot is still one of the attractions.

"The common misconception is that you can't have a small winery," Fenix says, speaking as a management professor as well as a proprietor. "You can, as long as you limit your labour costs, your production costs. And if you understand your local market and don't extend your sales and distribution channel too thinly. If you can serve a good local market as a small business, I think there is a lot of profitability in a winery business."

He is applying his ideas at the university as well, by getting the university's management faculty to launch a wine program. Now that a significant number of wineries have been opened on the islands, he sees such a program as a logical adjunct to the degrees the university already offers in marketing, tourism, and hospitality. There is room, he believes, for university-level business programs for the wine industry. "I am surprised it hasn't happened already," he says.

GARRY OAKS WINERY

OPENED: 2003

1880 Fulford-Ganges Road, Saltspring Island, BC V8K 2A5
250.653.4687
www.garryoakswine.com
When to visit: Open daily noon – 5 pm during summer, weekends only spring and fall

RECOMMENDED

PINOT NOIR
PINOT GRIS
GEWÜRZTRAMINER
FETISH
PRISM
ZETA

DURING SALTSPRING ISLAND'S LONG SUMMERS, MARCEL MERCIER, WITH HIS floppy white hat shielding him from the sun, can usually be found clipping and tucking the vines on the steep Garry Oaks vineyard. Elaine Kozak is there too unless she is in the winery. The parental concern they lavish on the vines clearly works, judging from the crisp, clean flavours found in their wines.

Marcel and Elaine left fast-paced professional careers in 1999 to establish this vineyard — not because grape growing is easy but for exactly the opposite reason. "We wanted a very strong intellectual challenge and we wanted a very strong business challenge," Marcel explains. "And we wanted to be in a healthy environment." They get all that at Garry Oaks.

Elaine, the granddaughter of Ukrainian immigrants who homesteaded in Alberta, previously was a successful professional economist. When she switched careers, her mother lamented: "What am I going to tell my friends?" Marcel, who grew up in Edmonton, did postgraduate work in land and environmental management.

He grins now when he relates that, when he was at college, an aptitude test suggested he should really become a farmer. Instead he went on to work on a range of consulting assignments around the world.

Eventually the demands of travel got to him. "You'd go into a hotel in Kuala Lumpur and all of a sudden you couldn't breathe," he remembers. "I have a bit of asthma. I realized it was time for a decision." With Elaine also ready for a change, they decided to grow wine. They were characteristically methodical in their property search. Marcel developed his own climate and soils map and then applied that to the Saltspring road map to find properties good for vines and well located for wine tourism. "This area came up best," he says.

The property, called Garry Oaks after the trees preserved on the south-facing hillside, once was part of an 32.3-hectare (80-acre) orchard. Marcel and Elaine retained a few of the heritage fruit trees.

Since 2000, when they began planting, Marcel and Elaine have developed three hectares (7½ acres) with early-ripening varieties, including two clones of Pinot Noir, an Alsace clone of Gewürztraminer, Pinot Gris, Léon Millot, and, with plants sourced from Austria, the island's first Zweigelt. Ever the scientist, Marcel carefully matched the vines to root stocks that further ensure early ripening. And as the vines were becoming established, Elaine got an oenology diploma from the University of Guelph. The couple retained consulting winemaker Ross Mirko to guide them through their initial vintages (made with grapes purchased from the Okanagan). By the time Ross moved to New Zealand in 2005, Elaine was a thoroughly capable winemaker.

They continue to buy Okanagan grapes to support their Bordeaux red, called Fetish, which has acquired a strong following. However, most of their production, around 1,500 cases per year, is from the estate vineyard. The terroir, they believe, produces flavours that are distinctive as the grapes ripen gently in Saltspring's dry and cool season.

"We are seeing a consistent character presenting itself," Elaine says. "You see it more in our Pinot Gris. The fruit is brighter here [than in Okanagan wines]. There is a brightness and a cleanness and a minerality which is really complementary." And these flavours arrive at lower levels of alcohol than in the Okanagan. "You always get the best expression of a fruit at the northern-most edge of its climate zone," Marcel asserts. "Here the Pinots, the Gewürztraminer, and the Zweigelt are performing well, and this is definitely the northernmost edge of the zone. The fruit that we get has berry flavours. We don't get jammy, cooked prune flavours — rather, we get really fresh berries."

In early 2008, when Marcel marked his 60th birthday, they listed the winery for sale. The $2.9 million asking price had attracted no acceptable offer by fall. "Marcel and I are still here," Elaine said, "and given the global financial turmoil, unlikely to be going anywhere soon."

GEHRINGER BROTHERS ESTATE WINERY

OPENED: 1986

> Highway 97 at Road 8, Oliver, BC V0H 1T0
> 250.498.3537 | 1.800.784.6304 (toll free)
> www.sunnyosoyoos.com/webpages/gehringer_winery.htm
> When to visit: Open daily 10 am – 5 pm May to October. Closed weekends
>   November to April

RECOMMENDED

RIESLING DRY
RIESLING PRIVATE RESERVE
SAUVIGNON BLANC
SCHÖNBURGER-GEWÜRZTRAMINER
PINOT GRIS PRIVATE RESERVE
AUXERROIS
EHRENFELSER
OPTIMUM PINOT NOIR
MERLOT
MINUS 9 EHRENFELSER ICEWINE

WHEN THE NEW GENERATION RECENTLY SHOWED AN INTEREST IN CONTINUING the Gehringer legacy, Walter Gehringer found himself strangely conflicted. On the one hand, having their sons follow in their footsteps would make Walter and his brother, Gordon, proud. On the other hand, they would have to make a long-term commitment to the winery so that the new generation could learn the ropes. "If we sold it, we could retire," Walter points out.

Surely he's not really serious, since he and Gordon run a business started for them by their own parents. The Gehringer family bought this vineyard property in 1981 specifically to create the winery for the brothers. Walter, born in Oliver in 1955, had graduated in 1978 from the wine school at Geisenheim in Germany (the first

Canadian graduate) and was honing his craft at Andrés in Port Moody. Gordon, four years younger, was just completing studies at Weinsberg, another German wine school. Their father, Helmut, said he would run the vineyard for a couple of years until the boys took over. "He never left," Walter says. It is probable that Walter's son, Brendon, and his nephew, Kevin, will get a similar commitment from their parents.

The quality of the wines and the friendly welcome at the tasting room show that wine is not just a business for the Gehringers; it is a lifestyle. "There's a personal reward in it," Walter says. He likes nothing better than wheeling about the meticulous vineyards in his all-terrain vehicle as the grapes are turning colour. "I still get butterflies about the crush," he admits.

Helmut came to the Okanagan from Germany in 1952, becoming a car dealer. His brother, Karl, soon followed him and ran the resort at Cathedral Lakes. When Gordon and Walter went to Germany to become winemakers, Helmut and Karl undertook a seven-year study of the climate in the South Okanagan before the 1981 purchase of the south half of what is now the 26-hectare (64-acre) Gehringer property. The north half, now called the Dry Rock Vineyard, was acquired in 1995. The property is on a plateau on the Golden Mile side of the Okanagan Valley, south of Oliver.

On the original parcel, hybrid grapes were replaced with premium German whites, including Riesling, Auxerrois, Ehrenfelser, Gewürztraminer, and Schönburger, in part because they believed these to be winter-hardy. Winters were colder in the 1980s. They routinely covered young vines with sawdust as protection against the winter cold — and even that was not enough to safeguard their first planting of Pinot Gris. "Nobody has to bury a vineyard in its first year anymore," Walter says now. "The winters are warmer."

When the winery first opened, the brothers followed an unabashedly German winemaking style, complete with baroquely scripted labels. Off-dry whites suited the tastes of BC consumers. As tastes changed in the 1990s, the winery responded with drier wines, including dry reds when Dry Rock's vines began producing. Because they perceived that the climate was warming, the Gehringers planted entirely different grape varieties in Dry Rock, including Chardonnay, which they had spurned initially because it is not a German wine grape. They also planted Sauvignon Blanc, Merlot, Cabernet Franc, and Cabernet Sauvignon — all mainstays of French winemaking. It was "a definite change in direction from where we initially were, allowing us to round out our winemaking style, rather than just making Germanic whites," Walter says. "We've evolved to make wines for certain wine styles, so that I can pretty well boast a wine for anybody's palate."

That includes icewine, first made by the winery in 1991. That fall a sharp freeze snapped across the Okanagan on November 1, six weeks to two months earlier than the typical icewine freeze. The Gehringers quickly picked the Riesling grapes still hanging on the vines. When the cold weather persisted, they bought some frozen Ehrenfelser the next day; and finally, on the third consecutive frigid day, they pressed some Chancellor for a red icewine. Since then Gehringer has become a leading icewine producer, in part because the brothers are always prepared for the unexpected.

In the vintage of 2002 the unexpected happened again when the temperature plunged at the end of October. This time the weather only stayed cold enough for two hours early on the morning of October 31. Because their pickers were standing by, the Gehringers harvested part of their grapes on what was the earliest icewine picking date in the Okanagan's history. No other Okanagan winery picked for icewine that morning. It was late January before it was again cold enough for icewine.

The Gehringer wines show impeccably clean and fresh fruit. This applies equally to the whites and to the reds because, for many years, the brothers disdained using oak. They have revised their approach as they have begun making more red varietals, notably Pinot Noir and a Cabernet/Merlot blend. But even having made this change, the brothers still aim for an unpretentious style. "I'm not looking for that real heavy red," Walter says. "I'm looking for that pleasant, nice glass of red — something you can drink sooner."

Although he believes the winery can grow these varieties in Dry Rock successfully because of climate warming, Walter remains nervous about how permanent the change is. "We're far out on thin ice," he worries. But if the change is as permanent as it seems, the climate is evolving slowly enough that no abrupt planting changes are expected. "I don't think we have to remove the Riesling that quick," Walter says of the variety that remains the flagship at Gehringer Brothers.

GLENTERRA VINEYARDS

OPENED: 2000

3897 Cobble Hill Road, Cobble Hill, BC V0R 1L0
250.743.2330
www.glenterravineyards.com
When to visit: Open 11:30 am – 5 pm Thursday through Sunday. Closed in January
Restaurant: Thistles Cafe open 11:30 am – 3 pm and 5:30 pm – 8 pm Thursday
    through Sunday

RECOMMENDED

PINOT BLANC
PINOT NOIR
PINOT GRIS
VIVACE
BRIO

SCOTS ARE SURELY WEARY OF THE FRUGALITY CLICHÉ, BUT JOHN KELLY IS ONE
who validates it. He and his partner, Ruth Luxton, have built Glenterra Vineyards
into a Cowichan Valley gem by husbanding limited resources. It was almost a
decade before a winery website was created. The couple had better uses for cash,
such as planting multiple clones of Pinot Noir and opening a café to show off her
skill as a chef and his as a winemaker. Sensible priorities.

Located on Cobble Hill Road just off the Island Highway, Glenterra's seven-
hectare (17-acre) property was previously called Ayl Moselle. John and Ruth bought
it in 1998 from John Harper, who worked the vineyard until he was 84. Harper, who
died in 2001, had spent half his life on private grape-growing trials, both in the
Fraser Valley and on Vancouver Island. He left behind at Ayl Moselle about an acre
of vines comprised of nearly 40 varieties — many of which are obscure German
grapes (such as Huxelrebe and Helfensteiner). John considered pulling them out.

Then his frugality kicked in and he chose to blend them into one red and one white wine, since he had no other producing vines at the time. Vivace, the white blend, and Brio are now among Glenterra's best-selling wines.

John identified other value as well in the Harper vines, which included 32 vines of Früburgunder — a German red similar to, but earlier to ripen, than Pinot Noir. John had extended his vineyard to 2.2 hectares (5½ acres) by 2007, a difficult cool and wet year that made the vintner change plans when preparing vines to plant an additional hectare. He reduced his Pinot Noir order and had about one thousand vines created from Früburgunder cuttings. "A growing season like this puts everything in perspective," he said.

Born in 1955 in Glasgow, John has lived in Canada since 1969, so long that he has lost most of the Scots inflection in his soft, lilting speech. He honours his heritage in the winery name. *Glen* is what Scots call a valley while *terra* acknowledges that his mother's homeland is the Mediterranean island of Malta. Becoming interested in wine in the 1970s, his passion was fired by a 1988 European backpacking vacation that included the vineyards of Bordeaux. "I was still buying inexpensive wines, of course, because I was on a budget," he recalls. "When I got back, I started paying more for wines to educate my palate. It was an expensive education. You've got to drink the good stuff to know what it's supposed to taste like."

John nurtured his growing interest in wine while running a successful, if mundane, Vancouver business that made traffic signs. "Around 1995 I was fed up with what I was doing and I thought it was time to make a change," he remembers. He investigated winemaking courses at the University of California at Davis. Deterred by the cost there, he enrolled in the two-year program at Okanagan University College in Penticton, where he could study during the week, run his Vancouver business on weekends, and begin searching for a vineyard property. He and Ruth, who prefer living near the west coast, chose the Cowichan Valley because it was the only region outside the Okanagan with enough wineries to attract wine tourists. "We had to be where there are other wineries, so we could at least have half a chance of succeeding," John said.

Planting continuously since 1999, John now grows primarily Pinot Gris, Pinot Blanc, Pinot Noir, and Gewürztraminer. His first estate-grown wine, a 2000 Pinot Noir, won a silver medal at the NorthWest Wine Summit. "Against all those Oregon wines," John says with quiet pride.

Like several other island wineries, Glenterra launched itself primarily with wines made from grapes purchased in the Okanagan. John could not afford to wait until his own vineyard was producing. Glenterra endured some criticism for this from several Cowichan wineries that are exclusively estate producers. John shrugged it off as "petty political crap" as he sought out the grapes needed to make good wine. His first Meritage, a blend of Bordeaux red grapes from the

1999 vintage, earned Glenterra a silver medal at a subsequent All Canadian Wine Championships.

He made an award-winning Chardonnay with Okanagan fruit but discontinued that wine when his own Pinot Blanc came available. Barrel-fermented and oak-aged, the winery's Pinot Blanc can take the measure of most Okanagan Chardonnays. Glenterra now uses primarily Vancouver Island grapes, although, especially in difficult vintages like 2007, John supplements with Okanagan fruit to achieve his target production of about seven hundred cases per year.

Ruth has come to wine through the food industry. "I'm a chef and I have a full-time job here on the island," she says. When they lived in Vancouver she worked with several catering companies before starting her own. Since late 2006 she has presided over the 40-seat Thistles Cafe, which was added when the Glenterra winery expanded from its original quarters, the unheated building that had served as John Harper's work shed.

The bright, airy café, which now includes the winery's tasting bar, offers vineyard views through heritage windows with leaded panes. The windows, which John found in a Vancouver Island antique store, are originally from the now-demolished Park Royal Hotel in West Vancouver. It was, John says wistfully, one of his favourite pubs.

GODFREY-BROWNELL VINEYARDS

OPENED: 2000

4911 Marshall Road, Duncan, BC V9L 6T1
250.715.0504
www.gbvineyards.com
When to visit: Open daily noon – 5 pm February 1 to December 24 (to 6 pm summer
   weekends); by appointment from December 25 to January 31. Picnic patio

RECOMMENDED

CURRENT RANGE NOT TASTED

THERE IS A REASON WHY SOME OF THE GODFREY-BROWNELL LABELS HAVE
such a literary ring: William Maltman Double Red, Colette, Scarlatti Sisters,
Winston's Solera. David Godfrey is the only winery owner in British Columbia to
have won a Governor General's Award for English language fiction (in 1970, for a
novel set in Africa called *The New Ancestors*). He is the retired head of the English
department at the University of Victoria, where he taught creative writing, and a
former owner of several publishing houses, one of which published early books by
Margaret Atwood and Michael Ondaatje.

What is a literary lion doing running vineyards and a winery in the Cowichan
Valley? Well, farming is in the Godfrey blood. His grandparents homesteaded in
Saskatchewan. During the Depression, the Godfreys lost the farm. While the grandparents moved to the Saanich Peninsula on Vancouver Island, the rest of the family
headed east. David was born in Winnipeg in 1938 but grew up near Toronto, becoming a university English professor.

"The family myth was to get the farm back, so I actually went out to Saskatchewan
and tried to buy it back," he recalls. "But that was when regulations said you had
to be a Saskatchewan resident to buy a farm." So he bought a small farm north of

Toronto, growing grain and raising cattle until moving to Victoria in 1978. Besides teaching he wrote more books, including one that listed every computer retailer in Canada. With his wife, Ellen, he established a pioneering Internet service provider and a software company.

His taste for wine started with making wine before he was of legal drinking age, growing up in an enclave of Italian home winemakers who imported Zinfandel grapes by the carload every fall. When David decided to farm in British Columbia, he settled on wine growing. Farming is a tough business but, as he once remarked, at least a vineyard owner can drink his profits. The Godfreys spent about five years looking for suitable property until, in 1998, they bought 24 hectares (59 acres) just next to Dennis Zanatta's pioneering Cowichan Valley vineyard. In an amazing coincidence, David discovered a family connection to this land. The property had been settled in 1886 by a homesteader called Aaron Brownell. "He was my grandmother's second cousin," David says. "So we felt we had to put the Brownell in the winery name."

The first five hectares (12½ acres) were planted in 1999; subsequent development has taken the vineyard to nearly eight hectares (20 acres). And in 2006 he bought a four-hectare (10-acre) vineyard on nearby Mount Prevost, now called Basking Turtle, that had been planted (with Gewürztraminer, Pinot Noir, and Pinot Gris) a few years earlier by a Vancouver doctor.

Opening the eighth winery in the Cowichan Valley, David took note of what his predecessors, especially Zanatta, had planted. "We really benefited from everyone else having experimented for almost 10 years," he says. "So we planted an acre of Bacchus and an acre of Maréchal Foch. Those are our insurance crops. And we planted three acres each of Pinot Gris and Pinot Noir and two acres each of Chardonnay and Gamay Noir. Except for the Chardonnay, somebody was already growing them and doing quite well."

In subsequent plantings Godfrey added Agria, Lemberger, Dunkelfelder, and a selection of the hardy Blattner hybrids. In 2007 he planted several Bordeaux red varieties, determined to make a big red. David recognizes that this is optimistic, saying that Pinot Noir should emerge as the winery's flagship red. The big red currently is the blend of Foch and Gamay that is called William Maltman Double Red. It sounds literary but it is actually named after a favourite relative who taught him how to drink, or so the story goes. One is never quite sure with David where literary licence begins.

Godfrey-Brownell opened with wines made from Okanagan grapes but, with its own vineyards in production, has used only island fruit since 2003. At the same time he began making wines from blackberries, planting about a hectare (2½ acres) on his property to supplement purchased berries. A light, refreshing sparkling blackberry wine — one of several sparklers in the Godfrey-Brownell portfolio — has been popular and is sold only at the winery. In fact, it is reserved largely for the bucolic brunches on the winery's shaded patio each summer.

David often presides over the patio or the wine shop, adding his particular thespian touch, which makes Godfrey-Brownell a popular stop in the island's wine tours. The welcome is relaxed and the picnic tables are freely available even to parties arriving with their own picnics, as happens from time to time. David happily sells them a glass or two, even a bottle or two, of whatever Godfrey-Brownell wine they prefer to drink.

"We try to give everybody that wants it the winemaker's tour," he says. "Take them in and let them taste what's in the barrel, not just what's in the bottle. It's fascinating because you are running six to seven thousand people a year through your winery, tasting wine at different stages. That's the best kind of market research you can possibly do. There is almost no relationship between what consumers like in wine and what the experts say they should like. It is quite amazing. The wine experts are a very small subset of the human population."

GOLDEN BEAVER WINERY

OPENED: 1995 (AS GERSIGHEL WINEBERG)

29690 Highway 97, RR1, Oliver, BC V0H 1T0
250.495.4991
www.goldenbeaverwinery.com
When to visit: Open daily 10 am – 6 pm April 15 to October 15; noon – 5 pm
    Wednesday through Sunday in winter. Closed from first week of December through
    first week of January

RECOMMENDED

VIDAL
VIOGNIER
MERLOT VIN DE CURÉ

JUST BECAUSE WINE IS SERIOUS BUSINESS, THERE IS NO REASON WHY IT should not also be fun, as Bruno Kelle and Stella Schmidt demonstrated by putting a beaver in yellow pants on the label and name of their winery when they bought it in 2006. The following year they toned down the label because it was a bit loud for most restaurants. However, it remains the Okanagan's first "critter" label. In fact, the idea was inspired by a bottle of [yellow tail]®, the hugely popular Australian brand that launched a flood of animal labels. It seemed obvious to them that a Canadian winery should choose a beaver as its critter. As Bruno and Stella explained it, they worked like beavers to renovate the rustic winery. "So, we can have fun with the name, too, can't we?" they once said on their website.

    Golden Beaver is perhaps more intuitive than Gersighel Wineberg, the name under which the winery opened in 1995. The first owner, Dirk De Gussem, a flamboyant Flemish farmer who brought his family to the Okanagan in 1986, concocted that moniker from first syllables of the given names of his three children.

When Dirk decided to sell in early 2006, the winery's excellent roadside location caught the eye of Bruno and Stella, Calgarians looking for a winery after being smitten by the winery lifestyle that, in Bruno's case, had begun in California. Born in 1958 in Tillsonburg, Ontario, he grew up on a tobacco farm. Although he was trained in electronics and engineering, farming was so much in his blood that he helped his family diversify into culinary herbs and, after moving to Calgary in 1996 as a sales and marketing executive for a technology company, even considered opening his own herb farm.

His Calgary employer had clients close to California's wine regions, including one near San Luis Obispo. Bruno particularly enjoyed servicing that client. "There are a lot of wineries in that area," he recalls. "So we got into a routine of stopping in a few wineries and doing some tasting before we got to the office. I fell in love with the whole romantic idea of having a winery [but] I thought it would be too expensive to get into it." Then during a 2005 wine tour, he and Stella came across several Okanagan wine properties they could afford. One was Gersighel, a small struggling producer with a "fixer-upper" tasting room and untidy vineyard but great roadside location.

Stella, born in Calgary in 1967, is a wine lover from way back. "I actually joined my first wine club when I was about 21," she remembers. A bookkeeper, she also shares Bruno's passion for farming. That showed immediately when they imposed order on the unkempt vineyard and turned the tasting room into an appealing and professional venue.

They eased into their new career with help from consultants and colleagues. "We quickly learned an immense amount about viticulture and winemaking, with the help of [consultant] Gary Strachan and many lovely winery owners and winemakers, particularly Bill Eggert of Fairview Cellars," a grateful Stella recounted early in 2007. By the end of that year, she reported, "Bruno and I are going it alone."

Golden Beaver's vineyard is only three hectares (7½ acres) in size but it grows a great many varieties. There was a note of astonishment in Bruno's voice as, soon after taking over the property, he ticked off for me what he was growing. "Merlot, Pinot Noir, Cabernet Franc, Cabernet Sauvignon, Chardonnay, Pinot Blanc, Riesling, Gewürztraminer, Tokay, Pinot Gris, Siegfried Rebe, and Vidal. That's 12. And I forgot Viognier . . . 13, oh, my God!" At least. Zweigelt also popped up in the list of Golden Beaver wines after the 2007 vintage, along with 50 cases of cherry wine made with fruit from a neighbour's orchard.

Perhaps Golden Beaver's signature wines are its vin de curé wines, made from grapes that are carefully air-dried after being picked before being pressed. This process concentrates both the flavours and the natural sugar, resulting in dessert wines that hold their own against icewine. Bruno has made these wines with Merlot, Pinot Blanc, and Vidal. Vin de curé has a long tradition in Europe, but in Canada it may be a niche that Golden Beaver has all to itself.

GRANITE CREEK ESTATE WINES

OPENED: 2004

2302 Skimikin Road, Tappen, BC V0E 2X0
250.835.0049
www.granitecreek.ca
When to visit: Open daily 10 am – 5 pm in summer or by appointment. Picnic area

RECOMMENDED

SYRAH
CABERNET SYRAH
EHRENFELSER SELECT LATE HARVEST

GRANITE CREEK IS A PARTNERSHIP OF TWO OF THE THREE GENERATIONS OF the Kennedy family that have farmed in the Tappen Valley since 1959, when Robert Pemberton Kennedy moved there from the Fraser Valley. Gary Kennedy, Robert's son, was completing a doctorate in agricultural engineering at the University of British Columbia when a family crisis required him to return to the farm. Doug Kennedy, Gary's son, was born in Vancouver in 1972 while his father was at university. Doug and Mayka, his Polish-born wife, juggle winemaking with bringing up daughter Gabriella and pursuing international careers in the oil industry. And Heather, Gary's wife, looks after the tasting room when she is not cuddling her granddaughter. Granite Creek offers the complete family winery experience.

Once an organic farm and likely an organic vineyard in the future, the Kennedy farm formerly produced livestock and dairy products. After leaving that business — most of his family were not interested in dairying — Gary canvassed other opportunities to keep farming his land. He compared the Tappen Valley's climate with wine regions in Europe and New Zealand, brought in two consultants, and settled on vines. Cautiously.

"We're right out in pioneer country here," he observed a few vintages into the project. In 2003 the Kennedy family planted four hectares (10 acres) of vineyard and, a few years later, cleared another hectare (2½ acres) on a hillside. There is considerable potential for more vines as the winery grows.

The vineyard was planted primarily with Gewürztraminer, Maréchal Foch, Kerner, a significant test plot of Pinot Noir, and small plots of about 10 other varieties. As a professional agrologist, Gary Kennedy is proceeding carefully to determine the vines best suited to the site. Doug hopes that Pinot Noir in particular will be one of the successes of this test. "If it works out, it could create quite a unique wine in our area," he says. His father believes it will be 2010 before they will know with some certainty whether Pinot Noir will succeed. Foch, on the other hand, is doing very well.

Other varieties, including Syrah, Merlot, and Gamay, are produced for Granite Creek by contract growers near Oliver. Climate change one day might bring the Tappen Valley's growing conditions closer to those of the Okanagan. For now, however, the valley has a shorter season, cooler nights, and more rain — so much that several vineyards in the area have not installed irrigation. Initially Granite Creek, named for the creek flowing through the property, also installed no irrigation. Gary, noting a long-term trend to drier weather, has decided to irrigate new plantings, if only to get the vines well established.

Gary calculated that his vineyard project would really become viable with the opening of a winery, the third in the Shuswap Lake region. The idea was embraced enthusiastically by Doug and Mayka. "My wife and I have been home winemakers for years," Doug says. Trained in computer science, Doug started his business career in northern British Columbia with Schlumberger Ltd., an international oil field service company operating in a hundred countries. Doug soon found himself promoted to management and working in central Africa and Russia. He and Mayka, a chemical engineer and also a Schlumberger employee, have travelled Europe's wine regions extensively.

Starting with an initial production of two thousand cases, Granite Creek is on its way to a target of five thousand cases. The long-term plans call for building a new winery into a mountainside, using gravity in the production process and burying the cellars. The tasting room is currently on the ground floor of Gary and Heather's home, with the existing winery just visible across a forested ravine. There is a picnic area and a seven-kilometre (4½-mile) trail system that the Kennedy family has developed for hikers. It connects with a more extensive network of trails on adjoining crown land, popular with horse riders.

And it is well worth making an appointment for a tour. The family is thorough about it, spending up to 90 minutes on a leisurely walk through the winery and its bucolic surroundings.

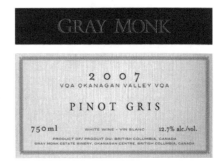

GRAY MONK ESTATE WINERY

OPENED: 1982

1055 Camp Road, Okanagan Centre, BC V4V 2H4
250.766.3168 | 1.800.663.4205 (toll free)
www.graymonk.com
When to visit: Open daily 9 am – 9 pm July and August; 10 am – 5 pm spring
    and fall; and 11 am – 5 pm Monday through Saturday and noon – 4 pm on
    Sunday in winter, except closed on Sunday January through March
Restaurant: Grapevine Patio open 11:30 am – 4 pm daily plus dinner hours
    during summer

RECOMMENDED

ODYSSEY SERIES (INCLUDING BRUT, BRUT ROSÉ, PINOT GRIS, PINOT AUXERROIS,
    AND ODYSSEY III PORT)
GEWÜRZTRAMINER ALSACE CLONE
PINOT GRIS
SIEGERREBE
ROTBERGER
CHARDONNAY UNWOODED
MERLOT
LATITUDE 50 SERIES

GRAY MONK IS THE ONLY WINERY IN BRITISH COLUMBIA (AND LIKELY IN
Canada) that boasts a fourth generation of the founding family involved in the
business. In Europe this is no big deal. In the New World, however, wine traditions
are just taking root. At Gray Monk the Heiss family is celebrating its legacy with
a triumphal renovation of their generation-old winery. With a plan calling for two
towers and gabled windows, it will look like a tradition-laden winery transported from
Europe to the shore of Okanagan Lake. There is a practical side to the renovation: the
tasting room had to be enlarged because, when it became crowded, visitors were
seen abandoning bottles because the wait for the cashier was too long.

The first generation of the family to enter the industry was Hugo Peter, a German immigrant who, in 1968, moved to an orchard near Okanagan Centre and planted grapes at a time only five wineries existed in British Columbia. His venture inspired the next generation — his daughter, Trudy, and his son-in-law, George Heiss, who were hair stylists in Edmonton, so successful that they were often booked months ahead. On a superb slope next to the Peter vineyard, they planted their own vines in 1972 and laid plans for a winery. They were such novices that, as George said later, uncorking bottles summed up their wine know-how.

George, born in 1939, grew up in the rich culture of Vienna, one of the few world capitals that has vineyards and wineries within city limits. One day when he was a teenager, his father told him it was time to come down to the salon and learn the trade. He did as he was told, learning from a parent who was a European champion hair stylist. George and Trudy, who was born in a village near Berlin, met in Edmonton, where both had hair salons.

Being novices, the couple initially planted what everyone else was growing — French hybrids such as Maréchal Foch and Rosette (Seibel 1000). They delayed applying for a winery licence after tasting wines from hybrids and studied Hugo Peter's German wine-growing publications. When he travelled to Europe in 1975, they asked him to source vinifera vines through the Alsace research station in Colmar.

This was the turning point: they imported the first Pinot Gris and the first Alsace clone of Gewürztraminer to the Okanagan. They were among the first to import Auxerrois and Kerner. Three varieties arrived for planting in the spring of 1976: 2,000 Pinot Auxerrois vines, 10 Gewürztraminer vines, and 50 Pinot Gris vines. There was also enough Pinot Gris budwood to produce about 4,000 vines for planting in 1977. Meanwhile the Heisses continued to dress hair, this time in Kelowna, and worked the vineyard in what spare time they had. George once ploughed the vineyard on Christmas Day.

In 1980 the Heisses revived their application for what became the Gray Monk winery when it opened in 1982. (The name is a translation of Grauer Mönsch, one of the many German synonyms for Pinot Gris.) And they brought the third generation into their wine dream when they sent George Jr., one of their three sons, to train as a winemaker at the Weinsberg technical institute in Germany. Gray Monk's first vintages were made by consultants John and Lynn Bremmer (now growing Merlot for Gray Monk). George Jr. took over when he returned from Germany in 1984. The varieties that had been imported from Alsace gave George Jr.'s wines an immediate advantage in quality. Throughout the 1980s the winery dominated BC wine competitions with its vinifera wines, easily besting wines made with hybrid varieties.

The Heisses did not keep the vinifera advantage to themselves. They levered a friendship with Helmut Becker, a leading German grape scientist, into a grape-growing trial benefiting all BC vineyards. Becker, who was consulting to Washington State, travelled to the Okanagan in 1975. He offered the Heisses, free of charge, about two dozen varieties from the Geisenheim research institute for trial plantings. They enlisted their fellow grape growers in a seven-year trial of the Becker vines that, by the time it ended in 1985, had identified many of the varieties now grown widely in the Okanagan.

With their boundless viticultural curiosity, the Heisses have embraced varieties not grown (or rarely grown) by others, with the result that Gray Monk has a larger wine portfolio than most of its peers. They have what is believed to be the only North American planting of Rotberger, a German-developed rosé variety. George Heiss took a chance on it without first tasting the wine, planting six rows. He sacrificed some of those vines a few years ago to expand the winery parking lot but kept enough to retain Rotberger's loyal following. Siegerrebe, an exotically aromatic white, continues to be grown because it is Trudy's personal favourite.

Gray Monk has grown to an annual production of 70,000 cases, with fruit from 20 hectares (50 acres) of family-owned vineyards, including the original Peter vineyard, now farmed by George Jr. The winery also buys from growers throughout the Okanagan, all of which display large signs identifying them as "proud" Gray Monk growers. Pinot Gris remains the signature variety (about 9,000 cases). First launched in 1990, the bread-and-butter brand — white, red, and rosé, totalling half the winery's production — is called Latitude 50. The winery is just a short distance north of that latitude, coincidentally the same one that runs through Schloss Johannisberg, just north of the Rhine.

The winery's growth has drawn the rest of the family in. George Jr.'s younger brother, Steven, brought his software and marketing skills to Gray Monk in 1994. The oldest brother, Robert, a former meteorologist, moved into winery operations in 2004. The fourth generation is represented by Robert's son, Keiran, a student of viticulture.

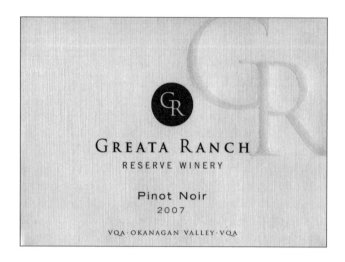

GREATA RANCH
RESERVE WINERY

Pinot Noir
2007

VQA·OKANAGAN VALLEY·VQA

GREATA RANCH RESERVE WINERY

OPENED: 2003

> 697 Highway 97, Peachland, BC V0H 1X9
> 250.767.2768
> www.greataranch.com
> When to visit: Open daily 10 am – 6 pm mid-May through mid-October, 11 am – 4 pm
> November to April

RECOMMENDED

> RESERVE CHARDONNAY
> RESERVE PINOT NOIR

SENATOR ROSS FITZPATRICK, THE FOUNDER OF CEDARCREEK ESTATE WINERY, knew about Greata Ranch long before he bought it. He purchased the lakefront property in 1994 for a vineyard but has since unlocked the other values of this spectacular setting, with plans to create a luxury residential community complete with its own winery. There is nothing quite like it in the Okanagan.

"I used to come up here with my dad," the now retired senator says. His father, Bud, managed an Oliver packing house and bought fruit from Greata Ranch. "This was a big beautiful peach orchard. At one time Greata was the largest single orchard in the Okanagan Valley." It could become the largest vineyard community in the valley with, when complete, about five hundred exclusive homes next to the vines and the beach.

Named for George H. Greata, a British immigrant who came to the Okanagan in 1895, the ranch occupies a bench on the west side of Okanagan Lake, eight kilometres (five miles) south of the current village of Peachland. Still visible are ruins of the wooden pipeline that brought irrigation water from nearby Deep Creek when Greata (pronounced *Gretta*) began planting fruit trees.

He sold the ranch in 1910 to a British investment syndicate that appointed John T. Long, another British immigrant, as manager. Thirteen years later, Long and his family bought the property. After a larger 46.6-kilometre (29-mile) irrigation line was built to Brenda Lake, Long expanded the orchard until, in 1945, the ranch boasted 55 hectares (136 acres) of fruit trees. The ranch had its own packing house and a dock on the lake where railway cars loaded with fruit were transferred to barges and shipped to the nearest railhead. The Longs (descendants still live in the Okanagan) sold the ranch in 1965 — just before a hard winter killed many of the trees. Over the next two decades, squatters moved into lakefront shacks; a condominium project in the early 1980s failed; and people began using the property as an informal dump. It was derelict when the senator bought it.

He believed that the ranch, in spite of its slight northeastern exposure, would be a good vineyard because peaches — superb peaches, as he remembered them — once thrived here. "This was too far north to grow really good peaches but they did it successfully at Greata, so I took a chance." Greata Ranch benefits from a local microclimate. The valley narrows dramatically here as the lake executes a dogleg toward the north. The granite cliffs on the east side radiate the heat of the day back across the water onto the vines in the evening. The funnel effect of the narrow valley creates beneficial morning and evening breezes that ward off frost.

CedarCreek planted 16 hectares (40 acres) of grapes, leaving the remaining two-thirds of the ranch for the vineyard community. The varieties grown here mirror those in the CedarCreek estate vineyard across the lake: Pinot Blanc, Pinot Noir, Chardonnay, Gewürztraminer, and Merlot. The quality proved as good as the senator's fondly remembered peaches. CedarCreek launched its Platinum, or reserve, wines in 1998 when Greata Ranch grapes first became available.

CedarCreek did not plan a separate winery here until prompted by evident demand. The appealing green vines are visible from Highway 97. Soon Greata Ranch's vineyard manager, who lived on the property, found tourists at his door, looking for a winery tasting room. The solution was to open the Greata Ranch winery in 2003. For the next several years most of the wines were made at CedarCreek. The original Greata Ranch wines, with labels inspired by the historic packing house, were all value-priced.

Since the 2006 vintage, however, Greata Ranch added up-market wines. Winemaker Corrie Krehbiel, who had been an associate winemaker at CedarCreek, took over with the mandate to make primarily reserve-quality wines. The winery was repositioned to burnish the image of the real estate development, Greata Ranch Vineyard Estates, where the buyers of the homes will get first crack at the reserve wines. The plan now is to produce about five thousand cases per year, divided between premium and value wines.

Born in Kelowna in 1975, Corrie got an unusual introduction to the wine business. While in high school she got a casual job on the CedarCreek bottling line, applying VQA stickers. Ann Sperling, then CedarCreek's winemaker, took the time to explain other winery processes. "I got hooked," Corrie recalls. She took an honours degree in food sciences at the University of British Columbia, which included six months studying oenology at New Zealand's Lincoln University.

"I worked at CedarCreek essentially all the way through university, in just about every capacity there was," she says. On graduating in 1998 she moved into the laboratory and cellar at CedarCreek, then spent a few years at Blue Mountain and at the Summerland research station. In 2002 she returned to CedarCreek as an assistant winemaker, having decided that "the wine end is where I love to be."

Her first wine at Greata Ranch was a reserve Chardonnay, followed by a reserve Pinot Noir and a reserve Bordeaux blend. And the wines look and taste different from those made across the lake at CedarCreek. That is deliberate. "They are two completely distinct wineries," Corrie explains.

HERDER WINERY & VINEYARDS

OPENED: 2004

2582 Upper Bench Road, Keremeos, BC V0X 1N4
250.499.5595
www.herder.ca
When to visit: Open daily 10 am – 6 pm May through October by appointment

RECOMMENDED

JOSEPHINE (BORDEAUX RED BLEND)
MERLOT BELLAMAY VINEYARD
PINOT NOIR BELLAMAY VINEYARD
CHARDONNAY TWIN BENCHES
THREE SISTERS
PINOT GRIS

FEW KNOW THE TERROIR OF THE SIMILKAMEEN VALLEY AS INTIMATELY AS Lawrence and Sharon Herder. Since 2002 they have planted four different vineyards in the valley, one of them twice. The hard-driving Lawrence took on so much work that he even aggravated a cardiac problem that, thankfully, was treated successfully.

Their first vineyard near Cawston was two acres of Syrah and Cabernet Sauvignon. Those vines suffered frost damage, and earlier-ripening Gewürztraminer and Pinot Noir replaced them. Syrah and Viognier were then planted in 2007 on a windswept 5.6-hectare (14-acre) knoll just east of Keremeos; this planting survived an early frost that autumn. In 2008 they sold the property to Kettle Valley Winery. They also sold their original winery and relocated to a view property on Upper Bench Road — a farm less prone to frost and more suited to growing the big red wines that are Lawrence's Holy Grail.

Born in California in 1967, Lawrence has been consumed by winemaking since he was 14 and tasted his aunt's amateur wine at his family's dinner table. "I was so enthused with it that I went into the attic and fired up a winemaking kit we had," he recalls. He made wine from both fruit and grapes. "I was quite popular as a teenager," he says with a laugh. Ultimately he enrolled at Fresno State University's winemaking program. "Anybody can become a winemaker," he says, "but the advantage of having the training about chemical defects is to know what to do when something goes wrong."

After working briefly for other wineries, he established his first winery in 1995 on a 13-hectare (32-acre) vineyard near Paso Robles. "You get your MBA on your first project," he reflects ruefully. Having committed so much to a large vineyard, he ran out of money just as the vines were starting to produce. He managed to find a buyer and retreated to Burnaby to help his wife run a family-owned printing company. The business made "tons of money" but it bored him. He was soon back at winemaking, doing two vintages at Jackson-Triggs and one at Golden Mile Cellars (now Road 13 Vineyards) in the Okanagan while getting the second Herder winery started at Cawston in 2004. The Similkameen, more affordable than the Okanagan, impressed him as good red wine country.

The valley, a dry, hot, and windy trench wedged between mountains, then had just two wineries, neither with the cult status that Herder Winery acquired almost from the day it opened its doors. While the Herders struggled with their original postage stamp vineyard, they relied on other new Similkameen vineyards for their first wines, starting with the 2003 vintage. "The original goal there was to take Similkameen grapes and perform winemaking to establish a reputation for grapes grown in the Similkameen," Lawrence says. Subsequent vintages have included wines made from selected Okanagan vineyards as well, notably Lanny Martiniuk's vineyards at Oliver. As a consulting winemaker, Lawrence also made the launch vintages when the Martiniuk family opened their own winery, Stoneboat Vineyards, in 2007.

Among the several Similkameen vineyards from which Herder buys grapes, Bellamay Vineyards near Keremeos produces fruit so well grown that Lawrence honours the grower by making single-vineyard wines. The winery developed a strong following for Bellamay Merlot and Bellamay Pinot Noir. A modest crisis occurred at the winery in 2006 when two of Herder's growers, including Bellamay's owners, Johan Boshoff and his wife, Helga, decided to sell their vineyard. The Boshoffs changed their minds a year later.

In 2006 a group of Vancouver business persons asked the Herders to partner with them in developing the Clos du Soleil Winery. They had chosen a former orchard on Upper Bench Road, a rock-strewn property backing against a mountainside. Lawrence was engaged to plant Bordeaux varieties here in 2007. As he was working there, Lawrence noticed that the six-hectare (15-acre) farm next door was for sale. Then an orchard with a two-year-old plot of Pinot Noir, it impressed Lawrence as a superb vineyard site. "It's a hunch," he says. "This belt [on Upper Bench Road] will be our best Cabernet Sauvignon and Merlot country." The south-sloping property backs against a massive cliff, creating a frost-free microclimate sheltered from the valley's persistent winds. The Herders sold their original winery in the summer of 2007 and relocated to Upper Bench Road after crush that fall.

The Upper Bench farm's previous owner, Herb Keller, had built a grand house with a commanding view over the Similkameen Valley. This appealed to the Herders, who installed a winery on the ground floor and the bright, airy tasting room on the second, along with their living quarters.

"Putting the winery downstairs gives me more peace of mind during crush," Lawrence says. "In the morning I can check my tanks when I wake up at five and have a peaceful coffee time without slurping back two cups and running over to the winery because I am worried." His cardiologist would approve.

HERON RIDGE ESTATES WINERY

OPENING PROPOSED FOR 2009

1682 Thrums Road, Thrums, BC V1N 4N4
250.764.5413
www.heronridgeestateswine.com
When to visit: To be established

A DOZEN YEARS AGO, WHEN PAUL KOODRIN FIRST APPLIED FOR A LICENCE
to make blueberry wine, the regulators told him there was no such category. He
asked again a few years later when he saw other fruit wineries opening, only to
be discouraged by the taxes then imposed on wine sales. "I was making more for
my berries that I would have with my wine," he says. "I decided to keep selling
blueberries." It was only after government gave fruit wineries that same favourable
tax treatment as estate grape wineries that Paul revived his plans for the Castlegar
area's first winery on the banks of the Kootenay River.

   Born in Nelson in 1943, Paul is a welder and pipefitter. During more than four
decades working throughout British Columbia, he maintained roots on this riverside family farm near the village of Thrums, just north of Castlegar. A few hobby
blueberry bushes were planted in the 1970s. Once numerous orchards grew in the
area, but agricultural experts recommended against blueberries. However, Paul's
bushes thrived. He planted a few more, then more again, until he had about three
thousand bushes on 1.6 hectares (four acres).

   Sometime in the late 1990s, the region's elk population increased sharply. Some
of the big animals, as they grazed along the river, began trampling Paul's blueberry
patch. They were not chewing on the trees, just barging through the middle of the
patch. Paul's guard dogs had some success in chasing the animals away. However,
a neighbour, complaining that the dogs were harassing the elk, summoned a game
warden. Paul went over the warden's head to Victoria and was told that, if the ani-

mals were interfering with legitimate farming, he could shoot. It was not a solution; Paul is not a hunter and does not even own a rifle. The berry patch struggled until recently, when he began fencing against the elk.

During a down cycle in the demand for welders, Paul opened a country store and restaurant beside the highway at Thrums. It thrived as a family business until both his first wife and his father died and the store was sold. While Paul owned it, however, he tried to develop a winery as part of the complex. The regional district told him that he did not have the proper zoning. Paul put the winery plans on hold for a few years. When he revived them, he located it on the family farm, where he had no zoning issues.

Paul became an occasional home winemaker. He remembers that his first batch of blueberry wine was not appealing. "But I made another batch and it got better," he says. "Then I started working with different recipes and I got real nice wine from it. That's when we decided to build a winery. And the government laughed at us because there was no category." He just continued making wine periodically through the many years it took to get the licence for Heron Ridge (named for the birds that live along the river).

His research included tasting blueberry wines already in the market, sometimes with hilarious results. He had a fruit winery in Nova Scotia send him a case, only to conclude it was no more appealing than his first batch. Then while on vacation in Oregon with his second wife, Irene, he spotted in a wine store what he took to be blueberry wine. He was disappointed to discover that he had actually purchased a blueberry-flavoured white Zinfandel. "It was just atrocious," he recalls.

His own winemaking pleased him more. He set out to make a bold blueberry wine by air-drying the berries to concentrate the sugar and the flavours, then by fermenting with an alcohol-tolerant yeast. "This is a port type with 18 percent alcohol," he says as we share a well-aged bottle. "It is a very heavy wine. The last bottle we had tasted like a good bottle of Shiraz."

The recipe, he says, was developed at the University of Michigan (the state is a big blueberry producer). Paul got it through the Internet and has made some of his own modifications, notably using a large volume of berries. "I use six pounds of blueberries for a gallon of wine," he says. "Most wineries use two, three, maybe four pounds."

In addition to this port-style wine, he plans to offer a sparkling blueberry wine, a sweet blueberry wine, and a sweet apple wine. He is undecided about making additional fruit wines. "If we have time," he says. "I don't want to get too big. It gets too complicated."

HESTER CREEK ESTATE WINERY

OPENED: 1983

> 13163 – 326th Avenue, Oliver, BC V0H 1T0
> 250.498.4435
> www.hestercreek.com
> When to visit: Open daily 10 am – 5 pm Easter to Christmas and Monday through
>   Friday January to Easter
> Accommodation: Six mountaintop villas

RECOMMENDED

> TREBBIANO DRY
> MERLOT RESERVE
> CABERNET FRANC RESERVE
> CABERNET SAUVIGNON RESERVE
> PINOT BLANC
> PINOT GRIS

THE SIX LUXURY VILLAS THAT HESTER CREEK BUILT ON THE HILLSIDE ABOVE the winery in 2007 look over one of the Okanagan's most historic vineyards. Italian-born Joe Busnardo, the first owner of the vineyard, started planting vinifera here in 1968, ignoring advice to plant hybrids instead. For a test planting, he brought in 26 varieties from Italy and another 56 from California. He paid a price for being one of the earliest vinifera growers in the valley: the few wineries then in business refused to pay a premium for the grapes. Famously stubborn — even his father, visiting from Italy, told him to pull out the vines — Joe left the grapes in the ground, while he worked as a heavy-duty mechanic in Penticton. "I closed the farm down," he said years later. "I didn't even prune the grapes."

The turning point for this vineyard was the severe winter of 1978–79, when a deep and early freeze did so much damage to vines that 43 percent fewer grapes were produced in the Okanagan in 1979 than in the year before. Joe noted that his vinifera grapes came through the winter well. He applied for a winery licence, opening Divino Estate Winery in 1983 with mainstream vinifera wines like Chardonnay, Merlot, and Pinot Blanc in the portfolio. Due to his endless vineyard trials — he said he may have tested as many as 128 varietals here — Joe also offered Italian varieties no one else had, then or now. Garganega and Malvasia are long gone, but the Okanagan's only planting of Trebbiano thrives here. A crisp white, it sells so well that Hester Creek's current owners extended the Trebbiano planting.

In 1996 Joe sold the vineyard and winery, re-establishing Divino in the Cowichan Valley (see page 109). The new owners renamed the winery for nearby Hester Creek (which itself was named after the daughter of Judge J. C. Haynes, a pioneer Okanagan rancher and customs officer). During the past decade viticulturists there have had a considerable chore to unscramble the potpourri of varieties. Even today there are some vines in the vineyard known simply as Italian Merlot. The winemaker is not sure what they are, but they do yield good wine.

And that's the thing about this 30-hectare (74-acre) vineyard. Joe picked an excellent site on the west side of the valley on the Golden Mile, a long and broad plateau with a bit of a crown in the middle. The general exposure is southeast but there are also a few mild northeast exposures, creating microclimates that readily support the still numerous (if reduced) number of varieties that flourish here.

The early 2000s were tumultuous around Hester Creek, which was in receivership when it was purchased in 2004 by Curt Garland, the wine-loving Prince George trucking company owner. A self-made man, Curt, who is now in his early 70s, started logging at age 17 and trucking a few years later. He once owned a sawmill and a plywood plant; when he sold that in 1988, he invested in a tree farm in Uruguay and ran that until 2007. A trucking company he started in 1979 grew into one of British Columbia's largest operators, delivering specialized services for forestry and mining companies.

Hester Creek is a far cry from what he had in mind when he first began looking at Okanagan vineyard property. "I went down originally just looking for five acres as a hobby," he says. Most of the properties he saw came with large houses, and he was not interested in that. "I was just sitting in the hotel there one evening and saw an advertisement the receiver had in the paper [for Hester Creek]," he recalls. "So I phoned him and never did get an answer. That made me even more interested. I pursued it then." Competing against Quails' Gate, he won with a superior offer to the court.

Hester Creek has been revitalized dramatically. A new $4 million winery was built in 2008, with the cellar set into the hillside. The tasting room has an expanse of windows overlooking the vineyard. Espousing green values, the new Hester Creek winery is set into the bedrock on three sides, with only the tasting room and the offices exposed, a design for efficient heating and cooling. Capacity is about 35,000 cases per year.

The design was supervised by Robert Summers, an experienced winemaker hired by Curt in 2006. Born in Ontario in 1962, Robert has an honours degree in food science from the University of Guelph. He progressed through several boutique Ontario wineries before becoming the national winemaker for Andrew Peller Ltd. It was in that role that he first saw the Hester Creek vineyard. While supervising Peller's winemaking in British Columbia, he visited Hester Creek to buy grapes. The potential of the site impressed him so deeply that he tried to raise money to buy it before Curt did. He jumped at the chance when Curt's unsolicited job offer arrived.

"It just was a no-brainer," Robert recalls. "Coming back to a small winery after 18 years in the wine business, taking all my experience and making it all come together. The main thing here is the vineyard site. It's a great site for Bordeaux reds and maybe even Syrah." Ironically, a quarter of the vineyard is planted to Pinot Blanc, and Hester Creek has no difficulty selling four to five thousand cases of that wine each year. Robert calls this variety a "horse to run with" along with Pinot Gris, another popular variety. The Hester Creek stable now also features a growing selection of reserve reds.

HIJAS BONITAS WINERY

OPENED: 2008

20623 McDougald Road, Summerland, BC V0H 1Z6
250.494.5208 | 1.866.534.4527 (toll free)
www.hijasbonitas.com
When to visit: Open daily 11 am – 5 pm April through October

RECOMMENDED

MERLOT
PINOT GRIS
PINOT NOIR

WHEN HE WAS NAMING HIS WINERY, IT CROSSED LAWRENCE HOPPER'S MIND that, since he speaks Spanish, he would field dozens of questions about whether he is Mexican. He shrugged off that concern. Hijas Bonitas (pronounced *EE-ass bon-EE-tas*) means beautiful daughters. The name is a tribute to his daughters, Edmonton businesswoman Chelsie Hutchinson and her younger sister, Teira Hopper, an emerging artist with canvasses for sale in the winery.

The touching relationship he has with his daughters has included listening to their advice as he edged into wine growing, planting vines in 1997 in a former lakeside orchard. "You have to understand that I knew nothing about wine," he says candidly. "I am a millwright by trade." He grows only four varieties in this three-hectare (7½-acre) vineyard. The first variety he planted, on the advice of Calona winemaker Howard Soon, was Gewürztraminer, followed by Pinot Gris, another vine suited to his cool site. Daughter Chelsie, who once managed a restaurant, weighed in with advice of her own. "She told me that serious wine drinkers eventually go to red and that I had to plant some red grapes," Lawrence recalls. "That's how I ended up with a small block of Merlot."

Wiry and athletic with a perennial Okanagan sunburn, Lawrence was born in Cobden, Ontario, in 1954 and raised in Edmonton in a single-parent home, the oldest of nine children. His mother was a hairdresser — "and she taught us a good work ethic." After working as a millwright in Fort McMurray, Hopper became a brewery salesman. His passion for beer has only been overtaken recently by a rising appreciation for wine.

He was 32 when he moved to the Okanagan, attracted by the fact he could ski for five months of the year and play golf pretty well year-round. He is such a golf enthusiast that he has a driving range in his office. On inclement days in winter, he estimates that he will drive up to two hundred balls. Since moving to the Okanagan, he has represented a Texas manufacturer of specialty lubricants, something he continues to do even with the winery open. "Most people in the Okanagan Valley will have two jobs, just so they can stay here," he suggests. "I am no different."

After living in Kelowna for a few years, he bought this picturesquely set orchard overlooking Okanagan Lake, just north of Summerland, at the end of winding McDougald Road. Although it is only a few minutes from the highway, the location is appealingly private. Here in 1994 he built a gleaming white Mediterranean home, cleverly designed so that anyone walking through the front door is stunned by the panoramic view of water and mountains beyond the home's vast expanse of plate glass. He has 300 metres (1,000 feet) of lake frontage. There is a comparable view from the sandy-hued winery, which is perched at the top of the vineyard, its back against the sage-covered hillside. The winery includes a bright tasting room and a second-floor gallery for Teira's art and for winemaker dinners.

One of the ideas behind moving to this stunning property was retirement by 50. Lawrence discovered quickly that he was not going to manage that with a basic orchard. For a while he considered converting to high-density cherry trees, cherries being more lucrative than apples. But with cherries, he reasoned, "After harvest, the year is over. I thought to myself, 'I like the idea of grapes.'" And he recognized there is a certain prestige attached to vineyards. "There are not a lot of people that run around and say, 'I own a cherry orchard,'" he says and grins.

In 1999 when he got the first harvest from his vineyard, he tried his hand at winemaking, producing 200 litres (45 gallons) that, to his chagrin, turned totally to vinegar. "It was a lesson," he says. He has not taken any chance with the Hijas Bonitas wines, retaining Brad Cooper, Township 7's winemaker, to make his wines while he himself acquires the skills of a cellar master.

Lawrence continues to regard the winery as something of a retirement project, but a very active one, because of what he perceives as the appealing quality of life that he gets to enjoy here, especially in the vineyard. "There is nothing better than riding around on the ATV," he says. "And when I want a break, I go down to the water. It is just a way of living."

HILLSIDE ESTATE WINERY

OPENED: 1990

1350 Naramata Road, Penticton, BC V2A 8T6
250.493.6274 | 1.888.923.9463 (toll free)
www.hillsideestate.com
When to visit: Open daily 10 am – 5:30 pm May through October and on weekends in
   April. Winter hours by appointment
Restaurant: Barrel Room Bistro open for lunch daily May through October and for
   dinner during the latter half of each week

RECOMMENDED

MERLOT RESERVE
MOSAIC
SYRAH
PINOTAGE
MUSCAT
CABERNET FRANC
OLD VINES GAMAY
GEWÜRZTRAMINER

ON MANY THURSDAYS, BILL AND KATHY CARPENTER INVITE THE STAFF AT
Hillside Estate Winery to tastings at which Hillside wines are pitted against
comparable Okanagan and international wines. It is an excellent way to avoid
acquiring cellar palates, the tendency to prefer one's own wines if that is all you
taste. The Carpenters honed their international palates during a quarter century of
travelling and working outside Canada before investing in Hillside in 2000.

   With 25 cases of wine made in the 1989 vintage, Hillside in 1990 was one of
the first two wineries to open on Naramata Road. It began in a roadside farmhouse
with a postage stamp vineyard planted by Czech immigrants Vera and Bohumir
Klokocka. Hillside's Old Vines Gamay, one of its tastiest reds, comes from vines

that the original owners planted in 1984. They also produced the Okanagan's first Cabernet Sauvignon and popularized aromatic Muscat Ottonel, still the flagship white wine at Hillside.

Vintage Holdings, a Calgary company, bought the winery in 1996 and rebuilt the farmhouse into a 1,400-square-metre (15,000-square-foot) structure. The Old World styling, with a 22-metre (72-foot) tower and thick walls of solid river rock, was designed (successfully) to draw in wine tourists — as if anyone could miss such a massive building almost at the very edge of the road. In fact, the best place from which to appreciate, and photograph, the winery is from the Kettle Valley hiking trail, which runs along the mountainside above the winery. Hillside's barrel cellar is dug into that mountainside.

The cost of the building nearly bankrupted the winery, which sought additional investors. By the time the Carpenters came on the scene, Hillside had 92 other Alberta shareholders. Initially Bill Carpenter involved himself in vineyard development and matters of wine quality. By 2005, however, the Carpenters had restructured the business by buying out the other shareholders. Moving to the Okanagan from Calgary, they built their home in Hillside's Hidden Valley Vineyard, the source of such varieties as Syrah, Malbec, and Petit Verdot. The vineyard, only five minutes from the winery, is tucked in a sun-bathed valley not visible from Naramata Road.

Soft-spoken but intense, Bill Carpenter was born in 1955 in Moosomin, Saskatchewan. After growing up in an oil patch family, he also became a geologist. Soon after graduating from university, he and his wife, Kathy, an accountant as well as a chef, took jobs that enabled them to travel the world. "We spent three years in Australia, six years in Indonesia, five years in Britain, a bunch of years in the United States, Venezuela, Algeria . . . all over the place," he says. "I think that is where we honed our palates for good wines and for good food."

A bout of malaria in Venezuela triggered a return to Calgary. Then Bill, who had started making wine, enrolled in the master's program in winemaking at the University of California. He also got hands-on experience, spending a year at Iron Horse Vineyards in the Sonoma Valley. To fund his new passion for wine, he returned to Alberta and started an oil exploration company. "Three oil and gas companies later, we did the takeover of Hillside," he says.

He had become involved with Hillside shortly after returning from California, at the request of the Alberta investors. He had a hand in developing the Hidden Valley Vineyard, where planting began in 2001. At the time the winery owned only two hectares (five acres) of vineyard, relying on purchased grapes for 95 percent of its needs. Today Hillside owns or controls five times that acreage, all of it on the Naramata Bench. That provides the winery with close to half of the grapes it needs for its annual production, about ten thousand cases. Better control of its grape sources has meant better-quality wines.

Although Hillside employs Kathy Malone, a professional winemaker, Bill is very much a hands-on owner. His California training comes into play in the styling and blending decisions regarding Hillside's wines. "We spend a huge amount of time on the blends," he says. "Ultimately the decision rests with me. I won't let a wine go out of here unless I consider it meets our Hillside standards."

Like many Okanagan wineries, Hillside formerly had a large wine portfolio (15 wines on a 2000 list, including icewine). The Carpenters reduced the list, in part for a tighter focus. Icewine, a challenge to make and to sell, has been replaced by more popularly priced dessert wines, including an exquisite late-harvest Muscat Ottonel. Riesling has been dropped, even though Bill likes the variety, because Hillside already has three aromatic whites. The portfolio choices also reflect the grapes available to the winery. For example, Bill has the typical winemaker's passion for Pinot Noir — but Hillside does not have that variety.

While Hillside made the Okanagan's first Cabernet Sauvignon varietal, its big reds now are Syrah, Cabernet Franc, Merlot, and a Bordeaux blend called Mosaic, first made in 2002. The name is meant to suggest, as the winery says, "small pieces coming together to create a work of art." This is a blend of all five Bordeaux varieties, led by Merlot and Cabernet Sauvignon.

Aside from Hillside's spacious tasting room, the best place to sample the wines is with food in the winery's Barrel Room Bistro, a room with the ambiance and menu of a fine French country restaurant. "If we offer wines at a reasonable price and provide that Okanagan experience, then we have done our job," Bill says. "If we ever get to cult status with our wines, fantastic." Arguably the Reserve Muscat Ottonel already has that status and Mosaic is on the verge.

HOLLYWOOD & WINE ESTATE VINEYARDS

OPENED: 2007

> 9819 Lumsden Avenue, Summerland, BC V0H 1Z8
> 250.494.0311
> When to visit: Open daily 11 am – 5 pm

RECOMMENDED

GEWÜRZTRAMINER
PINOT GRIS
LÉON MILLOT
CRANKY OLD MAN

THE SIGNED PHOTOGRAPHS HANGING IN THE WINE SHOP AT HOLLYWOOD & WINE Estate Vineyards make the connection to the winery's name. Harrison Ford, Donald Sutherland, Angelina Jolie, the cast of *Star Trek*, Bob Newhart, Morgan Freeman, Virginia Madsen. They are all friends of Neil Massey — friendships formed in a career of driving the big support trucks for movie and television sets across British Columbia. When he and Betty, his wife, opened this boutique winery in Summerland's Dale Meadow Valley, they turned it into a tribute to their Hollywood acquaintances.

It would be fair to say that wine growing seduced them gradually, for when they opened Hollywood & Wine they were at an age when most people are retiring. Neil was born in Selkirk, Manitoba, in 1940 and Betty was born a year later in Saskatoon. In 1965 they moved to Vancouver, where Neil began his trucking career with a grocery chain. Having been raised on farms, however, they decided to live on a four-hectare (10-acre) rural property in the Fraser Valley, with horses, cows, and a small garden. Having grown up with a mother who made berry wines, Neil continued the tradition, making numerous fruit and berry wines. "I made a beautiful blackberry wine," he remembers.

Betty's creative side is expressed with oils and canvas. "When I was in school I was always drawing, drawing, drawing," she says. "One day, I was drawing a lady in a bikini and my teacher caught me, and he made me stay in after class and draw him some more!" Today her paintings often depict western scenes, with sensitively drawn horses and riders. For a few years when the couple were starting to grow grapes, the pressure of work had her set the easel aside. "The vineyard is my canvas," she said. She has now resumed painting, both with designs for wine labels and paintings for the art gallery planned for the second floor of the new winery.

The couple moved to the Okanagan in the 1990s after Neil had begun driving trucks for film crews. They found their Summerland property in 1998. Dale Meadow is one of those quiet and attractive valleys hidden away behind Summerland, a rural idyll even though it is only a five-minute drive from downtown. The farm was a long-established apple orchard.

Betty took a dim view of apples because she found harvesting the old trees a considerable challenge. "Two thousand apple trees," she recounts. "I did not think that it was very romantic, climbing those high ladders and putting a bag behind you and filling it up." From the top of the apple ladders, she could see the vineyards elsewhere in the valley and thought they looked "so pristine and nice. So I said, 'Why don't we put a vineyard in?' " That was how the seduction of wine began.

In 2002, after removing the apple trees, they planted vines on the undulating landscape. They now have about 3.25 hectares (eight acres) of grapes — Pinot Noir, Pinot Gris, Gewürztraminer, Léon Millot, Zweigelt, and a little Merlot. Right from the beginning they chose to grow the grapes organically.

At first Neil and Betty were not planning a winery but thought they would sell grapes and grape juice. The more they thought about it, the more appealing a winery became. They would not have to negotiate grape sales with other producers. They would make a product they both enjoyed. Best of all for this gregarious pair, they could sell from their own wine shop and have a lot of fun with their visitors. So they retained a consultant to develop the business plan. To make the wine they retained Bordeaux-trained Christine Leroux, who also directs winemaking at several other wineries.

They were taken by surprise in the summer of 2007 when the Hollywood & Wine tasting room opened. Not only did visitors find them, but so many did that the line, on some days, stretched beyond the front door. That propelled the decision to dig a wine cellar into a nearby bank, with gravity-flow production and with a larger wine shop. Neil also scaled back his hours as a trucker to the Hollywood crews to spend more time on the vineyard tractor and, with Betty, to experiment with products other than table wines. "I would love to have a port of some sort down the road," Betty says.

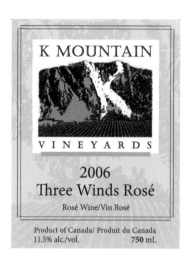

HOLMAN LANG WINERIES

HEAD OFFICE

1751 Naramata Road, Penticton, BC V2A 8T8

250.490.4965

www.holmanlangwineries.com

K MOUNTAIN VINEYARDS

OPENED: 2008

3045 Highway 3, Keremeos, BC
VOX 1N1
250.499.7052
www.kmountainvineyards.com
When to visit: Open daily 10 am –
6 pm May 1 to Canadian
Thanksgiving

RECOMMENDED

PINOT GRIS
THREE WINDS ROSÉ
SYRAH

LANG VINEYARDS

OPENED: 1990

2493 Gammon Road, Naramata, BC
VOH 1NO
250.496.5987
www.langvineyards.com
When to visit: Open daily 10 am –
6 pm May 1 to Canadian
Thanksgiving, 11 am – 5 pm to
October 31, and 11 am – 4 pm
Wednesday through Sunday in
winter. Closed in January

RECOMMENDED

RIESLING FARM RESERVE
GRAND PINOT
GEWÜRZTRAMINER
MARÉCHAL FOCH
ICEWINE

MISTRAL ESTATE WINERY

OPENED: 2005

250 Upper Bench Road South,
Penticton, BC V2A 8T1
250.770.1733 | 1.800.610.3794
(toll free)
www.mistralestatewinery.com
When to visit: Open daily 11 am –
5 pm May 1 to Canadian
Thanksgiving. Closed in winter

RECOMMENDED

GAMAY
CHARDONNAY RESERVE
GRAND RESERVE (RED)
VIOGNIER
CABERNET FRANC

SOARING EAGLE WINERY

OPENED: 2007

1751 Naramata Road, Penticton, BC
V2A 8T8
250.770.1733
When to visit: Open daily 10 am –
6 pm May 1 to Canadian
Thanksgiving, 11 am – 5 pm to
October 31, and 11 am – 4 pm
Wednesday through Sunday in
winter. Closed in January

RECOMMENDED

GEWÜRZTRAMINER
PINOT GRIS
VIOGNIER
PINOT MEUNIER
MERLOT
SYRAH
ICEWINE

SPILLER ESTATE WINERY

OPENED: 2003

Penticton, BC V2A 8T4
250.490.4162 | 1.800.610.3794
(toll free)
www.spillerestates.com
When to visit: Open daily 11 am –
5 pm May 1 to Canadian
Thanksgiving. Closed in winter

RECOMMENDED

PEAR
CHERRY DESSERT WINE
FUJI FROST ICED APPLE
PEAR FROST ICED PEAR

STONEHILL ESTATE WINERY

OPENED: 2001

170 Upper Bench Road South,
Penticton, BC V2A 8T1
250.770.1733
www.stonehillwines.com
When to visit: Open daily 10 am –
5 pm May through October,
11 am – 4 pm Wednesday through
Sunday November to April. Closed
in January

RECOMMENDED

PINOT BLANC
PINOT GRIS, ZWEIGELT
ESPRIT DE CABERNET SAUVIGNON
ESPRIT DE GAMAY
ESPRIT DE GEWÜRZTRAMINER

ZERO BALANCE VINEYARDS

OPENED: 2008

1865 Naramata Road, Penticton, BC
V2A 8T7
250.493.3470
www.zerobalancevineyards.com
When to visit: Open daily 10 am –
6 pm May 1 to Canadian
Thanksgiving. Closed in winter

RECOMMENDED

IN THE PINK
SAUVIGNON BLANC
VIOGNIER
PROJECT 743 WHITE
MALBEC

KEITH AND LYNN HOLMAN OPENED ZERO BALANCE, THEIR SEVENTH WINERY, IN 2008 and almost began working on an eighth. No other owner in the Okanagan, not even Vincor Canada, has as many individual wineries. Keith has an explanation for his aggressive approach. "This is not an infinite opportunity. It is finite and the doors are closing. If you are not moving fast, you are going to be left behind."

Their first winery, Spiller Estate, which opened in 2003, was a fruit winery. It was an appropriate way for them to get into the wine business. The Holmans are veteran orchardists. Lynn's family has grown fruit for three generations, beginning with Cedric Sworder, her grandfather. She and Keith have managed more than 40 hectares (100 acres) of fruit trees near Penticton for more than 25 years. As the profitability in apples declined, they diversified into late-season cherries. The winery was launched to add value to their fruit. It gets its name from the late Elbert Spiller, a pioneering Okanagan fruit grower who built the 1930s-era house next to the winery. The Holmans had purchased the house in the late 1990s, converting it into a cozy bed and breakfast.

Opening the fruit winery revived an interest in wine. Keith, who was born in Salmon Arm in 1948, has a marine biology degree that he has never used. He and Lynn spent two years in France, travelling and house-sitting. They returned to the Okanagan in 1978 so immersed in the French way of life that they were about to return to France and buy a vineyard when Lynn got a teaching job. Keith, who had always wanted to farm, bought an Okanagan orchard instead.

In February 2004, less than a year after opening the Spiller winery at the inter-section of Upper Bench and Naramata roads, the Holmans picked up another Upper Bench property, their first vineyard. Just as they were getting a licence for what they called Mistral Estate Winery, they also bought the winery next door. Now called Stonehill, it was developed originally as Benchland Vineyards by Klaus Stadler, a German brewmaster who moved to the Okanagan in 1998 and converted an orchard to vines. He decided to go back to Germany in 2004 and the Holmans took over the winery just before that fall's crush. Benchland appealed to Keith because the winery was well-equipped and was supported by a large vineyard. Keith recognized that a critical shortage of grapes was developing in the Okanagan.

As their winemaker, the Holmans hired Craig Larson from the nearby Red Rooster winery, putting him in charge of their three wineries, all clustered along Penticton's Upper Bench Road. In the summer of 2005 Craig, a Saskatchewan native who learned winemaking in Washington State, announced that he was thinking of joining a winery either there or in Oregon. Although Craig did not leave until the following year, the announcement alerted Keith that he was in a vulnerable position, given the shortage of trained winemakers in the Okanagan.

The solution was near at hand. Lang Vineyards, which had a good wine-maker, was for sale. The winery had been opened in 1990 by Günther Lang, a former Mercedes-Benz management trainee in Stuttgart who was charmed by the Okanagan during a 1979 vacation. He and his wife, Kristina, bought a property above Naramata Road for the view more than for the vineyard. When they came to like growing grapes, they updated the vineyard, replacing undesirable hybrid varieties primarily with Riesling. Ever since the winery opened, Lang has had a solid following for its Riesling wines. By 2005 the demand for Lang wines was so strong that Günther had to expand his grape purchases substantially or sell to someone who had grapes. As it happened, Keith was just beginning to plant additional vineyards and had grapes to spare.

Lang Vineyards had two things Keith needed. The Lang brand was well known and the winery had sales agents in place, whereas neither Mistral nor Stonehill were known brands. Second, Günther had just hired Bernhard Schirrmeister, a Geisenheim-trained winemaker. Born in Germany's Rheingau in 1965, he worked with several wineries there, honing expertise with Riesling, Pinot Noir, and sparkling wine. He was also attracted to the Okanagan during an earlier vacation. Keith took over Lang Vineyards and engaged Günther as general manager for the emerging winery group, with Bernhard as the group's chief winemaker. At the same time, Laurent LaFuente, a French-trained winemaker with expertise in distilling, came along and Keith hired him to run the two pot stills installed in a back room at Stonehill. "If you have the right team, there is nothing that can stop you," Keith believes.

He was just beginning to roll. He bought the storied Hermani farm, a plateau running from Naramata Road to the cliffs at the edge of Okanagan Lake. Little is known about Mr. Hermani. It is believed he was a German who, at the height of the Cold War, came to the Okanagan to build himself a very large house with a bomb shelter and a funicular cable car to access the beach below the cliff. After his death the house was destroyed by fire and the land, despite its spectacular setting, was derelict until Keith bought it for a vineyard. The Soaring Eagle Winery opened here in 2007.

Originally Soaring Eagle was the premium brand for oak-aged Lang Vineyard wines. However, as Keith and Lynn developed their wineries, they assigned each one a different style of wine, motivating wine tourists to visit each Holman Lang winery. "We're trying to create a cellar experience," Keith says. "The wineries we have on the bench here, every one has a distinct style."

Lang Vineyard has returned to its roots, offering fresh, fruit-forward wines that, for the most part, are fermented in stainless steel. Soaring Eagle has medium-bodied reds and whites with moderate oak aging. Mistral's mandate is to make the big, oaked wines, including reds designed for long cellar aging. Stonehill is designated as the "innovative" winery in the group because of the fortified wines being created here. As well, the Stonehill vineyard grows the only Pinot Blanc in the Holman Lang group.

The Zero Balance winery is just north of Soaring Eagle, on a four-hectare (10-acre) vineyard capable of supporting a 2,500-case winery, the smallest in the group aside from Spiller. The winery name, Keith explains, suggests wines that are in perfect balance. Its mandate is to produce premium wines meriting the winemaker's signature on the labels.

Although most of the Holman Lang vineyards are between Naramata and Penticton, Keith acquired parcels totalling 56 hectares (140 acres) in the Similkameen Valley in 2007. "I believe the Similkameen will supply some of the biggest reds and the most interesting wines because of the terroir," Keith says. His Similkameen winery is K Mountain Vineyards, and it operates from an organic fruit stand on the main street of Keremeos. The name is taken from the mountain on the river's south side, overlooking the town. Long slides of debris have carved channels down the side of the mountain that, from a distance, resemble the letter "k." No one else in the industry, Keith says confidently, has a bigger winery sign than that.

HONEYMOON BAY BLACKBERRY WINERY

OPENED: 2004

9940 South Shore Road, Honeymoon Bay, BC V0R 1Y0
250.704.6111
When to visit: By appointment

RECOMMENDED

BLACKBERRY WINE

BUT FOR A CHANCE MEETING BETWEEN RAY MOGG AND DIANA KRESIER, THE Honeymoon Bay Blackberry Winery might have closed in 2008. Busy with his cement business, Ray had little time to sell wine. Diana, a Victoria native with a cottage on Cowichan Lake, is an experienced wine salesperson. Soon after meeting her, Ray appointed her Honeymoon Bay's sales representative. She not only took on the job, she also became the winery's managing partner and winemaker and quickly re-energized the winery with new wines, new labels, and new packages.

Five years in the planning, the Honeymoon Bay winery was conceived by Merna and Walter Moffat, who had retired to Honeymoon Bay in the early 1990s from Prince George. They saw the winery as a modest economic development project in a community making the transition from forestry to tourism. The project was delayed after Merna Moffat had a heart attack and required surgery. Ray became involved as an investor, opening the winery in 2004 on his four-hectare (10-acre) lakefront property. A year later, Diana included the blackberry wine in the portfolio of wines she was selling on Vancouver Island.

A petite brunette with a silvery laugh, Diana has been in sales for many years, starting with furniture retailing. As the mother of three looking for part-time work, she switched in 1996 to wine sales for an agency operated by Seagrams and later the Kirkwood Group, a successor to the Seagram agency. Having become passionate about wine, she immersed herself in the subject by enrolling in the rigorous program of courses under the auspices of the Wine and Spirit Education Trust.

"I looked at this as a career move, to learn more about making the wine as well as selling the wine," she says of Honeymoon Bay. "I have always been in sales and marketing. I thought it would be interesting to learn how to make the wine."

Honeymoon Bay had been a very low-profile winery without a formal tasting room and open primarily by appointment. Sales were slow, in part because not much effort was going into sales and in part, Diana believed, because the labels and packaging had a homemade look. The labels, she found, were made with an ink-jet printer and applied by hand.

She took over early in 2008 as managing partner and, after making enough wine to keep the licence in good standing, she began overhauling Honeymoon Bay's labels and packages. "Since I changed the label, my sales almost doubled in two months," she said in June 2008. The new labels, done for her by a graphic designer, include — a rare label feature — the wine's sweetness code. The Wild Dry Blackberry is 01. "I put it right on the label because a lot of people who buy fruit wines think they are sweet," she says. "A lot of fruit wines are dessert style, but this is dry and you can pair it with food."

The winery also makes rhubarb and pear wines, including an off-dry pear wine spiced with cloves that is aimed at lovers of mulled wine. For dessert wine consumers, the winery makes what it calls Ice Berry, made by crushing frozen blackberries in the style of cryo-extracted icewines. However, the main focus is, as the winery's name makes clear, on making wine with the wild blackberries that grow profusely on Ray's property and pretty well everywhere else on Vancouver Island. "Blackberries, I believe, are one of the greatest fruits on Vancouver Island," Diana insists. "They have so much flavour."

Diana believes that the clientele for fruit wines is quite different from those who buy grape wines. The wines, she suggests, are comfortable entry wines for consumers new to wine because, served chilled, they are good refreshment beverages. She advocates chilling fruit wines, maintaining that "they don't taste very good when they are warm." She also explores the food pairing possibilities of Honeymoon Bay's dry wines. "I have used the pear as a marinade with pork," she says. "The rhubarb wine goes well with salmon."

HOUSE OF ROSE VINEYARDS

OPENED: 1993

> 2270 Garner Road, Kelowna, BC V1P 1E2
> 250.765.0802
> www.houseofrose.ca
> When to visit: Open daily 10 am – 5 pm

RECOMMENDED

WINTER WINE

IN THE 2008 VINTAGE MOST OF THE GRAPES FROM THE TWO-HECTARE (five-acre) House of Rose vineyard were sold to other wineries and the winery itself was advertised for sale. "I am 81 now and I really want to retire," Vern Rose, the founder, said. One of the Okanagan's most popular winery owners, Vern now had a different priority: recovering from a stroke he suffered in 2007.

Vern has long been the most senior Okanagan vintner. He began growing grapes almost since he retired from teaching at 55. Until his health problem, he was passionate about his second career at this winery not far from the Kelowna airport. "I love what I am doing," he said when he turned 76. "It has been a great fling. It is something that turned me on."

A native of Saskatchewan, Vern spent 35 years either teaching (physical education, mathematics, and sciences) or administering in Edmonton schools. He moved to the Okanagan after leaving teaching, purchasing a vineyard in 1984 in a neighbourhood called Belgo, near the Kelowna suburb of Rutland. With a collection of the hybrid varieties then standard in the Okanagan, including Okanagan Riesling, he settled down to learn viticulture and he sold the grapes to Calona Vineyards.

In 1988 his life was changed by two events. First, growers were paid to pull out varieties like Okanagan Riesling because wineries, about to lose protected status with the new free trade agreement, stopped buying the hybrid grapes. Vern took the cash to pull out almost all of the Okanagan Riesling, replacing it over the next few years with Chardonnay, Merlot, and Maréchal Foch. But he was attached to the heritage varieties because they grow so well on his cool site. He regenerated some Okanagan Riesling, some De Chaunac, and some Verdelet. He became almost the only producer making wines from these varieties. "I think somebody should," he argued. "They may regret it if they don't have the vines around. And some people come because they want to taste the wines. Nobody else is selling them."

Ironically, in the same year that his grape-growing plans were upset by the pullout, Vern achieved his lifetime dream of travelling to New Zealand. "From the time I was five years old, it was one of the few places that I really had a huge desire to visit." But rather than go as a simple tourist, he attended a conference on viticulture, then volunteered at a winery to lay irrigation pipes. He returned to the Okanagan inspired to open his own winery. "I figured the only way to become a viable operation was to make your own wine out of your grapes and sell the wine," Vern concluded. The first vintage was made in 1992, and the wine shop opened in 1993 in a modest room adjoining the family farmhouse.

At the New Zealand conference Vern met an emerging Swiss plant breeder named Valentin Blattner, some of whose early-maturing vines are now growing on Vancouver Island and the Gulf Islands. Those vineyards obtained the Blattner vines through commercial nurseries. The small but expanding plot of Blattner vines in the House of Rose vineyard got there somewhat more informally. After their meeting the two men became friends. Vern, who enjoys hunting and fishing, took Valentin on fishing trips. Valentin, in turn, provided a handful of grape seeds of a hybrid crossing of Maréchal Foch and Cabernet Sauvignon. The variety is winter-hardy and makes wines tasting like Cabernet. That is how Vern got the Cabernet Foch variety in his vineyard.

Having winter-hardy varieties is a priority in the vineyard, set on a plateau surrounded by apple orchards and far from the moderating influence of Okanagan Lake. While the so-called Belgo Breeze, which blows across the plateau most after-noons, protects the vines from early autumn frosts, winter can be hard. One of the previous owners of the property was trying to raise earthworms until a cold winter wiped out that business.

Vern has made as many as 28 different wines in a vintage, including numerous proprietary blends. Early in his winemaking career he registered Winter Wine — a blend of icewine and late-harvest wine — as a House of Rose trademark. When the wine attracted fans and won prizes, he extended the brand to include rosé and red versions of Winter Wine.

Vern's retirement from the wine tour leaves a hole. He was renowned as an entertaining tour guide, both at his winery and at wine festivals. His trademark was the white Tilley hat he always wore. In fact, he owned two — a newer one kept for wearing at festivals and an older one for working in the vineyard.

HOWLING BLUFF ESTATE WINES

OPENED: 2007

1086 Three Mile Road, Penticton, BC V2A 8T7
250.490.3640
www.howlingbluff.ca
When to visit: By appointment
Accommodation: The Inn at Howling Bluff (three suites)

RECOMMENDED

SIN CERA
PINOT NOIR
SAUVIGNON BLANC

ASK LUKE SMITH TO EXPLAIN SIN CERA, HIS FLAGSHIP RED, AND HE LAUNCHES into history. When the cost of top-quality marble started getting out of reach during the Italian Renaissance, some sculptors switched to inferior porous marble and hid the imperfections with wax, a fraud soon exposed by the burning sun. This deception became common enough that the reputable sculptors advertised their work as being *sin cera* — without wax.

That phrase is the root of the word "sincerity." "I think that perfectly describes what I am trying to do," Luke says of his second career as an Okanagan vintner. "Totally truthful, totally sincere, and making the best wines I can from these estate grapes." To focus totally on wine growing, he retired in 2008 at the age of 50 from his first career as an investment advisor with a major Canadian brokerage firm.

He had begun juggling the two jobs in 2000 when he started coming to the Okanagan to help Paul Gardner, a former Vancouver neighbour, at Gardner's Pentâge Winery south of Penticton. In 2003 Luke purchased a three-hectare (7½-acre) property just off Naramata Road and moved his brokerage office there from Vancouver. The property was then an orchard with a bed and breakfast (still operating) and a captivating view over Okanagan Lake from its highest point. That has been reserved for a home and for a gravity-flow winery. Luke's one regret is that he did not buy more land when it was still affordable.

Born in Vancouver, he started his wine education at home, where his mother was secretary of an International Wine and Food Society chapter. He became a broker after studying economics at the University of British Columbia. He also began collecting good wines; at one time he had cellars in three different cities. "In 1986 I had a new car, a sports car, and I went down I-5 as every young man does, and I turned right into Napa," he recalls. "I started at Calistoga and went all the way down the valley. I fell in love with it and thought one day that is something that I would like to do."

The Naramata property's appeal included the topography — slopes in every direction. "These slopes have something about them, about the way they move the air, the way the vines are tilted toward the sun," he believes. "It makes for better grapes." In 2004 he planted his first 7,600 vines, half of them Merlot and the remainder split between Sauvignon Blanc and Pinot Noir. Luke had not intended to plant Pinot Noir until told it is a difficult variety. The challenge immediately appealed to his contrary nature. "I don't care how hard Pinot Noir is to make," he decided, subsequently planting enough that he can make 10 or 12 barrels a year.

Over the next four years Luke added more Sauvignon Blanc and, with a white blend in mind, planted Sémillon as well. For the Sin Cera program, he added more Merlot along with four other Bordeaux varieties: Cabernet Sauvignon, Cabernet Franc, Malbec, and Petit Verdot. The idea is to blend these into one wine, although Luke is keeping his options open. "I probably will keep any leftovers for personal use because I am not sure I want to come up with, say, 50 cases of Malbec," he says. With his own vineyard and contiguous contracts, he has about eight hectares (20 acres) of vineyard to support a production expected to top out at three thousand cases a year.

The vineyard is called Summa Quies, a name with a monastic reference that Luke spotted in a wine book. At first this was to be the winery name as well. "I thought that was a fantastic name," he says. "When we told everyone it would be called Summa Quies, people did not comprehend what we were saying." Howling Bluff, inspired by the winds sweeping across the vineyard, emerged from a family brainstorming session. The label on the first release, a 2006 Sauvignon Blanc, included a sketch of a dog howling at the sky. The design became a work-in-progress after his clients told him the wines were more serious than the label.

The wines show the hand of an experienced winemaker. Luke struck a deal with nearby Lake Breeze Vineyards that allows their winemaker, Garron Elmes, to also make Howling Bluff's wines. Born in South Africa, Garron arrived at Lake Breeze (then owned by a South African émigré) in 1995 and has quietly built a reputation vintage after vintage. Luke is content to let Garron teach him the cellar craft necessary for managing Howling Bluff's wines when the winemaker is busy elsewhere.

Over the years Luke has tasted many great Bordeaux reds in the classic style — made to age two decades before being ready. His flagship Sin Cera, however, is more of a New World wine, approachable on release but also cellar worthy. "What I want is a wine I can pull out five years after it's been bottled and say, 'Holy cow, look what's going on now. I wish we hadn't drank so much of it two years ago.' "

Red-Tailed Hawk by Allan Brooks

Hunting Hawk
Vineyards

Merlot
Remuda Vineyard
2001
RED WINE • VIN ROUGE   13.3%
750ml   PRODUCT OF CANADA • PRODUIT DU CANADA   alc/vol
HUNTING HAWK VINEYARDS, SPALLUMCHEEN, B.C., CANADA

HUNTING HAWK VINEYARDS

OPENED: 2002

4758 Gulch Road, Spallumcheen, BC V0E 1B4
250.546.2164
www.huntinghawkvineyards.com
When to visit: Open daily noon – 4 pm June 15 through September 10 and during Fall
Wine Festival or by appointment

RECOMMENDED

MARÉCHAL FOCH
GEWÜRZTRAMINER

IN 1991, WHEN HE WAS 34, RUSS NILES GOT HIS PRIVATE PILOT'S LICENCE. HIS ability to sustain the capital costs of a winery — and briefly two wineries at the same time — flowed from that decision. It opened to him a career in aviation writing that supports his twin passions for flying and for running a postage stamp winery. "I tell visitors here that we are the smallest winery in BC, and that we wake up every morning dedicated to that prospect," he says with characteristic enthusiasm.

Russ was born in Victoria in 1957. His father was in the air force and the family moved frequently, with Russ attending 14 different schools. "It really made me want to settle down — that's why I bought this piece of property," he says, referring to the vineyard about 10 minutes north of Armstrong (now absorbed into the municipality of Spallumcheen). A journalist, he edited the *Vernon Daily News* until that newspaper closed in 1996 and briefly edited a replacement that also closed. At this time the owner of the local flying club alerted him that an aviation website had posted a job offer. Russ began writing for www.AVweb.com and eventually became editor of what he says is the world's largest general aviation website, with 200,000 subscribers. He also edits *Canadian Aviator* magazine and pilots his Cessna 140 around the Okanagan.

He and his wife, Marnie, who has operated a plant nursery, began developing a hillside vineyard on their property after the newspaper closures gave Russ the time to build a winery. His appetite had been whetted earlier when he was among many investors in Vernon's now-closed Bella Vista Winery. "I love wine," says Russ, a lively man who bounds around his winery as if on a pogo stick. "I love tasting wine, I love appreciating wine."

He conceived his vineyard, now neatly terraced, after growing Pinot Blanc vines from cuttings taken from a neighbour's garden vineyard. Subsequently he planted other varieties, including Maréchal Foch and Ortega. "This piece of land has been highly experimental," Russ said in a 2008 interview. "We have one-year-old, two-year-old, and three-year-old vines. I think our main white will be Ortega." Believing that climate change will soon enable the North Okanagan to grow what now succeeds in the South, Russ planted about one hundred Chardonnay vines in 2006. "If they don't ripen I can always make Champagne," he suggests. To be on the safe side, he also planted a trial plot of an early-ripening Blattner red hybrid.

The idea to call his winery Hunting Hawk was born when, on assignment from the *Vernon Daily News*, Russ toured a proposed Vernon-area golf course. The developers were thinking of calling it Emerald Dunes. Pointing to the native hawks wheeling about the sky, he suggested something like Hunting Hawk would be stronger. The golf course became Predator Ridge while Russ kept his idea for the winery. The labels are anchored by paintings of red-tailed hawks and other local birds, reproductions of work by Vernon artist Allan Brooks, who had a studio there in the 1940s.

Three years after opening Hunting Hawk in 2002, Russ opened a second winery at Vernon's historic O'Keefe Ranch. He planted almost a hectare (2½ acres) of grapes at the ranch and opened a wine shop in the ranch gift shop, expecting to catch the tourist traffic. He discovered, however, that these are not classic wine tourists. "They are families looking for something to do for the day," Russ says. "They do buy wine but we found that we don't really sell very much more wine having two locations than we would having one." In 2008 he decided he would either sell the O'Keefe Ranch winery or simply close it to concentrate on his original winery.

He would like Hunting Hawk to make entirely estate-grown wines. However, he has also established relationships with several vineyards farther south in the Okanagan that serve him well. His Gewürztraminer, for example, comes from Summerland, a terroir renowned for the quality of that variety. Nor will he pass up a good opportunity when it comes along. In the 2007 vintage he bought 1,000 litres (220 gallons) of Pinot Noir icewine juice to make Hunting Hawk's first icewine. "Boy, did it ever turn out well," he says.

INNISKILLIN OKANAGAN VINEYARDS

OPENED: 1980 (AS VINITERA ESTATE WINERY)

Road 11 West, Oliver, BC V0H 1T0
250.498.6663 | 1.800.498.6211 (toll free)
www.inniskillin.com
When to visit: Open daily 10 am – 5 pm May through October, 10 am – 4 pm weekdays
only through the rest of the year

RECOMMENDED

ZINFANDEL
MALBEC
CABERNET SAUVIGNON DARK HORSE VINEYARDS
TEMPRANILLO
MERITAGE
CHENIN BLANC
PINOT GRIGIO
MARSANNE ROUSSANNE

WHEN WINEMAKER SANDOR MAYER SET OUT TO REPLANT THIS WINERY'S NINE-hectare (22-acre) Dark Horse vineyard in 1990, he got a surprising bit of advice from a professional he consulted. Sandor was advised to plant no vinifera at all.

"Imagine that!" Sandor says. "And we committed to Cabernet Sauvignon and it just worked out fine." Those vines, among the earliest Cabernet Sauvignon in the South Okanagan, have been producing since 1993, yielding serviceable wine in cool vintages like 1999 and superb Cabernet in most other years. "Cabernet loves this place and I love Cabernet Sauvignon," the winemaker says.

The vineyard, a hot, rock-strewn, south-facing slope on a plateau just above the winery, was first planted with hybrid vines in 1967 by a grower named Joseph Poturica. He and his sons launched Vinitera Estate Winery in 1979, unfortunately making rustic wines. The wines got no better after a Vancouver car dealer took over in 1982, renaming it Okanagan Vineyards. When the car dealer gave up and sold in 1987, Alan Tyabji, a former accountant at the Calona winery, took over. The following year a government-financed program enabled Alan to uproot the hybrids. He hired Sandor to replant with the vinifera varieties that unlocked the vineyard's potential.

Born in Hungary in 1958, the soft-spoken Sandor began making wine at 14 with his father before getting a university degree in winemaking and viticulture. He went to work with Hungary's major wine research institute, then moved on to a vineyard manager's job in the country's famed Lake Balaton region. When neither the salary nor the opportunities were adequate, he and his wife, Andrea (also a winemaker), slipped out of Hungary. An uncle in the Okanagan sponsored their immigration to Canada in 1989 in time for the vintage at Quails' Gate. Here Sandor dissuaded the winery from discarding botrytis-affected grapes as rotten; he knew that Hungarians were using similar grapes to make great sweet wines.

Since there were few winemaking jobs in the Okanagan at the time, Sandor accepted Alan's offer to replant Dark Horse. Typical of the prevailing viticultural knowledge, Alan ordered a smorgasbord of varieties, hedging his bets since no one could tell him reliably what vines would flourish. Half the vineyard was dedicated to the three major Bordeaux reds and to Pinot Noir. The other half was planted with five whites: Chardonnay, Riesling (now mostly for icewine), Pinot Blanc, Muscat Ottonel, and just over half a hectare (1½ acres) of Gewürztraminer. Over several vintages, Sandor learned that the vineyard is just too hot for the latter two whites. Merlot replaced Muscat in 1999 and, in 2005, the Gewürztraminer vines were grafted over to Tempranillo, a Spanish red with great promise in the Okanagan.

The Okanagan Vineyards winery has been known as Inniskillin Okanagan since 1996, when it was acquired by Inniskillin Wines, Ontario's pioneering estate winery. Located near Niagara-on-the-Lake, Inniskillin was founded in 1975 by Donald Ziraldo and his Austrian-born winemaking partner, Karl Kaiser. After merging Inniskillin with what became Vincor, Donald set out to add Okanagan production, giving Inniskillin a national presence for table wines as well as icewine. Vincor was taken over in 2005 by New York–based Constellation Brands, the world's largest wine group. "I am very happy to work inside the organization," says Sandor. "We express our philosophy here without interruption."

Within the group Inniskillin Okanagan has the unique role of developing varieties that are new, or relatively new, to the Okanagan for what it calls its Discovery Series of wines. This arrangement plays to one of Sandor's strengths: in Hungary he made many experimental wines to prove up new varieties. The Discovery project began in the 2002 vintage when, with grapes from a nearby Vincor vineyard, Sandor made 250 cases of the Okanagan's first Zinfandel. As those vines became established, Sandor increased the volume to about one thousand cases per year.

The Discovery Series has since expanded to include varietals made with Malbec, Petit Verdot, Pinotage, Viognier, and Chenin Blanc. In 2006 a new vineyard downhill from Dark Horse, called Discovery Vineyard, was planted with two Rhône whites: Roussanne and Marsanne. More recently Inniskillin added the Okanagan's first planting of Grüner Veltliner, the important Austrian white variety, as well as two Italian clones of Pinot Grigio, backing up Inniskillin's signature white wine.

"We would like to try the potential of these varieties," Sandor explains. "Different wines for wine enthusiasts and wine lovers. If any of these do not perform well in the future, we will drop them and bring another one into the group. It is an evolution. The most important is the wine quality." The wines are ornaments in the winery's portfolio, where Meritage, Cabernet Sauvignon, and icewine have leading roles. Yet while the Discovery Series wines are small lot wines, Sandor tries to make enough so that many consumers, not just the lucky few, get to drink them.

Inniskillin Okanagan relies on Vincor vineyards for the grapes to produce about two-thirds of Inniskillin Okanagan's annual output of 25,000 cases of wine. The other third, generally premium wines, comes from Dark Horse, a rugged property with so much sharply broken rock that it is difficult to cultivate the lean soil, "This vineyard is very significant," Sandor says with a certain paternal pride. "This is the cream of all the wines we make."

ISABELLA WINERY

OPENED: 2007

11491 River Road, Richmond, BC V6X 1Z6
604.288.0608
www.isabellawinery.com
When to visit: Open daily 10 am – 6 pm

RECOMMENDED

SIKERA (ICEWINE AND APPLE CIDER)
FRUIT WINES

THE FIRST THING YOU SEE ON ENTERING THE TASTING ROOM AT ISABELLA Winery is owner Tony Ouyang's library of wine books, including fat books on Burgundy and Bordeaux. They look well-thumbed, a good indicator of Tony's infatuation with the subject. "Ever since I was a boy I dreamed of making wine," he says.

He was born in Taipei in 1965. Taiwan has a richer wine culture than is generally supposed. Many people make fruit wines at home and there are a surprising number of wineries around the island, notably in Nantou County. Tony spent some time at one of these wineries, trying to pick up pointers, before immigrating to North America. After living in San Francisco, he moved to Vancouver in 1992. Here he established a business manufacturing health food supplements, sold through his own chain of six stores in the Vancouver area. The success of that business, he says, enabled him to follow his passion by opening Isabella Winery. "I make money from that and I lose money from here," he says with an easy laugh. "This is a hobby."

In his first run at getting into the wine industry, Tony thought he might become a distributor, offering his Asia connections to Okanagan wineries. He recalls visiting every winery in the North Okanagan with this proposition. Vern Rose, the famously gregarious owner of the House of Rose winery in Rutland, invited Tony to stay at his home for a few days and regaled the would-be agent with wine talk.

"When I heard his story and his history, his dream became my dream," Tony recalls. Vern held out the idea of a partnership but Tony's finances were already tied up elsewhere. But he did agree to become the House of Rose distributor to Asian markets. "Over 10 years I sold lots of red wine, white wine, late-harvest, and icewine to export markets," Tony says. He also suggested that Vern make a dessert wine tailored to the Asian sweet tooth. The result was Winter Wine (a term that Vern promptly trademarked), a "secret blend" of Verdelet icewine and other varieties picked late in the season. This wine became the best-seller in the House of Rose wine shop as well as with Tony's Asian buyers.

When Tony set out to open his own winery, he was tempted to buy House of Rose when Vern, then in his late 70s, offered to sell it. However, with children in school and a burgeoning health food business, moving to Kelowna was not an option. Instead Tony bought a building on the banks of the Fraser River and plunked the winery in the middle of an industrial and commercial area. One neighbour is a fish packing plant. Tony did not discover that right away because he bought the property in winter when there no occasional odours to drift next door. The irony is that Isabella's building previously housed a restaurant. The building was renovated to make the most of its faux-castle appearance; there is now a spacious wine shop with two tasting bars. At the rear of the winery Tony added a large deck where, if regulations allow it, customers should be to enjoy a glass of wine while watching the passing river traffic.

Tony considered giving the winery a name alluding to its riverside location before settling on Isabella, for complex reasons. That was the name of one of the earliest Spanish ships to sail into this area. Secondly, the Spanish allusion recalls that brief period in the early 17th century when the Spanish, from their base in the Philippines, established a fort and a colony on the north end of La Isla Hermosa, as they called Taiwan. The colony, meant to hold off Spain's rivals in the area (the Dutch and the Japanese), did not last long but still seems to resonate in Taiwan's history. Thirdly, Tony maintains that a Latin version of his winery's name means "service to God." "What I have today, everything comes from God," he says.

Not having room for the vineyard or the orchard needed for a land-based winery, Tony opened Isabella under a commercial winery licence. He has taken advantage of that licence to import wine in bulk from the United States, favouring Washington, for Isabella's grape wines. However, the winery also sources VQA wines, notably icewines made for Isabella in the Okanagan and, occasionally, in Ontario. Consulting winemaker Charles Herrold, one of the owners of Langley's Blackwood Lane, helped the winery find Okanagan grapes and wines.

Charles was retained because Tony's expertise is in making Isabella's fruit wines. "I have my own recipes," he says. His cranberry, raspberry, and blueberry dessert wines are remarkably full-bodied, reflecting the high volume of natural juice that goes into making the wines. Some competing fruit wines are thin because, he says provocatively, water is cheaper than juice. In time he would like to master making grape wines after being swept off his feet by Blackwood Lane's flagship Alliánce red wine. "I want to make a wine like that, no more, no less," he says. "The wine is perfect for me."

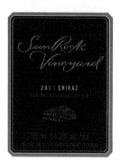

JACKSON-TRIGGS VINTNERS

OPENED: 1981 (AS BRIGHTS WINES)

38691 Highway 97 North, Oliver, BC VOH 1T0
250.498.4500 | 1.866.455.0559 (toll free)
www.jacksontriggswinery.com
When to visit: Open daily 10 am – 6 pm April 2 to October 31 and 10 am – 4:30 pm
November through March. Winery tours by appointment only

RECOMMENDED

SUNROCK VINEYARD WINES
ICEWINES (NOTABLY SPARKLING ICEWINE)
SHIRAZ
MERITAGE
MERLOT
CHARDONNAY
VIOGNIER
SAUVIGNON BLANC

OF THE MANY WINE AWARDS WON BY JACKSON-TRIGGS OVER THE YEARS, arguably the most remarkable was the International Wine & Spirits Competition's award for what winery publicists liked to call "the best Shiraz in the world." The phrase was a stretch since not all of the world's Shirazes were competing. Never mind: enough top Shirazes were entered that it was astonishing for an Okanagan Valley Shiraz made with fruit from young vines to be judged best in a fairly rigorous competition.

The South Okanagan has begun to gain renown for Shiraz (or Syrah, to use the other name for the grape that produces rich red wines). A lot of credit for this is due to Jackson-Triggs. While Nichol Vineyard planted a small block of Syrah in 1991, it was Jackson-Triggs that planted the first serious acreage of this variety in 1998 and 1999 on its new Osoyoos Lake Bench vineyards. By 2006 the winery had 24 hectares

(60 acres) of Shiraz, with more plantings coming in the next few years. The winery's best block of Shiraz is in a vineyard now called SunRock. The vines run up a south-facing slope that ends against a huge rock outcrop. The heat-loving Shiraz is in the hottest part of the vineyard, against this rock (hence the name).

Bruce Nicholson, who was then the winemaker at Jackson-Triggs, knew he had something special from his first vintages. The 2001 Shiraz was judged the best Canadian red wine at the following year's Canadian Wine Awards. Since then every single Shiraz vintage has won medals and acclaim. If anything, the success of this variety almost overshadows the other remarkable wines being made by Jackson-Triggs. "Merlot is where we started to make our name for red wines," Nicholson has said.

The Jackson-Triggs winery, now sprawling north of Oliver like an aircraft hangar, evolved from the controversial winery built on this site in 1981 by T. G. Bright and Company, a predecessor company. Because the site was (and still is) leased from the Osoyoos Indian Band, critics in 1981 — including other First Nations bands — were incredulous at locating an alcohol-producing facility on an Indian reserve. Sam Baptiste, the Osoyoos chief at the time and now manager of the band's Inkameep Vineyards, rejected the protests. Today the winery is the leading employer on the reserve. Jackson-Triggs is also a partner at Nk'Mip Cellars, the band-owned winery that opened in 2002 at Osoyoos.

The legendary Shirazes, among other varieties, emerge from the close relationship between the winery and the band. Vincor, the parent of Jackson-Triggs (and five other Okanagan wineries) operates almost 400 hectares (1,000 acres) of vineyard. The majority of this property, including the 32-hectare (80-acre) SunRock Vineyard, is leased from the band, whose reserve extends across the South Okanagan. Generally sun-baked and sandy, these are among Canada's best vineyards. They thrived under the professional management of Mark Sheridan, a seasoned viticulturist from Australia, who worked here from 1999 to 2009. The most extensive plantings are Merlot and Cabernet Sauvignon. Sauvignon Blanc and Riesling grow on the slightly cooler sites just southeast of Oliver.

The Jackson-Triggs name was coined in 1994. It comes from Donald Triggs and Alan Jackson, two of the founding partners of Vincor. They managed to put a real face on this large, corporate winery by having their names on the front labels and their signatures on the back labels. Even the wine quality tiers tied into this image: top-rung Proprietors' Grand Reserve, mid-range Proprietors' Reserve, and value-range Proprietors' Selection. (This somewhat confusing set of tiers was being simplified as this book went to press.) The single-vineyard SunRock wines, made in limited volumes, are on par with the Grand Reserve tier.

When Nicholson returned to his native Ontario in 2006 to take over making the wine at Inniskillin, Jackson-Triggs promoted his two assistants. The white wine maker is Derek Kontkanen, who was born in Midland, Ontario, in 1978. He moved to Jackson-Triggs in the Okanagan in 2004 while still completing a master's degree in oenology. His master's research involved icewine fermentation, a handy skill at a winery with a track record for superb icewines.

The red wine maker is Brooke Blair. Born in 1978 at Mount Gambier in Australia, she trained at the University of Adelaide, starting out in commerce before switching to wine, in part because winemakers get to travel. She worked three years at Hollick Wines, a family-owned winery in Coonawarra, did a vintage in Spain, and was thinking of Italy when she landed the job at Jackson-Triggs in 2004. Three years later she became a permanent resident of Canada, "which is an indication of how much I enjoy it here," she says.

That enjoyment stems from the quality of the grapes she gets to work with, allowing her to make both single varietals and sophisticated blends, notably the Meritage: a blend chiefly of Cabernet Sauvignon, Merlot, and Cabernet Franc. But it should be no surprise to discover what her favourite variety is. "I love working with Shiraz," she confides.

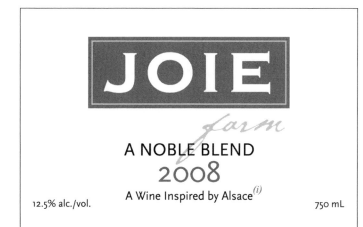

JOIEFARM

OPENED: 2004

2825 Naramata Road, Naramata, BC V0H 1N0
250.496.0073 | 1.866.422.5643 (toll free)
www.joie.ca
When to visit: No tasting room

RECOMMENDED

DEDICATION PINOT BLANC
A NOBLE BLEND
RESERVE CHARDONNAY
UNOAKED CHARDONNAY
MUSCAT
ROSÉ
RIESLING
PTG

TWO OF THE MOST ORIGINAL MINDS IN OKANAGAN WINEMAKING, HEIDI NOBLE and Michael Dinn, dared to launch Joie with a business plan that could only be called contrarian. In 2004 when consumers were scrambling for big reds, they began making only aromatic whites and a rosé while running a cooking school on their farm. By 2007, the year in which they won a Lieutenant Governor's Award of Excellence in BC Wines, they closed the cooking school permanently to make way for a new winery producing seven times as much as the one thousand cases in the 2004 vintage. And these self-taught winemakers still were not making a really big red.

Their grounding in the restaurants and wine agencies, where they had a chance to taste many fine wines, explains Joie's quick success. "We are coming at this backwards, from an experience of palate first and then winemaking skills,"

Heidi says. Rhetorically, Michael asks: "If you don't know what good wine tastes like, how can you achieve it?"

Heidi, petite and vibrant, was born in Toronto in 1974 and grew up in Edmonton. She began cooking as a teenager. "I had my first kitchen job at 14," she recalls. "I loved it. So I worked after school and all through the summer while I was in high school." A gold medal student at the University of Western Ontario, she earned degrees in both philosophy and literature but turned down an academic scholarship to enrol in the renowned Stratford chefs school. By the time she was 25, she was running the kitchen for a Vancouver caterer until, after a decade in food service, she switched careers. She completed a sommelier diploma and began working for a wine agency.

She met Michael, now her husband, through the sommelier program. Born in Victoria in 1967, Michael worked as a waiter while getting a university history degree. That experience came in handy in 1994 when, during a post-graduate tour of Europe, he replenished his funds by working in a fancy London wine bar. From that experience he recalls tasting an expensive Australian red "that actually made me understand why people paid $100 a bottle" for fine wine. Returning to Vancouver, he became one of the city's top sommeliers, studying wine with a burning intensity. Initially he had wanted to be a screenwriter until he accepted that his true talent and passion was for wine.

In 2000, burned out after 16 years in restaurants, Michael became a wine agent while he and Heidi laid plans for Joie. They opened the cooking school on their Naramata property in 2003. When they closed it in 2007 — the winery now consumed their lives — Heidi celebrated it with a handsome book, *Menus from an Orchard Table*.

They made their first vintage in 2004 at the nearby Poplar Grove winery, benefiting from Ian Sutherland's tutelage. They moved to the Pentâge winery in Penticton for several vintages until building their own winery. Their production had expanded from one thousand cases in the first vintage to seven thousand in the first year under their own roof; and they had taken on Vancouver wine writer Kenji Hodgson as an associate winemaker.

The wines are inspired primarily by wines of Alsace, Burgundy, and Germany. For the most part, these are aromatic wines that are dry but with vivid fruity flavours and aromas. Five varieties are blended into A Noble Blend, perhaps Joie's flagship white. It gets its name not so much from Heidi's surname as from the Alsace white blend inspiring it — Edelzwicker, which means "noble blend." They give a nod to Chablis for influencing their Chardonnay styles, even if the dash of Muscat that turbocharges the aromas of Joie's unoaked Chardonnay would be unorthodox in Chablis, if not downright against the appellation's rules. The red, a blend of Gamay and Pinot Noir, is called PTG because the model is Burgundy's Passetoutgrain blends. The same two varieties also produce Joie's exceptional rosé, a wine that sparks the producer's memories of the south of France.

The delicately perfumed Muscat, the wine with which Joie won its Lieutenant Governor's award, recalls Heidi and Michael's travels through northwestern Italy's wine country. When they planted the Joie vineyard in 2007, they began with just under a hectare (2½ acres) of Moscato Giallo, an Italian clone of that variety. "These wines are all genuine passions of ours," Heidi says.

Michael and Heidi are as spontaneous and refreshing as their wines, a youthful couple with ideas so synchronized that they finish each other's thoughts. Unfortunately, their fans won't always get to see this. They have chosen not to have a tasting room at what they now call JoieFarm, partly for practical reasons (fewer bureaucratic inspections to deal with) and partly because the wines are all sold directly to clients on their mailing list.

KALALA ORGANIC ESTATE WINERY

OPENED: 2008

3361 Glencoe Road, Westbank, BC V4T 1M1
250.768.9700 | 1.866.942.1313 (toll free)
www.kalalawines.ca
When to visit: Open daily 10 am – 6 pm April through October, 11 am – 5 pm
    Wednesday to Sunday November through March

RECOMMENDED

PINOT GRIS
RIESLING
MERLOT
ZWEIGELT
ICEWINE

KARNAIL SINGH SIDHU IS THE GO-TO MAN FOR MANY ORGANIC GRAPE GROWERS, his expertise acquired when he was a new immigrant just trying to earn a living. Born in 1968 in Punjab, he followed two brothers to Canada in 1993. Because of the currency restrictions then enforced by India, Karnail arrived at Vancouver Airport with only $40 US in his pocket. "For five family members," he says. "We started working right away, picking berries. We made some money every day."

Karnail had a diploma in electrical engineering but, even though he upgraded some of his skills at the British Columbia Institute of Technology, he could not get his professional qualifications recognized in Canada. He had also studied agriculture in high school — Punjab, after all, is India's bread basket — so he went to the Okanagan in 1995 and found work in a vineyard. The following year, he joined the Summerhill Pyramid Winery's pruning crew, a job that led to his career in organic grape growing. Summerhill wanted to convert its 19 or 20 growers to organic methods and turned over the grower relations job to Karnail. "They had talked about it but nobody had mobilized it," he recalls.

He remained on Summerhill's payroll for 10 years, learning organics but also applying some of his engineering talents. "It was always Karnail coming to a rescue when the presses would blow apart," remembers Joshua Scott, a winemaker who also worked at Summerhill and made the debut vintage with the versatile Karnail at Kalala. "He is an electrical engineer, plus he can do pruning," Josh says. Karnail shrugs off the accolade. "I do all kinds of work," he says. "For me, work is work."

Besides managing Summerhill's vineyards, Karnail, partnered with two brothers, branched into the agricultural supply business in 1997, setting up a company called Kalala Agriculture. The company sells products and advice for organic grape growers. An associated trucking company in Surrey is run by his brothers, part of an extended family unit that works together on whatever task is at hand. When, for example, icewine grapes need to be picked, Karnail can count on his family to help out. An associated business, which sells bird netting, was set up in partnership with Dave Dhillon, a retired prison warden and a long-time friend. When Dave decided in 2005 to develop what is now the Chandra Estate Winery, Karnail agreed to be his mentor.

The Kalala winery project began in 2001 when Karnail leased a four-hectare (10-acre) vineyard on the Glenmore plateau overlooking Westbank and Okanagan Lake. Here he grows organic Gewürztraminer, Riesling, Pinot Noir, Pinot Auxerrois, Zweigelt, and Merlot. Subsequently he acquired a second property on the Golden Mile south of Oliver, with about two hectares (five acres) of grapes, most of which are sold to another winery.

The winery gets its name from Karnail's hometown in the Punjab. Kalala means "miracle place." According to legend, the town was relocated to the spot where a wolf and a lamb were found living peacefully together. To Karnail, the Okanagan has comparable serenity. On the back label of the wines, he points out that the winery's "organic grapes are grown in harmony with their environment and nature's elements."

100% Natural
Wild Berries

KERMODE WILD BERRY WINES

OPENED: 2006

8457 River Road South, Dewdney, BC V0M 1H0
604.814.3222
www.kermodewildberry.com
When to visit: Open daily noon – 6 pm

RECOMMENDED

BLUE ELDERBERRY
EVERGREEN BLACKBERRY
HIMALAYAN BLACKBERRY PORT
SITKA MOUNTAIN-ASH
RED SALMONBERRY
BLACKCAP RASPBERRY PORT
MOUNTAIN CRANBERRY LIQUOR
SASKATOON BERRY LIQUOR

THE WINES MADE BY KERMODE WILD BERRY ARE BRITISH COLUMBIA'S MOST original. Every wine is made from berries that grow in the wild. The berries are often hard to find, difficult to harvest efficiently, and challenging to ferment into acceptable wines. "If it was easy, everybody would do it," says Fritz Sprieszl, who established this winery with his brother, Bob. They believe there are perhaps 40 edible wild berries in British Columbia. Since their first vintage in 2005, they have been determining which make palatable wine and which should be left to the bears with which they compete. They respect the bears: after all, the winery is named after the so-called Kermode spirit bear, a white genetic mutation of the black bear.

Fritz and Bob are the sons of a Hungarian immigrant who came to the Fraser Valley in 1964 and, after working for a railroad, opened his own shingle mill. Fritz, born in 1967, and Bob, born in 1974, went to work after high school in their father's mill and, when it closed, for other mills in the Mission area. Those jobs petered out when cedar logs became scarce. Bob took off to ski, first in New Zealand and then in northern Japan, following a Japanese woman he had met in Canada. When romance blossomed with Kana, Bob became a farm worker, spending seven years in Japan. He returned to Canada in 2005 to help Fritz with the winery. Kana, now his wife, runs the winery's tasting room.

When the shingle mills closed, Fritz looked for other ways to earn a living from the forest. "When we walk into the forest, we see dollars," he says, smiling. He started as a mushroom picker and was soon earning more than at the shingle mill. When mushroom season ended in northern British Columbia, he went to the Queen Charlotte Islands in the summer of 1999 to visit a friend. He could not believe the profusion of wild berries. "I thought, 'There has to be a market for this,' " he recalls. Soon he was shipping loads of huckleberries to the Lower Mainland. He followed up by opening a moss harvesting business in the Fraser Valley and, for a time, prospered by selling dried moss to florists and craft dealers.

During his stay on the Queen Charlottes, he became friends with an islander who was making quite drinkable wine from the huckleberries. That put the idea of wild berry wines into Fritz's mind and, when the moss business weakened, he developed this ingenious winery. "They didn't know where to put me," he says, laughing at the reaction from the regulators when he applied for a winery licence. He received a land-based winery licence in 2005 because the family's property near Dewdney on the north side of the Fraser River includes acres of the ubiquitous wild blackberries. The tasting room opened in late 2006 with eight wines: three from blackberries, two made with alpine blueberries, a blue elderberry wine, a red salmonberry wine, and a blackcap raspberry port. Additional wines have joined the portfolio since.

He and Bob have taken on an exceptional challenge, beginning with finding the berry patches. They rely on their own knowledge of the forests along with tips from their wine clients and, increasingly, calls from the freelance berry pickers they hire. Unlike cultivated berries, wild berry production is wildly cyclical. Fritz has learned the bushes yield bumper crops only once every two or three years. Each berry requires a different harvesting method and some fleetness of foot. The harvest of the blackcap raspberry, which makes one of Kermode's most delicious wines, is easily ruined by sudden rain. Some berries, notably the very acidic Oregon grape, challenged all of Fritz's considerable winemaking skills. "When I told some winemakers about the acid level in this Oregon grape, they laughed and said, 'Don't even try,' " Fritz says. He did, making a dry, pungent, and earthy wine not unlike a red grape wine.

His Sitka Mountain-Ash Berry Wine, with its tawny colour and smoky aroma, recalls a single malt Scotch — if Scotch had only 12 percent alcohol. "It's never been done here," Fritz believes. One can, however, find home winemakers in England using the fruit, called rowan berry there. The tree bears abundant bright red berries.

In medieval times, small crosses fashioned from rowan wood served to ward off witches. There is a long tradition of country wines in Britain, and Fritz has consulted the recipes for making what he calls his "wild-crafted" wines.

"Perhaps next year I will be able to add a highbush cranberry wine," Fritz said in the fall of 2008; he was also considering making rosehip wine. "I try to add at least two or three new wines every year. There is *so much* fruit out there."

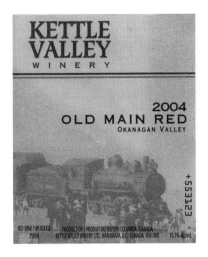

KETTLE VALLEY WINERY

OPENED: 1996

2988 Hayman Road, RR1, Site 2, Comp 39, Naramata, BC V0H 1N0
250.496.5898
www.kettlevalleywinery.com
When to visit: Open daily 11 am – 5 pm May to mid-October or by appointment.
  Groups of more than eight should book an appointment

RECOMMENDED

OLD MAIN RED
SHIRAZ
CREST CABERNET SAUVIGNON
PINOT NOIR (BOTH RESERVE AND HAYMAN)
MCGRAW ESTATE MERLOT
KING MERLOT
MALBEC
GEWÜRZTRAMINER
STARBOARD

THE STORIED KETTLE VALLEY RAILWAY STOPPED CARRYING FREIGHT OR passengers about 50 years ago. However, the railroad's history lives on not only in the name of this winery but also in the names of its wines — Old Main Red, Adra Station Chardonnay, Brakeman's Select, Caboose, Derailer, and, most recently, Naramata Bench Reserve Extra 4079. This blended red was named for the last train to climb the Coquihalla Pass on November 23, 1959, just ahead of four washouts that doomed the line. The rail bed in the Okanagan, now a hiking trail, snakes along the mountainside above the Naramata Bench vineyards, visible from the door of this winery's tasting room. It gave Bob Ferguson and Tim Watts the idea for the winery name when they opened Kettle Valley in 1996.

These railway history buffs came to winemaking in 1980 as amateurs. Bob was born in Scotland in 1950, grew up in Canada, and became a chartered accountant in Vancouver. Tim, eight years younger, was born in Victoria and became a geologist. After marrying sisters, they discovered a shared interest in winemaking and started buying Okanagan grapes. In 1985 Tim and his wife, Janet, bought a home near Naramata and put in a test block of Chardonnay and Pinot Noir. When these succeeded, the partners began acquiring vineyard acreage and easing out of their former careers.

The Old Main Vineyard was planted in 1990 to Cabernet Sauvignon, Cabernet Franc, and Merlot, one of the earliest plantings of Bordeaux varieties on the Naramata Bench. Today Bob and Tim own or manage about 14 hectares (35 acres), including a significant Syrah and Viognier vineyard at Keremeos in the Similkameen Valley, purchased in 2008. "We are farming 11 different vineyards," Tim says. "It's a difficult way to farm."

Wines made from Naramata Bench fruit now are released with the unofficial Naramata sub-appellation on the labels. Wines made from Similkameen fruit are, for the most part, bottled separately so that neither terroir is submerged into the other. An admirable practice, it makes for a large portfolio. "My wife [Colleen] tells me that we have 29 different wines," Bob says and laughs. She would know because, when Kettle Valley releases its wines, she takes the orders.

The Naramata Bench is one of the best terroirs in the Okanagan. With the nearby lake to ward off frosts, the bench vineyards ripen grapes longer than anywhere else in the valley. Kettle Valley's photogenic Old Main Vineyard slopes gently down toward the lake. The reds planted here are often not picked until early November. This vineyard, visible from the winery parking lot, is always netted against birds late in the season, because it is one of the last vineyards still hanging succulent red grapes.

The Similkameen Valley has a shorter but hotter season. That should suit Bob and Tim's winemaking style. "Our style has always been bigger, robust, ripe, full-bodied wines because that is the style we enjoy," Bob says. "The luxury of being small is that you can afford to do that. We have certainly tried to make wines that are very intense and full-bodied."

The signature wines have been the reds, which are seldom released until they have spent at least two years in barrel and bottle. The winery opened its tasting room in 1996 (in what formerly was a three-car garage) with a Pinot Noir from 1992. Boldly Burgundian, that Pinot Noir remained vibrantly alive a decade later. Wines like that have built Kettle Valley's reputation as a top Pinot Noir producer. At the same time, the winery releases memorable Bordeaux reds and Shiraz. Nearly all of Kettle Valley's reds are built for longevity.

During the winery's first 15 years, the white wines seemed to be made with a red wine philosophy, beginning with skin contact on quite ripe grapes. These full-flavoured high-alcohol wines were given long aging in barrel. Some wines, like the rich barrel-fermented Gewürztraminer, departed markedly from the Okanagan mainstream. In the 2007 vintage there was a distinct change in style. Bob and Tim chose to pick the whites a little earlier, keeping more fresh acidity in the wines and, with less barrel aging, making wines that are still complex but now show a refreshing fruitiness. In that vintage they also made Kettle Valley's first Riesling, balanced to be slightly off-dry and, in the German style, with just nine percent alcohol. "It's the first low-alcohol wine we have ever made," Bob says. It will not be the last because they have now planted some Riesling vines.

Although the winery is approaching an annual production of ten thousand cases, the partners continue to make small batches of most of their wines. For example, 197 cases of the 2005 Pinot Noir Reserve, 256 cases of 2007 Gewürztraminer, 90 cases of 2007 Schönburger, and 820 cases of 2005 Old Main Red. It is obvious that, after a quarter century either as amateurs or professionals, they continue to be exhilarated by winemaking. And backed by their wives, they do it largely by themselves.

"We want to be hands-on," Bob says. "We want to be involved in the process. The whole idea of being involved in the wine business was to *do it*, not to give the good jobs to someone else while you turn out to be the management."

LIQUEUR MUSCAT
NV
375 ml   740 Naramata Rd, Penticton   18.5% alc./vol.

LA FRENZ WINERY

OPENED: 2000

740 Naramata Road, Penticton, BC V2A 8T5
250.492.6690
www.lafrenzwinery.com
When to visit: Open daily 10 am – 5 pm May to October and by appointment

RECOMMENDED

LA FRENZ RESERVE
MERLOT
PINOT NOIR
CHARDONNAY
SHIRAZ
SÉMILLON
PINOT GRIS
VIOGNIER
ALEXANDRIA
LIQUEUR MUSCAT
FORTIFIED TAWNY

BECAUSE THE LA FRENZ WINES SELL SO QUICKLY, JEFF AND NIVA MARTIN rarely enter wine competitions, with the exception of a few each season. One of these is the NorthWest Wine Summit. Because it is held in Oregon, it gets many entries from Washington wineries, producers of some of the world's best Merlot. In the 2007 competition, a La Frenz Merlot not only won gold, it also was best in class, the first time an Okanagan winery had bested Washington competitors at this show. "You still get people saying, 'Will BC make great red?' " Jeff said after that win. "I don't think it's a serious question these days. I think we've been making great red for a few years now."

The desire to make his mark in an emerging wine region is why Jeff is in the Okanagan, not back in his native Australia. He and Niva can refresh their roots every morning by looking at the La Frenz tasting room. With its squat metal roof and big overhangs, it resembles a typical Australian farm building. Jeff was born in 1957 in Griffith, the New South Wales town where the McWilliams family has one of its large wineries and where Jeff became a trainee when he was 20. He impressed his employer, who helped finance him to a winemaking degree at Charles Sturt University. By 1989 he was the chief winemaker at the McWilliams premium winery.

With Australian wanderlust in their blood, the Martins came to the Okanagan in 1994, and Jeff, over five impressive vintages, helped put Quails' Gate on the map. Wanting to strike out on their own, they returned to Australia, only to find new wineries opening every two or three days, or so it seemed. Within months the Martins were back in the Okanagan. "Where was I going to be likely to succeed?" Jeff had asked himself as he considered the tidal wave of competitors. "In my 20-some years in the industry, it would have been the worst time to start a winery back there."

Instead the Martins purchased Okanagan grapes in 1999, making their wine at the Poplar Grove winery and selling through Poplar Grove's tasting room until establishing their own Naramata Road winery nearby. They purchased a roadside apple orchard and, in 2002, planted a 2.4-hectare (six-acre) vineyard to Merlot, Shiraz, and Viognier and built a winery. The first La Frenz tasting room consisted of planks over barrels in the winery's front corner. "I keep it pretty lean," Jeff said at the time.

As the winery became established, he leased additional vineyards and developed a four-hectare (10-acre) property south of Oliver on the Golden Mile. He calls this stony site his Rocky Fella Vineyard; it provides Petit Verdot, Malbec, Cabernet Franc, and Shiraz. In 2008 the Martins purchased another Naramata Road property not far from the winery. Here Jeff replaced fruit trees with two hectares (five acres) of Pinot Noir. He grows five selected clones of the variety designed to give him a bold wine. "I don't want to make strawberry jam," he says. "I want to make a big serious wine." He now has grapes to support an annual production of ten thousand cases. "That's a good family business," he says.

There is a story behind the La Frenz name. It is not, as it might seem, inspired by a bibulous evening drinking Foster's with "la friends." It is, in fact, the surname of Martin's paternal grandfather, an old family name from the Schleswig-Holstein region of northern Germany. But his parents divorced when he was a teenager and Martin grew up using his mother's maiden name.

Jeff's prize-winning wines — he has also won a Lieutenant Governor's Award of Excellence — reflect his experience. His vibrant "peaches and cream" style of Chardonnay, unique in the Okanagan, has been served at dinners for the Queen and has a strong following. He is adept at barrel-fermenting wines, letting reds do their final "fizz" in the barrel. The gentle aeration that wine undergoes in barrels is important to the development of texture as well as taste. Australian wineries often use chips or blocks of wood to impart oak flavours to inexpensive wines. "You can use bags of oak chips," Jeff agrees. "But you really can't replicate barrels yet." He even has learned some of the cooper's trade, taking used barrels apart and refreshing them by shaving the inner sides.

Jeff once took exception to the cliché that wines are made in the vineyard with the rejoinder that "winemakers also make wines." Even so, he pays a great deal of attention to his vineyards. In recent years he has begun to employ biodynamic methods. "Sustainability," he explains. "We haven't used synthetic fertilizers in here. We do a seaweed spray once a year for micronutrients. We want the wines to have more terroir effect and have more of the soil come through in the wine."

He has set the bar high for La Frenz. "I have come to the opinion, especially with all the new wineries popping up, there is just no place for average wine. I have a finite production capacity. Why would I want to do average? It's way easier to sell the better wines."

LAKE BREEZE VINEYARDS

OPENED: 1996

930 Sammet Road, Box 9, Naramata, BC V0H 1N0
250.496.5659
www.lakebreeze.ca
When to visit: Open daily 10 am – 6 pm July and August; 11 am – 5 pm May, June,
    September, and October; weekends in April. Winter visits by appointment
Restaurant: Mahdina's Patio (250.496.5619) open for lunch daily (except Monday) July
    and August, weekends May through September. Reservations recommended
Accommodation: Two rental cottages

RECOMMENDED

TEMPEST
SEVEN POPLARS SERIES (INCLUDING CHARDONNAY, MERLOT, PINOTAGE,
    PINOT NOIR, SAUVIGNON BLANC)
MERITAGE
SÉMILLON
PINOT BLANC
EHRENFELSER
PINOT GRIS
BLANC DE NOIR ROSÉ
ZEPHYR BRUT

ANYONE SITTING DOWN TO LUNCH AT THIS WINERY'S RESTAURANT PATIO WILL
understand the origin of the Seven Poplars label on the top wines from Lake Breeze.
Those stately poplars beside the patio provide welcome shade on hot Okanagan
days. There are few more attractive places than this patio for relaxing with a glass
of wine. More than one visitor has come away from the experience with a desire to
have a winery of their own. That more or less is what happened in 2001 when the
current owners of Lake Breeze, four Albertans, came to the Okanagan for a wine
country vacation, discovered that Lake Breeze was for sale, and bought it.

The winery was established by a Swiss-born South African businessman, Paul Moser, who came to the Okanagan in 1994 with his wife and bought a picturesque vineyard on the Naramata Bench. The winery he built, with its soothing white stucco exterior, echoed the architecture of Cape wineries in South Africa. Paul put a firmer South African stamp on Lake Breeze in 1995 by recruiting winemaker Garron Elmes, a fresh graduate from Elsenburg College of Agriculture in Cape Town. Born in 1972 in Cape Town, Garron, who is now a Canadian citizen, has continued to make the wine at Lake Breeze through three ownership changes. This accounts for the consistency in the style of the wines at this property.

Paul put a South African imprint on the vineyard by planting Pinotage, South Africa's iconic red grape variety. The variety was created in 1925 at the University of Stellenbosch when Professor Abraham Perold crossed Pinot Noir and Cinsault. It only began being released as a named varietal in the 1960s. Since then the variety has carved out an important place in South Africa, even having its own association. Paul only planted about an acre of Pinotage. However, the wines made by Garron created enough interest that at least two other Okanagan wineries (Inniskillin Okanagan and Stoneboat) also planted Pinotage.

Paul sold Lake Breeze in 1998, moving on because, as he explained to a journalist at the time, "Once business becomes administration, I become bored with it." The next set of owners, former operators of a helicopter company, came to a similar conclusion three years later. To date, however, the lifestyle of winery owners has continued to appeal to the current owners: Gary Reynolds and his wife Tracey Ball, and their partners, Drew and Barbara MacIntyre.

Gary, a chartered accountant formerly with the Edmonton School Board, is the working partner at Lake Breeze, the one, as he puts it on the winery website, with "dirty fingernails and new calluses." With the winery now making about 6,500 cases a year from its seven-hectare (17-acre) vineyard, the three other owners have kept their day jobs. Tracey is the chief financial officer of Canadian Western Bank. Drew MacIntyre is a Calgary investment banker and Barbara is a chartered accountant. "We should be able to figure things out," Gary quips.

Their involvement with the Okanagan is a typical story. Gary and Tracey started out looking for a property with "house-of-the-future potential." They had also been discussing a joint venture with the MacIntyres. The foursome came to the Okanagan in the spring of 2001, found that Lake Breeze was available, and moved quickly to snap up what Gary calls a "unique property" before the opportunity slipped away.

One of their first moves after taking over that fall was to build and equip a substantial new winery. Garron, their patient winemaker, had been working in extremely tight quarters: the previous owners had squeezed out every inch of space with unusual square wine tanks. The new quarters allowed Garron to move his laboratory from the owners' house, while he shifted wines from a garage into a climate-controlled cellar. Most importantly, Lake Breeze was able to accommodate a serious number of new barrels in its cellar. The result was an immediate jump in the quality of Lake Breeze wines, including the launching of the winery's "best barrel reserves" in the Seven Poplar series. One of those is Pinotage, of which only 125 cases are made annually.

Lake Breeze has offered at least a dozen different wines, although the portfolio has been reduced slightly. Gary is always hesitant to drop a wine. "In a small winery with a lot of its sales from the walk-in trade, when there are many varieties, someone always walks away with something because there is something for everybody," he says. The Lake Breeze reds, in addition to Pinotage, include Merlot, Meritage, and Pinot Noir. The white wines here include Pinot Gris, Pinot Blanc, Gewürztraminer, and Ehrenfelser, with a Chardonnay and a Sauvignon Blanc offered only in the Seven Poplars range.

Lake Breeze makes one of the few examples of Sémillon in the Okanagan, a Bordeaux white variety not as well known as it should be because it is usually blended with Sauvignon Blanc. On its own Sémillon can be full-textured with a refreshing grapefruit tang. "Some people find it over-the-top," Gary says. "There are some really robust fruit flavours in there. We continue to make it. It's got a great place in the vineyard."

LARCH HILLS WINERY

OPENED: 1997

110 Timms Road, Salmon Arm, BC V1E 2P8
250.832.0155 | 1.877.892.0155 (toll free)
www.larchhillswinery.com
When to visit: Open daily 9 am – 5 pm; in winter, check road conditions

RECOMMENDED

ORTEGA DRY
ORTEGA LATE HARVEST
TAMARACK ROSÉ
SIEGERREBE LATE HARVEST

JACK MANSER HAS A SIMPLE, IF PAINSTAKING, METHOD FOR EXPANDING THE vineyard at Larch Hills. Whenever he needs more vines, he takes cuttings from dormant vines during wintertime pruning. The cuttings develop new roots in his greenhouse, preparing them for spring planting. He laughed when the previous owner, Hans Nevrkla, worried about whether or not Jack knew how to do this. "I did thousands of cuttings from willows and poplars during my forestry career," Jack reassured him.

Born in eastern Switzerland in 1957, Jack had a 20-year forestry career before coming to Canada in 1992. When he could not get a visa to work here as a forester, he bought a small mixed farm in Alberta. That generated a modest living until the farm was divided to settle a divorce, triggering a search for an agriculture business with more potential. He settled on wine growing, a business giving him control from the vineyard through to the sale of the final products. "I like to be self-employed," he adds.

Jack and Hazel, his new spouse, toured the Okanagan twice before buying Larch Hills in mid-2005. "I like a green country," Jack says, explaining why they chose not to settle in the desert landscape of the South Okanagan. That was the same reason why Hans and Hazel Nevrkla, the founders of Larch Hills, chose to plant vines here in the first place, after buying 29 hectares (72 acres) of heavily forested slope in 1987. The government's grape expert advised against it but they went ahead with test plots and, by 1992, had begun to figure out what varieties would grow here. Hans proved the naysayers wrong when the winery opened in 1997 with quite tasty wine. "After that, all kinds of people told me they always knew it would work here," Hans said later, just before retiring from the successful winery.

Jack grew up on a mixed farm in Switzerland. The crops included apples, cherries, and plums, some of which his family turned into wine or distilled for personal consumption. He had some understanding of winemaking when taking over the winery, but not grape wines, so Jack arranged that the previous owner would be available as a consultant for a couple of vintages. Hans, a native of Vienna, is an experienced winemaker; he even taught other home vintners in Calgary before moving to the Okanagan. In retirement he continues to consult to other emerging producers in the burgeoning wine district around Shuswap Lake.

When they decided to retire, Hans and Hazel Nevrkla had Larch Hills making about 2,500 cases a year, a comfortable volume that they could make by themselves and sell effortlessly, mostly from the tasting room. The Mansers have approached Larch Hills more aggressively, more than doubling production. But they have not tampered with the Larch Hills style of making crisp and fruity wines, with perhaps one exception. The winery's popular Tamarack Rosé originally was a blend of red and white wines. Looking for a darker and more concentrated rosé, Jack now relies on only red grapes.

This is British Columbia's highest vineyard, at 700 metres or 2,300 feet above sea level, and one of the most northern. From the top of the vineyard, the northern end of the Okanagan Valley can be seen stretching into the distance. The vines grow without irrigation — rare in interior British Columbia — on slopes that pitch steeply toward the south and southwest. This ideal exposure is the main reason that certain wine grapes can be matured here.

"I believe this is white wine country up here," Jack says. He has continued to propagate the varieties that were already succeeding here when the Mansers bought the winery: Ortega, Siegerrebe, Madeleine Angevine, and Madeleine Sylvaner. He is considering planting Pinot Gris and Gewürztraminer, varieties the winery now purchases from contract growers. The flagship variety is the Ortega, an early-ripening German variety that gets both its Muscat-like fruitiness and its mid-season maturing from Siegerrebe, one of its parent varieties. Siegerrebe ripens even earlier, with intense aromas and flavours that show best in dessert wines — if the wasps, who are attracted to the vineyard by the aroma, have not decimated the harvest.

The only red at Larch Hills, so far, is a Hungarian variety called Agria. Maréchal Foch would do well here but, to date, Jack has been able to get the grapes from a contract grower, along with the other reds in the Larch Hills portfolio. Jack would prefer to grow more of his own red grapes rather than having to depend on distant growers in the South Okanagan. He has plenty of room on his slope. "A guy could add another 30 acres," he muses.

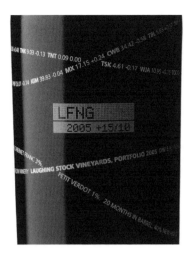

LAUGHING STOCK VINEYARDS

OPENED: 2005

1548 Naramata Road, Penticton, BC V2A 8T7
250.493.8466
www.laughingstock.ca
When to visit: By appointment

RECOMMENDED

PORTFOLIO
BLIND TRUST
CHARDONNAY
PINOT GRIS

WHEN DAVID ENNS IS NOT TEARING DOWN HIGHWAYS ON ONE OF HIS THREE motorcycles (two BMWs and a gleaming Ducati), he and Cynthia, his wife, often find time to taste in wine regions around the world. In the late 1990s they educated themselves on Rhône wines by visiting about 250 Rhône producers over three years. Recently they made a quick trip to France to taste the white Burgundies that inspire the style of Laughing Stock's Chardonnay. "We go over there regularly to develop a palate that is truly global," David says. "That is the underpinning of what we are trying to do here, to understand what it takes to make global wines."

If there seems a disconnect between that goal and the winery's whimsical name, here is the explanation. In their previous careers as financial consultants, they had many clients and friends in the investment industry. They plunged into wine so abruptly that associates feared they might make fools of themselves. They met the challenge head-on by calling the winery Laughing Stock and setting out to prove otherwise. Portfolio, the flagship red first released in the 2003 vintage, has become one of the Okanagan's most collectible wines, a bold red based on Merlot and the other Bordeaux reds, carefully aged in top-quality French oak and structured to be cellared, like any serious world-class red. "I'd be happy if this wine tastes fabulously developed after five or seven years," David says. "Five to ten years, anything in that range, is like a home run."

Wines like that come from benchmarking them against good wines from around the world. Born in Edmonton in 1957, David is the son of an air force officer who had European postings. "I got to see the world before I was a teenager," David says. He and Cynthia, who has a master's in business administration, shared a passion for wine when they met and collected a substantial personal cellar.

David's impulsive decision to make wine dates from a five-day winery tour in Washington early in 2000 with Vancouver wine merchant John Clerides. David noted the varied backgrounds of the winemakers he met. "That sort of opened my eyes," he recalls. "Anybody with some passion can get into the business. You don't need to have a winery that's been passed down six generations."

In 2001 he bought a half-ton of Cabernet Sauvignon and made his first wine in his White Rock basement, picking the brains of contacts in the wine industry for pointers. Because the grapes came from one of the best Washington vineyards, the wine turned out well. David, who took a couple of years of science in college, purchased Washington-grown Syrah in 2002 and jetted to the University of California at Davis for winemaking courses.

He and Cynthia had already begun looking for winery property. "We looked through Europe," he says. "The only region we never checked out was the Okanagan." He had been at high school in Kelowna in the 1970s when local wines were poor. At an Okanagan wine festival in 2001, they discovered how enormously the wines had improved. They narrowed their search to the Okanagan and, in March 2003, bought 2.2 hectares (5½ acres) on Naramata Road with 1.2 hectares (three acres) of young Merlot vines.

The secret of Laughing Stock is how shrewdly Cynthia and David, perhaps because they have been consultants themselves, tapped experts to get up to speed quickly. They retained Valerie Tait, one of the Okanagan's top vineyard consultants, to teach them how to run the vineyard. She quickly disabused David that good wine is made primarily in the winery, a common misconception among amateur winemakers. "Val taught us very early on that there are more decisions made in the vineyard than there are in the winery," David said late in 2003. "I challenged her at first, but having gone through a growing season, I understand."

It was through Valerie that David established a mentoring relationship with Poplar Grove winemaker Ian Sutherland. One of the Okanagan's best self-taught winemakers, Ian guided David in making Laughing Stock's 2003 and 2004 vintages, both produced in Poplar Grove's winery. By 2005, when the new Laughing Stock winery had been built on the hillside at the top of the vineyard, David was comfortably flying solo. "We've learned so much so quickly," David says. "You can't learn unless you do it." During the winery's first five vintages, production increased tenfold, to about five thousand cases. That is the capacity of this high-ceilinged, multilevel winery, which has all the usual winery equipment plus a good sound system. David's eclectic taste in music to work by runs from blues legend Jack Johnson to modern rock (with soothing classics when he is doing laboratory analysis).

The small Naramata vineyard is not nearly big enough to support five thousand cases. In 2007 David purchased nine hectares (22¼ acres) in Osoyoos growing six hectares (15 acres) of Bordeaux reds, along with Syrah and Viognier. With that property, Laughing Stock controls three-quarters of its own grape supply.

It also increased the range of wines David makes. Initially Laughing Stock intended to make only Portfolio and two whites (a Chardonnay and a Pinot Gris) with Cynthia arguing strongly for a tight focus. "It is hard as a winemaker not to dabble in other stuff," David says. When he was able to buy Pinot Noir in 2004, that variety joined the Laughing Stock lineup. Inspired by a taste for blended whites, he extended the production to include Pinot Pinot, made by co-fermenting Pinot Gris and Pinot Blanc. A second red was added to provide a home for the barrel-aged reds not needed in the final three-thousand-case Portfolio blend. It is called Blind Trust and the varietal composition, which changes from vintage to vintage, is never revealed. "The winemaker has full discretion over the assets," Cynthia says and laughs. "You just have to trust him."

The Osoyoos vineyard, along with some purchased grapes, has given David the chance to make a Rhône blend like those he came to admire a decade earlier in France. He believes that Syrah, co-fermented with up to five percent Viognier, yields a "seductive" wine. "A deep rich red wine with the aromatics of the Viognier, a white," he says. "When you co-ferment, special things happen."

LE VIEUX PIN

OPENED: 2006

> 34070 – 73 Street, Oliver, BC
> V0H 1T0
> 250.498.8388
> www.levieuxpin.ca
> When to visit: Open daily 11 am –
> 5 pm; appointments
> recommended

RECOMMENDED

> ÉPOQUE
> APOGÉE
> BELLE
> VAÏLA ROSÉ

LASTELLA

OPENED: 2008

> 8123 – 148th Avenue, Osoyoos, BC
> V0H 1V2
> 250.495.8180
> www.lastella.ca
> When to visit: By appointment
> 11 am – 5 pm, Tuesday to Saturday

RECOMMENDED

> MAESTOSO
> ALLEGRETTO
> VIVACE

THE SOUTH OKANAGAN IS A DESERT WITH ANNUAL RAINFALL AVERAGING 20 inches per year. That is why every vineyard is irrigated. Or almost every vineyard. Harold Gaudy, the vineyard manager for Le Vieux Pin and the sister winery, LaStella, virtually dry-farms this winery's established vines. The production is about half that of neighbouring vineyards; the vines are forced to yield small but intensely flavoured grapes. The object of such extreme viticulture is to make powerful wines remarkable for their aromas and flavours: wines with the potential to leave what winery co-founder Saeedeh Salem terms "a legacy."

Saeedeh and Sean Salem, her husband, do not have typical wine industry backgrounds. Now Vancouver entrepreneurs, both come from families that left Iran after the 1979 revolution. Her family lived some years in Europe before coming to British Columbia in 1988. Her management degree from Simon Fraser University equipped her to succeed in real estate development and to apply her disciplined, detail-oriented direction to running Enotecca Winery and Resorts, the holding company for the wineries. Sean, who was born in 1966, grew up in southern California, where he pursued a variety of businesses, including food distribution. "I started drinking wine in California," Sean says. "The friends I had were all wine drinkers, a bunch of Italians" — including Celestino Drago, a renowned chef. Saeedeh was introduced to wine when Sean was courting her. "Without Sean's passion for wine, I wouldn't be in the wine business," she says. "My wine knowledge is not quite that great."

It was their partner in the wineries, Greg Thomas, who talked them into it. A former broker and manager of junior mining companies, he had been asked to raise money for the company then controlled Hester Creek Estate Winery (prior to Hester Creek's bankruptcy). Greg turned that down but his interest had been sparked. "It sort of stuck with me that if this was approached properly, this would be a good business," he says. He wrote a business plan for a group of boutique wineries and a resort in the Okanagan and, because of their expertise in real estate, took it to the Salems, his close personal as well as business friends. "Going into this business was one of the biggest risks that I ever took," Saeedeh admits.

Sean, who is spontaneous to the point of being impulsive, took to the wine business as if born into it. Between 2004 and 2008 he put at least 50,000 kilometres (about 31,000 miles) per year on his leased vehicles, commuting to the Okanagan to buy 20 hectares (50 acres) of vineyard and to launch two new 3,500-case wineries. The business plan calls for a third winery but Greg, more conservative than his partners, had that project put aside for the time being.

Le Vieux Pin (LVP), off Black Sage Road just south of Oliver, opened in 2006. The winery, named for the old pine on a nearby ridge, is designed by Penticton architect Robert Mackenzie. The substantial overhang of the roof gives the winery the appearance of a railway station. There is a purpose to the large eaves. Robert incorporates green design elements in his buildings, including small windows, thick walls, and large overhangs to shield the interiors from the summer heat.

While LVP launched primarily with Pinot Noir and Merlot, the four-hectare (10-acre) vineyard adjacent to the winery is planted to Syrah and Viognier. Here winemaker James Cambridge will shift the portfolio to Rhône varieties as the vineyard matures. A graduate of the Niagara College winemaking program, James began his career at the Creekside winery in Ontario and worked at the Henry of Pelham winery before moving to the Okanagan. Here he spent a few years at Summerhill Pyramid Winery before taking over at LVP. He took over from Daniel Bontorin, the first LVP winemaker, who moved to the second winery, LaStella, on the northwestern shore of Osoyoos Lake.

Given grapes that are virtually dry-farmed, Daniel crafts swaggering wines like LaStella's $85 Maestoso 2006, a Merlot with 15.3 percent alcohol and a port-like richness. Born in Surrey in 1976, Daniel kicked around at several jobs in the Okanagan, including importing motorcycle parts, until 2000, when he recognized that the real future was in wine. After courses at Okanagan University College, he worked in the cellars at several wineries, including Fairview Cellars, Domaine Combret (now Antelope Ridge), Hillside, and Hester Creek. Then he did a vintage in northern Italy, returning just in time to join LVP for the 2005 vintage.

"My wife and I are both Italian," says Daniel, who holds dual citizenship, and the couple both have relatives in Italy. "We decided to go for a trip," he explains, "and we figured to make it worthwhile, I will do a vintage over there." In addition to getting useful experience, he returned with special Italian yeast strains that he has used to make some of his iconic wines.

LaStella's name was inspired by the diamond-bright stars in the Osoyoos sky. The winery, built in the style of an Italian winery, is sited at the foot of its vineyard. The tasting room deck looks out toward the lake, where LaStella has private beach frontage. The 10-hectare (25-acre) vineyard folds across several slopes, including a cooler northeastern exposure where Sauvignon Blanc has been planted. Some of the vineyard's Pinot Gris has been grafted to Sangiovese. The major variety for LaStella's wines is Merlot, a variety that, in the view of the Enotecca owners, is responsible for many of the world's great wines. The vineyard across the road, planted for the new delayed third winery, gives both winemakers interesting options: the varieties growing there include Tannat, Monastrell, and Muscat Blanc.

To reinforce the point that they are not making me-too Okanagan wines, they have relied on proprietary names in preference to varietal names. LaStella has adopted musical terms: Maestoso and Allegretto for two Merlots and Vivace for Pinot Gris wines.

At LVP the rosé is called Vaïla, the name Harold Gaudy gave to his daughter who was born in 2005, the year LVP made its first rosé. The Pinot Noirs are called Belle and Périgée, and the Merlots here have been called Apogée and Époque. The Sauvignon Blanc is Aurore. Anthony Burée, the now departed general manager, dipped into film lore for that name. "If you watch the movie *Casablanca*, when the two main characters first meet in Paris, they are in a café and if you look in the window, spelled backwards is Café Aurore," he says. "That's where we got the name. It felt right."

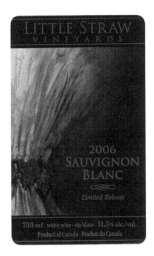

LITTLE STRAW VINEYARDS

OPENED: 1996 (AS SLAMKA CELLARS)

> 2815 Ourtoland Road, Kelowna, BC V1Z 2H7
> 250.769.0404
> www.littlestraw.bc.ca
> When to visit: Open daily 10 am – 5:30 pm April through October

RECOMMENDED

> SAUVIGNON BLANC
> PINOT NOIR
> TAPESTRY
> AUXERROIS ICEWINE

WINEMAKER PETER SLAMKA'S ORIGINAL TRAINING WAS IN INTERIOR DESIGN, a skill he used in construction before opening Slamka Cellars, as this winery was formerly called. In 2005 he drew on that skill again to design an attractive and functional 700-square-metre (7,500-square-foot) winery, triple the size of the cramped original winery. "I designed the building based on having to work here," Peter explains, as he shows off the new building's efficiency. "I don't mind working hard — I just don't like hard work."

The winery nestles on a ridge, with views from its large windows over vineyards and the cluster of neighbouring wineries. This "king of the castle" positioning is ironic, given Peter's down-to-earth personality and his practical approach. "I don't have any razzle-dazzle formula," he says. "Winemaking's been around for thousands of years. I just keep it simple."

The Slamka family — Slamka translates as "Little Straw" — has been growing grapes since 1969 when Joe Slamka, Peter's father, converted an orchard. The elder Slamka had left his native Czechoslovakia in 1948 and, after a decade as a machinist in Edmonton, moved to an orchard near Westbank. Poor returns from tree fruits triggered his subsequent switch to grapes. He was one of the earliest to plant Auxerrois, the fruity white from Alsace that is one of the winery's flagship wines. Peter Slamka underlines the maturity of the vines by producing what he calls an Old Vines Auxerrois. And he uses the same grape to make one of the Okanagan's most complex icewines.

The new farm winery designation that was created in 1989 opened the way for the Slamka family's winery. Peter, born in 1954, began making wine in small volumes for family consumption. In 1993 he took off with his wife on a seven-month world tour that included a visit with winemaking cousins in Austria and another visit with wineries in Australia's Barossa Valley. He made what he calls his first "official" vintage for his winery in 1994, opening to the public two years later.

Little Straw relies almost exclusively on estate-grown grapes from a 5.6-hectare (14-acre) vineyard, with room for more because the entire property is nine hectares (22¼ acres). The varieties grown include Riesling, Viognier, Sauvignon Blanc, Pinot Noir, Merlot, and a little Syrah.

The winery has a rising reputation for Sauvignon Blanc and Pinot Noir. But Auxerrois — the old gnarled vines are just below the winery — has a special place in Peter's affection. The Auxerrois is made in several styles. The Old Vines Auxerrois, rich and full on the palate, takes aim at Chardonnay palates. About a third of the wine in the blend is aged in French oak and spends time on the lees; the remainder of the wine is done in stainless steel, retaining fruitiness. Peter's second version is called Pinot Auxerrois; fruity and off-dry, it is aimed at palates attuned to Germanic wines. Little Straw is among only a handful of wineries in British Columbia that still make Auxerrois. The variety has an undeservedly low profile among consumers and sells best when hand-sold in the tasting room. When Slamka released the winery's first Sauvignon Blanc in 2002, he exulted that, at last, he had a white "that I don't have to explain."

Peter likes dealing with his customers. He tries to give them what he calls "the winery experience" that comes from meeting actual winery owners. A winemaker who does not work the tasting room, he argues, misses the chance to sound out consumer reactions. "To me that's the best part of the business," he says. "I like being out front, selling wine. For me it's a challenge, seeing how many bottles of wine I can sell, and getting people excited. You have about 15 seconds to connect with them. You know, you can be as nice as you want, but even if you are just off a little bit, they notice. I had people come in and I spent 20 minutes with them. They bought nothing, they left. I could hear one of them through the window, saying, 'He was nicer last time.' " He sighs at the memory. "It's valuable experience. You get to know your customers and you see what they like."

The winery's best-selling white is Tapestry, an off-dry blend of Auxerrois, Riesling, Siegerrebe, Schönburger, and Traminer. (The small planting of Traminer, rarely seen in the Okanagan, was developed from 10 plants that Peter's grandmother had in her luggage on returning from a 1970s visit to Austria. While the provenance was unorthodox, Peter assures that the vines came from a nursery certified free of disease.) Tapestry's creative blend yields a lively wine with spicy flavours.

Little Straw's primary red is Pinot Noir. It seems a variety suited to the Slamka vineyard, a site that could be described as cool because of its southeastern exposure. Like so many Pinot Noir producers, Peter regards his award-winning wine as a work-in-progress. "I notice the Pinots are all very delicate and very smooth, where ours has a little more meat and potatoes," he says. When he bought additional acreage in 2000, he planted more Pinot Noir. "We didn't have enough tonnage. Now we're able to thin down to one cluster and get some intense flavours. No sense making four hundred cases of mediocre Pinot Noir. You've got to make two hundred cases of the best you can make."

LOTUSLAND VINEYARDS

OPENED: 2002 (AS A'VERY FINE WINERY)

28450 King Road, Abbotsford, BC V4X 1B1
604.857.4188
www.lotuslandvineyards.com
When to visit: Open 11 am – 6 pm Wednesday through Saturday, noon – 5 pm Sunday
and Monday. Closed Tuesday

RECOMMENDED

ORTEGA
PINOT GRIGIO
CHARDONNAY
ENIGMA (RED BLEND)
CABERNET FRANC

IT SEEMS THAT DAVID AND LIESBETH AVERY KEEP REINVENTING THIS WINERY.
In the most recent chapter, the winery is being shaped into one of the greenest in
British Columbia, with solar panels on the buildings and organic practices in the
vineyard. "And all of our vehicles run on used vegetable oil," David says.

They launched the winery in 2002 as A'Very Fine Winery. The pun turned out
to be a little too clever. A year later they changed to Lotusland Vineyards. "Our old
name was kind of cutesy but it required too much explanation," David explains.
"Plus, it made us look like a 30-year-old winery."

The rebranding was handled by Vancouver marketing guru Bernie Hadley-
Beauregard, who had just scored a home run by rebranding Blasted Church as
the very effective successor to Prpich Hills. Lotusland is a term that has been
used for years to describe the West Coast's temperate climate and easygoing lifestyle. (There is even a botanical garden in California with that name.) The Avery
winery's vineyard is a reclaimed gravel pit just west of Abbotsford. "Why don't

we just take the approach of having a vineyard in the city?" Bernie asked. He created labels meant to celebrate Vancouver. The 2001 Merlot label, for example, has photographs of 21 individuals who have made a difference in the city. The strategy gave Lotusland a visibility that the winery lacked under its original name. "Their old brand was just not working," Bernie said at the time.

Lotusland's owners came to wine through David's amateur winemaking and through Liz (as she calls herself) Avery's gardening. Born in Toronto in 1955, David was managing an office supply company until the winery and vineyard demanded his full-time attention. Liz was born in Paraguay, the daughter of a farmer who moved to Canada in 1973. The roadside property near Abbotsford was just a hay-field when the Averys bought it in 1996. They concluded that vines would thrive on the field's sandy soil, with its contoured south-facing slope.

Before ordering vines from an Ontario nursery in 1997, they sought advice from experienced growers in the Okanagan and nearby in the Fraser Valley. Claude Violet, the owner of Domaine de Chaberton, had been growing grapes near Langley since 1982. Most of Violet's vines are white varieties suited to the comparatively cool climate of the valley and to what consumers were drinking in the 1980s. But the trend had changed. "Plant red," Violet advised. Almost half the vineyard was planted to early-ripening clones of Pinot Noir, supplemented with several rows each of Pinot Meunier, Merlot, Cabernet Franc, Gamay, and Zweigelt.

David and Liz managed their vineyard organically, although they did not seek organic certification until recently. "I've always been a gardener and I've always done it without poisons and herbicides and insecticides," Liz Avery says. "If I can do it on a small scale, we figured we could do it on a larger scale." They are more at ease with the environment in their chemical-free vineyard. "We've walked around vineyards that use heavy herbicides and pesticides and walked around in our own," David says. "Our own is full of butterflies and bees and ladybugs. We've got a really nice balance in the vineyard." They have promoted their ideas by hosting individuals who want to experience organic farming through an organization called World Wide Opportunities on Organic Farms.

David made the first commercial vintage in 2000, producing 2,800 litres (620 gallons). He made an enthusiastic jump to 54,000 litres (12,000 gallons) in 2001 (with the help of purchased grapes) but then concluded that small is beautiful. By 2003 he was limiting his production to his own vineyard and to fruit from nearby Fraser Valley growers.

He had by then emerged as a consultant in developing new vineyards, primarily planted with the hybrids developed by Swiss plant breeder Valentin Blattner. Some of these varieties ripen earlier in coastal climates and require less vineyard management than traditional vinifera. "I reduce my tractor time by 60 percent and I use less fuel," David says. "And that fuel is biodiesel." In 2007 he replanted most of the 2.4-hectare (six-acre) Lotusland vineyard with Blattner vines. It is among the 49 vineyards (and counting) where he has helped introduce Blattner varieties.

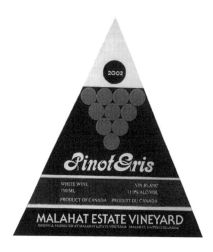

MALAHAT ESTATE WINERY

OPENED: 2005

> 1197 Aspen Road, Malahat, BC V0R 2L0
> 250.474.5129
> When to visit: Open daily 10:30 am – 5 pm

RECOMMENDED

CURRENT RANGE NOT TASTED

UNTIL RECENTLY LORNE TOMALTY, WHO WAS BORN IN 1923, SPENT THE summers clambering up the 30-degree slope of his vineyard with a spray pack on his back. It took perhaps two and a half days to cover the terraced two hectares (five acres), with the top of the vineyard 26 metres (85 feet) higher than the bottom. He was motivated both by his interest in growing grapes and by the perennial shortage of vineyard help on southern Vancouver Island. In 2008 his son David, a construction worker, took charge of the picturesque vineyard, giving Lorne more time for the wine shop. A voluble man, he enjoys interacting with the drop-in customers.

Including this four-hundred-case winery, Lorne has packed more into his life than most. Born in Ottawa, he spent World War II as an armoured corps officer. Upon being discharged, he enrolled in economics and political science at the University of British Columbia. When he tried to enter the job market in 1949, his education attracted two offers: one as an airline ticket agent and the other as an insurance salesman. So he worked as a miner in the Yukon until he could afford to return to university for a master's degree in public administration.

Upon graduation in 1952, he joined the British Columbia government as a personnel assistant. By the time he retired in 1985, he had become what he calls the government's "czar of manpower." He and his wife, Peggy, a nurse, bought a

4.6-hectare (11½-acre) property near the scenic summit of the Malahat, north of Victoria. After clearing some trees, he decided to plant grapes. With an elevation of 192 metres (630 feet), this likely is Vancouver Island's highest vineyard.

Lorne's interest in wine arose from years of making wine at home with friends of Italian heritage. When he began planting vines in 1995, he sought advice (and cuttings) from the vineyard manager at the Newton Ridge vineyard on the Saanich Peninsula. As a result, the Malahat vineyard mirrors the sound choices made at Newton Ridge, which also is on a mountainside but not as high. Lorne grows Ortega, Pinot Gris, and Pinot Noir.

His initial winery application was filed in 1997. Ironically, the civil service he had once worked with managed to lose the paperwork. Later he concluded this was good fortune because his preparations then were still premature. "I'm an Irishman," he chuckles. His forebears came from Ireland five generations ago. "The luck must still be there."

Six years later, when the second application was filed, Lorne was much more prepared. He had begun to make wine, with Glenterra's John Kelly as his mentor, and he converted a large double garage on the property to accommodate the winery and tasting room.

Malahat vineyard's whites are crisp, reflecting the cool site that gets the morning sun but not the evening sun. The grapes certainly ripen adequately, especially in a warm year like 2003, when the Ortega in particular delivered good sugars and moderate acidity. As well, the Pinot Noir has surprised Lorne with good colour to match the fruitiness. With more vines coming into production, he was able to make three barrels of Pinot Noir in 2003. However, since Pinot Noir is relatively light-bodied, Lorne in 2006 addressed the demand for a big red wine by buying Merlot grapes from a South Okanagan grower. He was so impressed with the quality that he ordered more Merlot in 2008.

Perhaps the main challenge of the Malahat vineyard arises from its location on a mountain abundant with birds and deer. The solution to the bird problem is to net the vines, even if that is not easy to do in a terraced vineyard. The deer are kept at bay with a solid fence and guard dogs.

The tasting room is just a short distance from the well-travelled Malahat section of the Trans-Canada Highway and the luxurious Aerie Resort. The drop-in traffic has made Lorne something of a barometer of how tourism is faring on Vancouver Island. At one time the majority of his visitors were Americans. "I see a drastic reduction in the number of American tourists," he noted in the summer of 2008. Fortunately, he can still rely on the loyalty that Vancouver Island residents have toward what is grown on the island. "Vancouver Island is a unique place," he says. "A large percentage of the people buy local products."

MARICHEL VINEYARD

OPENED: 2007

1016 Littlejohn Road, Naramata, BC V0H 1N0
250.496.5884
www.marichel.ca
When to visit: By appointment

RECOMMENDED

SYRAH
VIOGNIER

AT MARICHEL, FORMER AIRLINE PILOT RICHARD ROSKELL AND HIS WIFE, Elisabeth, have given themselves the goal of making the "quintessential" BC Syrah. Fans of the wine may be frustrated that there will never be much of it, and even less of Marichel's other wine, a Viognier. "I'll be surprised if we ever make it to one thousand cases a year," Richard says. "We have our heels dug in. We are not going to get big. We are going to stay personally focused on the vineyard and in the winery, and we will stay faithful to the terroir it comes from, and that will be the Naramata Bench."

They grow grapes on one of the most picturesque properties on the bench. The sculptured vineyard dips sharply down a slope, pauses for a rise, resumes on the top of the rise, then disappears toward the beach. An excellent photographer, Richard has captured calendar-quality images of the vineyard that he shares through the winery's website. Half of this 7.3-hectare (18-acre) property remains in its natural state. Since 2000 Richard and Ellie (as he refers to her) have planted three hectares (7½ acres) of Syrah and Viognier.

It took them three years to find this property and diligent sleuthing to buy it. Richard, born in North Vancouver in 1952, spent 30 years with Air Canada, retiring in 2005 when the jet lag associated with long-haul flying became intolerable. The Okanagan had attracted him some years earlier, first to a home in Kaleden and then to Naramata in 1997, when he and Ellie married. The former owner of a dental laboratory, she was born in Germany in 1954. Her fluency in German proved crucial to the purchase of this farm.

The property was not on the market when they spotted it, noted the great view, and set out to buy it. "We were attracted by the rugged beauty," Richard says. The owners were two Germans who bought it in 1980 but did not develop it after their business relationship fell apart. A search of public records elicited the names of the owners, both now living in Germany. Through the Internet, Richard assembled a lengthy list of similar names and German telephone numbers. Ellie called one number after the other until she found one of the owners and then, in six months of delicate negotiation, convinced the partners to sell in October 1999. "That Ellie was a German speaker was invaluable," Richard says.

During his travels as a pilot, Richard had been able to educate his wine palate. "Ellie and I both have a strong affinity for Rhône wines," he says, explaining why they decided to plant two Rhône varieties. "It was the farming side of the vineyard that really captivated us," he says. Initially they intended to sell their grapes, but in 2005 Richard took online winemaking courses from the University of California and retained half of his crop for wine trials. The six barrels of Syrah he made were the first release when Marichel (the name is a contraction of family names) opened in 2007. He also made a small quantity of Viognier in 2006 but, perhaps because the alcohol was over 17 percent, did not sell it. He succeeded with the 2007 vintage of Viognier, making an intensely fruity wine with more moderate alcohol. "Ellie has suggested that we would be better off to get a consultant," he says and smiles. "I definitely understand the wisdom of that but I am stubborn. I always had the goal and the vision that we would do everything."

In the 2006 vintage, when he kept all his grapes, Richard "pulled out all the stops" in the vineyard to make an attention-getting wine. "I kind of went overboard, with the thought in mind that I wanted to make something really special," he says. "I really wanted to let people know we are here and to catch their attention." He produced 11 barrels of a big, bold Syrah.

The objective is that Marichel will produce bold wines primarily from estate-grown grapes and always with fruit grown on the Naramata Bench. "Our focus is intentionally very limited," Richard says. "We hope to make the very best wine that we can and that is a basic expression of the land that it was grown on."

NOVINÉ RED
PRODUCT OF CANADA - RED WINE
PRODUIT DU CANADA - VIN ROUGE
12.5% alc./vol.   2003   750 ml

MARLEY FARM WINERY

OPENED: 2003

> 1831D Mount Newton Cross Road, Saanichton, BC V8M 1L1
> 250.652.8667
> www.marleyfarm.ca
> When to visit: Open daily 11 am – 6 pm May through September, 11 am – 3 pm
>   Wednesday through Friday and 11 am – 5 pm weekends October through April

RECOMMENDED

> KIWI SOLERA
> NOVINÉ WHITE
> NOVINÉ RED
> ELDERFLOWER
> RASTABERRY

THE REAL ESTATE AGENT'S SIGN AT MARLEY FARM'S FRONT GATE IN 2008 signalled a potential change in the character of a winery that echoed Jamaica during its first five years. In some quarters, there was relief when the sign was removed and, due to global financial conditions, the farm was taken off the market, at least for the time being. Visitors will continue to get a traditional Jamaican greeting, the occasional Jamaican mango chutney, and whimsically named products like the Rastaberry dessert wine.

The 19-hectare (47-acre) farm was purchased in 1995 by Michael and Beverly Marley, both Jamaica natives who had come to Canada in 1975. Theirs is a surname made famous by Bob Marley, the giant of reggae music and a second cousin of Michael. However, Michael succeeded as a land developer and the owner of a couple of Vancouver Island pubs. When the winery opened, he was outraged to discover that he could not serve Marley wines in the pubs. An old rule in British Columbia, the tied house rule created when breweries sought to own hotels, prohibits wineries from selling in any licensed establishment they own. The only exception is the winery's own restaurant. Several winery owners in addition to Michael have pressed for a change of that archaic rule, without success.

When Michael and Beverly parted in 2005, she and daughter Danielle took over the winery that had been launched, in part, as a venue for her interest in making fruit wines. Over the years the winery also has developed a portfolio of grape wines from its own 2.4 hectares (six acres) of vines and from purchased grapes, partnering the creative array of wines from berries and fruits. Few tasting rooms cover as many bases for the wine consumer as Marley Farm. And the wine shop commands a bucolic view of the farm's roadside vineyard where, in the right season, Muscovy ducks are on insect patrol between the vine rows.

The winery's signature grape wines are the red and white blends released under the Noviné label, a self-deprecating jest born from Beverly's inexperience in the winery's early days, when she inventoried the vines on a neglected vineyard not far from the farm. The vineyard, a tangled mess of wild blackberries and broken posts, had been someone's experimental block, with several rows each of about 18 varieties. "I went up there in the rain one day to see what kinds of grapes they had," Beverly recounted later. "At the end of each row, there is a little metal tag that tells you the variety. So I wrote everything down. At home I got out all the books, because I had never heard of some of these varieties. By the end of the afternoon, I was frustrated. Not for anything could I find Novine. It wasn't in any book. And then it dawned on me: 'It isn't Novine — it's No Vines!' "

The winery was launched with the help of Okanagan winemaker Eric von Krosigk, who became a long-running consultant to Marley Farm when a decision was made to plant vines in 2000. The Marleys were among several property owners on the Saanich Peninsula who were persuaded to plant vines by Fraser Smith, the founder of the Vancouver Island Grape Growers' Association (now the Wine Islands Growers Association). Smith was also behind the establishment of Victoria Estate Winery, which intended to buy grapes from the peninsula but ultimately failed as a winery. So several growers, including the Marleys, opened their own wineries. The farm was planted primarily with Pinot Gris, Pinot Noir, and Ortega, but since it takes three or four years for new vines to produce, Marley Farm debuted with berry wines.

"It's very new territory for me," Eric von Krosigk admitted at the time. By the time the winery opened in 2003, he had crafted wines with an array of fruits and berries, including blackberries, loganberries, raspberries, blueberries, apples, pears, rhubarb, and kiwi. Physically, kiwi wine is difficult to make because the fuzzy hide is unwanted in the fermentation vat. So the acidic fruit must all be peeled by hand. The first serious batch of kiwi wine was made using two tonnes (2¼ tons) of fruit; Beverly and friends who volunteered to help took nearly a week to deal with the kiwis. In subsequent years the kiwi squeeze, as it is called, was turned into a festive weekend party in January, with so many volunteers that they had to reserve a spot.

"One of the fruits that has the most potential for wine is the kiwi," argues Jeff Mesinchuk, who took over as the winery's general manager in 2008. To his palate the dry kiwi wine has flavours recalling tangy Sauvignon Blanc. Marley Farm exploits the versatility of this fruit with its delicious sherry-style Kiwi Solera. The wine, fermented to 17 percent alcohol and aged two years in oak, is rich with nut and caramel flavours.

Eric, who remains the consulting winemaker, is famously obsessed with making sparkling wines. One result is Marley Farm's sparkling elderflower. "A friend of mine in Austria made a sparkling elderflower and I just loved it," Eric says. The white elderberry flowers, after being separated laboriously from the stalks by more of the winery's friends, are immersed in sugar water and fermented. It is a light, refreshing wine with only three percent alcohol and with a dramatically aromatic nose. "It is just a delightful drink," the winemaker says. It is also a Canadian first.

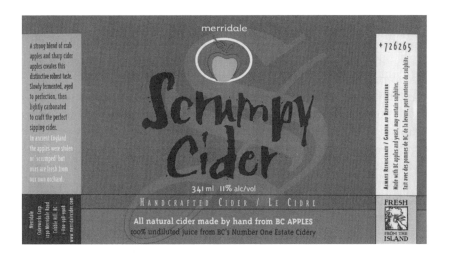

MERRIDALE ESTATE CIDERY

OPENED: 1992

1230 Merridale Road, RR1, Cobble Hill, BC V0R 1L0
250.743.4293 | 1.800.998.9908 (toll free)
www.merridalecider.com
When to visit: Open daily 10 am – 5:30 pm
Restaurant: La Pommeraie Bistro. Reservations recommended

RECOMMENDED

SCRUMPY
SOMERSET CIDER
TRADITIONAL CIDER
CIDRE NORMANDIE
CYSER
WINTER APPLE

MOST OF US DO NOT KNOW THE TASTE OF AUTHENTIC ENGLISH APPLE CIDER.
Until 2000 that would also have included Janet Docherty and Rick Pipes, who took
over Merridale that year and now are evangelists of cider. "We basically have
had to educate our cider drinkers one at a time," Rick says. They have done that
by improving Merridale's formerly rustic ciders and by turning the farm into a
destination jammed with visitors. Yet if they had not purchased Merridale when
they did, the cidery would surely have closed and the 5.2-hectare (13-acre) orchard
of rare cider apple trees would have fallen into neglect.

Merridale was incorporated in 1987 by Albert Piggott, a retired Scottish
teacher. He decided to pursue a lifelong cider passion when he moved to southern
Vancouver Island in 1954 and found that the climate and the soils compared well to
England's best cider regions. He opened the cidery in 1992. Struggling to develop
the cider market, he soon began advertising for investors or buyers for the business.

Rick and Janet arrived with a purchase offer in the nick of time. "We were Al's last ditch," Rick says. "He was already prepared to shut it down when we came along and started negotiating with him."

Rick is a Victoria commercial lawyer and Janet is a commercial realtor. Both have commerce degrees and natural entrepreneurship; they wanted to run a business together, in particular, a business that included a rural lifestyle. New wineries in the bucolic Cowichan Valley had started to draw tourists. That made Merridale appealing — if they could just increase the farm gate sales of cider from an anemic 10 percent of volume to a profitable 50 or 60 percent. "From the outset our goal has been to make it a destination," Rick says. In the decade since acquiring Merridale, they have tripled the cider house, opened a year-round restaurant, and created events for every season, from orchard tours to cidermaster dinners. In 2007 they added a $65,000 German still, a space-age unit gleaming with copper and polished stainless steel, making Calvados-style apple brandy.

There is a medieval ring to the names of the cider apple varieties grown here. On tours of the orchard, Rick cautions against biting into some varieties. "Nobody swallows a bite of Tremlett's Bitter," he says and chuckles. "The English call it a spitter." It is one of about 18 varieties here, with unfamiliar names such as Michelin, Yarlington Mill, Dabinett, Chisel Jersey, Kermerien, Julienne, Judaine, Frequin Rouge, and Hauxapfel. Some taste bitter, some are sweet, some are acidic. Blended together, they produce ciders comparable to the classic ciders of Britain and France. These varieties give the ciders complex flavours seldom found in ciders made with common dessert apples. "A cider made from an eating apple is like a wine made from Thompson Seedless grapes," Janet maintains.

The authentic personality of Piggott's ciders was expressed particularly by a tannic cider called Scrumpy, a traditional farmhouse cider drawing its name from English slang: to *scrump* an apple was to steal it. An educated palate is required to appreciate traditional ciders, particularly so with Scrumpy, which the new owners of Merridale considered dropping. "Neither of us could drink it," Rick recalls. "But some people said they really liked the Scrumpy and were very loyal to the product. They would phone us up here and say, 'Ma's Beer and Wine Store is out of Scrumpy.' These were people who would go in every day and pick up their bottle of Scrumpy." Rather than dropping it, Rick adjusted the blend to make the robust beverage less rough and more appealing. "They complained a little bit when I reformulated it but they are drinking it," he reports. "We gained more sales than we lost." And Merridale's improved Scrumpy won both gold and silver medals at a major American competition in 2002.

Rick knew little about cider making when the couple bought Merridale. He had to learn in a hurry when Piggott, after selling the business, took a long overseas vacation and Piggott's cider maker died in a traffic accident. Rick used his university-level science — he had once planned to become a doctor — to help him grasp the art of cider fermentation. "The first batch I made here was really bad," he remembers. "I don't know why anybody bought it." He used the Internet to research cider techniques and get advice from English cider consultants. Very quickly Merridale ciders, which had been variable in Piggott's day, achieved consistent quality.

The quickest way to taste Merridale's cider styles is by ordering a tray of samples in the bistro. Tasters start, of course, with Scrumpy, which is strong, full-bodied, and dry. Somerset is the Champagne-style sparkling cider. Traditional and House Cider are accessible, mainstream styles, similar except that House is a lighter pub-style draft cider. Cidre Normandie is a dry, oak-aged cider with 12 percent alcohol, made to take the place of wine at dinner. Sweeter palates might prefer Cyser, made with honey, or Merriberri, where blackcurrant, raspberry, and cherry juices are mixed with the cider. Finally, Winter Apple is rich and buttery.

The still has created many new possibilities for Rick. Since late 2008 Merridale has released a growing line of fortified wines and what they call Oh de Vies (a play on *eau de vie* or water of life, as spirits sometimes are called). These include an oak-aged Calvados-style brandy called Pomme de Vie.

Meyer Family Vineyards
Micro Cuvée
Chardonnay
2006

13.4% alc./vol.   Single Vineyard - Naramata   750 mL

MEYER FAMILY VINEYARDS

OPENED: 2008

965 Old Main Road, Naramata, BC V0H 1T0
250.496.5300
www.mfvwines.com
When to visit: No tasting room

OKANAGAN FALLS WINE SHOP
4287 McLean Creek Road, Okanagan Falls, BC V0H 1R0
250.497.8553
When to visit: To be established

RECOMMENDED

MICRO CUVÉE CHARDONNAY
TRIBUTE SERIES CHARDONNAY
PINOT NOIR

THE WINE GODS CERTAINLY LOOKED AFTER JOHN "JAK" MEYER AND WIFE, Janice Stevens, in 2008 after they launched Meyer Family Vineyards in February with just a few hundred cases of premium Chardonnay. By year-end, JAK had chanced upon, and hired, a seasoned winemaker, and had snapped up a bankrupt Okanagan Falls vineyard and winery. And he had enlisted most of his large family in what surely will be a boutique producer to reckon with.

JAK had come a long way from when, as a young stockbroker, he asked colleagues how to become a wine expert. "Right-hand column ordering," he was told. In other words, run your finger down a wine list's right-hand column until you find the most expensive wine and order that. JAK, who tells the story on himself, quickly developed a taste for the best California Cabernets. In time he moved on to other varietals, including the big Shiraz wines from Australia. White wines did not figure prominently on his table until he became a Chardonnay producer.

JAK was born in Calgary in 1958 and grew up there and in Edmonton. A volleyball scholarship took him to Grant McEwen Community College, where he was so intent on the sport that he stretched two years of business studies to four. Upon graduating he became a broker and then, after moving to Vancouver, branched into developing and investing in real estate projects there and in the Okanagan. In recent years his development business has been conducted from a base in the Okanagan.

A mutual friend introduced him to Vancouver wine educator James Cluer, a youthful Briton who earned his Master of Wine designation while concurrently teaching MW-level courses through his own company, Fine Vintage Wine Ltd. They discovered a shared passion and, in what JAK recalls as a "handshake over a beer," James agreed in 2004 to guide JAK on starting a winery. Determined to use grapes he controlled, JAK looked for a vineyard for two years until he found one just off Naramata Road, with 1.4 hectares (3½ acres) planted entirely to mature Chardonnay. (The previous owner had been selling the grapes to the Kettle Valley winery.) Because he did not yet have his own winery, JAK arranged to have the Meyer Chardonnays made at Road 13 Vineyards in 2006 and 2007. It proved a very good choice. Michael Bartier, Road 13's winemaker, is especially adept at making this variety. It was no accident that European wine critic Steven Spurrier pronounced the two initial Meyer wines as "the best dry white wines I have ever tasted from Canada."

Such critical acclaim seemed to put the wind in JAK's sails. By the fall of 2008 he had Penticton architect Robert Mackenzie working on drawings for a showpiece winery on Naramata Road. Meanwhile Christopher Carson, a New Zealand–trained Canadian winemaker with expertise in Pinot Noir, returned to Canada with his wife, also a winemaker, to raise their child here. JAK hired him on the strength of his impressive resumé. "I was pretty lucky," says JAK.

Born in Edmonton in 1971, Chris's interest in wine began when he was backpacking in New Zealand in 1996 and found a casual job with Gibbston Valley Wines in Central Otago. When his visa expired he returned to Canada to become an assistant viticulturist with Lake Breeze Vineyards in May 1997. He returned to New Zealand in September 1998 for formal winemaking studies at Lincoln University. He took time off to do the 2001 vintage with Calera Wine Company, a California specialist in Chardonnay and Pinot Noir. Back in New Zealand he advanced his career at a succession of vineyards and wineries there. He has done a couple of crushes in Burgundy and, in 2003, with Quails' Gate in the Okanagan. Since Chris is a friend of Garron Elmes, the winemaker at Lake Breeze, he made Meyer's 2008 vintage at that winery.

JAK planned to build his own Naramata Road winery by the 2009 crush, but he put that on hold when he was able to buy the Stone Mountain Vineyard in a court-ordered bankruptcy auction. This is one of a proposed trio of wineries that a former

Kelowna native, Gordon Pekrul, intended to fund with revenues from his real estate development business in Arizona. Two of the wineries never materialized. Stone Mountain, with 5.6 hectares (14 acres) of established vines, began making wine in the 2005 vintage. Inexplicably, it never opened a tasting room on its property, which is just a few kilometres east of Okanagan Falls. When the Arizona real estate market collapsed, Stone Mountain also failed. JAK paid about $2 million for all the assets except for the wine (which was sold to other wineries).

The attraction for JAK was the vineyard. "At the end of the day, you have to own the grapes," he believes. Stone Mountain, renamed McLean Creek Road Vineyard, gives him additional Chardonnay along with Pinot Noir, Gewürztraminer, Merlot, Cabernet Franc, and other varieties (Gamay, Siegerrebe, Perle of Csaba) that JAK will sell. He wants to keep Meyer focused primarily on Chardonnay and Pinot Noir. He calculates that, with this vineyard and the Old Main Road Vineyard at Naramata, Meyer will quickly achieve its initial target of three thousand cases per year, with some opportunity to grow to a maximum of five thousand cases.

The word "family" is not a cosmetic addition in this winery's name. JAK is the youngest in a family of five. So far he has involved two sisters, Terry and Laura, in the winery full-time. Other family members are called on when the opportunity arises. When 17 of his relatives arrived for Thanksgiving in 2008, JAK enlisted them to pack bottled wines into wooden presentation boxes.

MIDDLE MOUNTAIN MEAD

OPENED: 2004

3505 Euston Road, Hornby Island, BC V0R 1Z0
250.335.1397
www.middlemountainmead.com
When to visit: Call for hours
Accommodation: Ambrosia House and Cottage rentals

RECOMMENDED

MEAD OF INSPIRATION
CRANBERRY MEAD
BLACK MEAD
ROSE MEAD

HELEN GROND HAS A MASTER'S IN GEOLOGY AND A DEEP KNOWLEDGE OF THE platinum group metals, but since opening British Columbia's second meadery, she has become equally fluent in old Norse mythology. Mead is central to some of those myths because, as the primary fermented beverage, it was integral to Norse life and ceremony. One legend attributes poetic inspiration to a rather gruesomely produced batch of mead. It involves a murdered god whose blood was mixed with mead to create the mead of inspiration, drops of which subsequently were scattered, inspiring poetry and insight from those on whom the drops fell.

A drop or two seems to have fallen on Helen. In 2008 her Middle Mountain Mead added a new product called the Mead of Inspiration. "I have always been more driven by the historical significance of mead than by anything else," she says. "Mead of Inspiration may be the most famous historical mead. All human creativity derived from this substance. There is no reality to it, but it was a legend that was passed on for eons." She learned of it while researching the Norse and Saxon origins of mead. "Finally I got around to crafting a recipe. Obviously I am not using the blood of famous poets. We did find it was a good opportunity to use a lot of very interesting things that grow here. What we ended up with is something that is wildly unique and exotic. It does not taste like any other wine that I have ever come across."

That explanation speaks to the arcane art of meads, which range from pure honey wines to complex blends. Helen spent four years making a sweet rose mead, adding more rose petals each year to the blend to build layers of aroma and flavour. That is a simple product compared to the Mead of Inspiration, which incorporates 10 berries in the blend along with numerous herbs and botanicals. These two are among 10 or 11 meads in this producer's portfolio.

Mead making evolved from Helen's passion for gardening. In 1992 she and Campbell Graham, her former husband (also a geologist), moved from Vancouver to Hornby Island, looking for a quiet community in which to raise their children. They purchased a five-hectare (12-acre) property near the south end of the island. On its well-drained, gravelly hillside, Helen began cultivating a number of berries, fruits, and, especially, herbs and lavender. While researching uses for herbs, she came across *metheglin*. An old Welsh word for medicine, it refers to herb-infused mead. That suggested to her that mead making would be a natural complement to the farm's herb production.

Mead begins by fermenting honey. As with Middle Mountain's Olde Meade, this unadorned base wine develops character by aging in barrel and then in bottle. "The aging process with mead is just astounding," Helen says. "We can make mead that comes out of the tank in eight months to a year and be delicious. But a year later it has transformed into something else." Olde Meade is only released after aging long enough to develop rich caramel flavours.

Flavoured meads — most of Middle Mountain's meads are flavoured with berries or herbs or even green tea — often go by exotic names with Celtic roots: *cyser, melomel, pyment,* and *metheglin.* Said to be the world's oldest fermented beverage, mead was important in the rituals of the Celts and the Norse. For example, wedding celebrations could go on for a month, during which the newlyweds ensured fertility with regular draughts of mead. Mead makers maintain that this is the origin of the word "honeymoon."

"The farm is totally dedicated to the meadery," Helen says. That includes 10 beehives, as many as can be supported on Hornby, a tiny island without berry farms or orchards. Helen buys much of the honey she needs from a beekeeper at Fort St. John in northern British Columbia. There, the source of the honey is clover and wild blueberries. "Our goal is to try to keep our honey as pure as possible," she says. The meads are produced essentially to organic standards although they are not certified organic since it is impossible to assure that bees visit only organically grown plants.

A compact cabin on the farm was turned into the meadery, with production on the ground floor, a tasting room on the second floor, and a rooftop deck with a panoramic view of herb fields and, beyond these, the Strait of Georgia and the mountains on the BC mainland.

Middle Mountain makes about 5,000 to 6,000 litres (1,100 to 1,300 gallons) per year and has the capacity, although perhaps not the ambition, to double that output. "We have never really looked for customers," Helen says. "We are still just trying to meet the demand from customers who come to us."

RESERVE
SHIRAZ
VQA Okanagan Valley VQA
2002

MISSION HILL FAMILY ESTATE

OPENED: 1966 (AS MISSION HILL WINERY)

1730 Mission Hill Road, Westbank, BC V4T 2E4
250.768.7611
www.missionhillwinery.com
When to visit: Open daily 10 am – 6 pm (5 pm in winter). Tour program includes
deluxe tours and private tastings. Charges apply. Consult website for details
Restaurant: Terrace (250.768.6467) open daily for lunch May to October, weather
permitting

RECOMMENDED

OCULUS
QUATRAIN
PERPETUA
SELECT LOT COLLECTION WINES
RESERVE WINES
FIVE VINEYARDS PINOT GRIGIO

TIMELESS ARCHITECTURE AND A MOUNTAINTOP SETTING COME TOGETHER
to make Mission Hill stunningly attractive. It is Canada's most beautiful winery,
reminiscent of a golden hilltop monastery in Tuscany. This is astonishing, considering
that Mission Hill had dirt floors when Anthony von Mandl bought it in 1981 and set
about to turn it into one of the world's 10 best wineries. Perhaps he is not there yet,
but he has made enormous progress and he is still only in his 50s.

The original Mission Hill Winery was also the talk of the Okanagan when a
syndicate of local businessmen opened it in 1966, modelled on the architecture
of California's Spanish missions. They reasoned that an attractive winery with a
stunning view would draw many wine tourists. They were correct: Mission Hill
today attracts about 150,000 visitors per year. It could not do that in 1966, when

winery tasting rooms were still banned in British Columbia. Soon the winery was virtually bankrupt.

It was purchased by Ben Ginter, a rough-hewn Prince George brewer who had made a fortune in heavy construction and squandered it on making wines like Hot Goose and Fuddle Duck. Ginter changed the winery's name to Uncle Ben's Gourmet Wines and later, after another brush with failure, to Golden Valley, before selling it in 1981 to Anthony, who reverted to the fine original name. Later he modified that to Mission Hill Family Estate, signalling that he intends to leave a legacy. "I firmly believe it is going to take my lifetime and beyond to realize the full potential of this incredible region and this incredible valley," he says today.

Born in 1950 to parents from Czechoslovakia, Anthony got the idea of an Okanagan winery in the 1970s. Working as a young wine merchant, he wrote a report on such a venture for Josef Milz AG, a German winery whose wines Anthony sold in Canada. Milz decided against investing in the Okanagan, but Anthony had grasped the region's possibilities when few others in the wine world took it seriously. Shortly after taking over Mission Hill, he predicted in a speech that the valley one day would have "world-class vinifera vineyards" and wine tourism like California's Napa Valley.

A Mission Hill wine put the Okanagan on the map. In 1992 Anthony hired John Simes, an experienced New Zealand winemaker. Arriving just before vintage, he found one of Mission Hill's growers had exceptional Chardonnay grapes. John ordered new American oak barrels and fermented a wine that won the top trophy at the annual International Wine & Spirits Competition in London in 1994. Mission Hill enthusiastically called it the "world's best Chardonnay" and, on the strength of that award, began buying vineyards of its own. Today, with 400 hectares (1,000 acres), Mission Hill is the largest vineyard owner in the Okanagan.

It grows vines on the Osoyoos Lake Bench, the Black Sage Bench, the Naramata Bench, in East Kelowna, and on the slopes of Mount Boucherie, beside the road leading to the winery. These enviable sites give Mission Hill the ability to make everything from powerful Bordeaux and Rhône-style reds to elegant Burgundies and even icewines. In 2008, echoing the win a decade and a half earlier, Mission Hill's 2006 Riesling Reserve Icewine beat the world as the best icewine in the International Wine Challenge in London, said to be the world's largest wine competition.

It seems that no expense has been spared to turn Mission Hill into a legacy winery. "I wanted to create a winery and a structure that would be enduring, that would be as relevant in two hundred years, three hundred years, as it is today," Anthony once told me. "To me a sense of timelessness was absolutely essential." The reconstruction, completed in 2002, took six years and many millions.

The outcome is a visually spectacular winery that offers the complete visitor experience, including educational wine tastings and culinary lessons. In 2008 a leading American travel magazine called the Terrace restaurant, an open-air dining venue with unexcelled views of vineyards and lakes, one of the world's five best winery restaurants.

"It was clear to me that a landmark showcase winery was absolutely essential to the future of the Okanagan," Anthony told me. "It certainly is now bringing visitors from many countries, and not only to Mission Hill Family Estate. People that have never heard of the Okanagan are reading about Mission Hill and are coming here."

And no expense has been spared, both in viticulture and in the winery, to make sure the wines deliver. Winemaker John Simes continues to call the final shots; recently, however, he has been bringing Michel Rolland, the world's most sought-after wine consultant, into the Mission Hill cellar for technical advice and for help in blending the premium wines.

The result has been wines like Oculus, now one of Canada's icon wines. This red blend based primarily on Merlot, Cabernet Sauvignon, and Cabernet Franc was first made in the 1997 vintage. The wine has become progressively more complex with each passing vintage, as Mission Hill's vines have matured and as Rolland's styling has made an impact.

2007
Gewurztraminer

Product/Produit of
British Columbia, Canada | 14.1% alc./vol.

750 ml | White Wine/Vin Blanc

(M) Mistaken Identity
VINEYARDS

MISTAKEN IDENTITY VINEYARDS

OPENED: 2009

164 Norton Road, Ganges, BC V8K 2P5
250.538.9463
www.mistakenidentityvineyards.com
When to visit: To be established

RECOMMENDED

CURRENT RANGE NOT TASTED

IN JUNE 2007 CLIFF BROETZ, AN INVESTMENT ADVISOR AT NANOOSE BAY ON Vancouver Island, had what he remembers as a "life-changing" lunch with his friend and client, Nanaimo chartered accountant Dave Baker. Both men are in their 50s — Cliff was born in Winnipeg in 1955 — and were speculating on what they might do when they retired from their current professions. They learned that they shared a mutual passion for wine. By the end of that summer they owned a Saltspring Island vineyard.

Cliff comes to wine as a consumer. Before he and his wife, Barbara Steele, moved to Vancouver Island in 1989, both worked for Chevron Canada in Vancouver. She was in charge of installing a new computer system and spent several months working with it in Chevron's San Francisco offices. When Cliff visited on weekends, they toured Napa Valley wineries and were soon seduced by the romance of wine. "That's where it really hatched for me," Cliff recalls.

During that lunch Cliff learned that Dave Baker and Dave's brother, Ian, were even more "consumed" with wine that he was. Inspired by Ian's award-winning home winemaking, the Bakers had been looking for potential vineyard land in the Cowichan Valley. About six weeks after that lunch, Dave came across an Internet listing for a vineyard on Saltspring Island. Only a kilometre (about two-thirds of a mile) from Ganges, the largest community on the island, it already had about three hectares (7½ acres) of grapevines just coming into production. Within half a day, the Bakers and Cliff were on the island with a purchase offer. "Not that we make quick decisions," Cliff says, "but this place just called out to us."

The vineyard had been started six years earlier by Ted Bishop, the operator of a U-brew shop, and his wife, Daria. When they found that the demands of 7,500 vines were a substantial burden on top of a business and a young family, they decided to sell. Before Cliff and the Bakers came along, the property was very nearly bought by an individual who would have uprooted the vines and pastured horses.

The vineyard has the varieties appropriate for the coastal climate. The whites include Madeleine Angevine, Madeleine Sylvaner, Siegerrebe, Ortega, Reichensteiner, and Pinot Gris, with a small plot of Chardonnay. The reds are Zweigelt, Pinot Noir, and Léon Millot. The three partners (along with their spouses) took over the vineyard just in time to pick the 2007 crop. Not having a licence yet to make wine, they crushed about two tonnes (2¼ tons) of grapes, storing the must in a commercial freezer until the following vintage.

That idea emerged from Ian's experience as a member of the Nanaimo Winemakers, a club of keen amateurs that often use frozen grapes so that vintages can be juggled with members' other autumn interests (hunting, travelling). Ian joined the club a dozen years earlier when he got serious about making wine at home.

Born in North Vancouver in 1959, Ian has a degree in business. After finding office work confining, he joined the Department of Fisheries and Oceans in order to work outdoors. He was transferred to Vancouver Island to run a fish hatchery. When that was closed during a government downsizing, he and Wendy, his wife, set up a successful landscape maintenance business at Qualicum Beach. Like so many amateur vintners, he started with wine kits before moving on to Okanagan grapes. At the time he was so green that an unscrupulous grower sold him mouldy Pinot Noir by saying there was frost on the grapes. Then he joined the wine club, where the experienced home vintners tutored him. "That totally changed me," he says. He became one of the best white wine makers in the club, notably for his Gewürztraminer wines, gold medal winners twice in national competitions.

With their partners looking after the details of getting the winery licensed, in 2008 Ian and Wendy moved to Saltspring Island to deal with the vineyard and to build and equip a winery.

After struggling to come up with a winery name, the partners turned to Traction Creative Communications, a Vancouver design company, which came up with Mistaken Identity. "We want to be taken seriously but when they came up with Mistaken Identity, we really felt it spoke to us and that was the right name for us," Cliff says. "They said that the safe name is pretty dangerous but a dangerous name is safe."

MORNING BAY VINEYARD & ESTATE WINERY

OPENED: 2005

6621 Harbour Hill Drive, North Pender Island, BC V0N 2M1
250.629.8351
www.morningbay.ca
When to visit: Open 10 am – 5 pm Wednesday through Sunday in summer, 1 pm –
5 pm Friday through Sunday in winter. Licensed picnic area

RECOMMENDED

RESERVE MERLOT
MERLOT
ESTATE BIANCO
ESTATE CHIARETTO (ROSÉ)
ESTATE GEWÜRZTRAMINER-RIESLING

WINE IS ALL ABOUT PATIENCE. KEITH WATT BOUGHT A FORESTED OCEAN-VIEW
property on Pender Island in 1992 and spent the better part of a decade deciding
what to do with it. Having been a farm journalist, he found that farming was in his
blood. But what, he wondered, could you do on the steep slope of Mount Menzies?
The answer came from across Plumper Sound, on Saturna, the neighbouring island.
From his island home, Keith watched Saturna Island Vineyards being developed in
the mid-1990s. In 2002, after clearing the trees and creating 20 terraces on a slope
that spans 80 hectares (almost 200 acres), he began planting 2.8 hectares (seven
acres) of grapes. The first vintage took place four years later, and in 2007, a full
15 years after buying the Pender Island property, Watt proudly released the very
first Pender Island wines.

The wines are distinctive, reflecting an island terroir that is different from the
Cowichan Valley and much different from the Okanagan. This is real cool-climate
viticulture, producing wines notably aromatic that are refreshing and crisp due to

their vibrant acidity and their moderate alcohol levels. The slope and the southern exposure of Morning Bay's vineyard capture heat during the growing season, but the nearby ocean ensures average temperatures during the long, moderate growing season. This is not a place for growing big reds, which is why Morning Bay contracts Okanagan fruit for its powerful, barrel-aged Merlots and for several whites. Hence the winery's attractively appointed tasting bar amounts to a sensory tour of both the Gulf Islands wine style and that of the much hotter Okanagan.

"I come to agriculture with my eyes open," Keith says. Born in Winnipeg in 1951, he once worked for an impecunious Ontario farmer whose barn had burned. He helped the farmer salvage and straighten used nails for its reconstruction. As a broadcaster for the Canadian Broadcasting Corporation in Edmonton, Keith produced farm shows and won awards for his agricultural documentaries. He was a media instructor at North Vancouver's Capilano College when he bought the island property. Initially part of it was turned into an organic fruit and vegetable farm (still being operated), with the decision to grow vines coming later.

"I really inaugurated this project on my 50th birthday," says Watt. He took a one-year sabbatical from his college job in 2001, volunteering at Saturna Island Vineyards to gain experience. In 2002 he spent a month in New Zealand, touring wineries and vineyards, returning with insights on the wine business and the concept for Morning Bay's simple gravity-flow winery.

Keith unsettled his neighbours along Razor Point Road (which leads to Harbour Hill Drive), who were apprehensive about a destination winery rising near the end of the road on a quiet property once owned by an elderly female sheep herder. He himself noted that this end of North Pender Island had once been a no man's land. It is believed that British naval ships in Plumper Sound used the cliffs for target practice. In modern times the island (like all the Gulf Islands) has been populated by intellectuals, artists, and organic farmers.

Keith's neighbours formed what they called the "Save Razor Point" committee to lobby against the winery, leading to a furious exchange of letters in the local papers and with various regulators in Victoria. "We do not want to operate a 7 day, 12 hour 'drinking establishment,' " Watt tried to reassure the opponents in one letter to *Island Tides*, the local paper. "Our sewage permit, approved by the health department, does not allow for it. We have not planned to operate a bar in our business plan. We do not think it is appropriate in a largely residential neighbourhood."

The anxiety subsided once the winery opened and residents saw it being run responsibly. To be sure, there is more going on at the end of Razor Point Road than formerly, including winery dinners and a daylong music festival each year on the September long weekend. The festival's acceptance may have something to do with the presence of numerous Pender Island entertainers.

The climate on Pender Island limited Keith to planting varieties suitable for cool sites. These include four clones of Pinot Noir, some of which are found in

Chiaretto, the winery's crisply dry rosé. Watt also grows Pinot Gris, Gewürztraminer, Riesling, Schönburger, and Maréchal Foch. The objective is that island grapes will supply at least half Morning Bay's needs, increasingly likely now that other island farmers have begun to plant vines. In 2008 Watt planted Pinot Noir, Ortega, and Siegerrebe on an island farm committed to selling him the grapes. He also was in conversation with other farm owners.

The big reds — Morning Bay has produced several brawny Merlot wines — are made from grapes grown in the South Okanagan. They are made into wine there by Tilman Hainle, Morning Bay's consulting winemaker. "Crushing close to the source of the grapes is critical," Watt maintains.

Morning Bay's winery was built with kiln-dried lumber produced from trees logged to make room for the vineyard. The two-level winery is set amid towering forest with views of the vineyard. The large tasting room door rolls back, allowing visitors to sit outdoors on the deck. It is a design that aims to impress. "When people visit your winery and find that the building is serious, they approach your wines seriously," Watt reasons.

MORNINGSTAR CREEK WINERY

OPENED: 2008

403 Lowry's Road, Parksville, BC V9P 2B5
250.954.3931
www.cheeseworks.ca
When to visit: Open daily from 9 am Monday to Saturday

RECOMMENDED

CURRENT RANGE NOT TESTED

THIS FRUIT WINERY WAS CREATED TO ADD ANOTHER ATTRACTION TO THE BUSY farm that is home of Clarke and Nancy Gourlay's Little Qualicum Cheeseworks. It reflects the farming philosophy set out by the Gourlays in their periodic classes on cheese making. "One of the points we make is that the only way to earn an income from farming in the long haul is to do value-added and retail," Clarke says. "Wine is a tremendous example."

Farming is but the most recent of Clarke and Nancy's colourful careers. Clarke was born in Toronto in 1964 but grew up in various communities across Canada, his father being a much-transferred banker. After graduating in international politics from McGill, Clarke and his bride, Nancy, went to Turkey as missionaries. A year and a half later, the first Gulf War broke out and the Gourlays went off to work in Kurdish refugee camps on the Turkey-Iraq border.

It was the start of what would be nine years working in humanitarian aid, which included a stint in Afghanistan spanning the last months of Taliban rule and their ouster. "In a less than ideal world, you have a choice between safety and freedom," Clarke reflects. "You choose your poison. It became much freer but much less safe when the Taliban left." Because they had children beginning school, they returned to Canada, with Clarke spending another two years with a humanitarian agency based in the Fraser Valley. Most of the work involved fundraising, which he did not find as satisfying as the work in the field.

While abroad, they spent two years in Switzerland in the headquarters of an aid group. There they discovered the glories of cheese. In 1999, now living in the Fraser Valley, they began researching agricultural pursuits and "identified the cheese making opportunity, which is absolutely huge," Clarke recounts. "Neither of us come from agricultural backgrounds." Nancy took a course to learn how to manage dairy cows. Then she went back to Switzerland on a self-study cheese making program. On her return to Canada they leased a small farm near Qualicum, on Vancouver Island, and launched Little Qualicum Cheeseworks in 2001.

Three years later they relocated to nearby Morningstar Farm (named for the creek running along the 27.5-hectare/68-acre property), taking along the one-time school portable that had become an efficient little cheese plant. They built their dairy herd to about 60 and opened the farm to the public, complete with miniature horses and other animals that can be petted. A bustling retail store opened to sell an expanding range of cheeses, including Rathtrevor, a Swiss-inspired hard cheese with an island brand name.

Starting a fruit winery was Clarke's idea. "A no-brainer, wine and cheese," he says. "We'd been selling cheese to several wineries for some years." For wine-making, Clarke turned to Phil Charlebois, who had previously joined the Gourlays as a farmhand but made himself increasingly valuable. Born in Edmonton in 1963, Phil had spent two years in theology school, decided that did not suit him, and moved to a lumber mill, where he eventually became the manager. Tiring of that, he moved to Vancouver Island to help in a start-up business that, unfortunately, did not succeed.

"Clarke needed help on his farm," Phil recalled. "Originally it was just working with the cows and doing farm work. Then I got involved in making cheese as well. When I started, I told Clarke I was just not interested in merely having a job. We have been working on something to keep going." Winemaking is the most recent example. Because Phil's winemaking experience is limited, Morningstar has also tapped the expertise of veteran consulting winemaker Ron Taylor to help him master the skills.

"Our primary wine is blackberry," Clarke says. "We have planted two acres of blackberries and about three-quarters of an acre of raspberries and some rhubarb. But we are not going to limit ourselves to that. The biggest blueberry farm on the island is four or five kilometres from here while our neighbours are growing grapes." The current licence prevents Morningstar Creek from making grape wines alone, but fruit and grape blends are allowed. Success depends on how creative Phil and Clarke can be. "I have no shortage of ideas," Clarke says.

MT. BOUCHERIE ESTATE WINERY

OPENED: 2001

829 Douglas Road, Kelowna, BC V1Z 1N9
250.769.8803
www.mtboucherie.bc.ca
When to visit: Open daily 10 am – 6 pm

RECOMMENDED

FAMILY RESERVE 2004 (CABERNET/SYRAH BLEND)
SUMMIT RESERVE SUMMIT (BORDEAUX BLEND)
SUMMIT RESERVE SYRAH
SUMMIT RESERVE ZWEIGELT
EHRENFELSER
SÉMILLON
PINOT GRIS
GEWÜRZTRAMINER
CHARDONNAY
PINOT NOIR

"WE ARE PROUD OF BEING FARMERS AND GROWERS, FIRST AND FOREMOST," declares Nirmal Gidda, who with brother Kaldep runs 85 hectares (210 acres) of vineyard in the Okanagan and the Similkameen valleys. "Having your own vineyards, you can control the quality of the grapes that come into the winery." That is as desirable as it is obvious: just ask winemakers Robert Thielicke and Dave Frederick. Few have as broad a range of varietals to work with as they do.

The Gidda family has been in grapes since buying a vineyard near Westbank in 1975. They intended to convert to apples but soon realized that, even then, there was more money in grapes. The brothers have farming in the blood. Mehtad Gidda, their father, was a farmer in India until, at the age of 29, he brought his family to British Columbia in 1958. He laboured in sawmills while investing in orchard property. He insisted his sons get educated before becoming farmers. Nirmal earned a science degree and Kaldep, the younger brother, trained as a mechanic. The oldest brother, Sarwan, a graduate in business administration, was a partner in the vineyards and wineries until selling to his brothers in 2008. He retained some vineyards near Westbank for an independent business.

Their father grew apples for six years before buying the family's first vineyard. The family did very well with labrusca and hybrid grapes but, alert to trends in the wine industry, began switching to vinifera wine grapes before the 1988 vintage. That fall many growers accepted government payments to remove surplus vineyards. The Gidda family did not take pullout money but instead expanded their vineyards at a time when many doubted that the BC wine industry would even survive.

Their Westbank vineyards were expanded to 22 hectares (54½ acres). In 1991 they looked at several properties farther south, including acreage on Black Sage Road that had been fallow since the 1988 pullout. Finally they acquired what was called the Sunrise Vineyard near Okanagan Falls. The big attraction was a two-year-old house on the vineyard, because Kaldep's home had just been razed in a fire. But the property also came with 16 hectares (40 acres) planted to desirable wine grapes, including Merlot.

The brothers lined up wineries for this fruit and looked for other properties so that they could grow grapes in differing terroirs. In 1998 they bought a 36-hectare (89-acre) producing vineyard near Cawston in the Similkameen Valley. At the time Sarwan maintained that the Similkameen is one of the best vineyard sites in the world. "I've seen the Napa Valley and I think we can grow just as good as them." Kaldep now manages that vineyard as well as Okanagan Falls. The brothers grow "everything" in the Similkameen, including Riesling, Gewürztraminer, Lemberger, Kerner, Pinot Gris, Chardonnay, Merlot, Bacchus, Syrah, Cabernet Sauvignon, Pinot Noir, Gamay, and Zinfandel.

In 2007, when Sarwan was leaving the partnership and taking Westbank vineyards with him (Gewürztraminer and Gamay), the Giddas acquired a 30-hectare (74-acre) former cattle ranch near Okanagan Falls. Here they have planted 20 hectares (50 acres) of vines, with an equal planting each of seven varieties: Cabernet Sauvignon, Malbec, Petit Verdot, Syrah, Viognier, Pinot Gris, and Gewürztraminer. This astonishing roll call of grapes gives the winemakers a lot of options.

The Mt. Boucherie winery opened in 2001 in a boxy, high-ceilinged facility big enough at 1,850 square metres (20,000 square feet) to accommodate growth for the next decade as the winery's production climbed beyond 25,000 cases a year. The building is large enough that Mt. Boucherie has done custom winemaking for emerging producers. The 2000 vintage, the first made here, was produced before the builders had time to put a roof on the winery; that was completed only in December. "It was a little tough to get the malolactic ferment started," says Nirmal, referring to a process that requires a relatively warm environment.

Mt. Bouchierie's initial vintages were made by consultant Alan Marks. When he moved on in 2003, he was succeeded by Graham Pierce. Born in Vancouver in 1971, Graham came into wine through an early career in food service. He came to the Okanagan to work at the Summerhill winery restaurant. When an interest in wine took precedence, Graham became a Mt. Boucherie cellar hand under Marks and immersed himself in winemaking courses at Okanagan University College. When he moved on to manage Black Hills Estate Winery in 2008, he was succeeded by Robert Thielicke, who had been assistant winemaker for five years and who had previously worked with Kettle Valley Winery. Robert's new assistant, Dave Fredericks, is a banking graduate from the University of Western Ontario. Attracted more by wine than by banking, he worked at several Okanagan wineries before joining Mt. Boucherie in 2008.

Mt. Boucherie attracted notice first for its flagship Pinot Gris, its Gewürztraminer, and its budget-priced Pinot Noir. During each succeeding vintage, the winery has added big reds and complex white blends under a premium tier called Summit Reserve. Recently, a super-premium tier called Family Reserve has been created for wines considered exceptional, such as the 92 cases of 2004 Family Reserve Cabernet Syrah that was released at $50 a bottle in the fall of 2008. "We have not produced another since 2004," Nirmal said in 2008. By the time it is sold out, there will be a small vintage of 2007 Family Reserve Zinfandel. Family Reserve, Nirmal says, "is something we may not do every year."

MT. ST. MICHAEL WINERY

OPENING PROPOSED FOR 2010

> 2350 Mount St. Michael Road, Saanichton, BC   V8M 1T7
> 250.652.4559
> When to visit: To be established

RECOMMENDED

CURRENT RANGE NOT TASTED

KERRY SPANIER WAS BORN IN WINNIPEG IN 1960, THE SON OF AN INSURANCE executive. From an early age, however, Kerry was drawn to farming. "My uncle, Stanley, had a farm and it was one of my favourite places to go," he says. It was only in 2003 that Kerry and his wife, Cindy, found acreage on the Saanich Peninsula, where they realized a shared interest in agriculture by planting 1.2 hectares (three acres) of Gewürztraminer.

Kerry grew up in Coquitlam, to which his parents moved in 1967. When he finished high school, he chose a marine career by qualifying both as a diesel mechanic and as a yacht captain. When his parents retired to Vancouver Island, he decided the island would also suit him. There he met Cindy, and they are raising their two children on their Saanich farm. Kerry established Vector Yacht Services Ltd., a yacht repair business, in Sidney. Now semi-retired from that business, he still keeps his hand in yacht repair.

During the summer he also signs on to captain large private yachts sailing the ocean between Washington State and Alaska. He has the advantage of being a captain who also knows how to fix a diesel marine engine. "If you have a diesel mechanic aboard your large yacht," he observes, "it is a nice thing to have when you are all by yourself up in Alaska." He does not go cruising in the Caribbean in winter, preferring to be home with his family. And while Cindy and Jerry, his father, look after the vineyard in summer, Kerry makes sure he is home at harvest.

The vineyard site is on the cool eastern side of Vancouver Island; the ocean can be glimpsed in the distance. Gewürztraminer is a challenging variety in many of the island vineyards, but Kerry is succeeding with the variety. "We wanted to grow something different than everybody else's Ortega and Siegerrebe, because there is so much of that on Vancouver Island," he explains. Every April he tents the entire vineyard, a greenhouse technique that kick-starts vine growth early in the season. By accelerating vine growth after bud break, Kerry's grapes get adequately ripe by early fall. He usually picks his low-cropped Gewürztraminer with sugars between 21 and 23 Brix. "I am looking for quality, not quantity," he says.

While other small Saanich vineyards sell their grapes, Kerry figured out that he had to make wine as well. "I recognized really quickly that if I just grew grapes, it wasn't profitable," he says. "I had to make the farm more viable, so I decided to take the next step and learn how to make wine."

He describes himself as "a one-step-at-a-time person." The next step, after the Spaniers had committed to a vineyard, was to enrol in the winemaking and viticulture course that the University of California offers as a distance learning program. Although his father has years of experience as a home vintner, Kerry recognized that he needed appropriate training in order to make wine commercially. Working under the eye of consulting winemaker Todd Moore, Kerry began making wines in the 2005 vintage. All of Mt. St. Michael's early vintages have been sold in bulk to other wineries on Vancouver Island. "I am a bit of a perfectionist," Kerry explains. "I want to make good wine before I put our name on it. This is a process of hands-on growing the proper variety for the site and gaining experience in the craft."

His preparation included a major tour of wineries throughout France in 2006. "They are maybe a little more on the artistic side and not so much focused on chemistry and biology," he concluded. "They make lovely wine but I wanted to look at things from a scientific approach. I am trying to blend art and science."

He has built a 372-square-metre (4,000-square-foot) winery and has equipped it with a full laboratory and tanks with cooling jackets so that he can ferment the white wines at the low temperatures that preserve their fruitiness. In addition to his own grapes, Kerry also buys Pinot Blanc from another small Saanich vineyard. He is open to buying other grapes, but within his one-step-at-a-time strategy. "I'd like to move into other varieties as well but I am going to get this right at first," he said just before the 2008 vintage. That is likely to involve replacing the Gewürztraminer with earlier-ripening Siegerrebe, a decision he reached after completing the University of California studies in viticulture.

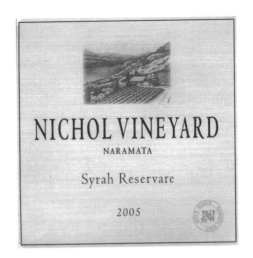

NICHOL VINEYARD & ESTATE WINERY

OPENED: 1993

1285 Smethurst Road, RR1, Site 14, Comp 13, Naramata, BC V0H 1N0
250.496.5962
www.nicholvineyard.com
When to visit: Open 11 am – 5 pm Tuesday through Sunday late June to Canadian
  Thanksgiving and during wine festivals or by appointment

RECOMMENDED

GEWÜRZTRAMINER
PINOT GRIS
SYRAH
CABERNET FRANC
ST. LAURENT
PINOT NOIR

ROSS HACKWORTH BEGAN NEGOTIATING TO BUY NICHOL VINEYARD ON LABOUR
Day in 2004. Then a Vancouver pulp and paper salesman, he laid down the condition
that Alex and Kathleen Nichol take time to tutor him in wine growing before they
retired. When they departed in February 2006, leaving Ross on his own, he was
flattered to hear that they had told a friend that he had "good instincts."

"A lot of the instinctual part of it was growing up in an orchard," Ross believes.
Born in California (not far from wine country), he was 10 years old when his parents bought a Penticton-area orchard in 1973. "It was the best thing they could
have done for me," he says, crediting his disciplined work ethic to being brought
up on the adjoining orchards belonging to his parents, his uncle, and his maternal
grandparents.

As a youth he competed in karate at a high enough level (he was on the Canadian
Olympic team) to spend time in Japan and acquire skills with the language. That led

him into a business program at the British Columbia Institute of Technology, a few years as a metals broker, then work as a partner in an granite importing firm. In 1991 he became a sales executive in the Vancouver office of Oji Paper, a Japanese pulp and paper giant.

"It was a great career," Ross says. "The one thing that was very tiring was the travel. I was travelling two or three weeks a month. It makes it hard to maintain any type of relationship, be it personal or professional, because you are just never there." In 1999, when a high school friend bought the heritage hotel in Naramata, Ross spent weekends helping renovate it. Rediscovering his Naramata roots, he bought a small house in town and had begun looking for his own vineyard when he learned that Nichol Vineyard was for sale.

"It was perfect," Ross says. "I knew Nichol wines. I had been drinking them for years. I wasn't really sure about the vineyard itself, but I thought if that's the quality of product that is coming out of the site, at the very least it is worth a good hard look." He knew what he was getting into. "A couple of years ago, just out of curiosity, I enrolled at the University of Guelph in their distance learning program in oenology and viticulture," Ross says. "I was flying back and forth to the east coast quite a bit [selling paper]. You are on a plane for five to six hours at a time. I was making best use of my time, taking those courses. I realized that this was something I am definitely interested in and I wanted to pursue it."

A decision to change jobs for the lifestyle resonated with the Nichols. Alex had had a long career as a double bass player with the Vancouver Symphony and Kathleen was a corporate librarian. But in 1989 they sold their Vancouver home to buy a Naramata orchard where they replaced the trees with vines. In 1991 they were the first in British Columbia to plant Syrah, now the fourth most widely grown red variety in the Okanagan. John Vielvoye, then the provincial government's grape specialist, recommended Syrah to the Nichols. John had come to this conclusion, Alex remembered, while hosting a group of French nursery owners on an Okanagan tour in 1990. "They had told him that all the Bordeaux and Rhône varieties could be grown in the valley," Alex says. He ordered 1,350 Syrah vines from a Rhône nursery and made the first vintage from the young vines in 1994, a superbly warm season. The wine, inky black and rich on the palate, put Nichol and Syrah on the map in the Okanagan.

Nichol Vineyard had a portfolio of 10 wines when Ross took over. Other than dropping a few blends but adding Gewürztraminer, Ross makes the same wines that Alex made and in the same style. "I knew the wines he had made for years fit my sensibilities, because the wines were always soft, always approachable, always food-friendly," Ross says. "That's what I like in wine."

Famously thrifty, Alex made his wines in an absurdly cramped winery, producing between 700 and 1,200 cases per year. Ross laughs that the winery expansion he completed in 2007 would have struck the Nichols as a "Wal-Mart store." He explains that "I made the footprint as big as possible and got myself a nice working environment." The winery now has the capacity to make 10,000 cases per year, although Ross does not plan to go beyond 3,500 cases.

"I left that [pursuit of unending growth] in the corporate world," he said in 2008. "I have a boat. I have been out on it maybe six times this year, which is four times more than last year. And the two times I went out last year is twice as many as I went out the year before. At the end of the day, I would like to go out and picnic or water-ski, or take a book and do nothing."

NK'MIP CELLARS

OPENED: 2002

>1400 Rancher Creek Road, Osoyoos, BC V0H 1V0
>250.495.2985
>www.nkmipcellars.com
>When to visit: Open daily 9 am – 5 pm
>Restaurant: The Terrace at Nk'Mip open 11 am – 4 pm daily May to September and
>   until 7 pm in July and August. Occasional First Nations salmon barbecues

RECOMMENDED
_____

>MERITAGE QWAM QWMT
>MERLOT QWAM QWMT
>CHARDONNAY QWAM QWMT
>PINOT NOIR QWAM QWMT
>SYRAH QWAM QWMT
>RIESLING ICEWINE QWAM QWMT
>PINOT BLANC
>RIESLING

A HAUNTING RECORDING OF FIRST NATIONS CEREMONIAL MUSIC OFTEN PLAYS softly in the Nk'Mip Cellars elegant tasting room, evoking the centuries of tradition behind this very modern Okanagan winery. When Nk'Mip opened, it was the first winery in North America owned by Aboriginal people — the entrepreneurial Osoyoos Indian Band. The winery's symbol is a pictograph (one of many found on rock faces throughout the valley), the outline of a turtle with an arrowhead for a head. The turtle symbolizes wisdom and vision while the arrow represents power. The premium wines are identified with a phrase from the consonant-rich Okanagan language, *Qwam Qwmt*, which means "achieving excellence." And that is what the 370-member Osoyoos band has achieved, first as grape growers and now as vintners.

The oldest of the dozen or so businesses run by the band is Inkameep Vineyards, a 97-hectare (240-acre) vineyard near Oliver first planted in 1968. "I imagine most vineyard producers have dreams and ideas about opening up their own wineries," says Clarence Louie, elected band chief since 1985 and grandson of an earlier chief. "The Osoyoos Indian Band is no different." In 1980 the band took its first step — controversial at the time — by erecting a building near the vineyard that was leased as a winery to T. G. Bright & Company, a predecessor to Vincor. Now the Jackson-Triggs winery, it has become the Okanagan's largest winery and a major provider of jobs for band members.

Nk'Mip Cellars was conceived by the band as the anchor for its resort development overlooking Osoyoos after the band was unsuccessful with a casino application. Needing an experienced winery partner, the band approached Vincor, a company already closely aligned with the band. As well as the Jackson-Triggs winery, it leases almost 400 hectares (1,000 acres) on the Osoyoos reserve for vineyards. Vincor offered the band capital to build a winery. "What we really wanted was a joint venture," says Chris Scott, the band's economic development officer. "I wanted a partner that would assure us that when that winery starts up, it has the expertise of a management team behind it, specifically in the marketing." Vincor took a 49 percent interest in the winery and provided vital technical services: the first two vintages for Nk'Mip Cellars were made by the winemakers at Jackson-Triggs.

In 2002 winemaker Randy Picton was recruited from CedarCreek. Born in Yorkton, Saskatchewan, in 1958, he has a business administration diploma from Calgary's Mount Royal College. After an industry recession derailed his first job in the purchasing department of a lumber company, Randy and his wife ran a Penticton campground and motel. When that business was sold, Randy spent 10 years as a tree planter. "It was extremely physically demanding work," he says. "I decided I should start looking at other options."

He enrolled in the inaugural winery assistant program at Okanagan University College in 1995. "At the time what I knew about wine was that it was either white or red." In April 1996 he joined CedarCreek as a cellar hand. Within five years he was the associate winemaker. On several occasions he filled in as interim winemaker during staff changes. "We didn't have anybody else in the cellar," Randy recalls. "I had to go down and put my boots on and do all that, and then come up and make sure we were getting things done properly in the lab and that the paperwork was being done. It was a good learning experience."

At Nk'Mip Cellars, Randy has mentored two emerging First Nations winemakers. Justin Hall, who is a member of the Osoyoos band and who has relatives working at Jackson-Triggs, previously worked at the band's golf course. He joined Nk'Mip Cellars early in 2004, just in time to clean the tanks from the previous vintage. Far from being discouraged, Justin took winery assistant and viticultural training at Okanagan University College and did the 2005 crush at the Goundrey winery in

Western Australia. Nk'Mip's other cellar supervisor is Aaron Crey, a member of the Cheam Indian Band in the Fraser Valley. He joined Randy's team in the fall of 2003 after doing clerical work at the Nk'Mip Resort. He is also a product of OUC's training and has supplemented that education by visiting wineries in France and Italy.

The winemaking team makes award-winning wines because they get grapes from choice vineyard plots, including the eight hectares (20 acres) around the winery and select blocks in the Inkameep Vineyards that are pampered to produce the best fruit. Some of the vines at Inkameep grow in east-west rows, following the contours of the site. This means that the grapes on the north, or slightly shaded, side of each row ripen a week or so later than those on the sun-drenched south side. At Randy's request, the vineyard picks the north side of rows later, ensuring that all grapes achieve optimal ripeness before being crushed for wine. "There are probably not a lot of vineyards that would go to that length for you," Randy says. "It is nice to be working with a vineyard that will."

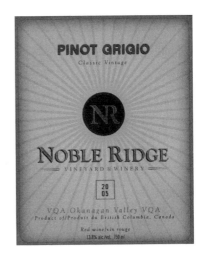

NOBLE RIDGE VINEYARD & WINERY

OPENED: 2005

> 2320 Oliver Ranch Road, RR1, Site 3, Comp 43, Okanagan Falls, BC V0H 1R0
> 250.497.7945
> www.nobleridge.com
> When to visit: Open daily 11 am – 5 pm May 1 to October 9

RECOMMENDED

> KING'S RANSOM
> MERITAGE
> PINOT NOIR
> CHARDONNAY
> PINOT GRIGIO

DURING A 1998 FAMILY SABBATICAL TO EUROPE, CALGARY LAWYER JIM D'Andrea was instructed by several colleagues to look for wineries in which, as partners, they could invest. He found two properties in the south of France but his partners backed away. Jim remained interested, even more so after a subsequent hiking holiday in Tuscany with Leslie, his wife. On returning to his practice, he began looking in Ontario and in the Okanagan until 2001, when he purchased a 10-hectare (25-acre) property south of Okanagan Falls. "We loved the beauty of it," he says. "It overlooks Vaseux Lake."

Born in Welland, Ontario, in 1954, Jim moved to Calgary in 1982 after graduating from law school. His entire career has been with Bennett Jones, the firm that was founded in 1897 by the future prime minister, R. B. Bennett, and that employs about 250 lawyers today. Jim heads the firm's employment practice group and has written several books on this field of law. In his spare time he referees minor-league hockey.

"Leslie and I have always liked wine," Jim says, explaining the decision to launch a winery. He and his wife had come to know the Okanagan during family vacations. They were soon adding an increasing number of BC products to a wine cellar reflecting their catholic tastes for both New World and Old World wine. Leslie, born in Toronto in 1958, has a master's in health administration. Recently, however, she has switched her interest to viticulture through courses at Okanagan University College. Her husband found himself putting aside his law books to read her texts. "It's contagious, once you get the bug," he admits. Curious about all aspects of wine, both have also taken sommelier courses. Jim has even thought about learning to be a winemaker. "At this point it is not in the cards, because of the career," he admits. "Some day I would like to."

The property they purchased had 1.4 hectares (3½ acres) of grapes that had been planted in 1986, but the total plantable area was five times that large. The defining feature is a ridge with two slopes, one to the south and one to the north. The winery gets its name from the ridge and the noble varieties in the vineyard. The original planting included Cabernet Sauvignon, Merlot, and Chardonnay. Shortly after taking over the vineyard, the D'Andreas added another 1.6 hectares (four acres), split evenly between Pinot Noir and Pinot Gris. Encouraged by the quality of the first crop of Pinot Noir in 2003, they filled most of the remaining area with that variety and with Chardonnay. They added a little Pinot Meunier as a base for sparkling wine. "This is sparkling wine country," Leslie maintains.

They had Noble Ridge's first three vintages made at other wineries by consulting winemaker Michael Bartier until they built their own winery. The wine shop, an attractive facility featuring a curved marble bar, was opened first, perched on a ridge with vineyard and lake views. The question of where to put the production facility was resolved in 2006 when Jim and Leslie bought a vineyard on the other side of Oliver Ranch Road from a sometime winery operator, Don Gabel.

A retired trucking company owner, Don had applied for a winery licence as Desert Falls Winery. The winery produced, bottled, but never sold several vintages of profoundly ordinary wine. The processing facility was a massively strong barn-like structure designed to house big trucks. In 2006 Don and his partner, Brenda Bond, changed their minds about making wine. They were in the habit of spending their winters in the American Sunbelt and decided they preferred that to running a winery full time.

The winery building, along with its 2.4-hectare (six-acre) vineyard, was just what Noble Ridge needed. "Being able to obtain some land in our area is of great importance to us," Jim says. "We are strongly of the view that the Okanagan Falls 'appellation' is a premier wine-growing region."

With a winery building, Jim could hire a winemaker of his own. In the fall of 2006 he landed Philip Soo, who had just left Andrew Peller Ltd. to become an independent consulting winemaker. The son of immigrants from Hong Kong, Philip was born in Vancouver in 1969. He has degrees in microbiology and food engineering. When he graduated, he was offered jobs at a pharmaceutical firm and a company that produced gourmet salads but, having been a good amateur beer maker while in college, he took a job with a manufacturer of wine and beer kits "because it was in line with my hobby." After Peller bought the kit company, Philip transferred to Peller's winery in Port Moody in 2000. He left five years later when the winery closed.

Philip inherited a very disciplined portfolio at Noble Ridge with, for example, the Bordeaux grapes blended into a Meritage rather than released as separate varietals. That reflected the appreciation for blended reds that their travels in France had given Jim and Leslie. While the winery produces Pinot Noir as a varietal, the wine is a blend of the four clones that have been planted here. The only major addition since Philip arrived has been a sparkling wine. And to the winemaker's relief, Noble Ridge makes no icewine. "I prefer not to do icewine," Philip admits.

OLIVER TWIST ESTATE WINERY

OPENED: 2007

33013 Road 9A, Oliver, BC V0H 1T0
250.485.0227
www.olivertwistwinery.com
When to visit: Open daily 10 am – 5 pm May to October and by appointment

RECOMMENDED

PINOT GRIS
KERNER
CHARDONNAY
PINOT NOIR

NOTHING SEEMS TO FAZE BRUCE AND DENICE HAGERMAN, WHO, DURING THE past 40 years, have moved effortlessly from one career to another and even one country to another. In the fall of 2006 they found themselves in their brand new winery in the Okanagan with truckloads of grapes arriving for their first vintage. "I had never done a crush in my life," Bruce says, "but things just came together." As they always have for the Hagermans.

To launch the winery they took viticulture courses at Okanagan University College and retained consulting winemaker Christine Leroux. "I intend to make my own wine but that will be down the road," Bruce said in an interview prior to that debut vintage. (He has been a home winemaker since 1989.) He is so confident of mastering yet another skill that he says: "The day I think I know everything about this business is the day I get out of it!" For the moment, that seems unlikely. The Hagermans are having at least as much fun with their Oliver Twist winery as in any previous career.

The seven-hectare (17-acre) vineyard was planted in the spring of 2006, replacing the apple and cherry trees growing there when the couple bought the property in 2002. They had just returned to Canada from the United States with the intention of starting an Okanagan winery. However, for a few years they hesitated to pull out the fruit trees, concerned at offending the meticulous previous owner. They found creative ways of selling their produce, trucking it to customers in Grande Prairie, Alberta, a former hometown. They produced conserves and considered going into the jam and jelly business seriously. "I have never worked so hard in all my life on 17 acres of orchard," Bruce says. "I had 1,000 acres in Alberta, a small farm, and I didn't work as hard. The 6,400 trees here were a tremendous amount of labour. You were out there all the time, up a ladder. I had some monster trees."

They bit the bullet on converting the orchard after the 2005 season, when the return from selling fruit was not enough to pay the farm's bills. The following spring the trees were replaced with 27,000 vines (Viognier, Syrah, Chardonnay, Pinot Gris, and Merlot). Meanwhile a 446-square-metre (4,800-square-foot) winery was erected, contracts were signed for purchased grapes, a winemaker was hired, and Oliver Twist was ready for its grand opening within a year. It is typical of the fast pace at which the Hagermans wheel through life.

"I like to do different things," Bruce says. "I once asked a little old lady about the things she did in her life and what it was she regretted. She said, 'Sonny, it is not the things I did in my life that I regret, it is the things I didn't do.' That is my philosophy in life."

The couple met in high school, where Bruce was studying electronics. From there, he became a management trainee with the Woodwards department store chain, training that he then applied in 1975 to operating his own Radio Shack franchise in Edmonton. In his spare time he learned to fly, largely so that he and Denice could visit their families in Grande Prairie when they wished. For a time they ran a farm near that community; Bruce also learned the art of auctioneering and put it to work at farm equipment auctions. In 1983 he took over a large tools dealership in British Columbia as well as learning the locksmithing trade. During this period he also was a propane distributor.

"We took off in 1985 for three and a half years in a motorhome," Bruce recounts. "We spent all the summers in Canada and the winters in the United States and Mexico, just for the weather." They went from that to running a large recreation vehicle park in Ontario, selling it after several years because they preferred living in the West. Soon they were back in sunny California, living in Palm Springs. Bruce joined the police department while Denice helped manage the local tennis club. Hiking in their spare time led them to collaborate on a best-selling book about the area's hiking trails.

The September 11, 2001, attack on the World Trade Center in New York abruptly changed the mood in the United States, or so it seemed to the Hagermans, and they decided to return to Canada. Bruce cracks that they had "an allergy to snowflakes" that kept them from moving back to Grande Prairie. So they settled in the Okanagan, where the dry summers remind them of Palm Springs, and decided to go into the wine business as their next career. It was not a complicated decision. "There is so much romance about wine," Denice explains.

They run a jolly tasting room with characteristic élan. Bruce, who can be a wisecracking jokester, will tour visitors through the winery on the spur of the moment. And if he is not there, a row of windows along one side of the wine shop look down onto the winery's working floor, revealing tanks and barrels. The wine shop is also notable for wine prices that have been kept moderate. "I don't know what the perfect price is," Bruce says, "but I don't want to price my wines so that only the lucky few can afford them."

OROFINO VINEYARDS

OPENED: 2005

2152 Barcelo Road, Cawston, BC V0X 1C0
250.499.0068
www.orofinovineyards.com
When to visit: Open daily 10 am – 5 pm May through October. Picnic tables shaded
by almond trees

RECOMMENDED

PINOT NOIR
MERLOT
CHARDONNAY
RIESLING
RED BRIDGE RED
LATE HARVEST MUSCAT

THESE ARE WINES FOR THE SOCIALLY CONSCIOUS CONSUMER, BECAUSE Orofino is one of Canada's greenest wineries. Both the 204-square-metre (2,200-square-foot) winery and the cozy tasting room are built with straw bales, unique among Canadian wineries. Heating and cooling these naturally insulated buildings is so efficient that Orofino's annual power bill would be the monthly bill at many other wineries. If the design is rustic, the appearance is not. Clad with rose-hued stucco, this winery blends easily with the sage and sagebrush tones of the Similkameen Valley.

Natives of Saskatchewan, owners John and Virginia Weber had mature social consciences in 2001 when they took over this 2.4-hectare (six-acre) vineyard. High school sweethearts who were both born in 1969, John taught school and Virginia is a nurse. John took several breaks from university to work in Brazil, first with street children and then returning for nearly four months to work "with the poorest farmers you can imagine." Virginia, meanwhile, spent time nursing in India.

As students they also travelled and worked in Europe. "We both spent some time in France in 1990," John remembers. "That triggered our interest in wine. It is pretty hard not to fall in love with the whole wine history and scene when you are living amongst it." Still under the spell a decade later, they bought this Similkameen vineyard, embarking on totally new careers. "We spent that first year on a huge learning curve, trying to do our best," he says.

Located on a flat bench near Cawston, the vineyard was planted in 1989 by Sandor Mayer, now the winemaker at Inniskillin Okanagan, who sold it when Inniskillin's Dark Horse Vineyard required his full attention. Both Sandor and Matt Leak, the subsequent owner from whom the Webers bought the property, planted enough varieties to support a good wine portfolio. These include Pinot Noir, Merlot, Cabernet Franc, Pinot Blanc (now grafted over to Pinot Noir), Chardonnay, Riesling, three different varieties of Muscat, and small numbers of other trial plots. The mature vines proved a big advantage, yielding intensely flavoured wine grapes.

After selling grapes for several vintages, the Webers in 2003 began having wines made for Orofino Vineyards — Spanish for "fine gold" and also the name of the mountain overlooking the vineyard. While taking wine courses at Okanagan University College, John engaged various consulting winemakers, tapping their expertise until he could go solo. "The idea was to hire a winemaker and apprentice right here, on our property, but wean ourselves off, so that eventually Virginia and I, but mainly myself, became the winemakers," John says.

The wines were very well received. The 500 cases that Orofino opened with in the spring of 2005 were gone by the end of the summer. Since then, with the help of purchased grapes, the winery has increased production to about 2,500 cases per year. And the winery is still sold out by the end of the season; at times between releases, the Webers shut the tasting room temporarily until new wines are ready for sale. The validation of what they are producing can be seen in the astonishing list of blue-ribbon restaurants that carry Orofino wines.

Along with the quality of the wines, the decision to build a straw bale winery has clearly burnished Orofino's image. "I wouldn't say we sell more wine because of it, but it can keep my customers here a little but longer," John says. "We show the building off, talk about it. They can look through the little glass window and see a straw bale in the wall. It's got this real nice organic feel to it."

It is odd that no other small winery has chosen this method of construction. The technique, used for other buildings in the Similkameen Valley, is inexpensive and easy. Orofino's tasting room was completed in five days by volunteers learning the art; more volunteers helped a professional crew erect the winery itself. "And the straw that we used is a renewable resource," John notes.

OSOYOOS LAROSE ESTATE WINERY

OPENED: 2004

Jackson-Triggs Winery, Oliver, BC V0N 1T0
250.498.4981
When to visit: No tasting room

RECOMMENDED

LE GRAND VIN
PÉTALES D'OSOYOOS

ABOUT 96,000 VINES FLOURISH IN THE OSOYOOS LAROSE VINEYARD, MOST OF them planted in 1999 and 2000 on a gentle slope on the west side of the Okanagan Valley overlooking Osoyoos Lake. French-born winery manager Pascal Madevon is on first-name terms with each vine. "I spend 80 percent of my time in the vineyard and 20 percent of my time in the winery," he says. "The terroir is the most important thing to making good wine. If you have a fish in the kitchen and it is bad, you can do nothing. It is the same with grapes." His attention to detail is why he has made some of the Okanagan's best red wines, vintage after vintage since the debut wine in 2001.

Osoyoos Larose is a joint venture between Vincor, Canada's largest wine producer, and Groupe Taillan, a French giant that owns at least seven top estates in France. The winery's name neatly melds Osoyoos with Taillan's most distinguished estate, Château Gruaud-Larose. Until the partners build a winery on the vineyard, Pascal continues to make the wines in a self-contained corner of Vincor's massive Jackson-Triggs winery north of Oliver. Vincor's strategy was to sit back and learn from the French, who sent out their vineyard consultants, ordered the vines, and recruited Pascal before the first vintage.

The Okanagan surprised them. Unlike premium Bordeaux wineries, which never use the fruit from young vines in their first-label wines but only in second-label wines, Osoyoos Larose did the reverse. The winery released Le Grand Vin right from its first vintage because the Okanagan-grown wine was just that good. "Incredible!" Pascal marvels. Pétales d'Osoyoos, the winery's second label, was not produced until the 2004 vintage, and not because he had second-rate wine. When he had finished the blend for 110,000 bottles of the 2004 Le Grand Vin, Pascal had wines that did not fit into that blend. They went into a slightly different blend for 21,000 bottles of Pétales.

"I arrived here in September 2001," Pascal remembers. "It was my first time in North America. The next day, at six in the morning, we began the harvest. When I saw the quality of the fruit, it was a big surprise." Born in Paris in 1963 and graced with a muscular build, Pascal took math in high school but chose to become a winemaker because he likes outdoor work. "I didn't even know how to drive a tractor," he admits. But he had an early passion for wine, acquired from his grandfather, who had a small vineyard in Burgundy. Most of his winemaking career in France was spent at Château La Tour Blanche, a cru bourgeois of Médoc. In addition to making wine, Pascal has written two wine books, one of which has gone through several editions and sold 25,000 copies.

He adapted quickly to the Okanagan and to the egalitarian way of doing things here compared with France. "I have a very nice friend here," he says. "He was one of my workers in the cellar. In France it is impossible that a manager would have a friend who is a worker. I like this sort of spirit in the workplace. I want to stay here a long time. I want to share two countries in my life — France and here." That also has something to do with the wines he found in the Okanagan. "I am very surprised by the quality of the wine here because it is a very young industry," he says. "If I compare it to the Médoc, except for the classified growths, there is very nice wine here."

The Osoyoos Larose vineyard, the location of which was chosen by Groupe Taillan's viticulturist, is planted exclusively with the five chief varieties grown for red wine in Bordeaux. The largest area is planted to Merlot, always the backbone of the Le Grand Vin blend (60 percent in the 2006 wine). The vineyard is about 40 hectares (100 acres), enough to produce 25,000 cases of wine, 10 times the quantity of the first release. The French deliberately chose a vineyard on the west side of the valley. When the sun drops behind the nearby mountains, the vines end the day considerably cooler than they would on the sun-baked eastern flank of the valley. Alain Sutre, the viticulture consultant from Groupe Taillan, says that the grapes at Osoyoos Larose mature more slowly, thus developing intense flavours.

The vineyard is farmed with surgical detail. The stylized map of the vineyard on Pascal's computer resembles a crossword puzzle, except that each square represents a block of five vines. The winemaker has entered data on the vigour of the soils and the productivity of the individual vines so that each block, or each group of blocks, can be farmed according to its vigour. Ultimately he hopes to balance the soils in each block so that the grapes develop as uniformly as possible. "We try, after five or six years, to have exactly the same vigour everywhere," he says. "But we never forget that we are not making a car. It is a vine. There is nature behind it."

Pascal's devotion to detail — "the amount of detail makes the difference, all the time" — extends into the superbly equipped winery. His French-made fermentation tanks are unlike any others in the Okanagan: squat steel tanks shaped like the historic wooden vats of Bordeaux that provide superior contact between the skins and the fermenting wine. His pump is gentle; and he avoids pumping wine at all if he can. When a barrel of wine needs to be emptied, it is raised by the forklift and gravity moves the wine. When Osoyoos Larose finally builds its winery on the spot at the top of the vineyard, the building will be set into the hillside, fully harnessing gravity.

"I try to progress all the time," he says. "I try to get better. We did not arrive from France believing we know everything." Although the style of Osoyoos Larose might well be compared with wines from the commune of Margaux, Pascal insists that he makes Canadian wine from Okanagan grapes, not French wine. That may be so, but Le Grand Vin is like a fine Bordeaux in its ability to improve with age. "I can drink the 2004 now," Pascal said when that vintage was released, "but I can also wait 20 years."

PACIFIC BREEZE WINERY

OPENED: 2007

> 6 – 320 Stewardson Way, New Westminster, BC V3M 6C3
> 604.522.2228
> www.pacificbreezewinery.com
> When to visit: Consult website

RECOMMENDED

> CHARDONNAY
> CABERNET SAUVIGNON
> GSM (GRENACHE, SYRAH, MOURVEDRE)
> SYRAH

THE SO-CALLED *GARAGISTE* WINES ORIGINATED IN THE 1970S IN BORDEAUX when small producers with modest facilities began releasing innovative wines that won high praise from wine critics like Robert Parker. The concept of making great *vins de garage* soon spread to other regions. In the Seattle suburb of Woodinville, many acclaimed wineries were launched in garage-like industrial warehouses. In turn, those *garagiste* wineries inspired Frank Gregus and Maurice Hamilton when they set up Pacific Breeze Winery in a warehouse, under the SkyTrain and beside a New Westminster street heavily travelled by trucks. In a space no bigger than a garage for a semi-trailer and its tractor, they manage to produce nearly three thousand cases annually of award-winning wines.

Most BC wineries have land-based licences and, thus, vineyards of their own. City-based Pacific Breeze owns no vineyard, at least not yet. It operates under a commercial licence that allows it to import grapes from California and Washington. In the tradition of most *garagistes*, Frank and Maurice have gone to great lengths to buy premium grapes from top vineyards. That's the only way to handcraft award-winners.

Frank, born in New Westminster in 1961, and Maurice, born in Nanaimo in 1951, are friends who began making wine as amateurs in the late 1980s. Their hobby, and now their profession, continues to be supported by careers in sales. Frank is an accounts manager with a soft drink producer while Maurice sells dental equipment. "We have been talking about this for years," Maurice said just as the winery was getting ready to open. "There are a number of other people that are also thinking about it. We are the only ones that have jumped in."

Pacific Breeze winemaker Dan Jones and his assistant, Don Kellet, have also come through the amateur ranks. Dan, who was born in Vancouver in 1952, was working as a plumber and gas fitter until a construction industry recession in the early 1980s. His trades training got him a job in 1984 with the Labatt brewery in New Westminster, and he stayed there until the brewery closed in 2005. Dan started making wine in 1982 when his wife gave him a kit. He progressed to grapes, including Okanagan grapes, and was twice provincial champion amateur winemaker. "It got to be a bit of a passion for me," Dan says. "When the brewery shut down, I decided to go into the wine industry."

He equipped himself by taking several courses from the University of California and working as a cellar hand at CedarCreek Estate Winery. When the Okanagan winery did not have a permanent position available, Dan moved to Pacific Breeze in late 2005, first in the laboratory and then as winemaker.

"As amateurs we made a lot of wine from BC," Frank says. "We had access to fruit from Fischer Vineyard [now site of the Tinhorn Creek winery]. We used to buy a lot of fruit on the Black Sage Bench." There was a shortage of Okanagan grapes in 2005 when the partners were getting ready for their first vintage. That June they began touring Napa Valley vineyards. They insisted on tasting wines made from the vineyards they were considering. Frank remembers that none of those wines delivered the "wow" factor they were looking for.

They found it the following month at a Seattle trade show when they tasted bold and intense reds from a vineyard in northern California's Lake County. They secured enough grapes to make 1,250 cases that vintage, all red wine, except for a Chardonnay from renowned Sangiacomo Vineyards fruit in Carneros. In 2006 they chanced on another Lake County vineyard with Grenache, Syrah, and Mourvedre grapes too good to pass up, so they added a gsm wine to their portfolio and raised production to 2,500 cases, close to the maximum they can squeeze from their garage.

"We'll pay a premium for the grapes," Frank says, "but that ensures that we get the best fruit." They have found that premium growers like to deal with small wineries because the grapes, rather than disappearing into large blends, end up as vineyard-designated wines. One of Pacific Breeze's top Cabernet Sauvignon suppliers is an Alexander Valley vineyard owned by two pun-loving doctors. They call the property ACure EState Vineyards. Geyser Peak Winery formerly bought the grapes.

"We are committed to grow," Frank says. "Our vision would be to be around 15,000 cases." The winery will remain in the Vancouver area, close to the market. The partners are open to buying Okanagan grapes, if they find consistent sources, and perhaps also buying a vineyard. "I'd love to own something on the Naramata Bench," Frank says. "That's a jewel in my opinion."

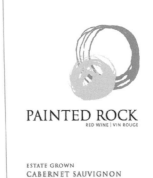

PAINTED ROCK ESTATE WINERY

OPENING PROPOSED FOR 2010

> 4850 Lakeshore Road, Penticton, BC V2A 846

RECOMMENDED

> MERITAGE RED
> SYRAH

JOHN SKINNER WAS A BIT TICKED OFF WHEN A FRENCH CONSULTANT, AFTER walking his Painted Rock property in the Okanagan, asked if he intended to make French wine or California wine. John's reply was the obvious terroir answer, that the French imbibe with their mother's milk: Painted Rock would make the wines that expressed that property. Right from the winery's first vintage, the wines are bold, concentrated reds that are Okanagan in style. If there is a slight bow to California, it is because John has friends among Napa Valley wineries from which he picked up winemaking pointers.

This vineyard, growing about 50,000 vines, has been developed on property south of Penticton and east of Skaha Lake that old-timers still call Braeside Farms. Before tree fruit production ended here, this claimed to have been the world's largest apricot farm. The property was sold in pieces, with Paul Gardner's Pentâge Winery planting its vineyard on the northern portion. John bought his parcel in 2004 from the former owners of Hillside Estate Winery.

The location, John believes, is magnificent. Grapes should thrive on this bench, with the towering Skaha climbing bluffs at the back, radiating the heat of the day over the vines long into the evening, while the lake out front insures a long, frost-free season. And, in a wine region full of great views, the Painted Rock winery has one of the best.

John was approaching 50 and ready for a change from a stockbroker's career when he took the plunge into wine. He was born in 1958 on a Manitoba military base, the son of a Canadian Forces fighter pilot. "I moved 20 times by the time I was 20," he says. Trish, his wife and his only partner in the winery, had an oil driller for a stepfather and thus also a peripatetic adolescence. Perhaps because of that, the Skinners settled down in West Vancouver. "But I think travel was very good for me," John says. "It either puts you in your shell or takes you out. I had new friends on a regular basis."

He became a broker when he left university before graduation. He had been financing his studies by working in a sawmill, until he saw how much more prosperous several of his friends had become as investment advisors. John promptly began a long and successful career in mining finance in Vancouver. And as part of a broker's lifestyle, he began acquiring a taste for, and interest in, good wines. The sharp quality jump in Okanagan wines that became apparent in the late 1990s led him to develop a winery of his own from the ground up. "There is not a lot of difference between distributing new issues of your latest vintages and distributing new issues of an underwriting," he figured.

He decided from the start not to cut corners. He hired consultants, including viticulturist Valerie Tait, to advise him. As the property was being shaped into an ideal grape growing exposure, vines — typically two clones of each variety — were ordered from France. About a quarter of the 10.5 hectares (26 acres) is planted to Syrah. Most of the remainder, except for a small Chardonnay block, is planted to Merlot, Cabernet Franc, and Cabernet Sauvignon, with modest blocks of Malbec and Petit Verdot. John calls the latter two varieties the "spice" for use in Painted Rock's big red blend.

Without a winery or a winemaker yet in 2007, John had Painted Rock's first vintage, 105 barrels of red wine, made at Poplar Grove by that winery's founder and winemaker extraordinaire, Ian Sutherland. "I know and trust Ian," John says. "I needed 'a safe place' to make sure it was done right." To ensure a differentiated style for the Painted Rock wines, John introduced some California-inspired winemaking techniques under the direction of Painted Rock's own consultant. John firmly resisted suggestions that he should make the wines. "I am not going to be the winemaker," he says. "I am an eager student but I really am intent on bringing in somebody who knows what they are doing." To make the second vintage, John hired Gavin Miller, who had been Ian's assistant at Poplar Grove.

John shelved his initial plan for an eye-catching destination winery and tasting room when he recognized that the site has insufficient access for large groups of wine tourists (even while he provides access to the climbing bluffs). Instead he is planning what he calls a vineyard community — townhouses and condominiums that can be rented by the day when owners are not using them. "That would by my revolving community of wine enthusiasts," he says.

PARADISE RANCH WINES

OPENED: 1998

901 – 525 Seymour Street, Vancouver, BC V6B 3H7
604.683.6040
www.icewines.com
When to visit: No tasting room

RECOMMENDED

ICEWINES (INCLUDING CHARDONNAY, MERLOT, RIESLING, PINOT NOIR)
LATE HARVEST MERLOT

PARADISE RANCH IS ONE OF JUST THREE WINERIES IN CANADA MAKING ONLY dessert wine, primarily icewine, but no table wine. (The others are Royal DeMaria in Ontario and Willow Hill winery near Oliver.) "Business has been good but it is not everyone's cup of tea," Paradise Ranch owner Jim Stewart admits. He exports to about 20 countries, mostly in Asia, to buyers with whom he has nurtured relationships. The paradox is that Canada is the world's largest icewine producing nation, but Canadians are not big consumers of the country's signature wine. "You spend a lot of time on airplanes," Jim says.

The winery was conceived in the 1990s by Jeff Harries, a Penticton physician who also ran a vineyard on a Naramata property called Paradise Ranch, a name coined by homesteaders because of the site's great beauty. To add value to the grapes being produced there, Jeff enlisted Vancouver lawyer and businessman Jim Stewart to partner in the winery, which was licensed in 1998.

"When Jeff suggested we get into this business, he told me that demand exceeded supply," Jim recalls. Paradise tested the waters with two icewines from the 1996 vintage, a Chardonnay and a Pinot Gris, then plunged ahead to make eight in 1997 — including a rare Viognier — six in 1998, and three in 1999. A few of these "historic" icewines remained in the winery's portfolio, evidence the demand does not necessarily exceed supply. "There had been a widespread assumption that if you make it, the consumers will come to you," Jim says. "That is not the case."

Fortunately Harries had chosen a business-savvy partner. Jim, after practising business law, became a director of Polaris Water Company. As well, he was the founder and chief executive of a successful software company. In almost a decade prior to running the icewine company, Jim developed personal credibility in Asia, the key market for icewine. "I had a lot of business contacts," he says. "Asia is very relationship-based." Quick to spot good promotional ideas, Jim snapped up an iconic website, www.icewines.com, before competitors grabbed it; and in 1999 he registered Whistler as a Paradise Ranch brand long before the resort had been selected for the 2010 Olympics. Whistler Icewine was released in 2007.

Initially a winery was planned for Paradise Ranch's idyllic lakeside vineyard with its two kilometres (just over a mile) of waterfront. However, in the summer of 2002, the Harries family sold the entire property to Mission Hill. Jim acquired the Harries interest in the winery, along with the Paradise Ranch name.

During much of its first decade, Paradise Ranch has been a nomad, making its icewines at a succession of operating wineries, including Red Rooster, Calona Vineyards, and Hester Creek. Divorced from its original vineyard, the winery purchased grapes at various Okanagan vineyards and relied on a succession of winemakers. Recent vintages have been made by Bernhard Schirrmeister, the German-trained winemaker for the Holman-Lang group of wineries. In 2007, however, Jim settled Paradise Ranch's production in a Kelowna warehouse and he purchased a small Naramata property. There in 2008 the winery planted 3.25 hectares (eight acres) of Chardonnay and Pinot Noir. This is intended to be the first of several vineyard acquisitions.

Paradise Ranch also has contracted an Ontario winery to make Vidal icewine under the Paradise Ranch brand. "There is an international demand for Vidal icewine," Jim says. "But the primary reason we did this was for certainty of supply." Making icewine successfully depends on winter weather delivering the required freeze (at least –8°C/18°F, by regulation) in early winter, and Jim bets that the conditions for icewine will be favourable each winter in at least one of Canada's two major vineyard regions.

He can recite a cautionary history. The winters of 2001 and 2002 were unusually mild in the Okanagan. The required freezing temperature came so late that Paradise Ranch was only able to make late-harvest wines. Even very good late-harvest wines, which they were, command only half the price of icewine. In 2006 a sharp November freeze meant an abundant icewine harvest; but the 2007 vintage was smaller because the grapes could not be picked until a freeze arrived in January 2008. Ontario icewine production also is hit by climate cycles, but the cycles are seldom the same as in the Okanagan.

PARALLEL 49 VINEYARDS

OPENING PROPOSED FOR 2009/10

Highway 97 and Road 8, Oliver, BC V0H 1T0

AS THE MARKETING EXECUTIVE BEHIND CALONA'S SCHLOSS LADERHEIM WINE, Bruce Schmidt scored one of the greatest successes in the Canadian wine business. A wine with the label and the taste profile of an off-dry German white, Schloss was launched in 1977. For a few years in the early 1980s, it was the top-selling Canadian brand and was widely copied. The durable brand, now a blend based on Emerald Riesling wine from California, is still being produced.

As he develops his own winery in the Okanagan, Bruce is ambivalent about Schloss. It is not the image the Okanagan wants to project today and not the style of wine that will emerge from his winery. That does not mean, however, that Bruce is apologizing for Schloss. It was a breakthrough wine in the 1980s, a time when, as he recalls, "if you could get people to drink anything with a cork, you were in good shape." He thinks it remains a wine style that many drink at home, no matter what they order in public. "That is a great lesson for me," he says. "There is room for all types of wines as long as they are technically sound."

Born in Kelowna in 1952, Bruce has been around wine for much of his career, even if his university degree is a bachelor of science in physics. As soon as he graduated in 1975, he got a marketing job at Molson; a few years later he moved to Nabisco Foods in Toronto as a brand manager. Nabisco then owned Calona Wines and transferred Bruce to the winery in 1980 as the national brand manager. He left fours years later when the Keg restaurant chain recruited him as its first vice-president of marketing.

"Basically, sales and marketing has been my talent base," he says. He launched his own consulting firm in 1987, working in areas including marketing and venture

PARALLEL 49 VINEYARDS   295

capital. In 1992 Strategic Equity Corporation, of which he was a principal, helped Blue Mountain Vineyards raise $1 million to launch a winery. "Blue Mountain has been a great teacher of how you do things right," he says.

When not involved with wine, he has run or been a director of several biotechnology companies. But wine has been a continuing interest; he has even belonged to the same 12-person wine tasting group for two decades. He began looking for vineyard property or a winery project about 2002. "I have always had this interest in a vineyard," he says.

In 2007 he acquired control of and began planting a 4.5-hectare (11-acre) property south of Oliver superbly located for a winery. It is at the northwest corner of Highway 97 and Road 8, at the only place between Oliver and Osoyoos where there is a left-turn lane on the highway. Currently that serves the wine tourists visiting Hester Creek and Gehringer Brothers, two popular wineries at the top end of Road 8. The property formerly was an orchard; it has a large, well-equipped packing house that Bruce will turn into a winery. "If anything it is just too big," Bruce says.

Two-thirds of the site has been planted with Merlot vines; Sauvignon Blanc and Viognier occupy the other third. Since the young vineyard will yield its first grapes only in 2009, Bruce will consider buying grapes for the winery's initial vintages. "At this point, however, I would like to be an estate producer and just make the best damn wine that I possibly can," he says.

As this book was being completed, Bruce still had decisions to make about the winery. Parallel 49 Vineyards is the working name. The final name for the winery remains to be chosen when he decides how to brand the winery. For the man who once managed the Schloss Laderheim brand, that should be a walk in the park.

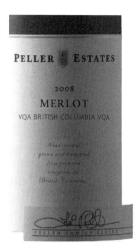

PELLER ESTATES

OPENED: 1961

> 1125 Richter Street, Kelowna, BC V1Y 2K6
> 250.762.9144 | 1.888.246.4472 (toll free)
> www.peller.com
> When to visit: Open daily 9 am – 6 pm

RECOMMENDED

> MERLOT PRIVATE RESERVE
> CABERNET SAUVIGNON PRIVATE RESERVE
> CHARDONNAY PRIVATE RESERVE
> CABERNET SAUVIGNON HERITAGE SERIES
> CABERNET MERLOT HERITAGE SERIES
> RIESLING HERITAGE SERIES
> PINOT BLANC HERITAGE SERIES
> TRINITY ICEWINE

ANDREW PELLER LTD. IS THE LARGEST CANADIAN-OWNED WINE PRODUCER. NOW headquartered in Ontario, it got its start in 1961 as Andrés Wines Ltd. with a winery in the Vancouver suburb of Port Moody. In 2006, after buying Calona Vineyards, Peller closed its Port Moody winery and moved its entire production into Calona's cavernous plant in Kelowna, completing one of the most significant takeovers in the Okanagan wine business. Why? Because the Peller wines suddenly got a lot better when Peller's winemaking moved closer to the grapes and came under the control of Calona's talented winemakers.

Hungarian-born Andrew Peller, whose grandson, John, now runs the company, established Andrés after a stint as a brewer in Hamilton. He came to British Columbia when the Ontario government would not give him a viable licence. (He had infuriated those regulators by flouting a ban on beer advertising.) His winery was built in the Vancouver suburb of Port Moody because, as Andrew recounted in his autobiography, the city "almost gave me the three and a half acres I had my eye on . . ." It made sense in that era, before wine tours were allowed in British Columbia, to build the winery close to the market, not close to the grapes.

It was another decade before Andrew acquired an Ontario winery and started to build a national company. By then its Port Moody winemakers created the products that fuelled the company's early growth. None is more famous than Baby Duck, a pink sparkling wine that was cheaper than other sparkling wines because the low alcohol content attracted less tax. The winery scored a huge success with the 1971 release of Baby Duck. "Within five years it had put us in a league we never anticipated joining," Andrew wrote of a wine that was once the best-selling Canadian wine. It still has a following.

Andrew Peller's given name was Andras. That give him the idea to name his winery Andrés, the French variant of his name, because, at the time, French wines had such an elite image. The Peller label was created only in the early 1990s. The idea was to associate the family name with the new wines from premium vinifera grapes that began to emerge from the Port Moody winery, where a skilled winemaking team had been assembled. When that team left (one for France in 1996, one for California in 1999), less seasoned cellar staff were placed under the direction of the national Peller winemakers in Ontario. The wines suffered. Too often grapes were being picked based on sugar level numbers reported back to Ontario and not on whether the grapes also tasted ripe. As good as Peller's national winemakers were, winemaking by email or fax just does not cut it.

The problem had been diagnosed by Robert Summers when he was Peller's national winemaker and started spending time in the Okanagan. "Once I got involved in BC [in 2003], I researched when we were picking in prior years and I think we were picking too early," Robert concluded. The Okanagan's long dry autumn permits grapes to hang until fully ripe. "In Ontario we don't see that level of ripeness on the Bordeaux grapes that we get out here." In the Okanagan's hot 2003 vintage, Robert let the grapes hang longer than in previous years. Plumper wines started to emerge. And Robert became so enamoured of the Okanagan that he moved there in 2007 as Hester Creek's winemaker. There he practically lives in the vineyard.

Good wine comes from winemakers who spend a lot of time in the vineyards as grapes develop, tasting them to determine if the ripe flavours have developed. That is what Peller gained by moving to Kelowna and tapping Calona's talent. Howard Soon, the winemaker at Sandhill and Calona, took over as the Peller group's senior winemaker in British Columbia. And he installed his protegé and associate winemaker, Stephanie Leinemann, at Peller, starting with the 2005 vintage. Both spend a lot of time in the vineyards, assessing the grapes before they are picked.

Stephanie is a Kelowna native who became enthused about wine while, during a break from college, she worked in a restaurant in Germany's wine country. Returning to Canada, she switched to Brock University's new wine school. She graduated with an honours degree in 2003, scoring so highly that she won the President's Medal as the top graduate that year. At the time the award was announced, she had already joined Calona, and made two vintages there before taking over at Peller.

Peller's Calona purchase in 2005 gave it control of the Sandhill Estate Vineyard on Black Sage Road. Since then Peller has made other bold investments to assure a supply of high-quality grapes. The company spent $10 million to plant 119 hectares (294 acres) of grapes, almost all them white varieties, on land leased at Covert Farms near Oliver. In 2007 it acquired full control of the 28-hectare (70-acre) Rocky Ridge Vineyard in the Similkameen that had been developed in 1997 with a partner. And the winery entered into an agreement to take the grapes from the 32-hectare (80-acre) Vanessa Vineyard, another Similkameen property planted in 2006 primarily with reds. These moves make Peller the third largest vineyard owner in British Columbia after Vincor and Mission Hill.

PEMBERTON VALLEY VINEYARD & INN

OPENED: 2000

> 1427 Collins Road, Pemberton, BC V0N 2L0
> 604.894.5857 | 1.877.444.5857 (toll free)
> www.whistlerwine.com
> When to visit: By appointment
> Restaurant: The Vineyard Restaurant open from 6 pm Wednesday through Sunday
>   May to October. Closed Monday and Tuesday. Open based on seasonal demand
>   November to April
> Accommodation: Bed and breakfast

RECOMMENDED

CURRENT RANGE NOT TASTED

BEARS OCCASIONALLY FORAGE IN OKANAGAN VINEYARDS, WHERE THERE ARE PLENTY of grapevines from which to choose. For the bears of the Pemberton Valley, the only game in town is the 1.2-hectare (three-acre) vineyard in the front yard at Patrick and Heather Bradner's winery and country inn. An electric fence might be an effective deterrent but Patrick is not certain about even that. He tempted fate in the fall of 2003 by leaving the vineyard's Chardonnay unpicked. Then an early November frost snapped across the vines, giving him his first chance ever to make icewine. He succeeded even though he was competing for frozen grapes with two bears.

Fortunately the bear population usually keeps to itself in the forested hills surrounding Pemberton. This rapidly growing village is less than half an hour's drive north of bustling Whistler, where Patrick sold real estate while his winery and inn became established. "The vineyard-winery is not a money-making thing yet," he conceded, interrupting the making of his 2003 icewine for an interview. "It's kind of a hobby out of control."

Born in Vancouver in 1957, Patrick is the son of a land developer who bought property in Whistler early in the 1960s, mostly so the family could ski when it wanted to. Patrick, who has a business degree from Simon Fraser University, followed his father into real estate. He also learned to enjoy wine at the family table.

"My dad always really liked wine," Patrick recalls. "Even when we were 12 or 13, he would let us have a glass of wine with our roast beef dinners on Sunday nights. I started to develop a palate for wine fairly young." By the time he was a teenager Patrick was making beer with his friends. Subsequently he became an avid home winemaker. In Whistler, where he and Heather moved in 1987, Patrick was part of a quartet that made an average of about one thousand bottles of wine per year with purchased grapes. By the time Pemberton Valley Vineyard made its first commercial vintage in 1999, Patrick had accumulated almost a decade and a half of experience.

The Bradners purchased their property on the northern edge of Pemberton in 1995. Because Patrick wanted to grow grapes, they first took a hard look at various locations in the Okanagan, including Naramata Road, where property prices had just begun to rise. Wearing his realtor's hat, Patrick chose the Pemberton Valley. Land prices were lower and he could continue his lucrative work selling Whistler real estate. And there was plenty of room for vines on the 2.8-hectare (seven-acre) property. In 1997 he planted about 3,500 vines of Chardonnay and Pinot Gris with vines obtained from the Okanagan. A few years later, after being impressed by a bottle of Quails' Gate Old Vines Foch, he planted about 500 Maréchal Foch plants.

Although the Pemberton Valley has a renowned seed potato industry, this is the valley's first vineyard. Patrick compares the climate for grape growing to that of the Cowichan Valley on Vancouver Island, with greater heat in summer. "The Pemberton Valley is kind of an east-west valley," he explains. "It has a bit of an arc in it, bending out to the south. We are right in the arc, so we get really good sun. In midsummer the sun is on our property from 6:30 in the morning to eight o'clock at night. That's one reason why this valley gets so hot. The sun doesn't cross it — it goes the length of it."

The growing season, however, is shorter than Vancouver Island's. Four years in five, Patrick has discovered, a frost at the beginning of May damages the buds. By 2006 he had suffered enough setbacks in the vineyard that he had to remove both the Chardonnay and the Pinot Gris. However, the Maréchal Foch — "an afterthought," he says — continues to thrive. In 2008 he was considering extending the Foch planting as well as planting a Blattner variety and perhaps some early-ripening aromatic grapes.

With his tiny vineyard still testing varieties, Patrick expects to rely on Okanagan grapes for some time. With that fruit he offers Chardonnay, Syrah, a Merlot/Cabernet blend, and an aromatic white blend. Production averages about five hundred cases per year, much of it sold at the winery's restaurant and its three-unit bed and breakfast. Each room is named for a wine region; naturally, the Champagne Room is the most luxurious.

PENTÂGE WINERY

OPENED: 2003

4400 Lakeside Road, Penticton, BC V2A 8W3
250.493.4008
www.pentage.com
When to visit: Call for hours

RECOMMENDED

PENTÂGE RED
MERLOT
CABERNET FRANC
SYRAH
SÉMILLON
PINOT GRIS
ROSÉ

THE PENTÂGE WINERY IS A TIGHT SHIP, CREWED PRIMARILY BY OWNERS PAUL Gardner (a former marine engineer), his wife, Julie Rennie, and winemaker Adam Pearce. "Every time you delegate a task, there is one level being removed from you," Paul believes. "Sometimes it leads to loss of control and, ultimately, quality." Many other wineries of this size, about five thousand cases per year, hire a mobile bottler several times a year. Paul bought a state-of-the-art Italian bottling line. "It's like everything else that I have done: if I can buy it and use it, I am not going to rent it."

That determination to be self-reliant seems to have developed during his 20 years at sea as a marine engineer on ocean-going towboats. Born in Singapore in 1961 and raised in Canada, he acquired a high level of comfort with machinery at sea, which has served him well in the winery. "I'm not afraid of machinery," he says. Bottling lines are finicky to run but he figures that if something goes wrong, he can fix it. Not all of his peers are as handy with a wrench.

Paul's interest in wine was turned on by people in his Vancouver social circle, some of them collectors of fine wine. Julie, the Scots-born daughter of a marine engineer, was for many years the executive assistant to one of the city's top mining financiers. However, the couple were not considering developing a winery until they were seduced by the beauty of the Pentâge site in the spring of 1996. They were taking a weekend break in the Okanagan, looking at getaway properties, when they came across a derelict orchard in south Penticton. It is an exceptional property, a high plateau sloping westward with high bluffs behind it and Skaha Lake sparkling far below. On a calm morning you hear the children playing on Skaha's beach. "I came up here and within the space of a weekend, decided that there was absolutely no reason not to do this," Paul says of the decision to plant vines.

An open-minded novice, Paul took advice where he could find it. "I found in the summer of 1996, when I was going through the valley talking to wine growers, that the information is available if you are willing to ask the questions and listen," he says. "I talked to all the people I could to get a good idea of what I should be planting based on what the public wanted and what would grow in the area."

His whites include Sauvignon Blanc and Gewürztraminer. A neighbour grows Pinot Gris on the hillside behind the winery. The reds at Pentâge are Syrah, Cabernet Sauvignon, Cabernet Franc, Merlot, and Gamay. The winery's name arose because Gardner started with five reds, inspiring a play on the Greek for five, *pente*. "I've always thought I would like to make a blend of five reds," he says. "And I didn't want the winery name to be another creek. I just wanted to use a single word."

He created more winemaking options when he doubled his vineyard with the 2006 purchase of 3.2 hectares (eight acres) nearby. It was planted with what he calls his "dirty dozen" varieties — Malbec, Cabernet Sauvignon, Zinfandel, Syrah, Petit Verdot, Merlot, Mourvedre, Roussanne, Grenache Blanc, Marsanne, Viognier, and Tempranillo. "I would still rather make small lots of interesting wine than big tanks of wine," Paul explains.

He is never happier than among his vines. "I am lucky because it is a pleasurable place to work. It doesn't seem like the drudgery that it could be," he says. "I also like machinery, and I have got to say that I have always felt that grapes are a logical engineering machine. They follow this genetic pattern. Basically all the species and varietals are different, but once you learn what a varietal will do, it will duplicate that time and time again."

Beginning with Pentâge's first vintage in 2000, Paul tapped consulting winemaker Ross Mirko for help. When the consultant left for New Zealand in 2005, Michael Bartier (now Road 13's winemaker) recommended one of his protegés, Dwight Sick, a meticulous winemaker with training from Okanagan University College. Dwight remained there for several vintages before moving on to Stag's Hollow. In 2008 he was succeeded by Thunder Bay native Adam Pearce, who was "bitten by the bug" when he spent 1999 working on Australian vineyards. A Niagara

College graduate in winemaking, he was previously the assistant winemaker at Fielding Estate Winery in Beamsville, Ontario.

For the first eight years the Pentâge wines were made in a temporary winery, a building originally intended to house vineyard machinery. Starting in 2002 Paul spent six years creating a cellar by excavating a huge cavern into bedrock at one of the property's high points. "It is as close to a cave as I can get without rock boring," he says. It has solid rock on three sides, a thick concrete ceiling slab, and insulated doors big enough for an aircraft hangar, all designed to be cooled naturally. On the slab above, or very nearby, Paul and Julie plan both a residence and a tasting room, several hundred feet above the lake.

At first they expected that Pentâge might be a two-thousand-case winery, but the demand for the wines and the vineyard expansion are allowing the winery to grow to more than three times that size before they cap growth. "This has been anything but boring, working with things that grow, right from the fruit to the finished wine," Paul says of his career change. "Ships were always waiting to sink or to be scrapped. I was maintaining things for a short period. Here I can create something that can last for years."

POPLAR GROVE WINERY

OPENED: 1997

1060 Poplar Grove Road, Penticton, BC V2A 8T6
250.493.9463
www.poplargrove.ca
When to visit: Consult website

RECOMMENDED

THE LEGACY
CABERNET FRANC
MERLOT
SYRAH
PINOT GRIS
CHARDONNAY
MONSTER WINES

IN 2004 TONY HOLLER CELEBRATED A BUSINESS SUCCESS WITH A NAPA
Valley vacation. He gushed at the vineyard landscapes as he and his wife, Barbara,
toured the valley, until she reminded him that the Okanagan, where he had grown
up, is far more attractive. After years of living in Vancouver, he had come to take
the valley for granted. "I came back from that holiday, contacted a real estate agent,
and told him to find a property on the lake," Tony remembers. In 2004 he bought a
lakefront orchard on the Naramata Bench, planted a small vineyard, and designed
a home on the beach.

His neighbour was the Poplar Grove Winery, and Tony struck up a friendship
with Ian Sutherland, the winery's co-founder. In 2007 when Ian needed a partner,
Tony stepped up to buy 75 percent of the business. "I had been drinking the wine
for some years before I knew Ian," Tony says. "I thought, 'This is a consistently
good wine.'" Already successful in the pharmaceutical business, Tony triggered

the expansion that is transforming Poplar Grove from a small artisanal winery to a major player capable of making 25,000 or so cases per year in one of the Okanagan's greenest wineries. "I am a business guy," he says. "I'm not getting into the wine business for fun."

Ian and Gitta Sutherland opened Poplar Grove just before the 1997 Okanagan Wine Festival and immediately won medals with two debut wines. Ian, who was born in Montreal in 1952, had developed a serious international wine palate after moving to the Okanagan in 1975. He supported his passion by working as a welder and pipefitter, becoming a keen home winemaker in his spare time. He and Gitta, a nurse, bought an apple orchard in 1991 and replaced the trees with Merlot and Cabernet Franc vines. After the winery opened, Ian burnished his self-taught winemaking skills during the Okanagan winters by working at New Zealand and Australian wineries for several consecutive vintages. He also learned cheese making at one of those working sabbaticals, launching the Poplar Grove Cheese Company, which Gitta now runs. The winery was making 6,500 cases of widely acclaimed wine by 2007 when Ian, to settle a divorce, brought in his new partner.

Born in Summerland in 1951, Tony grew up on a fruit farm, one of eight children. He became a doctor, spent 11 years as an emergency room physician in Vancouver, then became medical director of ID Biomedical, a Vancouver vaccine producer. He became the chief executive in 1999 and ran the company until 2006, when an international drug giant acquired ID Biomedical. Subsequently he became chief executive of another Vancouver biomedical firm, CRH Medical Corporation.

After Ian and Tony shook hands on their proposed partnership in 2007, Tony and Barbara moved aggressively to secure vineyards for an expanded Poplar Grove. They own or control 44.5 hectares (110 acres), about half on the Naramata Bench and the rest near Osoyoos. In Tony's view a winery needs to control its own vineyards to make the best wines. "Coming from a farm background, I know that the farmer's bias is to produce as much fruit as possible," he maintains. "Unfortunately, as production increases in the vineyard, quality goes down and the winemaker gets a poorer product. The farmer and the winemaker are never going to get along properly."

Poplar Grove's new winery is being built on the slope of Munson Mountain, a site that overlooks both the lake and the city of Penticton. The property had come on the market before Tony and Ian agreed to partner. In his typically decisive manner, Tony bought the land because the site is excellent for a winery. Most of the winery is buried into the slope, using gravity in its processes and geothermal technology for heating and cooling. The intent is an energy neutral winery secure against future energy price shocks.

Shortly after the partnership was struck, Poplar Grove rolled out a quirky second label, Monster Wines. Inspired by Ogopogo, the Okanagan's mythical lake monster, the label is used for affordably priced wines that do not fit the Poplar

Grove portfolio for one reason or another. "These are fun wines that people can enjoy on a patio in the afternoon," Tony suggests.

The intent, however, is to make as much wine as possible under the premium Poplar Grove label. "So long as we have the high-quality grapes, the majority of our production will go to Poplar Grove and we'll always produce less of the Monster label," Tony promises. "If you have the grapes to make the good wine, make the good wine!"

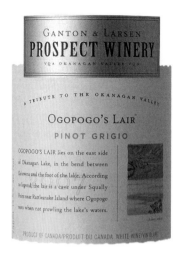

PROSPECT WINERY

OPENED: 2007

Box 474, Oliver, BC V0H 1T0
www.prospectwinery.com
When to visit: No tasting room

RECOMMENDED

- CHARDONNAY
- UNOAKED CHARDONNAY
- PINOT GRIGIO
- SAUVIGNON BLANC
- RIESLING
- SHIRAZ
- MERLOT CABERNET
- VIDAL ICEWINE

WHEN MISSION HILL CREATED PROSPECT WINERY IN 2007, THE WINES WERE branded to highlight the Okanagan and its history. None illustrate this better than the Haynes Barn Merlot Cabernet. The label includes the somewhat derelict cattle barn at the south end of Black Sage Road, once the property of John Carmichael Haynes, the "Cattle-King of the South Okanagan." His entry in the *Dictionary of Canadian Biography* relates that Haynes, who was born in Ireland in 1831, came to the colony of British Columbia in 1858 to join a newly formed police force. Later he became a judge and the customs inspector at Osoyoos while building his ranching operations to 8,400 hectares (20,760 acres) and 4,000 head before his death in 1888. The province named Haynes Point Provincial Park for him in 1962; now he is also remembered with a wine.

Prospect dipped into Okanagan lore, history, and nature to give its wines a sense of place. There is Ogopogo's Lair Pinot Grigio for the mythical lake creature;

Spotted Lake Sauvignon Blanc for the mineral-rich lake west of Osoyoos; Larch Tree Hill Riesling for the original name of the plateau above Osoyoos now called Anarchist Mountain. Since that begs another question, the answer is that the mountain now commemorates an early settler of Osoyoos remembered for extreme political views. In this way, every brand becomes a conversation piece. "Prospect Winery is about the salt of the earth of the Okanagan, the roots of the Okanagan," says Daniel Zepponi, the president of Mission Hill.

As this book went to press, there were only preliminary architectural drawings for the actual winery, which will be built somewhere between Oliver and Osoyoos. It will not be another grand winery like Mission Hill but rather a functional and well-equipped building, possibly with styling somewhat inspired by the Haynes Barn. However, Prospect has vineyard allocated to the brand among the 400 hectares (1,000 acres) that Mission Hill owns or leases in the Okanagan. As well, Wade Stark, a veteran of the winemaking team assembled by Mission Hill's John Simes, is now Prospect's winemaker.

The wines are intentionally not sold in Mission Hill's elegant tasting room (although they are widely available in wine shops and restaurants). The winery is to have an identity quite distinct from Mission Hill. Prospect emerged from a strategy at Mission Hill to build a wine group under a holding company, the Artisan Wine Company. Under Artisan's umbrella are labels and wineries aimed at different wine consumers, from the entry level to the collector level. Daniel Zepponi, a former executive with large wine companies in California, believes that successful brands are those that focus, not those that try to be everything for everybody.

The focus at Prospect is on making affordable wines whose quality will surprise. (All are currently priced under $20 a bottle except the icewine.) "We want people to pick it up and pour it and say, 'Wow, that is more than I expected,'" Daniel says. Within a year of being launched, Prospect was in the top five among Vintners Quality Alliance brands, well on its way to becoming a winery making about 50,000 cases per year.

The label debuted as the Ganton and Larsen Prospect Winery. In reaching — perhaps stretching — for Okanagan roots, the Artisan Wine marketers appropriated the surnames of two of Mission Hill's Okanagan growers. Although the sentiment was clever, Daniel concluded that there were too many names on the labels. In any event, Prospect Winery was always more prominent on the label.

The brief stories on each label should engage consumers to dig out more detail as well as pour that second glass. The biographical details on Judge Haynes came from an Internet search. Major Allan Merlot memorializes the late Allan Brooks, a Vernon naturalist and wildlife artist. Other labels are based on Okanagan plants or animals. Red Willow Shiraz is named for a plant also called the western dogwood that grows in the Okanagan. Rock Wren Pinot Noir takes its name from a wren that nests near Vaseux Lake. Townshend Jack, the name of the winery's unoaked Chardonnay, refers to a rabbit now extinct in the Osoyoos area.

Prospect even found a story for treasure hunters with its Lost Bars Vidal Icewine. Sometime in the early 1890s, gold was discovered at Camp McKinney, a mineral property on Mount Baldy, southeast of Oliver. One of the mine owners was robbed of three gold bars in 1896. The thief, later shot by police, managed to smuggle one bar into the United States. The remaining two are said to be buried still on the slope of Mount Baldy.

Prospect will run out of varietals before it runs out of colourful Okanagan history.

QUAILS' GATE ESTATE WINERY

OPENED: 1989

3303 Boucherie Road, Kelowna, BC V1Z 2H3
250.769.4451 | 1.800.420.9463 (toll free)
www.quailsgate.com
When to visit: Open daily 9 am – 7 pm in summer, 9 am – 6 pm in October, 10 am –
  5 pm November through spring
Restaurant: Old Vines Restaurant open daily at 11:30 am for lunch and dinner. Closed
  in January

RECOMMENDED

STEWART FAMILY RESERVE WINES (INCLUDING PINOT NOIR, CHARDONNAY, CHENIN
  BLANC, RIESLING)
LIMITED RELEASE WINES (INCLUDING MERLOT, PINOT NOIR, CHARDONNAY)
RIESLING ICEWINE
ROSÉ
OPTIMA BOTRYTIS AFFECTED

THE STEWART FAMILY, WHICH OPERATES QUAILS' GATE ESTATE WINERY, believe that their father, Richard, put in Canada's first successful planting of Pinot Noir in 1975. Today Quails' Gate is the Okanagan's largest producer of Pinot Noir, with seven clones on 16 hectares (40 acres) in its vineyard on the slope of Mount Boucherie. Pinot Noir comprises one-fifth of the winery's total production, now about 50,000 cases per year. Winemaker Grant Stanley was recruited specifically for his Pinot Noir experience, which underlines the winery's tight focus on this elusive red Burgundy varietal.

The Stewarts are one of the Okanagan's pioneer horticultural families. Richard John Stewart arrived from Ireland in 1906 and soon was followed by two brothers. First the Stewarts established nurseries. Then Richard John's son, Richard, bought the Allison ranch, as it was then called, and in 1963 began planting what has become the Quails' Gate vineyard. His son, Ben, left a career in banking to get involved with the vineyard and then launch the winery in 1989, as the family made its bet on Pinot Noir. "When Ben was first involved with the vineyard, he went over to Europe," recalls Tony Stewart, his younger brother and now chief executive of the winery. "He talked to people who said from what they knew of the Okanagan that Pinot Noir would be the only red vinifera they would recommend."

To this day the brothers regard Pinot Noir as the red variety with which the Okanagan can achieve an international profile. "We have the ability to make great Pinot here," Tony argues. "It doesn't mean we can't make other great wines, but it is the one I firmly believe we can export and not find that we are getting unfavourable observations from other regions."

Pinot Noir has been one constant at Quails' Gate; the other has been the role of southern hemisphere winemaking in shaping the portfolio. Quails' Gate started as a small farm winery with consulting winemakers while Ben Stewart gauged how well the new VQA wines would be received. When Vancouver restaurants embraced the wines, the Stewarts decided to expand and, in 1994, recruited Australian Jeff Martin, an accomplished winemaker then 20 years into a career with McWilliam's Wines, a family-owned winery in Australia. Now the owner of Naramata Road's La Frenz Winery, Martin made bold wines at Quails' Gate that set the tone for the winery. When he left in 1998 the Stewarts recruited two more Australians in succession before turning to New Zealand in 2003 for Grant Stanley, the current winemaker.

"We hired Grant based on his interest in Pinot Noir," Tony Stewart says. "If Grant had it his way, we would probably make only Pinot Noir. Not to say that he does not like making the other wines. He does, but his goal is to make the Pinot Noir as best as he can. The other wines make it possible for us to invest in the Pinot Noir program."

"You know, I am a Pinot guy," Grant admits. "I don't advertise it but with all the different varieties I make, I still spend about 80 percent of my time thinking about Pinot Noir. I think it has a positive spinoff on the other wines. There is a lot you can learn about Pinot that you can apply to other winemaking. It really is the tricky grape to make. If you can learn with it and understand it, you can ask: if that works for Pinot, will it work for Merlot?"

Grant was born in 1967 in Vancouver, the son of a printer and a dental technician, both of them New Zealand immigrants and neither particularly interested in wine. He developed his wine passion while working at restaurant and hotel jobs in London, England, New Zealand, and the Whistler resort. He and his British-born horticulturist wife, Annabelle, moved to New Zealand in 1991, with exquisite timing: the boom in New Zealand wines was just beginning. She got a job with the Cloudy Bay winery while Montana Wines, then New Zealand's biggest producer, gave him a job and then sponsored him to train as a winemaker. In 1998, after a few vintages with small wineries, Grant joined a legendary New Zealand Pinot Noir producer called Ata Rangi, where he did six vintages, plus guest winemaking in Oregon and France. "Ata Rangi opened doors for me," he says.

During an Oregon stint in 2001, he visited British Columbia to taste some wines. "I just couldn't believe it," he said. "When I left Canada, the Okanagan was a land of cheap white wine." He did not hesitate when Quails' Gate recruited him two years later.

The subtle and finessed winemaking style that he brought from New Zealand is well suited for the grapes and the terroir of Quails' Gate's 36-hectare (90-acre) vineyard on the toe of Mount Boucherie, an extinct volcano. In Okanagan terms, this is a cool site, ideal for the winery's signature wines, notably Pinot Noir. With good vineyard management, Quails' Gate also succeeds with varieties as diverse as Chasselas, Riesling, and Cabernet Sauvignon. "We have fantastic fruit and I like to let the fruit speak a little clearer in the wines," says Grant, who has a lighter touch with oak than his predecessors. He does not hesitate if he has to push the envelope to make a more interesting wine — perhaps crushing Sauvignon Blanc by foot or daring to ferment with wild yeast strains.

Starting with Jeff Martin, Quails' Gate has offered primarily two ranges of wine. Depending on the quality of the vintage, 10 to 15 percent of the production is released as Stewart Family Reserve, premium-priced wines built to cellar for five or ten years. But all the grapes are grown to the same exacting standard; Grant does not believe in growing grapes to achieve wines at differing prices. "That's a hard way to make wine," he says, preferring to choose the very best lots after fermentation for Family Reserve while still having commendable quality for the lower-priced Limited Release range.

"I take pride in some economy in the wine," he says over a glass of Limited Release Chardonnay, which he once described as his house wine. "I want people to be able to afford wines like this every night. When I am putting blends together, I send everybody home with a sample and say, 'Have that over a meal and tell me what you think.' Most of the time these wines are going to be drunk with a meal. They should look good with food and not just on their own."

QUINTA FERREIRA ESTATE WINERY

OPENED: 2007

34664 – 71st Street (Black Sage Road), Box 1062, Oliver, BC V0H 1T0
250.498.4756
www.quintaferreira.com
When to visit: Open daily 10 am – 6 pm

RECOMMENDED

OBRA-PRIMA
SYRAH
MALBEC
MERLOT
ROSÉ
VIOGNIER
MISTURA BRANCA (WHITE BLEND)
MISTURA TINTA (RED BLEND)
CHARDONNAY
VINHO DU SOL (DESSERT WINE)

BEHIND THE TASTING ROOM'S CURVED MARBLE COUNTER, JOHN FERREIRA IS wrestling a recalcitrant cork from a bottle of Syrah when a visitor suggests that he consider screw cap closures. He fixes the visitor with a gaze of utter disbelief. "I'm Portuguese," he protests. The country of his birth produces 60 percent of the world's favourite wine closure. John Ferreira will probably be the last vintner in the Okanagan to use any other.

He jokes that he got his first taste of cork when he was five and growing up in Portugal, where he was born in 1954. At times it was his task to have the family's empty wine container refilled at the corner store. Barely tall enough to see over the cork-surfaced counter, he chewed on it while waiting. His family migrated to Oliver in 1960. Another migration brought the family of his Portuguese-born future wife, Maria, to the Okanagan about the same time.

By the time he was seven John had learned to drive a tractor, helping his father, Antonio. The Ferreira family built a new life by starting as farm labourers, then leasing and later buying an orchard just south of Oliver. They kept wine on the table by making their own. "We could never really afford to go into the liquor store and buy wines, so we had to buy the grapes," John remembers.

A tough childhood bred a fierce work ethic. "School was a holiday," John recalls. "I didn't do very well in school because I was always being pulled out to make money. My parents were always saying, 'We need you to help out with the family expenses.' My parents would pull myself and my older sisters out for two to three weeks, to pick apples in Kelowna. So we would miss the first few weeks of school." But he made it through high school, graduating with practical industrial skills applied immediately to a packing house job and farming on the side.

In 1979 John and Maria took over the family farm, an eight-hectare (20-acre) property then growing apples, peaches, and cherries. Meeting their mortgage payments required them to sell some fruit privately, against the rules of the packing house co-operative. Expelled from the co-operative, they built their own packing house. In 2007 John turned that utilitarian building into a sage-and-sand-coloured winery with a Portuguese flavour. The baronial oak doors, specially commissioned by the Ferreiras, anchor the winery's European look. Quinta Ferreira is the first winery south of Oliver on Black Sage Road, perched on a hilltop overlooking the town. The eye-catching design makes it hard to drive past this tasting room.

John and Maria grew fruit for 20 years until, spurred by depressed fruit prices, they switched entirely to grapes. The 6.3-hectare (15½-acre) vineyard that emerged grows Merlot, Chardonnay, and Pinot Blanc, the dominant Okanagan grape varieties, along with Syrah, Viognier, Zinfandel, Petit Verdot, and Malbec, varieties now in wide demand. John still intends to plant Touriga Nacional, one of the classic Portuguese varieties for red wines and port.

"I didn't know the first thing about growing grapes when we put the first one in," John admits. "I was just tired of the fruit business." He acquired the skills to grow grapes by retaining veteran Okanagan grape grower John Bremmer as a consultant. At first John Ferreira sold his grapes to Township 7 estate winery. It is a point of pride that his first Syrah harvest was turned into a wine with which Township 7 won a Lieutenant Governor's Award of Excellence. His vineyard produces a Syrah with those attractive peppery notes often found in Black Sage Syrahs.

"I believe every man on earth would either like to have a vineyard or a winery," John maintains. "I have always wanted to have a vineyard but I never really thought about a winery." He pauses and reflects for a moment. "I am not sure what made us go to a winery. Maybe because I was so independent as a fruit packer that I wanted to stay independent."

The winery opened with vintages made by Christine Leroux, a busy consulting Okanagan winemaker. Ultimately Quinta Ferreira will keep it all in the family. Son Michael, who got a taste for winemaking by helping Township 7's former winemaker, Michael Bartier, has recently taken over as winemaker. He has begun to stamp a style on the portfolio with intriguing blends, notably a red that the winery calls Obra-Prima, Portuguese for "masterpiece."

RAVEN RIDGE CIDERY

OPENED: 2003

3002 Dunster Road, Kelowna, BC V1W 4A6
250.763.1091
www.ravenridgecidery.com
When to visit: Open seasonally at the KLO Farm Market
Restaurant: The Ridge open daily 11 am – 3 pm late April through October

RECOMMENDED

AMBROSIA ICE APPLE CIDER
BRAEBURN ICE APPLE CIDER
FUJI ICED APPLE CIDER
GRANNY SMITH ICE APPLE CIDER
D'ANJOU ICE PEAR CIDER

ALWAYS READY TO DIVERSIFY HIS APPLE BUSINESS, RICHARD BULLOCK IS open to new ideas. The technique for growing apples with logos on them was adapted from a practice he spotted during a 1990s business trip to Japan. Japanese orchardists put opaque bags over selected apples on the trees early each summer. The apples grow to full size without colouring. The bags are removed a few weeks before harvest. A decal is applied to each apple and the fruit, now exposed to the sun, acquires its normal colour — except for the decal, which is peeled off at harvest, leaving behind a vivid white image.

Each year now, corporate clients order significant quantities of apples with logos from the Kelowna Land & Orchard Company, the historic 61-hectare (150-acre) farm that the Bullock family has operated in East Kelowna since 1942. Richard thinks that some clients would find crisp, fresh apples with a corporate message more novel as gifts than baseball caps or pens.

The Raven Ridge Cidery, run by Richard's effervescent daughter Nicole, is a further extension of the apple business and uses the farm's busy market and gift shop as its storefront. Nicole, who was born in Kelowna in 1968 and has a degree in agriculture, credits her father with spotting the idea for cider. "My father was in Quebec a few years ago and saw the ice cider being produced there," she says. The idea sat on the back burner until the fall of 2002, when an unexpected October cold snap settled on the orchard while the three latest-maturing varieties — Fuji, Braeburn, and Granny Smith — remained on the trees. The Bullocks seized the opportunity to salvage apples no longer suitable for the fresh market and the Raven Ridge Cidery was conceived. "My mom, Jacqui, was the one who put up the money," Nicole says. "My brother, John, is the one that grows the fruit, and I do the rest." In 2007, faced with unsold D'Anjou pears on their trees, the Bullocks added a pear ice cider to the portfolio.

There is a long tradition of entrepreneurship here. The original Kelowna Land & Orchard Company was established in 1904, one of five land companies that developed Kelowna. The company that carries the name today was acquired in 1942 by Romanian immigrant John Bullock, Richard's father. It is still one the largest apple producers in the Okanagan. However, to counter cycles in the orchard trade, the Bullocks have exploited the tourist potential of their site. The farm occupies a plateau commanding a postcard-perfect view over the city and Okanagan Lake to the southwest. Tourists trek here every season for orchard tours, visits to the petting zoo, and elegant lunches at the Ridge restaurant. The ravens swooping across the skyline inspired the cidery name.

To take advantage of the October 2002 freeze, the Bullocks had to move fast. Not having a winery or a winemaker at the farm, they struck a deal with nearby Pinot Reach Cellars (now Tantalus Vineyards) to ferment and bottle the ciders. Subsequently production facilities were installed in a century-old barn on the Bullock farm. Winemaker Roger Wong, now at Gray Monk, makes the ciders and, occasionally, apple wine. Born in Vancouver, Roger started on a totally different career before falling passionately into wine. His 1987 degree from the University of British Columbia is in urban and economic geography. He became a cartographer and then a technical records keeper with the federal Department of Energy, Mines and Resources. But in 1995, chafing at his nine-to-five routine, he left the civil service and volunteered to help Tinhorn Creek pick its grapes that fall.

Roger, who had made wine as an amateur for a number of years, began working in Tinhorn Creek's cellar in 1996. He moved to Pinot Reach in 1998 and then to Gray Monk in 2005, while continuing to look after Raven Ridge's winemaking. The concept of ice cider is inspired by icewine. Unlike icewine, there are no stringent production rules for processing apples. Most producers of ice cider in eastern Canada simply freeze the apples commercially. Nicole says she would prefer to wait for nature to do the job, if only because "it makes a better story."

Raven Ridge, which produces about 4,500 litres (1,000 gallons) each year, chooses not to blend the three apples into a single cider. "We thought of it but I don't think it would fly," Nicole says. "People like varietals." The pear ice cider is attractively spicy. The product made with Granny Smith apples, notable for their natural acidity, is so tart and crisp that it has been served in the Ridge as a palate cleanser between courses. The cider made with the juice of Fuji apples, which are high in sugar, has a softness and sweetness appropriate to an after-dinner drink. The Ambrosia cider, with soft acidity, has flavours true to the apple itself. The most popular, Nicole says, is the ice cider made from the juice of Braeburn apples, a variety with good sugar and balancing acidity. "You can serve this instead of sherry before dinner," she says. It has flavours of caramel and baked apples, finishing with notes of spice and smoke. "To me it's the way a good hand-rolled cigar finishes," she says.

REAL ESTATE WINERY

OPENED: 2002 (AS GLENUGIE WINERY)

> 3033 – 232nd Street, Langley, BC
> V2Z 3A8
> 604.539.9463
> 866.233.9463 (toll free)
> www.realestatevineyards.com
> When to visit: Open 10 am – 6 pm
>   Monday through Saturday, 11 am –
>   5 pm Sunday

RECOMMENDED

CURRENT RANGE NOT TASTED

BACKYARD VINEYARDS

PROPOSED OPENING: 2010

> 29418 Simpson Road,
>   Abbotsford, BC
> When to visit: To be established

RECOMMENDED

CURRENT RANGE NOT TASTED

THE PUN WAS INTENDED WHEN REAL ESTATE WINERY WAS CHOSEN IN MID-2008 to replace Glenugie as this winery's name. Proprietor Ewen Stewart has made a living in real estate development ever since, in his fourth year at the University of Manitoba, he dropped out of science classes "to make some money." After buying Glenugie late in 2007, Ewen retained Vancouver marketer Bernie Hadley-Beauregard to rebrand the winery as well as to begin branding Pepin Brook Vineyards, his other winery project in the Fraser Valley.

Bernie has made a career by creating edgy winery names (Blasted Church, Dirty Laundry, just to name a few). Some of his ideas for Glenugie — such as Dangling Carrot — were too far out for the developer. But the developer did accept Backyard Vineyards for Pepin Brook and Real Estate for Glenugie.

"It seemed to us that the Glenugie name was a non-starter in the wine industry," Ewen said. A single malt distillery operated under that name in Scotland from 1834 until closing in 1983. However, that was not where the winery got its name. Founders Gary and Christina Tayler both had Scots roots. Her family once had a farm in the glen (or valley) of the Ugie River. That inspired the winery's original name. The winery was sold after the deaths of Christina in 2006 and Gary in 2007.

Gary had been both a real estate developer in the Fraser Valley and, in the 1980s, a grape grower in the Okanagan. He retired from construction in 1997 and made the sentimental decision to plant enough Pinot Noir on his property near Langley to make his own wine. Somehow a few vines grew to two hectares (five acres). Since that was far more than any home vintner needed, the Tayler family found itself developing a winery. As Gary said at the time, "You can't start off in a garage any more." He erected a functional winery whose unusual slit windows recalled a fortress. That was intentional. The windows are narrower than a human head and would, Gary hoped, deter thieves from breaking into the winery. It was this building and its superb winemaking equipment that caught Ewen's eye when Gary's family sold the winery.

Born in Winnipeg in 1948, Ewen moved to British Columbia in 1981. He found a niche as a developer who salvaged problem projects. That was how he got into the wine business in 2006 by taking over Pepin Brook Vineyard Estates not far from Abbotsford International Airport. Another developer had begun developing a subdivision here for about 235 homes on a remediated former gravel pit. In order to extract the property from the land freeze and have it rezoned for housing, the developer agreed to plant grapes and build a winery on 12 hectares (30 acres), about a third of the total property. The project went into receivership and Ewen took it over, agreeing to the ironclad condition that housing would be allowed only if the vineyard and winery went ahead.

Ewen had to replant practically all of the vineyard in 2007 because the vines in the initial planting had died from lack of water. After upgrading the irrigation system, he planted seven hectares (17⅓ acres) with seven varieties, including Pinot Noir and Pinot Gris, and left room to add up to three more hectares of vines. All are cool-climate varieties except for a small block of Merlot. "We did it as an experiment," Ewen says, adding hopefully that "Abbotsford does get pretty warm in comparison with the coast." As a cellar and winery was being designed for the Pepin Brook site, nearby Glenugie came on the market for $2.8 million.

Rather than be deterred by the stiff price tag, Ewen spotted immediate synergies between the projects. Glenugie had capacity to spare: it is a 20,000-case winery that had been making between 2,500 and 5,000 cases per year. Ewen reasoned that using Glenugie to make most of Pepin Brook's wine would get those wines on the market quickly, providing the revenue that start-up wineries seldom have in their first years. While some wine is being made at Pepin Brook's temporary facilities, Ewen is taking his time to build a winery with a tasting room commanding views of Mount Baker.

The residential subdivision retains the Pepin Brook name, taken from a nearby creek. However, Ewen decided to change the winery name. Dipping into the suggestions from Bernie, he chose Backyard Winery. Because the 235 houses also face Mount Baker, more or less, the winery, which is perched on the highest corner of the property, looks over all those backyards. It is also in Vancouver's backyard. The Backyard Winery is scheduled to open in the fourth quarter of 2009.

Ewen believes that his two wineries need to be significant producers and, like Domaine de Chaberton, destination wineries. Three such wineries should anchor the valley's emerging wine tourism. "We looked at it from a financial point of view and decided if we take a minimalist approach, it's going to be a marginal operation. If we think bigger and do this right, it could be a screaming success."

RECLINE RIDGE VINEYARDS & WINERY

OPENED: 1999

> 2640 Skimikin Road, Tappen, BC V0E 2X0
> 250.835.2212
> www.recline-ridge.bc.ca
> When to visit: Open daily 9 am – 6 pm July through September, 10 am – 6 pm April
>   through June and October or by appointment. Licensed picnic patio

RECOMMENDED

> ORTEGA
> SIEGERREBE
> MARÉCHAL FOCH
> PINOT NOIR ROSÉ
> PINOT MEUNIER
> RIDGEPORT

BY LAUNCHING THE RECLINE RIDGE WINERY IN 1999, THE MOST NORTHERLY winery in British Columbia, Michael Smith opened the Shuswap region to wine touring and grape growing. Although the Larch Hills winery opened two years earlier south of Salmon Arm, it is largely self-sufficient for grapes. Recline Ridge stimulated others to plant vineyards by buying locally grown grapes, supplementing the production from its own three hectares (7½ acres) of vineyard.

It's not as if visitors need incentives to visit the Shuswap. The azure and generally placid Shuswap Lake is Canada's capital for houseboats. The nearby Adams River is renowned internationally for the colourful salmon spawning run that coincides with the vintage each fall. For those interested in wine, Recline Ridge and the other nearby wineries, Larch Hills and Granite Creek, are value added and easy to find. Recline Ridge, with its tasting room in a gingerbread log house, is

14 kilometres (nine miles) west of Salmon Arm in the pastoral Tappen Valley, just off the Trans-Canada Highway.

Born in Ottawa, Michael Smith has been a serious home winemaker since 1975. He took to the hobby with ease. When he gave samples of his early wines to his parents, his father accused him of steaming labels from commercial wines. "I was incensed until I realized what a compliment he was paying me," Smith says. The name, Recline Ridge, originated as the label for his home wines, inspired by a ridge in northern British Columbia where he once relaxed in the sun while hunting elk.

The winery decision was somewhat impulsive. Michael was then managing Salmon Arm's cable television company and lived on this country property. It was cleared initially to provide horse pasture, for Susan, now his ex-wife, was interested in riding. A modest plan to plant a few vines for personal use grew by the spring of 1994 into a vineyard large enough to support a winery. Taking a cue from what was growing well at Larch Hills, Smith planted Ortega, Optima, Siegerrebe, Madeleine Sylvaner, Madeleine Angevine, and Maréchal Foch.

Pioneering wine growing in a new region raised a number of challenges, including dealing on one occasion with an inept grape supplier. Smith thought he had planted some Gewürztraminer, only to discover that the flourishing vines were Concord, a variety unsuitable for table wine production. He had to start all over again in that section of his vineyard but with Siegerrebe, a variety he already had and one that is comparable to Gewürztraminer.

The winery opened on July 19, 1999 — fortunately, a Friday when government offices in Victoria were open. "It was an open and closed day," Michael remembers. When a local health inspector discovered that the winery's water supply was the local creek, he ordered the winery closed and threatened to confiscate all the wine. He thought that the water was used in manufacturing the wine. After a few quick phone calls to the Victoria regulator who had approved the winery in the first place, Recline Ridge reopened by mid-afternoon. But Smith was required to put bottled water in the tasting room; to warn guests not to drink the tap water; and ultimately, to install his own chlorination system. For the record, Michael Smith would not add water to his wines. It would be illegal under VQA rules.

Two of the best varieties in his vineyard have been Siegerrebe and Ortega. Both ripen early to sugar levels that produce just over 11 percent alcohol, which is quite enough for the light, fruity style of the wines. The Siegerrebe has been one of Recline Ridge's most popular whites. The debut 1999 vintage of that varietal especially was remarkable in its vivid aromas and flavours.

To supplement his own vineyard, Michael purchased fruit from some of the other small vineyards in the Shuswap area as well as from the Okanagan. At times that has resulted in artful blends. Madeleine Sylvaner and Madeleine Angevine were blended into a light wine called Cuvée Madeleine. While the wine sold well, Michael figured it needed a bit more substance. He added Chardonnay from purchased grapes in subsequent years, producing a summer white now called Shuswap Serenade.

Like other wineries, Recline Ridge has had a strong demand for red wines, satisfied primarily by a sturdy Maréchal Foch made from estate-grown grapes and grapes from elsewhere in the Shuswap. Michael also turns to the Okanagan for varieties that do not thrive this far north. With grapes from a Naramata grower, Recline Ridge produces one of the rare examples of Pinot Meunier, a variety that shares many attributes with Pinot Noir. Michael also offers Pinot Noir from time to time, including a delightful rosé.

The winery has grown to produce about 2,500 cases per year. Recline Ridge sells them not only from its own wine store but through private wine stores and VQA stores. Where many small wineries do not submit wines to the VQA tasting panel — a voluntary panel — Michael has done this from the start. He appreciates the professional feedback that his wines get. VQA also helps to sell the wines.

In 2008 Michael opened a new chapter in his life by listing the winery for sale at just over $2 million. However, he did offer to stay as a consultant or to train the new owner.

RED ROOSTER WINERY

OPENED: 1997

891 Naramata Road, Penticton, BC V2A 8T5
250.492.2424
www.redroosterwinery.com
When to visit: Open daily 10 am – 6 pm April through October, 11 am – 5 pm
    November through March
Restaurant: Lunches on patio daily June and July; weekends May, June, and
    September to mid-October

RECOMMENDED

BANTAM
MALBEC
MERLOT
PINOT NOIR
SYRAH
GEWÜRZTRAMINER RESERVE
PINOT GRIS
PINOT BLANC

RED ROOSTER IS AN ART LOVER'S WINERY. JUST ASK OKANAGAN SCULPTOR
Michael Hermesh, the creator of a work called *Frank the Baggage Handler*. Both the
original and a full-scale copy are on display here, one on the winery grounds and
one in the tasting room.

The statue was commissioned from Michael as the centrepiece for the traffic
circle in front of Penticton's art gallery. It was immensely controversial because it
is a nude male with all its appendages. When vandals destroyed the offending bits,
Red Rooster's founders, Beat and Prudence Mahrer, stepped in to have the sculpture repaired. In 2005 they moved it to the safety of the winery, which already had
a permanent art gallery. Visitors to Red Rooster are comfortable with *Frank*. And

the sculpture fits in well with what general manager Blair Dufty calls Red Rooster's "whimsical" image.

The whimsy is the legacy of the Mahrers, who ran the winery until Andrew Peller Ltd. bought it from them during the 2005 vintage. They had arrived in the Okanagan in 1990 from their native Switzerland, where they had owned fitness centres. Too busy to have conventional pets, they started keeping chickens. They continued this practice in the Okanagan as they converted an apple orchard near Naramata to a vineyard. When they opened a winery, they named it Red Rooster for one of the birds in the coop at the end of the driveway.

For the grand opening in 1997, the Mahrers announced that Prince Charles had been invited. To no one's surprise, he declined the invitation with a polite letter, which hung on the tasting room wall for years. The self-described "fun-loving" owners of the winery replaced him with the winery's rooster, conveniently also called Prince Charles. In Portugal the rooster is thought to bring good luck. It certainly worked for the Mahrers. They outgrew their original winery within five years of its opening. In 2003 they had architect Robert Mackenzie design a new winery six times as large as the first one. The tasting room, now a separate building, is itself the size of that first winery (which is now the Therapy Vineyards winery).

Red Rooster's location and the architecture are eye-catching. Set just beside Naramata Road, the tasting room, with its gabled roof, recalls the genteel country homes that the Austrian aristocrats built in the days of their empire. The striking building does the job: the parking lot usually is full to overflowing during wine touring season.

The winery also caught the eye of Andrew Peller Ltd. when that big Canadian wine company went shopping in the Okanagan in 2005, buying Calona Vineyards and Sandhill Wines early in the year and then Red Rooster when the Mahrers decided they wanted a break. They retained Naramata Bench vineyards which, in 2008, served as the base for their new boutique winery.

As the presence of *Frank the Baggage Handler* shows, the Peller group has not messed with Red Rooster's whimsical image, nor with some of the other great ideas that the Mahrers had. One of them was the winery's Adopt-a-Row Club, which was launched when Beat Mahrer planted a one-hectare (2½-acre) vineyard on the west side of the winery.

This is a canny way to develop a loyal following. The object is to have club members pay $300 to rent a row of 50 vines for a year. In return they get a case of wine (six white, six red). Their names are attached to their rows and their names are displayed in the tasting room. They get a 10 percent gift shop discount (a significant saving for art collectors) and they are first in line for limited-release wines, such as the 145 cases of Red Rooster's first Malbec, released in 2006. The wine was made from grapes grown in the winery vineyard.

Under Peller ownership, Red Rooster's winemaking team has stabilized. In its first decade the winery had five different winemakers, including Beat (who worked with a consultant). The style of the wines, as a result, was a bit of a moving target. Beginning with the 2007 vintage, Karen Gillis became the winemaker. Born in Vancouver, she grew up in a family of chefs. She initially had the same career in mind when she completed a diploma in food technology at the British Columbia Institute of Technology in 1996. But after three years developing food products, she zeroed in on wine and joined Andrés (as Andrew Peller Ltd. was then called) as an assistant winemaker.

She moved to Calona Vineyards in 2006 and then to Red Rooster the following year. Karen's style is solid and practical. As she says: "I take the roll-up-your-sleeves approach to winemaking."

RIVER'S BEND WINERY

OPENED: 2005

15560 Colebrook Road, Surrey, BC V3S 0L2
604.574.6106
www.riversbendwinery.com
When to visit: Open daily 11 am – 6 pm Tuesday through Sunday. Closed Monday

RECOMMENDED

SYRAH
MERLOT
BLUSH
PINOT GRIS
CHARDONNAY

IN ONE OF THOSE LITTLE COINCIDENCES OF THE WINE WORLD, THE FAESSLER surname of the family behind this winery is Swiss German for "barrel maker." That is perhaps one of the few occupations that Court Faessler has not pursued. Born in 1928, he grew up in the Cariboo where his Swiss parents had a homestead. Court left school after the eighth grade and, after picking apples in the Okanagan, began working in construction in Vancouver.

Strongly entrepreneurial, he soon had his own company in 1952, the first of several that supplied wire rope and related supplies to contractors and logging companies. "I sold my company three times and started over," he said in a 2006 interview. "I am still in the wire rope business."

Responding to his agriculture roots, Court and Annette, his wife, found country property in 1990 — a low-lying, swampy duck habitat tucked into a bend of the Serpentine River in South Surrey. After modifying the drainage and adding about 1.2 metres (four feet) of soil, Court transformed it into farmland. "I told everybody I was going to grow grapes," he said. "I wasn't that serious about it. I was born and raised in the Cariboo and had never seen a grapevine. I thought it was a novelty to grow grapes." In 1992 he planted a modest selection of varieties purchased from local nurseries, liked how they grew, and gradually expanded the vineyard until he was growing six hectares (15 acres) of grapes. These included a number of table grapes, and the Faesslers developed substantial fresh-market sales.

"One of the problems with fresh-market grapes was the labour of packing," he recalled. "We had a lot of grapes that we couldn't sell to the fresh market. So I started making wine myself and giving it away at Christmastime and stuff like that." By the late 1990s, inspired by the rising number of Okanagan wineries, Court began expanding plantings of wine varieties and reducing the table grape production. The white wine varieties here include Chardonnay, Pinot Gris, Madeleine Angevine, Madeleine Sylvaner, Gewürztraminer, Pinot Gris, Ortega, Kerner, and some Geisenheim crosses. The reds include Maréchal Foch, Agria, Pinot Noir, Gamay, and Zweigelt.

Winemaking for River's Bend began with the 2003 vintage, with consultants in the cellar, while Court embarked on getting the winery built and licensed. Gary, his son, who is a chef, food writer, and photographer, says he tried to talk his father out of opening a winery. But when his parent went ahead anyway, Gary became involved, both as a manager and in shaping the style of the wines. "I don't oak the whites and I lightly oak the reds," he says. "I am not a fan of big, jammy fruit and high-alcohol wines."

The wine styles here have been in flux because several consultants have cycled through this winery. Starting with the 2007 vintage, winemaking has been done under the direction of Ron Taylor, a veteran of 25 years with Andrés Wines and latterly a busy consultant for several BC wineries. The cellar master as well as vineyard manager at River's Bend is George Phiniotis, the son of veteran Okanagan winemaker Elias Phiniotis.

This was South Surrey's first winery. The winery itself is a functional building with a shaded veranda along the two sides that looks over the vines. It had been constructed for a telecommunications company, and Court snapped it up at a good price when the company went bankrupt. The winery has the capacity to produce between two and three thousand cases per year. The strategy since opening has been to sell chiefly from the tasting room, which is open year-round except Mondays.

River's Bend makes a point of submitting its wines to the Vintners Quality Alliance tasting panel. The VQA seal eases wine onto restaurant lists. "It would be detrimental not to have VQA," Gary says. "They have spent millions on marketing."

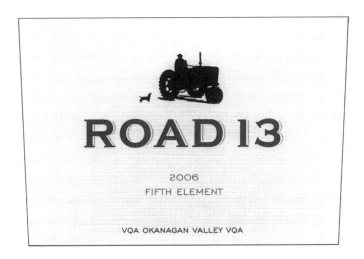

ROAD 13 VINEYARDS

OPENED: 1998 (AS GOLDEN MILE CELLARS)

> 13140 – 316A Avenue, Road 13, RR1, Site 28A, Comp 10, Oliver, BC V0H 1T0
> 250.498.8330
> www.road13vineyards.com
> When to visit: Open daily 10 am – 5 pm from the May long weekend to October 20; by
>   appointment in winter

RECOMMENDED

> JACKPOT SERIES (INCLUDING SYRAH, PINOT NOIR, CHARDONNAY)
> FIFTH ELEMENT RED
> CHARDONNAY
> CHENIN BLANC
> PINOT NOIR
> ZINFANDEL
> HONEST JOHN'S WHITE
> HONEST JOHN'S RED

SOON AFTER PAM AND MICK LUCKHURST BOUGHT GOLDEN MILE CELLARS IN late 2003, neighbouring vintners began asking when they would change the name of the winery. Long before the winery had been established, the west side of the Okanagan Valley south of Oliver was a viticultural district calling itself the Golden Mile (because there once were gold and silver mines in the hills here). In 2008 there was a collective sigh of relief in the neighbourhood when Pam and Mick changed the name to Road 13 Vineyards. "We're giving the Golden Mile name back to the wine industry," Pam said.

Golden Mile Cellars was the name chosen five years earlier by Peter and Helga Serwo when they opened the winery in an eccentric gold-hued castle designed and built by Peter with consummate European craftsmanship. He had been a builder in Germany before coming to the Okanagan in 1966 to grow grapes. They were proud of their castle. But after a winemaking daughter settled in Europe, the Serwos decided to sell. A Calgarian had all but wrapped up the purchase until he said the castle would be pulled down. The Serwos abruptly refused his offer and, in a handshake business deal, sold to the Luckhursts, who respected Peter's design and, partly in sensitivity to the Serwos, waited five years to change the winery name.

The moustachioed Mick calls himself a "high-energy" person. Born in Port Alberni in 1950 and trained in marketing, he has been a lumber broker, a real estate developer, and the operator of a Nanaimo building supply store. He spent a few years as a developer in Edmonton before stress led him to sell the business and take a sabbatical in the Okanagan in 2003. Here wine touring drew the Luckhursts to a new lifestyle. The strenuous farm work on his 14 hectares (34½ acres) of vineyards did not diminish Mick's enthusiasm for this lifestyle. Nor did it did take him long to grasp the importance of growing grapes well on good sites. The slogan chosen for Road 13 is "It's all about the dirt." Manchester-born Pam, a former flight attendant and long a partner in her husband's businesses, runs the tasting room with the same warmth that she and Mick experienced when they started wine touring.

In 2004, the Luckhursts' first vintage at Road 13, the winery made three thousand cases. With their life savings now committed to the wine business, the hard-driving couple doubled production the following year and then doubled it again. "For high-energy people, this growth is what you feed on," Mick says. "I get stressed out but if I didn't have it to do, I'd get stressed out the other way. It is already a lot bigger than we had originally envisioned. But you need to be profitable to weather the bad times and to take advantage of opportunities." One such opportunity was the purchase several years ago of a four-hectare (10-acre) Black Sage Road property. The sun-drenched site has been planted entirely to Rhône varietals, including Syrah, the grape that winemaker Michael Bartier predicts will be the Okanagan's signature red.

Michael joined the winery in 2005 and immediately began making award-winning wines for Road 13. Born in Kelowna in 1967, Michael is a weekend mountaineer and rock climber with a degree in recreational administration. A wine agency sales job after university fired his interest. In 1995 he took a cellar hand's job at Hawthorne Mountain Vineyards (now See Ya Later Ranch), quickly progressing to award-winning winemaking at a succession of wineries. Wines he has made at three different wineries, including Road 13, have taken the prized Awards of Excellence in competitions sponsored by British Columbia's lieutenant governor.

Michael's strengths include his blending skills. "Mike builds every wine," Mick observes. "We have about 35 fermentation vats in our winery." A case in point is Chardonnay, grown in three plots in the Road 13 vineyards. The grapes from each plot and even from different sections in each plot are picked at different times, fermented and aged in individual lots or barrels. Each lot of wine brings its own nuance of flavour and aroma for an ultimate blend that is more complex than the single lots. Fifth Element Red, one of Road 13's flagship wines, is another example. The wines blended for the 2006 release were chosen from the best 29 barrels of red wine among the 279 barrels in the winery.

Between 20 and 25 percent of Road 13's wines end up in the top-tier label, formerly called Black Arts but now called Jackpot (after a long-ago mine in the hills above the Golden Mile). Most of the production is released as varietals under the Road 13 label.

The entry-level wines are Honest John's White and Honest John's Red. Those are named for "Honest" John Oliver, who was premier of British Columbia from 1918 to 1927. He is revered in the South Okanagan, where the town of Oliver is named for him, because irrigation was brought to the region during his time in office.

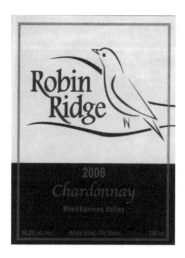

ROBIN RIDGE WINERY

OPENED: 2008

2686 Middle Bench Road, Keremeos, BC V0X 1N2
250.499.5504
www.robinridgewinery.com
When to visit: Summer weekends and during wine festivals

RECOMMENDED

CHARDONNAY
GAMAY
PINOT NOIR
MERLOT
RIDGE RED

TIM COTTRILL INTENDED TO BECOME A PHOTOJOURNALIST AFTER HIGH school, until he decided to treat himself to a year off before going to technical college. "When you take a year off, you might as well throw all your dreams away," he reflects. "You get sidetracked way too easily." But for that fateful decision, however, Tim might never have become a grape grower and, with Caroline, his wife, the owner of Robin Ridge. It seems that he has found another satisfying dream.

The son of a carpenter, Tim was born in Kelowna in 1966 and grew up in Summerland. As a teenager he spent his vacations and school breaks helping his father build houses. He continued to work in residential construction after high school until, at the age of 30, he had had enough. "We were tired of the boom and bust in construction in the Okanagan," he recalls. After looking for something else that involved working outside — something he really enjoys — he and Caroline decided to grow grapes. Caroline was not interested in tree fruits after growing up on a peach farm. "She recognized that grapes seemed to be an up-and-coming thing," Tim recalls. "And you never heard any grape farmers complaining."

In 1996 they found a four-hectare (10-acre) property in the Similkameen, more reasonable in price than raw land in the Okanagan and strategically situated near the valley's popular tourist attraction — the Grist Mill and Gardens on Upper Bench Road near Keremeos. The property was a hayfield on spare, stony soil. "It is really rocky," Tim says. "Grapes don't mind rocks. They always say rocks hold heat. But they are a pain in the butt to a farmer." While waiting for their vines to start producing, the couple found jobs to support themselves and their family of four. Tim became a manager with the local irrigation district while Caroline, with an accounting background, became a manager of a pharmacy in Keremeos.

Tim prepared himself by taking the viticulture course at Okanagan University College in 1997, starting to plant two years later. Chardonnay, now about a third of the 3.2-hectare (eight-acre) vineyard, was planted in 1998, followed by Gamay the next year, Merlot in 2001, and Pinot Noir in 2004. Tim also has small plots of Cabernet Sauvignon, Gewürztraminer, St. Laurent, Rougeon, and Sovereign Coronation, a table grape. "It's all been staggered because I have always worked," Tim says. "I end up doing my own work at night and weekends. It has made for a busy life."

Caroline had begun making wines at home in Summerland, gradually involving Tim in the hobby. When the couple moved to the Similkameen, he was able to increase his production, especially when his own vines started to produce. For several years the Cottrills sold their grapes to other small wineries. In 2005, partly encouraged by the praise Tim was getting for his home wines, the couple began planning their winery. "I told Caroline in the beginning that eventually we would always have wine to drink," Tim says and laughs. "Now we are sometimes too tired to drink it."

As good as his home wines are, Tim has shrewdly enlisted experienced consulting winemakers, notably Lawrence Herder of Herder Winery, to mentor him through his initial commercial vintages. "I need more science," Tim recognizes. "I didn't take much science in school. For me having a consultant is like insurance. I also bought a couple of those Australian [winemaking] books. They are $140 apiece, but if I can learn the equivalent of a couple of hours' worth of consulting from these books, they have paid for themselves."

All the careful preparation paid off. The first wines that Robin Ridge released early in 2008 won acclaim from wine critics and places on the wine lists of good restaurants. The winery opened its attractive tasting room in 2008. However, it is only open periodically at this stage in the winery's life. That is not because the Cottrills have kept their day jobs but because there is not yet that much wine to sell. In the 2007 vintage Robin Ridge made only one thousand cases. "We are not chasing ten thousand cases," Tim says. "We just want to make enough to make a living."

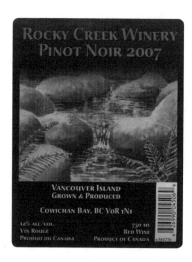

ROCKY CREEK WINERY

OPENED: 2005

1854 Myhrest Road, Cowichan, Bay, BC V0R 1N1
250.748.5622
www.rockycreekwinery.ca
When to visit: Frequent weekend tastings; consult website

RECOMMENDED

PINOT NOIR
PINOT GRIS
ORTEGA
BLACKBERRY

IT TOOK MARK AND LINDA HOLFORD'S ROCKY CREEK WINERY JUST TWO YEARS to outgrow its improbable first location, the basement of their former home in suburban Ladysmith. The five-year business plan with which they started had been realized in half that time. After finding a creative way to launch a winery without a vineyard, they could afford the vineyard. In the winter of 2008 they moved to a three-hectare (7½-acre) farm in the Cowichan Valley. It is unlikely that any other BC winery got established in quite the same way.

Mark is the third generation in his family to make wine at home but the first to go professional, realizing a long-held dream. The ambition was achieved on a shoestring, with a good day job to fall back on: he is an environmental engineer for Vancouver Island pulp mills.

Born in Deep River, Ontario, in 1968, Mark is a chemical engineer with a master's degree in environmental engineering. He met Linda in Calgary, her hometown, when he was completing a co-operative studies assignment with an oil company. She is an engineering technologist with management skills gained in the oil industry.

Because their Calgary home afforded him the space, Mark bought winemaking equipment and began making serious quantities of wine for the household and their friends.

"Ever since I was in my early teens, I helped my dad make wine," Mark recounts. "He did a lot of amateur winemaking and my grandfather in England did a lot." He became a popular student at university, making both beer and wine, and continued to be popular in his social circle. "After a lot of friends asked me to make batches of wine for them, I started to realize that it could be more than just a pastime," Mark says. "It could be something I could do as an occupation."

Before that could happen, however, the Holfords moved to Sarnia, where he worked in a petrochemical plant. Neither put down roots there; instead they started looking for opportunities to move to Vancouver Island. They were drawn by the perception of the cleaner island environment, particularly after visiting Linda's parents, who had retired to Victoria. They moved in the fall of 2001. Any possible hesitation about doing so vanished after the terrorist attacks in New York. "It was comforting coming out to Vancouver Island," Mark says. "The perception is that there weren't any [terrorist] targets out here. Chemical Valley in southern Ontario is definitely viewed as a potential target."

At this point the winery seemed a project they would put off until retirement, or at least until they could finance the vineyard needed for a land-based winery licence. Then they discovered that, in British Columbia, it is possible to open a landless winery with a commercial licence. Only after ordering tanks and other winemaking equipment did they discover that small commercial wineries are barely viable, because they are taxed far more heavily than land-based wineries.

It seemed a fatal setback until they made a critical discovery in the regulations. If their wines earned the Vintners Quality Alliance designation, the government would rebate much of the tax. Mark found (and subsequently leased) a small vineyard in nearby Chemainus. Because his wines were made from BC grapes, and were made well, they breezed through the VQA panel and Rocky Creek was in business. They made 600 cases in the 2005 vintage and nearly 900 cases in 2006. They pushed the capacity of their basement with 1,100 cases in 2007.

Perhaps their biggest concern (aside from negotiating regulations) was that they were selling out too quickly. The key to their following among local consumers and restaurants, aside from a clutch of early awards in competition, was their decision to use only island grapes. As a commercial winery they could have imported California grapes (as New Westminster's Pacific Breeze Winery does). A government official, in fact, pointed out that California grapes might be cheaper. The Holfords remained steadfast, thereby tapping the strong island pride in island-grown produce.

The Chemainus vineyard, which they now manage, gives them Ortega, Siegerrebe, Bacchus, Pinot Gris, and Pinot Noir. In the new Cowichan Valley vineyard, they had planted Maréchal Foch and some of Valentin Blattner's Swiss hybrids. They were also required to plant about a hectare (2½ acres) of blackberries. Rocky Creek's port-style blackberry wine is made mostly with the wild blackberries that thrive in endless abundance on Vancouver Island. In spite of that, recent regulations require fruit wineries to grow some of their fruit, however pointless it seems. The blackberry wine is Rocky Creek's only sweet wine. "We warn people when they come here that we make wines the way we like to drink wines," Mark says. "That means dry."

ROLLINGDALE WINERY

OPENED: 2006

2306 Hayman Road, Kelowna, BC V1Z 1Z5
250.769.9224
www.rollingdale.ca
When to visit: Open daily 10 am – 6 pm

RECOMMENDED

CHARDONNAY
MERLOT
SWEET TOOTH SERIES ICEWINES
PORTAGE ICEWINE

AFTER THE INTIMIDATING GRANDEUR OF THE NEARBY MISSION HILL WINERY, Rollingdale brings visitors back to earth with its rustic informality. Until a planned new winery is built, Rollingdale can be found in a metal-clad industrial building; the approach is from an long, unpaved driveway that winds past the vines. A few vintages ago a portable toilet at one side of the property served (quite efficiently) as the winery's comfort station.

What is not immediately obvious is Rollingdale's most important attribute: since 2007 this has been one of only a small number of wineries that are certified organic producers. Steve and Kirsty Dale, the winery owners, have a long and passionate commitment to organic agriculture. Steve is frank about the reason. "I prefer to consume products that are as clean as they can be," he says. "I like to taste the untouched terroir of a vineyard clearly in the wine."

The Dales — she is his high school sweetheart — have had an interesting journey to this point. He was born in Owen Sound, Ontario, in 1971 and earned a degree in English literature at Carleton University on Ottawa. Kirsty, meanwhile, studied communications at Queen's University. Surprisingly, given that background, they then moved to British Columbia to open a gardening shop in Port Moody, where they specialized in making organic preparations and giving organic advice to local gardeners and greenhouses. After three years they were invited to join a horticultural consulting partnership in Switzerland. They spent four years doing projects around Europe, acquiring a taste for wine along the way.

Steve then sold his interest to his partners and took some time off. "We just wiggled our toes in the sand in Spain for a year," he says with a laugh. "Then we decided we would come back to Canada and open a winery in the Okanagan." In the fall of 2003 he enrolled in the winery assistant course at Okanagan University College, intending to work in a winery after that to hone his experience. As his first practicum he was assigned to help prune a vineyard then leased by the Hainle winery. By lunchtime his employers had learned that Steve wanted a vineyard of his own, and he discovered that they wanted to get out of their lease. "Within a day I had taken over the lease on that vineyard," he says. "It was just like that."

The Rollingdale winery now occupies that vineyard because the Dales, after leasing for a year, bought the property. The site is a strategic location for a winery. Just off Highway 97, it is the first of the six Mount Boucherie wineries that tourists find when driving south from Kelowna. "I didn't have to look very hard," Steve says. "It found me as much as I found it."

The vineyard, then just a little over two hectares (five acres), was divided almost equally between Maréchal Foch and Pinot Gris, with a few rows of Pinot Blanc. Steve admits he was not "too thrilled" with the Foch. He changed his mind late in 2005 when he left some Foch grapes to hang for a few litres of icewine, almost certainly the first time that variety has been used in this way. Steve was so impressed with the result, which he called Portage, that his very limited production of 32 bottles was priced at $840 a bottle. In 2006 nearly all of his Foch became Portage, selling, thanks to the large volume, for $70. Rollingdale has made icewine something of its specialty since opening and has done very well. In a dessert wine show in Spain in 2008, the winery's 2006 Pinot Gris Sweet Tooth Series icewine achieved a perfect score of one hundred.

To supplement the varieties in Rollingdale's vineyard, Steve has contracted grapes from growers in the southern Okanagan. The winery's portfolio includes Chardonnay, Merlot, a Cabernet/Merlot blend, and Pinot Noir. Some of his blends are announced with offbeat labels, such as the 2006 Riewurztrafelser. Described as tasting like a melon ball, the wine long since sold out to visitors who ventured down that dirt driveway and were lucky enough to be taken through a cellar tasting by the passionate winemaker.

Goodbye Ruby Tuesday,
who can hang a name on you....
This wonderful painting for the label was
created by our soul mate and brilliant artist
Jennifer Garant. The shoes represent the dreams
we all have...
Ruby Tuesday Winery produces wines from grapes
exclusively grown on the Naramata Bench. Our inaugural wine
is a blend of Shiraz and Cab. Sauvignon, reflecting the terroir. It
has been aged in new French Oak barrels for 10 months, shows rich
dark aromas, and is being released as a 'first' to celebrate our
comeback into the wine industry.   It's good to be back! Cheers,
Prudence and Beat Mahrer
917 Naramata Rd, Penticton, B.C. V2A 8V1

SHIRAZ CAB. 2007

Product of Canada / Produit du Canada
14.2% alc./vol   Red Wine/ Vin Rouge   750 ml

RUBY TUESDAY WINERY

OPENED: 2009

> 917 Naramata Road, Penticton, BC V2A 8V1
> 250.276.5311
> When to visit: Open daily noon – 5 pm

RECOMMENDED

CURRENT RANGE NOT TASTED

IF THERE WERE A SUPPORT GROUP FOR RETIRED WINERY OWNERS, PRUDENCE Mahrer would have joined it after she and husband Beat sold Red Rooster Winery in 2005 to Andrew Peller Ltd. Even though she had immersed herself in farming the 5.6 hectares (14 acres) of vines the couple retained, she missed the wine business acutely. So when their three-year non-compete agreement expired just after she turned 55, she launched Ruby Tuesday. "I can easily do another 10 to 15 years," she believes.

She has always been fit and seems eternally effervescent. The Mahrers operated fitness clubs in Switzerland until selling that business in 1990 to move to an orchard near Naramata. They began replacing the fruit trees with vines the following year. The original Red Rooster winery, so named because they kept chickens as pets, opened in 1997. When they outgrew those compact quarters, they had architect Robert Mackenzie design the elegant new Red Rooster, which opened in 2004 at a prominent bend on Naramata Road. Ruby Tuesday is next door, on a 1.6-hectare (four-acre) roadside property the Mahrers bought several years earlier to prevent someone from opening a competing winery next door. That was before Naramata Road's winery explosion showed that more wineries attract more visitors.

It has not always been like that. Prudence recalls that it was a struggle for sales when Red Rooster Winery first opened on quiet Debeck Road, nor far from the Naramata fire hall. It was much easier to pull in the visitors at the highly visible second Red Rooster, a winery with three or four times the capacity of the first. That also caught the eye of the Peller wine group when it went on an Okanagan buying spree in 2005.

Freed of running a winery, the Mahrers immersed themselves in their hobbies, including their Piper Super Cub float plane. Both are licensed pilots. However, Prudence stopped flying when she decided to open Ruby Tuesday. The signal to stop, she says, was when her pilot's licence, left in a garment pocket, dissolved in the laundry. "I could have asked for a new one but I said that was just it," she says and laughs.

The couple also travelled extensively — as far north as Tuktoyaktuk and as far south as Baja California. There, in the town of Todos Santos, the legendary Hotel California — memorialized in a song by the Eagles — caught Prudence's artistic eye. She took many photographs of the attractive colonial structure, now the inspiration for the Ruby Tuesday winery, designed by the Mahrers. No matter where they travelled, they always returned to the Okanagan in summer, so Prudence could climb back on her vineyard tractor. Just selling grapes, however, was not fulfilling enough.

Prudence is from the boomer generation, whose musical tastes were shaped by groups like the Eagles (sometimes still played on her home stereo) and the Rolling Stones, the inspiration for the winery name. In 1967 the Stones released an evocative single, "Goodbye Ruby Tuesday," about a free-spirited girl who, Prudence explains, "had a lot of dreams and was following her dreams."

It is an apt parallel for what Prudence is doing. Beat is her partner in the new winery, but it is definitely her dream to return to a business she missed so much. "I said to Beat, 'Listen, we have all the knowledge about the winery. We have all the vineyards.' I love to sell what we produce. That is the most beautiful thing."

She had made up her mind by the 2007 vintage. She hired consulting winemaker Philip Soo to make eight hundred or so cases of red wine so, when the tasting room opened in the spring of 2009, Ruby Tuesday would be offering ready-to-drink Syrah, Cabernet Sauvignon, and Merlot as well as Viognier, Riesling, and Gewürztraminer from the latest vintage. Unlike Red Rooster, Ruby Tuesday is intended to remain a small winery making two thousand to three thousand cases per year, virtually all of it sold personally from the wine shop. "I love to be together with people," Prudence says.

750 ml
Product of Canada

2008
Cherry
fruit wine / vin de fruits

13.7% alc./vol.
Produit du Canada

RUSTIC ROOTS WINERY

OPENED: 2008

2238 Agar Road (Highway 3), Cawston, BC V0X 1C2
250.499.2754
www.rusticrootswinery.com
When to visit: Open daily 10 am – 5 pm (8 pm in summer), by appointment January
    through March

RECOMMENDED

APPLE PEAR WINE
CHERRY WINE
BLACKBERRY (FORTIFIED)

A FEW YEARS AGO ORGANIC FARMERS BRUCE AND KATHY HARKER WERE ASKING themselves whether, as they reached their 60s, it was time to sell the farm and go travelling. Then their sons, Jason and Troy, returned to the farm, along with their families; and daughter-in-law Sara initiated a fruit winery project. That ended any thoughts of selling. "When the kids came on board, all of a sudden, those roots are in pretty deep," Bruce discovered.

Generations deep, in fact. Sam Manery, Bruce's maternal great-grandfather, was the fourth settler's baby born in the Similkameen Valley. His parents settled in 1888 on the same seven-hectare (17-acre) farm that is now being transferred gradually to Bruce and Kathy's children. The Harkers moved to the valley later from Saskatchewan, with Ken Harker, Bruce's father, marrying into the Manery family. Ken is credited with opening the farm's first formal roadside fruit and vegetable shop in 1961. "My two older brothers started a fruit stand here, which they made out of wood boxes, in 1957," Bruce recalls. "At that time, that was not a paved highway, it was a gravel road."

Bruce, who was born in 1950, initially set out to study photography at Langara College in Vancouver. "I realized after spending three years doing that, that my heart was still on the farm," he says. In 1974 Bruce, now married to Kathy, his childhood sweetheart and also a Similkameen Valley native, returned to the farm. The couple began taking over the business the following year, converting the farm to organic practices. They also began wholesaling their produce and that of other Similkameen organic farms to organic food retailers, processors, and restaurants.

Such extensions of the business are all part of staying viable in farming in the face of ever-changing markets. Several years ago one of their most important processing clients, after an ownership change, switched to cheaper fruit sources from the United States. That caused the Harkers to produce their own fruit juices. They were soon selling substantial volumes at their busy fruit stand. But they were distressed that good-quality surplus fruit was still ending up in the compost. They decided it would be a much better idea to make wines with that fruit, reasoning that their fruit stand customers were just as likely to buy wine as other products.

The winery is Sara's project. She was born in Oliver in 1982, a member of a family that had emigrated from Hungary in 1956. The family's settlers' effects at the time included cuttings of Hungarian sour cherry trees. They were grown successfully in Kaleden, and Sara intends to plant some on the Harker farm for future wines.

She comes to wine through the restaurant business. After studying science for a year at Langara and then business administration at Okanagan University College, she spent eight years working at various positions at the Fairview Mountain Golf Course. Troy Harker, her husband, worked in heavy construction in Alberta for several years until the couple decided to return to the Harker family farm. Sara equipped herself for the winery by taking OUC's winery assistant program. To launch the winery the Harkers have enlisted Christine Leroux, a consulting winemaker for, among others, Elephant Island Orchard Wines. Sara plans to spend several years mentoring with Christine.

The winery debuted with wines made from apples, pears, cherries, and blackberries, in both dry table wine and dessert wine styles. One of the dessert wines is an icewine-style product made from the rare Sweet Orin apple. "Our goal," Sara says, "is to produce clean, crisp, fruit-forward wines. We want to showcase the fruit we are using."

Rustic Roots was chosen as the winery name for fairly obvious reasons. Rustic refers to the farm and roots to the generations — now six, counting Bruce's grandchildren — that have grown up here. "It is the association of the generations, the history, and the family that has been here for so long," Sara says. "Our goal in marketing is to focus on those things, and to have our wine shop family-friendly, because that is what we are about — family."

RUSTICO D'ASOLO WINERY

OPENING PROPOSED FOR 2009

31238 – 123rd Street, Oliver, BC V0H 1T0
250.498.2739
www.rusticowinery.com
When to visit: To be established

RECOMMENDED

CHARDONNAY
MERLOT

VANCOUVER MARKETER BRUCE FULLER'S EFFORTS TO OPEN AN OKANAGAN winery are driven by nostalgia. He was first inspired by memories of a village near Venice called Asolo. More recently he has been drawn to the story behind a sprawling sod-roofed log house in the South Okanagan in which he intends to base what he calls Canada's "most romantic" winery.

The story begins in 2003 when Bruce and Daniel Lagnaz, then his winemaking partner, launched wines under the d'Asolo Vineyards label, with 2001 Merlot and 2002 Pinot Gris made for them by Tinhorn Creek. Several subsequent vintages were made by the Mt. Boucherie winery. Bruce, who developed his superb marketing skills during 14 years with the Pattison Group and then in his own businesses, sold the wines to restaurants and private buyers. Although it may seem he had the cart before the horse, he was shrewdly establishing a brand for the future winery.

His initial dream was to build an Italian village in the Okanagan. Bruce has had a fascination with historic villages since his teenage years at Metz, in France, when he explored the gingerbread villages of Alsace. Years later, during a trip to northern Italy, a restaurateur friend introduced him to the quaint village of Asolo. One of Bruce's mementoes is a 1978 photograph of him in front of an Asolo wine shop, glass in hand, in the company of half a dozen Italians made cheery by their morning grappa.

Bruce first proposed the village project to the Covert family, the owners of a historic farm just north of Oliver. When that did not materialize, he acquired control of a former packing house and orchard at Road 8 on Highway 97 south of Oliver. His vivid imagination conjured designs that would have transformed the 780-square-metre (8,500-square-foot) building into a winery and Italian market. After a falling-out with his partners, Bruce moved his dream in 2007 to the log house farther south on the Golden Mile. The dream also shifted from the Italian village to a celebration of the South Okanagan's ranching history. While the financing for the dream was not assured as this book went to press, Bruce's dogged determination continues to move it along.

"I don't think there is any winery that has the story to tell like this one does," Bruce asserts. The 3.6-hectare (nine-acre) vineyard was begun in 1968 by a debonair individual named John Tokias, who came to British Columbia from Hungary in 1951 and who purchased this property, then raw crown land, in 1963. He worked for about 17 years in the silver mines near Beaverdell. As mines started to close, he acquired a log cabin bunkhouse. He relocated it log by log to his Okanagan property, apparently using his Volkswagen truck and a trailer to transport the logs gingerly around mountain highway curves. When he put the cabin back together, he added a massive sod roof. Over the years he hung bleached animal skulls on the exterior, a bizarre decoration only removed recently as Bruce prepared to welcome winery visitors. (The rustic appearance inspired the winery's name.)

Four years after John's death in 2000, his family sold the property to Don and Bonnie Bradley. A former brewer, Don had almost completed a new winery before he and his wife changed their minds and sold it to Bruce. When ill health sidelined Bruce's winemaking partner, he sold the grapes to other wineries and entered strategic agreements for finished wines when the tasting room opens. The proposed portfolio should reflect the major varieties in the vineyard: Merlot, Gewürztraminer, Zinfandel, and one of the few remaining blocks of Chancellor in the Okanagan.

Whether the romance theme or the history theme will win out remains to be seen. Bruce has collected fascinating artifacts from earlier decades, including records and photographs of the Tokias family. Serving history with a glass of wine is never a bad idea.

ST. HUBERTUS & OAK BAY ESTATE WINERY

OPENED: 1991

>5225 Lakeshore Road, Kelowna, BC V1W 4J1
>250.764.7888 | 1.800.989.9463 (toll free)
>www.st-hubertus.bc.ca
>When to visit: Open daily 10 am – 5:30 pm May through October, noon – 5 pm
>   Tuesday to Saturday November through April

RECOMMENDED

>CHASSELAS
>DRY RIESLING
>GEWÜRZTRAMINER
>PINOT BLANC
>MARÉCHAL FOCH
>PINOT BLANC
>ROSÉ
>SPARKLING ROSÉ
>PINOT NOIR ICEWINE
>PINOT BLANC ICEWINE

THERE ARE WINERY TOYS, AND THEN THERE IS ANDY GEBERT'S RADIO-controlled model helicopter, equipped with a camera. Aerial patrols of the vineyard, Andy has learned, are quicker than walking the property. The camera is effective at picking up problems among the vines. The camera also takes great vanity photographs of winery properties. That's why the helicopter is among the several pieces of equipment, including a mechanical harvester, that St. Hubertus rents to its neighbours.

Andy delights in posting aerial shots of the St. Hubertus vines on the winery website. Few Okanagan winery owners enjoy their vineyards like Andy and his brother Leo. Their joie de vivre, infectious in the St. Hubertus wine shop, has survived the severest of tests. St. Hubertus is the only Okanagan winery ever to have burned to the ground when a forest fire in Okanagan Mountain Park swept through the vineyard in 2003. Within 10 days the resilient brothers had reopened a tasting room in a nearby warehouse. Before the season ended they released two wines, Glowing Amber and Fireman's Red, dedicating revenue to a firefighters' relief fund.

As you might guess from the Chasselas on their wine list, they are Swiss. Leo was born in 1958 at Rapperswil, a picturesque agricultural community in the German-speaking part of Switzerland. He trained as a banker and then worked in the United States with a plastics fabricator. But as a student he spent his summers in small Swiss vineyards and ached to be a farmer. In Switzerland, landholdings are small, tightly controlled, and very expensive. In 1984 Leo and Barbara, his wife, moved to the Okanagan, attracted by the mountains and by the chance to buy a substantial vineyard in a single parcel. Subsequently the property, which is conveniently divided by a ravine, was split with his brother when Andy, who was born in 1965, followed him to Canada in 1990.

They have a seamless relationship. "We are brothers, we married sisters, we are neighbours, we are business partners, and that's as close as any family ever should get together," Andy says with a characteristic smile. (His wife's name is Susanne.) In life before wine, Andy spent several years skippering yachts in the Caribbean.

The brothers own one of the oldest vineyards in the Okanagan. It was planted in 1928 by J. W. Hughes, the Kelowna horticulturist who established five commercial vineyards at that time. For many years it was owned by pioneer viticulturist Frank Schmidt, who grew grapes for a winery in Victoria. Schmidt called it the Beau Sejour vineyard. The arched gate at the entrance to St. Hubertus, which surprisingly survived the 2003 fire, has the Beau Sejour name visible on the back of the St. Hubertus sign.

The Riesling block planted here in 1978 still produces excellent fruit, although the Gebert brothers have updated the rest of the varietal profile. Today the 23-hectare (57-acre) vineyards grow the varieties featured in the St. Hubertus portfolio, including Pinot Blanc, Gewürztraminer, Pinot Noir, Gamay, Merlot, and Maréchal Foch. The Chasselas, which is the major white in Swiss wines, was there already when Leo bought the vineyard, planted about the same time as the Riesling. The delicate wine made from these grapes has become the signature wine for St. Hubertus, even selling to Switzerland. "If it weren't a Swiss variety, I wouldn't plant it," Leo admits, concerned with the variety's winter tenderness.

The winery got help to make its early vintages from nearby wineries, including Mission Hill. The current style — crisp, fresh, and fruit-forward — reflects the work of two talented female winemakers. New Zealander Cherie Mirko (now back in New Zealand) was there from 1995 to 2001; Christine Leroux, a Bordeaux-trained Canadian, was there until 2008, when she was succeeded by German-born and

British-trained Hooman Haft Baradaran. For a number of years few barrel-aged wines were made because Leo was "no friend to oak." The barrel-aged Oak Bay wines released in recent years reflect Andy's palate.

The winery's ability to come through the 2003 forest fire was due both to good luck and to preparedness. In one terrifying night just before harvest, the fire roared down the hillside through the vineyard, destroying Leo's heritage home (circa 1930) and the original winery. The ripening grapes were saturated with smoke and fire retardant and were unsuitable for wine. "Even the birds would not eat the grapes," Andy quipped later. St. Hubertus made wines in 2003 with grapes, including Chasselas, made available by neighbouring wineries.

Fortunately nearly all the St. Hubertus wines from 2002 had just been bottled and were in the winery's recently built warehouse, which the fire spared. The brothers quickly opened a new wine shop there and set about erecting a new winery and replacing Leo's home, all of which had been fully insured. "Leo is very religious about that," Andy says admiringly.

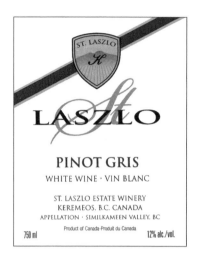

PINOT GRIS
WHITE WINE · VIN BLANC

ST. LASZLO ESTATE WINERY
KEREMEOS, B.C. CANADA
APPELLATION · SIMILKAMEEN VALLEY, BC

Product of Canada-Produit du Canada

750 ml   12% alc./vol.

ST. LASZLO VINEYARDS

OPENED: 1984

Highway 3, Keremeos, BC V0X 1N0
250.499.2856
When to visit: Open daily 9 am – 5 pm and later if necessary

RECOMMENDED

ROSE PETAL
RASPBERRY
PINOT GRIS LATE HARVEST

FOR MANY YEARS ST. LASZLO WAS THE ONLY WINERY IN THE SIMILKAMEEN Valley. Today there are more than half a dozen. Far from being dismayed at the competition, winemaker Joe Ritlop Jr. says: "The more, the merrier." The growing ranks of wineries give the Similkameen appellation the visibility needed to attract visitors and sell wine.

But no matter how many wineries open in the valley, St. Laszlo will always remain unique. The wine portfolio, with both grape wines and fruit wines, is one of the longest in the industry. Most of the products are open in the tasting room. Among the grape wines are American hybrid varieties that no one else grows in British Columbia. "It sets me apart from the rest," the winemaker says.

The winemaker's comment also reflects the Ritlop family's stubborn individualism. His father, also named Joe, launched the winery in 1984 after he could not get other wineries to buy all of his grapes. In a 1985 interview with me, he recalled telling wineries: "If you don't want all of them, I won't sell you any."

"We are not the go-with-the-flow crowd," Joe Jr. acknowledges. Winemaking is resolutely traditional, eschewing the use of sulphur as a wine preservative and using only the wild yeasts that come naturally from the vineyard. Joe Jr. is inclined to think of the certified oenologists employed at some other wineries as chemists. "We are vintners," he says. "We are from the old school of thought." His father once refused a wine writer's request for an interview, saying he was not going to give away the secret of his wines. These days Joe Jr. hints he has wines "on the drawing board" that he is not ready to talk about.

The elder Ritlop was born in Slovenia in 1933, into a family that had been making wine for at least three generations. He came to Canada in 1954 and made a living where he could find it. "In this country you work at what you can get," he told me the year after he opened the winery, initially called Keremeos Vineyards. He and Mary, his Saskatchewan-born wife, came to the Okanagan Valley in 1963 and, seven years later, bought an eight-hectare (20-acre) property on the outskirts of Keremeos. "I find this to be the most favourable climate," he explained later. "I can grow better-quality grapes here than in the Okanagan Valley."

Joe Sr. began planting grapes in 1976. The initial choices reflected an era when vinifera varieties had few champions. Like everybody else, Joe planted hardy hybrids, including Verdelet (still in production), Interlaken, and Clinton. The latter is an old and hardy American hybrid that has been grown as far afield as northern Italy (where it is no longer legal because Europe bans labrusca hybrids).

"I tried to select the hardiest I could," Joe said in 1985. "We have cold winters — a dry cold. So far most of my plants have survived." But while he chose winter-hardy varieties, Joe also took an early gamble on vinifera, including Chardonnay and Gewürztraminer. Among his first plantings was Riesling, which then was just being introduced to the Okanagan and Similkameen valleys. The proliferation at St. Laszlo occurred because Joe planted small test plots of numerous varieties. "Always," he vowed, "I am going to keep many varieties."

One of those freezing winters early in the 1980s snapped across the vineyard when there were still unpicked grapes. Jumping at the opportunity, the Ritlops made icewine. This style of wine was so unfamiliar in Canada at the time that St. Laszlo was prevented from entering it in the Pacific National Exhibition's 1985 wine competition because there was no icewine category. Credit for Canada's first icewine generally is given to Walter Hainle, who made a hobby-sized batch in 1974 (see also Working Horse Winery, page 457). When Walter and his son, Tilman, opened Hainle Vineyards (now Deep Creek) in 1988, they were able to offer icewines from vintages as early as 1978. Technically St. Laszlo could argue that it was the first BC winery to commercialize icewine, since the Similkameen winery opened three years earlier than Hainle. Today Joe Jr. just shrugs. Who was first is not an argument that interests him so long after the fact.

With the perception, or perhaps the reality, that winters have become milder, Joe Jr., who was born in 1957, has added or plans to add some mainstream vinifera to the vineyard. The varieties include Merlot, Pinot Noir, Pinot Gris, and Gamay. "We are evolving," Joe Jr. explains. "We're coming out with a whole new generation of products." He takes credit for being the first commercial winemaker with fruit wines, starting with raspberry.

His most intriguing non-grape wine came about in 2001 when he was asked if he would make a wine from rose petals. When he agreed, he was surprised to get 50 pounds (22.7 kilograms) of rose petals of assorted hues. The result was a wine that was light pink in colour and exotically spicy in aroma and flavour. It is in the St. Laszlo repertoire whenever Joe Jr. gets his hands on rose petals. As for the recipe, it is a brave person who will ask.

ST. URBAN WINERY

OPENED: 2008

47189 Bailey Road, Chilliwack, BC V2R 4S8
604.824.6233
When to visit: Call to ensure the winery is open

RECOMMENDED

CURRENT RANGE NOT TASTED

FOR CHRISTMAS 2003 PAUL KOMPAUER'S GIFT FROM HIS WIFE, KATHY, WAS a framed copy of his family tree. It shows winemakers were in the family in Europe at least since 1740. Paul was a 19-year-old university student when he left Czechoslovakia in 1968, just after Soviet tanks rolled in. While he became a successful civil engineer in Canada, the passion for making wine never left him. Now he has recreated his heritage in a most unlikely place — a flat, four-hectare (10-acre) farm east of Chilliwack, where the Fraser delta runs up against the mountains. "I am a seventh-generation winemaker from Slovakia," he says. "I made my first wine when I was 12, 13 years old, independently. And it was drinkable too."

Paul grew up in the village of Rača, a suburb of Bratislava, the capital of Slovakia, the country that emerged in 1993 when Czechoslovakia split. The Slovak wine route runs along the Danube here, through communities with small vineyards. Paul's older brother, Otto, runs the vineyard that was returned to the family when state-owned farms were disbanded.

After getting his engineering degree from the University of Alberta, Paul moved to British Columbia in 1976 because the milder climate reminded him of home. A specialist in structural engineering, he establishing his own consulting firm in 1986. Kathy, who was born in Winnipeg, is also an engineer, an authority on concrete technology.

In 1989 Paul began searching for a place to grow grapes and make wine. He and Kathy planted a tiny vineyard in Surrey, where they then lived, to grow Bacchus and Ortega. He found a desirable vineyard in the Similkameen Valley but, in a flat real estate market, failed to sell his Surrey home to raise the necessary cash.

Finally, in 2001, Paul and Kathy acquired what was then known as the Back in Thyme Vineyard, just east of Chilliwack and four kilometres (2½ miles) south of the Trans-Canada Highway. A previous owner, a dairy farmer, had planted table grapes about 15 years earlier. The vineyard was taken over by Dennis Sept, who came up with its poetic name. He put in three hectares (7½ acres) of wine grapes, including Madeleine Angevine, Ortega, Kerner, Siegerrebe, and Turan (the alternative name for Agria), selling the fruit to wineries and to amateurs who often won awards with the spicy Siegerrebe.

Dennis's plans for a winery died when a marriage breakdown led to the sale of the property. By the time the Kompauers took over the vineyard in the summer of 2001, it had been neglected for two years. "We had no idea how much we were going to harvest," Kathy says. "We had no idea about the quality. We were taking a big risk. But it was the location. It was an established vineyard on a busy corner."

That fall they were only able to harvest 800 kilograms (1,800 pounds) of Turan, an early-ripening Hungarian vine capable of producing dark, full-bodied, and some-what rustic reds. Turan takes well, however, to oak aging. Paul, who has a taste for moderately oaked reds, has most of it in French oak barrels.

Paul and Kathy have struggled to get the winery open and have had a very low profile in the Fraser Valley ever since. Part of the time was consumed by satisfying various picky inspectors. However, the toughest part was rejuvenating the vineyard and correcting some of the planting errors. "It's been kind of an uphill battle," Kathy said. "It didn't help that the vineyard had been abandoned for two years. We still fight mould issues." Paul decided he had too much Ortega and replaced much of it with Kerner, Zweigelt, Pinot Gris, Maréchal Foch, and St. Laurent. The winery also contracts Pinot Noir from nearby vineyards.

Their farm is one of the hottest locations in the Fraser Valley for growing grapes. In a hot, dry year like 2003, the early-ripening whites achieved enough sugar to yield bold, dry wines with 13 percent or more alcohol. The most significant chal-lenge, however, is the risk of rain in October when grapes still are on the vines. The heavy October downpour in 2003 forced the Kompauers to abandon some unpicked grapes. The next two years also were challenging, especially 2005, when spring rains reduced the fruit set by half. None of this, however, dimmed their determina-tion to develop the Fraser Valley's easternmost winery.

Chilliwack is a long way from the Slovakian wine trail. Nevertheless, Paul and Kathy recreate some of that Eastern European ambiance here. The tasting room décor, including the bright floral entrance, decorative glass in the windows, and two statues of the saint after whom the winery is named, is inspired by Slovakia's cosy wine cellars. "We were once visiting in this little town outside of Bratislava called Pezinok," Paul remembers. "It's an old wine town with a museum of wine and grapes. We went there and found a big party in the little courtyard. They were celebrating St. Urban's Day."

By the end of the merry party the idea had been born of naming his new winery after St. Urban, the patron saint of vineyards. Many Slovakian wine towns have statues of the saint to protect the vines from frost. It is not entirely clear how an individual who was Pope for eight years in the third century achieved this distinction, but tradition has it that spring frost never occurs after May 25, St. Urban's Day.

SALT SPRING VINEYARDS

OPENED: 2003

> 151 Lee Road at 1700 block Fulford-Ganges Road, Saltspring Island, BC V8K 2A5
> 250.653.9463
> www.saltspringvineyards.com
> When to visit: Open daily 11 am – 5 pm June 13 to September 1, noon – 5 pm Friday
>   through Sunday in September, weekends in October, and Saturdays in December
> Accommodation: Bed and breakfast

RECOMMENDED

> PINOT GRIS
> KARMA SPARKLING WINE
> MERLOT
> MILLOTAGE
> BLACKBERRY PORT

IN 2002, THE YEAR BEFORE THIS WINERY OPENED, DEVLIN AND JOANNE McIntyre bought property on Saltspring Island for their eventual retirement home. Six years later, retirement went on the back burner when they bought Salt Spring Vineyards and surrendered to a long-time desire to own a winery. They have had a hobby vineyard, about 70 vines, near Abbotsford since 1985; and they were founders of the Fraser Valley Wine Growers Association, a group of amateur grape growers. Recently they had become so serious about a winery that they had wine-growing friends in France scouting property for them.

Then in the spring of 2008, they learned that Salt Spring Vineyards founders Janice and Bill Harkley wanted to sell their winery. The McIntyres and the Harkleys hit it off and after a brief negotiation that was more like a whirlwind romance, the McIntyres bought 80 percent of the winery, a deal that keeps the founders and their experience available.

Bill was an Air Canada pilot until 2000, when he reached 60, the mandatory retirement age for airline pilots. He and Janice, an accountant and executive coach, had moved to Saltspring in the late 1990s, also to ease into retirement. "We thought, 'Buying land on the waterfront is nice — but when you build such a place, what else are you going to do but sit and enjoy it?' " Bill says, explaining why the couple bought two hectares (five acres) of land suitable for vines. "We liked to be more active." Technically Salt Spring Vineyards was the first of the two island wineries to get a licence, because the Harkleys received their paperwork about half an hour earlier than the owners of neighbouring Garry Oaks Winery.

By coincidence, the two wineries were put on the market in 2008 by their founders. The McIntyres did not consider Garry Oaks because they found soul mates in the Harkleys. "We had a lot of common interests and a lot of common goals," Joanne says. "A sustainable vineyard. Good wine. A beautiful property. We are avid sailors and like to travel. They are the same. We seem to fit together well."

Devlin, who was born in Thunder Bay in 1950, grew up in Regina and got a medical degree from the University of Saskatchewan. Joanne was born in Halifax in 1954. After getting a degree in oceanography, she almost completed a doctorate in microbiology but never got around to defending her thesis because she went to Queen's University to become a doctor. She met Devlin, who was there to become a surgeon. They practised briefly in Saskatoon before moving to Abbotsford in 1984. He spent the next 24 years as a general and vascular surgeon while Joanne worked in general practice.

The Fraser Valley hobby vineyard, still producing, was planted in 1985 to test what varieties would thrive in the coastal climate. Devlin succeeded with Siegerrebe, Madeleine Angevine, Madeleine Sylvaner, Ortega, Reichensteiner, and Schönburger. "We have been growing and making wine in an amateur way since that time," he says. As their interest in wines grew, the McIntyres began vacationing in wine country in Europe and the United States. They also found time to join various wine societies, including the Opimian Society. Devlin developed such a keen palate that he was the top Opimian wine taster in British Columbia three times. Now that they have plunged totally into wine, the McIntyres will only practise medicine to relieve other doctors. "I can't stretch myself too thinly," Devlin says.

Under the new owners Salt Spring Vineyards, which produces about 2,500 cases per year, relies on Saltspring or Vancouver Island grapes for 90 percent of its needs. "We are committed to the concept of producing locally," Joanne says. The top seller is Pinot Gris, a variety suitable to the coastal climate. In their own vineyard they also grow Chardonnay and Pinot Noir, some of which is destined for a bottle-fermented sparkling wine called Karma. In warm vintages the vineyard also produces a Pinot Noir that their winemaker, Paul Troop, turns into award-winning table wine. The only Okanagan wine here is a Merlot, for which the winery has an established following. "There are still people who want that big red," Devlin says. "And I very much like the wine."

It is not the winery's only big red. From a blend of Maréchal Foch and Léon Millot the winery makes a soft and juicy red called Millotage (a name created by Janice Harkley). And from the abundant local blackberries, the winery makes a port-style wine. "It is so popular," Devlin says. "We have to cut off sales around the first of July so we have some left over for people to buy as Christmas presents."

SANDHILL WINES

OPENED: 1999

> 1125 Richter Street, Kelowna, BC V1Y 2K6
> 250.762.9144 | 1.888.246.4472 (toll free)
> www.sandhillwines.ca
> When to visit: Calona Vineyards wine shop open daily 9 am – 6 pm June through
>   December, 9 am – 5 pm January through May

RECOMMENDED

> CABERNET FRANC
> CHARDONNAY
> GAMAY
> PINOT GRIS
> SANDHILL *ONE*
> SANDHILL *TWO*
> SANDHILL *THREE*
> ALL SMALL LOTS WINES (INCLUDING BARBERA. MALBEC. PETIT VERDOT.
>   SANGIOVESE. SYRAH, VIOGNIER)

SANDHILL WAS LAUNCHED IN 1999 AS A PRESTIGE LABEL OF CALONA Vineyards and has evolved into a stand-alone winery. While the wines have been made at Calona's cavernous winery for more than a decade, sites are reserved for a future winery on the Sandhill Estate Vineyard on the Black Sage Bench. Sandhill requires its own winery, if only to underline the distinctive philosophy behind the superb winemaking here. Every Sandhill wine is made from a single vineyard, not from a blend of fruit from several vineyards. The object is to show the terroir, or the personality, of the vineyards that supply the winery.

In the 1960s Calona partnered with grower Richard Stewart to plant the first substantial vineyard on Black Sage Road. When a Montreal conglomerate took over Calona in 1971, the vineyard was sold and Calona just bought grapes. History went full circle at the end of the 1990s, after Swiss investors acquired Calona. By then Burrowing Owl Vineyard founder Jim Wyse had replanted 116 hectares (287 acres) of Black Sage vineyard with premium vinifera grapes that Calona was buying once again.

In 1996 Jim and the Swiss formed a joint venture to develop the Burrowing Owl winery, coincidental with the creation of Sandhill. When the joint venture was unwound in 2002, the Wyse family ended up in control of the Burrowing Owl winery and 46 hectares (114 acres) of vineyard, leaving Sandhill with the remainder. The latter portion was also renamed Sandhill Estate Vineyard to eliminate the confusion that occurred when both wineries had the Burrowing Owl name on their labels.

The vines at Sandhill, most of which were planted between 1994 and 2000, have now reached their productive prime. The largest blocks are Merlot, Cabernet Sauvignon, Cabernet Franc, Syrah, and Chardonnay. There are slightly smaller blocks of Pinot Gris, Sauvignon Blanc, and Gamay. As well there are 1.5 hectares (3¾ acres) of Sangiovese and almost as much Barbera, the first examples of these Italian reds in the Okanagan. Winemaker Howard Soon releases these varietals on their own and also blends them with Merlot and Cabernet Sauvignon in Sandhill *three,* a wine inspired by Italy's Super Tuscan blends.

Richard Cleave, the veteran vineyard manager who supervises the Sandhill vineyard with his partner Robert Goltz, also runs his own Phantom Creek vineyard, only three hectares (7½ acres) in size. It was planted in the late 1990s just across the road from Sandhill, primarily with Syrah, Cabernet Sauvignon, and some of the Okanagan's first Malbec and Petit Verdot. In 2000 he asked Howard to make wine from his grapes. Howard was so impressed by the grapes that he rolled Phantom Creek into Sandhill's wine program. Syrah is grown both here and across the road at Sandhill but, in the Sandhill philosophy, the grapes are not mixed but made into distinctive vineyard-designated wines. Side by side tastings of the wines — the Phantom Creek is the richer of the two — validate Sandhill's dedication to what it calls "a true expression of the vineyard."

Just north of Phantom Creek is Robert Goltz's 4.8-hectare (12-acre) Osprey Ridge Vineyard. Sandhill's Viognier is grown here. The fourth vineyard currently in the Sandhill program is the 17-hectare (42-acre) King Family Vineyard on the Naramata Bench just north of Penticton. Brothers Don and Rod King, whose family has had an orchard here since the 1930s, replaced the fruit trees with vines in the early 1990s. When Calona began making award-winning Pinot Gris from the King vineyard, Howard launched a Sandhill Pinot Gris in 2001.

The Sandhill wines turned Howard into a late-blooming star winemaker. The grandson of a shopkeeper who emigrated from China in the 1880s, Soon was born in Vancouver in 1952. A University of British Columbia biochemistry graduate, he spent several years as a brewer before joining Calona in 1980. There he moved through the ranks from quality control to the wine master. Witty and engaging, Howard also is one of the Okanagan Valley's most popular wine educators.

The single-vineyard philosophy does not exclude blends, because Howard makes excellent blends from within each vineyard. Phantom Creek's flagship red, first made in 2000, is Sandhill *one*, with Cabernet Sauvignon as the backbone, supported with Petit Verdot, Malbec, and Merlot. By comparison, Sandhill *two*, also first released in 2000 but from Sandhill Estate fruit, is a blend of Cabernet Sauvignon with Merlot and Cabernet Franc.

The winery's Small Lots program, which began in 1999 with Barbera and Sangiovese, is Sandhill's reserve range. The wines are so named because production is limited. In the 2006 vintage, for example, the winery made only 338 cases of Sandhill *two* but, from the same vineyard, 5,466 cases of a Cabernet/Merlot blend.

To ensure that the terroir comes through, Howard has a light touch with oak or, in the case of the Pinot Gris, uses none at all. "Oak should not be the dominant factor in the aroma or taste of a wine," he maintains. "The core flavour of the wine comes from the vine, not from the barrel."

SANDUZ ESTATE WINES

OPENED: 2006

> 12791 Blundell Road, Richmond, BC V6W 1B4
> 604.214.0444
> www.sanduzwines.com
> When to visit: Open daily 11 am – 6 pm

RECOMMENDED

DRY BLUEBERRY
BLUEBERRY PORT
WHITE CURRANT
GOOSEBERRY
GEWÜRZTRAMINER
MERLOT

YOU HAD BETTER STICK TO TEA IF YOU CAN'T FIND SOMETHING TO SUIT YOUR palate in the elegant Sanduz wine shop, which happens to be at the geographic centre of Richmond. There were 27 grape and fruit wines available during one recent visit, ranging from an austere Alsace-style Gewürztraminer to seven dessert wines and two port-style fruit wines. The most popular are the several blueberry wines, from dry to port in style. "It's blueberry heaven here," co-proprietor Neeta Sandhu says with tinkling laughter.

So it would be. Neeta and Dave Sandhu, her husband, are among Richmond's leading growers of blueberries. They farm about 57 hectares (140 acres), sell locally and export internationally. Taking the lead from research in Japan on the health benefits of blueberries, they have developed products to make the blueberry a year-round food. The winery is a value-added extension to their business.

"There is no farming background in our families," Dave says. Born in India in 1966, he came to Canada with his parents when he was four. Nor sure what career he wanted, he studied business administration at Kwantlen College but also took courses qualifying him to work as a bailiff. Then, with a brother-in-law, he invested in a Fraser Valley farm, looking for a quick profit on real estate. There were blueberries on the property. "The only experience we had had with blueberries was as kids in Richmond," Dave admits. "You'd go pick and make a couple of bucks."

They were lucky enough to have bought the farm a month before harvest. The bushes were heavy with berries and prices were favourable. "We got the labour force in, picked the harvest, and made some good money at it," Dave recalls. Even though his father cautioned him that the family had no farming experience, he quickly leased or bought substantial acreage to become one of British Columbia's biggest blueberry producers.

Neeta, who was also born in India but raised in Canada, entered the wine business from an even more unlikely background. She has a social sciences degree from Ottawa University, with a major in criminology. After graduating, she joined the federal immigration department. Over a 12-year career there she worked in a variety of positions, including front-line jobs as an officer at the Vancouver International Airport. "I denied entry to people," she recalls. "I have done quasi-judicial inquiries. I've done policy and human resources. Then I said, 'I've done it all now. I want something else.' "

When one of Dave's Japanese customers ordered blueberry skins (to be powdered for cooking uses), the couple had to figure out what to do with the blueberry juice. They were introduced to Ron Taylor, the former Andrés winemaker who has reinvented himself this decade as British Columbia's busiest fruit wine consultant. The Sandhus quickly engaged him to develop their winery. "I am only an occasional wine drinker," Dave says, explaining the need to hire an experienced professional.

Ron, who has rarely seen a grape or a fruit that cannot be turned into wine, convinced Dave and Neeta to have a large portfolio. The amazing selection includes white gooseberry, which produces a uniquely smoky wine that seems to have more in common with Sauvignon Blanc than the berry. There is wine from cranberries, raspberries, strawberries, currants, Granny Smith apples, crabapples, and blackberries. And more.

"I want to have something for everyone," Neeta says. Thus the winery added a selection of grape wines (Merlot, Pinot Noir, Gewürztraminer, Cabernet Sauvignon, and Pinot Gris), with fruit from the Okanagan. The regulators required that Sanduz plant a small vineyard of its own. In 2007, on a corner of the Richmond property, Dave and Neeta planted just under a hectare (about two acres) of Reichensteiner vines. This white variety, created in Germany in 1939, matures to high sugar levels in cool climates. It is one of the most widely planted varieties in England, where the maritime wine-growing climate is somewhat similar to that of Richmond.

If that is not enough to choose from, there is more to come. If the grapes are available, Ron will make Viognier. He has also been developing blends of fruit and grape wine, based, of course, on blueberry.

SATURNA ISLAND FAMILY ESTATE WINERY

OPENED: 1998

8 Quarry Road, PO Box 54, Saturna Island, BC V0N 2Y0
250.539.5139 | 1.877.918.3388 (toll free)
www.saturnavineyards.com
When to visit: Open daily 11 am – 4:30 pm May 1 to October 12
Restaurant: Bistro open daily 11 am – 3:30 May 1 to October 12

RECOMMENDED

PINOT GRIS
GEWÜRZTRAMINER
PINOT NOIR
VINSERA FORTIFIED WINE

WITH FOUR VINEYARDS TOTALLING 24 HECTARES (60 ACRES) ON SATURNA
Island, this is the largest single planting of grapes on any of British Columbia's Gulf
Islands. The project took root during a jolly lunch in 1995 at Le Gavroche, one of
winery owner Larry Page's favourite Vancouver restaurants. A veteran securities
lawyer, Larry had partnered with a group to develop ocean-view housing on Saturna,
including a lot where he built a home for his family. After the lot plan was drawn
up, there remained 31.5 hectares (78 acres) of dormant farmland on a sunny slope.
Jean-Luc Bertrand, who then owned Le Gavroche, convinced Larry to plant vines
and moved there to develop Rebecca's Vineyard, the first of four planted between
1995 and 2000. Sadly, Jean-Luc died in 1997. Okanagan winemaker Eric von Krosigk
completed the plantings and for a number of years made the wine.

Initially Larry also owned a lodge on Saturna, but after selling it he opened a
winery bistro and added a permanent dock for the passing boaters. Within a few
years the bistro was serving as many as one hundred lunches per day in the peak

summer season. And Larry began planning a new lodge on the vineyard, another measure to generate sales for a winery that is hard to get to if you are not a boater.

Saturna Island's rich history adds colour to this winery. The island was named in 1791 after the seven-gun Spanish schooner *Saturnina*, one of the Spanish ships exploring the BC coast. Saturna is among the least-populated of the Gulf Islands (about three hundred residents). When Larry bought the farm that has become the vineyard, he discovered that the issue of the farm's beach access had triggered considerable litigation. The individual who purchased the farm in 1936 turned it over a decade later to his daughter and son. The property was divided after the two had a falling-out, with Robert Thomson, the son, settling in a beachfront cottage and leasing his farm acreage to his sister and her husband. He agreed to let them use a road across his land when they needed to send their sheep to market or to bring in materials.

Some of those sheep were destined for the renowned Saturna Beach lamb barbecue, which became an annual tradition after the first one in 1950. When Thomson decided to sell his property, including the leased acreage, in 1987, he said there would be no more beach barbecues. His sister, Jean Campbell, went to British Columbia Supreme Court, demanding beach access along the road, called Quarry Trail. She won there, and again at the Appeal Court, but she could not persuade her brother to sell her the farm. In 1990 he sold it to Larry — who allowed the annual lamb barbecue to resume.

The south-facing vineyards back against a soaring granite cliff that stores the heat of the day, releasing it to the vineyard during the cool evenings. Rebecca's Vineyard, named for Larry's daughter, grows Gewürztraminer, Pinot Gris, Pinot Noir, and Merlot. Robyn's Vineyard, named for Larry's wife, was planted in 1996 with Pinot Noir, Chardonnay, and Pinot Meunier. In 1998 and 1999, the five-hectare (12-acre) Longfield Vineyard was planted exclusively to Pinot Gris on a plot that had been called the long field in its previous farming history. The final block that was planted, beginning in 2000, has been called Falconridge because of the abundant population of falcons on the cliff above. A few more hectares remain to be planted, likely with Gewürztraminer.

In the winery's first five years, Saturna purchased Okanagan grapes until its nascent vineyard began to produce. When the winery began selling wine in 1998, it had 4,400 cases, all from Okanagan grapes. The winery stopped importing Okanagan grapes in 2003 and now relies on its own vineyards. Larry believes that the winery, which was established in 2001, can produce between 10,000 and 12,000 cases per year from its grapes. That is in an optimal vintage. In 2007 cool temperatures and rain at the wrong time resulted in small yields and a production of only 2,700 cases. After getting advice from Richard Cleave, the Okanagan's leading vineyard consultant, Larry was able to improve the yields in 2008.

SEA CIDER FARM & CIDERHOUSE

OPENED: 2007

> 2487 Mount St. Michael Road, Saanichton, BC V8M 1T7
> 250.544.4824
> www.seacider.ca
> When to visit: Open 11 am – 7 pm Wednesday through Sunday and on holiday
>   Mondays

RECOMMENDED

> KINGS AND SPIES CIDER
> PIPPINS
> RUMRUNNER CIDER
> POMMEAU CIDER

THE TASTING ROOM WINDOWS AT SEA CIDER LOOK OUT ON APPLE TREES AND, BEYOND the orchard, on Haro Strait. Those waters, Kristen Jordan believes, were plied by rum-running speedboats during the American Prohibition. Those accounts inspired her Rumrunner Cider, a tasty cider whose flavours are enriched by having been aged in barrels once used for Newfoundland's famous Screech rum. The product also marks Jordan for what she is: an original thinker on the subject of apple ciders.

"You are probably not as interested in apples as I am," she suggests. "It's all that I think about and all that I talk about." Her passion for apples began in her teens, when she inherited a Shuswap orchard. Now its heritage apples are among several sources of fruit for her ciders.

She developed a taste for classic ciders as a student at Atlantic College in Wales from 1985 to 1987. "I was always drawn to the cider," she recalls. "There was a small pub on campus and there were small pubs in two of the nearby villages. You could have a glass of cider, enough to be social."

Raised in Medicine Hat, Kristen first worked as an international consultant after studying economics at McGill. She spent three years working on Ethiopian agriculture projects. "All my mother's side are farmers and ranchers," she explains. When civil war flared up, she went to France to study economic geography and then, after a brief return to Ethiopia, did post-graduate work at Yale on food security issues. She worked several years for the United Nations before joining a Victoria consulting firm. In that city she met husband Bruce, a lawyer and former rugby player. After a lengthy search for a cider property, they found a former sheep farm on the Saanich Peninsula. They planted 50 varieties of apples on four hectares (10 acres) and built a cidery in 2006.

Sea Cider and the Merridale Cidery in the Cowichan Valley, unlike most of British Columbia's other cider producers, rely primarily on European cider apple varieties or heritage varieties rather than the dessert apples found in grocery stores. "The European apples give you quite an earthy, full-bodied cider, like a very big beer or a tannic wine," Kristen says. "The [heritage] North American apples give you more of a crisp and clean, high-acid product, like a really dry, acidic Riesling with quite a fruity nose." That aptly describes her effervescent cider, called Kings and Spies; one of the varieties is Northern Spy.

Kristen and Bruce, who no longer practises law, immersed themselves in the craft of cider by taking courses at Washington State University. In 2008 Alistair Bell, a fermentation scientist at the University of Victoria, joined them, bringing more than a decade of experience as a cider maker. "It is much like white winemaking," he says. And the ciders, with a tangy crispness and a touch of effervescence, do resemble cleanly made white wines.

Certain ciders, notably Rumrunner, derive character from aging in barrels. "Some cider makers in the UK use old Scotch barrels," Kristen says she found when she researched cider history. "There is a disconnect between the flavours." A British cider consultant advised her to find rum barrels. "We looked all over for barrels and found Newfoundland Screech barrels." Those are oak barrels originally used to age bourbon and then used by the Newfoundland and Labrador Liquor Corporation to age the Jamaican rum it sells under the brand Screech. The residual rum flavours enrich the taste of Kristen's cider, which acquires a pleasing fullness during its time in barrel. Subsequently Kristen and Alistair have begun cider trials using bourbon barrels.

Sea Cider has endeavoured to raise the image of ciders by packaging them elegantly in glass bottles patterned on traditional British ginger beer bottles. "Typically in the US and in Canada, you find cider in beer bottles," Kristen says. "It kind of gets plunked in with beer, and it really has much more in common with wine than with beer." The other advantage of glass, she notes, is ciders can be aged to develop additional complexity in the bottles. "This whole thing is about resurrecting a lost tradition," Kristen says of cider making. "It was such an important industry 100 to 150 years ago. That's all changed now. When we started looking into the history of orchards and cider making, it was like discovering a lost art in North America."

SEE YA LATER RANCH AT HAWTHORNE MOUNTAIN VINEYARDS

OPENED: 1986

Green Lake Road, PO Box 480, Okanagan Falls, BC V0H 1R0
250.497.8267
www.sylranch.com
When to visit: Open daily 9 am – 5 pm

RECOMMENDED

BRUT
PINOT 3
JIMMY MY PAL
PING
RIESLING
CHARDONNAY
GEWÜRZTRAMINER
EHRENFELSER ICEWINE

SEE YA LATER RANCH IS THE OKANAGAN'S ONLY WINERY WITH A PET CEMETERY beside its century-old tasting room — and with a dog on the labels of its wines. Tourists travelling with dogs are welcome here. This winery revels in its rich and colourful canine-filled history, so much so that two of its wines — Ping and Jimmy My Pal — are named for dogs that once lived here and, of course, are buried here.

The viticulture here is also remarkable. At an elevation of 536 metres (1,759 feet), this is the highest vineyard in the Okanagan. The largest part of this 40.5-hectare (100-acre) vineyard is planted to Gewürztraminer, believed to be the single largest block of that variety in North America. The vines are a massive green blanket across the slopes of Hawthorne Mountain. The recently erected electric bear fence around the perimeter is a reminder that this is on the Okanagan's frontier.

At the beginning of the past century this was the homestead of two brothers named Hawthorne. The property's colourful history began when it was purchased by a Montrealer named Major Hugh Fraser, shortly after World War I. According to research done by the winery, Fraser came to the Okanagan to visit a playwright friend and liked the wide open spaces so much (he had spent two years as a German prisoner of war) that he stayed.

There is an apocryphal story that he brought a British bride, who soon returned to Britain from the isolation of Hawthorne Mountain, leaving a note signed "See Ya Later." The major lived most of the rest of his life with a succession of 12 dogs, burying each one under its own headstone. A few years ago the headstones were all placed in a circle under a tree in front of the tasting room.

A more pedestrian explanation for See Ya Later was uncovered by the winery's recent research. The major was "a prolific letter-writer, staying in touch with dignitaries around the world . . . He would end each letter with the signature phrase 'See ya later.' " That phrase came to identify the ranch.

In 1961, five years before retiring to Penticton at the age of 81, the major planted the first vineyard with such varieties as Maréchal Foch, Chelois, Buffalo, and Bath for Andrés Wines. The grapes were sold commercially until Albert LeComte established the LeComte Estate Winery here in 1986. He made an inspired choice when he replaced Buffalo, a coarse labrusca variety, with Gewürztraminer, with which he soon was making medal-winning wines. That caught the attention of Sumac Ridge founder Harry McWatters, who needed more Gewürztraminer grapes to support his winery's most successful wine. When LeComte sold the winery in 1995, Harry bought it and renamed it Hawthorne Mountain Vineyards. The name changed to See Ya Later a decade later, a few years after Vincor bought both it and Sumac Ridge.

See Ya Later started as the label for the premium wines made at Hawthorne Mountain until Vincor decided to phase out the Hawthorne Mountain brand and, at the same time, get some mileage from the lively history of the major and his love of pets. Before he died in 1970, the major was active in the Society for the Prevention of Cruelty to Animals. According to a profile of him for the Okanagan Historical Society shortly before his death, he still had two collies named Lassie and Goldie and a 19-year-old parrot. Some of the revenue from the sale of Jimmy My Pal, a white blend, has been contributed to the SPCA.

The heritage home now serving as the tasting room was built by the Hawthorne brothers. Recent renovations have preserved its heritage qualities, notably in a private function room, while turning the house and its shady patio into an immensely relaxing stop on any wine tour. However, there have seldom been tours of the winery itself. The antique building did not make many good impressions because sanitation was so challenging. Eric von Krosigk, who was the winemaker there for a couple of vintages in the mid-1990s, complained about fishing frogs from the wine tanks. Finally, in 2007, Vincor moved wine production to its well-equipped and well-scrubbed Jackson-Triggs winery at Oliver.

That was the same year in which See Ya Later winemaker Dave Carson also became the senior winemaker in the Vincor group, a promotion that speaks volumes about his winemaking skills. Raised in Kelowna, he is deceptively quiet-spoken for someone who was formerly a nationally ranked bodybuilder and who still looks muscular enough to lift a barrel of wine. He cut his teeth on viticulture with part-time vineyard work when he was only 11. In 1980 he was hired to help Sumac Ridge plant its first vines. He just stayed on, doing almost everything in the winery, until he became Sumac Ridge's assistant winemaker in 1996. In 2003 he became See Ya Later's winemaker. (Also a dog lover, he once brought his dog to work but quickly found that the pet was too energetic to hang around a winery all day.) When Dave was promoted in 2008 to Vincor's senior winemaker in British Columbia, he was succeeded at See Ya Later by Mason Spink, a Victoria native who got his wine-making degree the year before at Brock University.

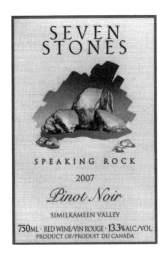

SEVEN STONES WINERY

OPENED: 2007

1143 Highway 3, Cawston, BC V0X 1C3
250.499.2144
www.sevenstones.ca
When to visit: Open 11 am – 6 pm daily May 1 to October 31 except Tuesdays

RECOMMENDED

CHARDONNAY
CABERNET FRANC
PINOT NOIR
MERITAGE
SYRAH

NEWCOMERS TO THE SIMILKAMEEN VALLEY, GEORGE HANSON AND HIS QUEBEC-born wife, Vivianne, have embraced its history by naming their winery after seven massive rocks that are freighted with Aboriginal history. Speaking Rock, for example, was a First Nations meeting place, while Standing Rock — Highway 3 jogs around it — is associated with a tale of a woman who rode her horse to the top. These and other stories are finding their way into this winery's labels.

Born in Alberta in 1957, George spent 25 years with the telephone company in the Yukon. Home winemaking fired his desire to retire on a vineyard. His interest in wine, he says, began when a brother married into an Italian family that included a father who was a good winemaker. When the phone company offered golden handshakes, he decided to invest his severance in a vineyard.

He was just getting discouraged after making several unsuccessful bids on property near Oliver when he chanced on his Similkameen property on the very day in 1999 when the owner put up the FOR SALE sign. George snapped it up immediately; had he delayed, it would have been acquired quickly by one of two wineries that were then sniffing around the Similkameen. The property, then a hay meadow, is ideally located beside the highway. The vines have been planted on a westward-sloping plateau with a natural gully that draws away the frost. There is a panoramic view of the mountains across the valley.

Since 2000 he has planted eight hectares (20 acres). Most of the vines are the big reds suited to the Similkameen's sunny summers: Cabernet Sauvignon, Cabernet Franc, Merlot, Pinot Noir, and Syrah. Conceding that there is always a call for white wine, he added one hectare (2½ acres) of Chardonnay. "I planted this vineyard with the intention of making a Bordeaux-style red and one white," says George, who has since planted both Malbec and Petit Verdot to complete the varieties needed for his Meritage. However, the remarkable qualities of his Pinot Noir and Syrah caused him to add those varieties to his wine portfolio. "This is an exceptional place to grow grapes," George believes. "We have been selling to four or five other wineries, and they are all making premium wines."

He calls the vineyard Harmony-One because, in his mind, there is a parallel between a conductor directing an orchestra and a grower managing his vines. That was also the tentative name for the winery when he had Lawrence Herder make an initial volume of red Meritage in the 2003 vintage. Then Vivianne came into his life. After they married the winery project was delayed by a year so that the couple could first build a house (which she designed). "Everybody in the industry told me that if we didn't get to build the house now, everything would go into the winery and I'll never have a house," she says and laughs.

Vivianne operated a health products store in Prince George for 10 years and is an avid herbalist. "I joked with George that our added value will be that I will sell tinctures to help people's livers so they can come and buy more wine," she says. She is very much in tune with the Similkameen's farming culture, where almost half the producers are organic. "I am in heaven here, with all this organic fruit," she says.

When the couple revived plans for the winery, they recognized that the Harmony-One vineyard's name lacked the appropriate resonance. "I like the ring of the Seven Stones," Vivianne says. "It has a bit of a magic to it. I read a lot of books and there are legends about the different rocks. It has lots of marketing potential because each rock has a story. We wanted to make it our own story too."

Still working with consulting winemakers, they resumed making wine for their winery in the 2005 vintage and opened the winery in 2007. By then George had taken over making the wines. Within a year he was adding to the winery buildings, providing more capacity to produce wines that had been very well received. "We've had an incredible year," Vivianne said in 2008 as she recited all of the white-tablecloth restaurants in Vancouver with Seven Stones wines on their lists.

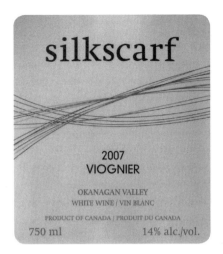

2007
VIOGNIER

OKANAGAN VALLEY
WHITE WINE / VIN BLANC

PRODUCT OF CANADA / PRODUIT DU CANADA

750 ml   14% alc./vol.

SILKSCARF WINERY

OPENED: 2005

4917 Gartrell Road, Summerland, BC V0H 1Z4
250.494.7455
www.silkw.net
When to visit: Open daily 9:30 am – 5:30 pm May 1 to October 30. Licensed patio

RECOMMENDED

MERLOT
VIOGNIER
CHARDONNAY
GEWÜRZTRAMINER
BLANC DE NOIR

IDAN MANOFF ADMITS IT: IT WILL BE A CHALLENGE TO MATURE THE TEST PLOT of late-ripening Malbec in the Silkscarf vineyard at the edge of Summerland. The variety is his father's idea. Roie Manoff would like to produce a Malbec because it would connect him to his roots. He was born in 1951 in Salta, the old Spanish city in northwestern Argentina. Malbec is the signature grape in Argentina, and that was one country that the Manoff family researched when considering where to establish a winery after deciding to emigrate from Israel.

Migrating is in the Manoff family history. Roie's grandparents lived in Odessa, in Russia, but fled anti-Jewish pogroms in the late 19th century to settle in Argentina. When Roie, whose Hebrew name means "shepherd," was five, his fervently Zionist parents moved to the young country of Israel. When Roie reached military age, he became a fighter pilot and spent 26 years as an air force officer, including three as Israel's air attaché in Washington. The winery's name, Silkscarf, comes from the early years of aviation, when pilots flying in open cockpits wrapped silk scarves around their throats. There is hardly any need for a scarf in the F4 Phantom jets that

Roie flew. The winery name is simply a romantic allusion.

Roie retired from the military to establish a successful Israeli software company, running it for 14 years with several partners, including a brother. "But wine was my passion for as long as I can remember," he says. There are good wineries in Israel, and they served as a starting point when Roie began to research a new career in wine. He also began taking winemaking courses and, as Idan recalls, reading widely about wine.

Soon the family began looking beyond Israel, if only because the domestic market is comparatively small. Besides Argentina they considered Italy, Spain, and Australia. When they learned that Canada also made wine, they looked at Ontario — and then discovered the Okanagan in 2002. "I think it was not so much where you can grow grapes and make wine but where you want to live," Idan recalls. "The Okanagan, with its beautiful scenery and the great outdoor feeling and the lake, was a personal choice."

Gartrell Road, where the Manoffs bought an orchard in 2003, is the winding suburban road that, with five wineries on it now, has become Summerland's wine road, with Silkscarf as the first winery on the road. The property's apple and cherry trees have been replaced gradually with vines. The major white varieties grown here are Gewürztraminer, Chardonnay, Riesling, Viognier, and Pinot Gris. The reds include Pinot Noir, Syrah, Malbec, and Cabernet Sauvignon; the latter is another late-ripening variety that Roie admires and that Idan sees as a challenge.

Idan, born in Israel in 1976, has a computer science and business education. With his father still winding up affairs in Israel, Idan was sent to the Okanagan to start planting vines in 2004. He brought with him practical farming experience gained in Israel, preparing him to farm grapes in the Okanagan. "A tractor is a tractor," he says. It was a couple more years before his father was able to spend more time on the winery than on the affairs of his business in Israel. By 2008 Silkscarf had 3.5 hectares (8½ acres) under vines on Gartrell Road. The winery supplements its own grapes with purchases from vineyards elsewhere in the Okanagan.

After using a series of consultants in its early vintages, Silkscarf engaged Philip Soo as winemaker in 2007. The style of the wines now has stabilized. The whites are typically crisp and fruity, including a Gewürztraminer somewhat in the commendable Alsace style. The crowd-pleaser on the wine shop's shaded patio deck is a slightly off-dry wine labelled Riesling Muscat. The wine's punch of fruit aromas and flavours comes from the Muscat variety in the blend, a mere four percent of intensely aromatic Perle de Csaba, an old Hungarian variety.

The Manoffs have a clear focus on what they want to do: operate a winery producing up to 2,500 cases per year of the best wine they can make. They intend to sell much of it directly from the wine shop with that personal touch that family ownership brings. "We really want contact with our visitors, our customers," Roie says, "to have a wine shop and to have the fun tasting the wine with them."

SILVER SAGE WINERY

OPENED: 2001

32032 87th Avenue, Oliver, BC V0H 1T0
250.498.0319
www.silversagewinery.com
When to visit: Open daily 10 am – 6 pm
Accommodation: Three guest suites in the winery

RECOMMENDED

PINOT NOIR "THE PASSION"
SAGE GRAND RESERVE
RASPBERRY DESSERT WINE
SUNSET DESSERT WINE
THE FLAME

IT IS AN UNDERSTATEMENT THAT THE WINES OF SILVER SAGE ARE CREATIVE.
The Flame is a memorable dessert wine quite unlike anything else in the Okanagan: there is a red pepper in each bottle. There should be a warning on the label that this wine will leave the palate tingling, to say the least.

Then there is Sage Grand Reserve, a table wine whose herbal flavours make it Canada's answer to Retsina, the resin-flavoured white wine from Greece. The base wine is Gewürztraminer, and the secret ingredient is the sagebrush that grows throughout the southern Okanagan. Winemaker Anna Manola favours a particular source of sage on a Golden Mile mountainside south of Oliver. The sage is picked in June and soaked in wine until the end of September to remove the stronger oils from the plant. The sage then goes into the tanks of fermenting Gewürztraminer wine and stays there until the wine is almost dry. The resulting wine is spicy, herbal, and relatively dry with the unique aroma of sage. Some of these recipes emerged from the imagination of Victor Manola. Since his accidental death in 2002, they have been polished by Anna. "It took me two years to perfect this wine," she says of the Sage Grand Reserve.

Victor and Anna grew up in wine country in Romania. "My father was a wine-maker," says Anna, who was born in 1954. He managed a 600-hectare (1,500-acre) vineyard. "I grew up in the winery, actually. I worked as a student for five years with my father. The wine business in Romania was not considered a job for a woman, so I became a teacher." Both her family and Victor's family owned vineyards that were taken over by the state. While her father continued to work in the state winery, Victor was an independent spirit who chafed under Communist rule. In 1975, when he was 20, he smuggled himself out of Romania, at considerable personal risk. After six months in an Austrian refugee camp he came to Edmonton. Once he established himself, he brought Anna to Canada in 1980.

Victor subsequently became a construction contractor in Vancouver while Anna returned to teaching mathematics (she had authored mathematics texts in Romania). A creative woman with an eye for colour, she also painted and created elegant needlepoint, examples of which hang in the Silver Sage tasting room. "Wine goes with beautiful things, with elegance, with nice ambiance, with companions," she says.

The Okanagan's beauty so appealed to them — Anna still maintains that V0H in the Oliver postal code means "valley of heaven" — that in 1996 they bought riverside vineyard property that had been fallow since 1988. It was a tangle of roots, posts, and wires, overgrown with sage. "Such a beautiful smell," Anna remembers. "That's where the winery name comes from." They began planting vines in 1997, ultimately putting in nine hectares (22¼ acres) of Pinot Blanc, Merlot, Pinot Noir, Gewürztraminer, and Schönburger. "It was just a labour of love. We were commuting from Vancouver every single Friday. I had a job, Victor had a company. And the boys, my sister, Victor's sister, his father . . . all the family came here. We were working seven days a week, without a day of holiday."

They also began to make fruit wines in 1996, initially for export. They only started to sell the fruit wines (along with grape wines) domestically in 2001 after the collapse of an export deal with a Japanese purchaser. The fruit wines give Silver Sage a deliberate point of difference from other wineries. "Before we went into this business, we visited quite a few vineyards and wineries," Anna says. "Not just in the Okanagan. We did the Napa Valley, Sonoma, and Europe." In this way they refined their vision for what they wanted to do. "I always said that Silver Sage would not have a chance, coming with just three or four more grape wines into such a well-established region like the Okanagan."

Anna learned to make fruit wine at her father's side. Working with such fruits as raspberries, blueberries, cherries, peaches, apricots, pears, and quince, she makes wines that are remarkable for their intensity of colour, aroma, and taste. She freezes the fruit to reduce the water content and thus concentrate the sweetness and flavour, then ferments the must slowly at cool temperatures. The wines are finished by fortifying them to 20 percent. The fruit wines blended with grape wine, such as Silver Sage Sunset, where Pinot Noir is combined with cranberry and raspberry, have about 14 percent alcohol. "I never produced a dry fruit wine," Anna says. "It's juicy, it's full of aroma, it's sweet. It's got that natural, natural fruit." She estimates that almost two kilograms (4½ pounds) of berries are required for each bottle of raspberry wine.

The baronial winery, a showcase of Victor's craftsmanship, was completed after his death. "It was a dream I couldn't let down," Anna says. "It would have been much easier for me to just sell it." The winery's large function room, complete with a dance floor, is a possible future venue for a cooking school. Three guest suites on the second floor are named for Anna's signature wines: Sage Room, Flame Room, and Passion Room. The latter refers to the winery's premium Pinot Noir, which Anna, in tribute to her late husband, calls The Passion. The purple label is similar to the shade of a widow's garb in Romania.

SILVERSIDE FARM & WINERY

OPENED: 2005

> 3810 Cobble Hill Road, Cobble Hill, BC V0R 1L5
> 250.743.9149
> wjaten@telus.net
> When to visit: Open daily 10 am – 6 pm July through September, 11 am – 4 pm
>   Saturday October through June

RECOMMENDED

> TAYBERRY WINE
> WILD BLACKBERRY PORT
> RASPBERRY DESSERT WINE

ASK JEANNE ATEN WHY SHE AND BILL, HER HUSBAND, BUILT A WINERY AT their blueberry farm in 2005 and she replies: "It sounds quite exclusive." Then she remembers the licensing hassles. "I didn't think much about being exclusive when I was going through all of the hoops of getting this okayed by the government. But we got through all of that."

They probably knew what to expect of bureaucracy. Bill, who grew up on a Salmon Arm dairy farm, spent 33 years as an engineer with the Ministry of Forests. Jeanne was a teacher until they purchased their Cobble Hill property in 1982 (naming it for the silver birch trees they planted beside the driveway). She left teaching to run the farm, something that is in her blood, since she grew up on a farm near Pritchard, in the BC interior. Initially the Cobble Hill property was going to be a mixed farm, with beef cattle, pigs, and chickens. The farm had come with a pregnant dairy cow. Within a few years they had a small dairy herd — and a lot of work. "We were both getting worn out, milking five cows morning and night," Jeanne recalls.

"So we had to decide whether we wanted to go into farming full time with a dairy herd or do something else."

Because the farm was not quite big enough for a commercial dairy herd, they took advice to plant raspberries and blueberries. The raspberries struggled on the heavy clay soil and were subsequently removed, but the blueberries thrived. Ultimately Jeanne has been selling as much as 8,200 kilograms (18,000 pounds) of fresh berries a year from her two-acre (0.8-hectare) patch, mostly to repeat buyers who start to reserve their berries in spring. Using her berries and purchased fruit, she also developed a steady trade in jams and jellies.

She and Bill had considered a winery to use up surplus fruit, but the real push came from a local home winemaker, Harold Moulton. "He'd been at this a long time," Jeanne says. "He kept bringing us a taste of what he was doing. It was always very good. Then he said, 'How about we work together?' " They had what Harold lacked — enough production from their own berries to support a land-based winery. They converted one of the farm buildings into a winery, with an adjoining tasting room. With Harold in charge, they began making wines from blueberries, raspberries, and blackberries (which grow wild on the farm). They started selling their wines just in time for Christmas in 2005.

By the time Harold retired as winemaker in 2008, Bill had the experience to take over. "I find that I like making wine," he says. The winery now produces about 4,500 litres (1,000 gallons) per year, all of it in small 225-litre (50-gallon) lots that are blended for consistency, aged between three weeks and two months in barrel, then for another three to six months in glass before bottling. The object is to let the wines clear naturally, without filtering, which can diminish the flavours.

Bill likes to leave a touch of sweetness in the table wines, believing this accentuates the natural berry flavours. "If you go dry with fruit wines, you could be drinking anything if you close your eyes," he maintains. The dessert wines are sweeter, of course, but are rich and balanced. Bill has modified the original wild blackberry "port" recipe that he got from his friend. Harold liked to fortify the wine with Grand Marnier, but government regulators would not allow that non-Canadian addition. Bill uses Canadian-made grain alcohol.

Although several nearby wineries have grapevines, Silverside Farm remains focused on berries. "Growing grapes is a way bigger job that growing blueberries," Jeanne observes. "You are constantly doing stuff with the vines. You prune the blueberries once in the spring and then you pick them and that's it — other than the weeding." Their simple farming model gives her time to pursue her other interest, creating paintings in a variety of media, including pastels, watercolours, and acrylic paints. Her canvasses, along with those by other Cowichan Valley artists, are also displayed and sold in the Silverside wine shop.

SKIMMERHORN WINERY & VINEYARD

OPENED: 2006

1218 - 27th Avenue South, Creston, BC V0B 1G1
250.428.4911
www.skimmerhorn.ca
When to visit: Open 11 am - 5 pm Friday through Monday
Restaurant: Bistro in wine shop

RECOMMENDED

MARÉCHAL FOCH
PINOT NOIR
PINOT GRIS
ORTEGA
ROSÉ
GEWÜRZTRAMINER

SKIMMERHORN WAS THE SECOND WINERY TO OPEN IN THE KOOTENAYS, perhaps laying the foundation for an emerging wine-growing region well off the beaten path. When they were preparing to launch Skimmerhorn, Marleen and Al Hoag figured there was little chance of finding a consulting Okanagan winemaker willing to drive three hours or more to Creston. Instead they got a winemaker from New Zealand, as improbable as that sounds.

The logic, however, is that southern hemisphere winemakers harvest their wines in our spring, leaving them free to make wine six months later in the northern hemisphere. Australia is full of flying winemakers, and the Hoags were planning to recruit there. Then a companion on Marleen's curling team came across a New Zealand quarter in her change and suggested that was where the Hoags should look. Thinking it over, Marleen recognized that "Australia is way too hot for what we are going to be doing here."

They knocked on winery doors across New Zealand's South Island until they found Mark Rattray, the Geisenheim-trained owner of Floating Mountain Winery in Waipara. Attracted by the adventure of pioneering a new wine region, Rattray agreed to make Skimmerhorn's initial three vintages and mentor the Hoags in subsequent years. "He has good experience with Pinot Noir and he's got some really nice, award-winning Pinots," Al notes. "That is one of the reasons we got Mark." His sure-handed winemaking got Skimmerhorn off to an excellent start.

The Creston Valley has a long agricultural history. The Hoags grew apples, cherries, and other tree fruits for 20 years before switching to grapes. Born in Alberta in 1958, Al Hoag grew up in Victoria and became a millwright. In 1984 he took over a Creston fruit farm from his father, operating it until selling the orchard in 2005 when apple prices no longer covered production costs.

Looking for added value, Al was well along in establishing a cidery when he had second thoughts. "The reality is that cider is a fairly small and specific market," he says. "It might be easier to get experience in a market that is a little more active. That's why we decided to do a grape winery. It may be a path of less resistance."

He recognized that vines would flourish in the same climate as apples and cherries. In 2003 the Hoags bought a well-sited property on the southern edge of Creston with a 1940s farmhouse. On its gentle south-facing slope beside the Goat River canyon, they planted 5.6 hectares (14 acres) of vines, carefully choosing varieties suited to the Creston Valley's short but intense season. The primary varieties are Maréchal Foch, Pinot Noir, Ortega, Pinot Gris, and Gewürztraminer, all relatively early-maturing varieties. They seem to have started a trend. In 2004 neighbour John Haley planted 1.2 hectares (three acres) of Pinot Gris and Gewürztraminer, which he sells to the Hoags.

The farmhouse at Skimmerhorn was renovated in a style that retains echoes of the 1940s. Possessed with an artistic eye, Marleen scoured the Internet to find period fixtures, giving the tasting room the comfortable ambiance of that earlier time. The tasting room's shaded hospitality patio overlooking the vineyard is enclosed with a wrought iron fence that Al found in a Cleveland salvage yard. The winery itself is in a separate building, a utilitarian structure but a well-equipped one.

The Hoags also reached back into local history when naming the winery. The Skimmerhorn name is prominent in Creston, where it is found on everything from a motel to a mountain. It is believed to refer to Frank Skimmerhorn, an American who moved to the Creston area in the 19th century, a possible fugitive from justice who became a pillar of the community north of the border.

"Creston is not a tourist destination, it's just not," Al says. However, his winery and any future wineries in this corner of the Kootenays might change that. Until Skimmerhorn opened, the only draw in town for visitors was the seasonal tours at the Columbia Brewery. Now the brewery and the winery refer visitors to each other and to the recently opened Kootenay Alpine Cheese Company.

SLEEPING GIANT FRUIT WINERY

OPENED: 2008

6206 Canyon View Road, Summerland, BC V0H 1Z7
250.494.0377 | 1.800.577.1277 (toll free)
www.summerlandsweets.com | www.sleepinggiantfruitwinery.ca
When to visit: Open daily 9 am – 5 pm, 9 am – 8 pm in July and August. Closed
   Sundays January through March

RECOMMENDED

PEAR WINE
GALA APPLE WINE
APRICOT WINE
PEACH WINE
BLUEBERRY WINE
CHERRY WINE
RASPBERRY WINE

THE SURPRISE IS THAT IT TOOK SUMMERLAND SWEETS, IN BUSINESS PROcessing fruit since 1962, so long to add a winery. The company has built a solid reputation for its jams, syrups, and other fruit products and draws at least 20,000 visitors a year to its attractive country store, tucked away on the edge of Summerland. Wine is a natural extension. "It's been a thought in the family for quite a while — five, six, seven years," manager Len Filek says. "With the other projects we had, we just kept putting it off."

Summerland Sweets was founded by a legendary Okanagan food scientist named Ted Atkinson. Born in Penticton, he came back to the Okanagan with an agriculture degree from Oregon State University to join the research station at Summerland. Ultimately he became the station's head of food processing and an internationally renowned authority. He would do "anything for the food industry," says Len, whose wife, Susan, is the scientist's granddaughter.

A very active Rotarian, Ted and a colleague at the research station developed fruit candies so that Rotary could raise funds by selling them. He could not find an existing processor to take over commercial production so, upon retirement from the research station, he launched Summerland Sweets. It was a small company still run by Ted, who was then in his 80s, when Len joined in 1984. Born in Kamloops in 1958, Len was a recent commerce graduate from the University of British Columbia when he sought a summer job at Summerland Sweets. It took a bit of selling with Ted. "He said he would never hire a commerce type," Len remembers. "He always wanted a food technologist." Len convinced him that the Okanagan had plenty of food technologists but not nearly enough marketers.

The company's big break came in 1986 when it was invited (along with many other BC food companies) to a major Vancouver trade show. Customers that Len signed up at the show, including the Overwaitea grocery store chain, continue to buy from Summerland Sweets. Much of the company's sales, however, have been built from its Summerland store, which provides visitors with samples of the delectable products, selling super-sized ice cream cones in summer. Until recently, there were also free tours. These stopped a few years ago when the company, which exports to the United States, was required to secure its processing area against unauthorized visitors to comply with American anti-terrorism legislation. Sampling continues, however, including generous tastings in a pine-paneled wine shop with its display of about six hundred bottles of wine.

Ted Atkinson's approach to quality was simple. "Whenever he made something, he had the same theory," Len recalls. "Put good fruit in it, put in lots of it, and you will create a good fruit product. You can't skimp with the raw materials." Len applies the same philosophy to the wines, launched under the Sleeping Giant label. The name is inspired by Summerland's most prominent feature, the small mountain called Giant's Head.

Sleeping Giant's winemaker is Ron Taylor, a veteran Vancouver winemaker who, after a 25-year career with Andrés Wines, has re-emerged as one of British Columbia's most active vintners of fruit wines. When the Spiller Estate Winery opened near Penticton in 2003, Ron was the winemaker. He had, in fact, crushed the fruit for Spiller's first wines at Summerland Sweets because the Spiller facility was then not ready.

At several of Ron's clients, the dessert style is favoured. Although Sleeping Giant offers dessert wines, Len decided that most of the wines should be dry, or relatively so, and designed to be consumed with food. He believes the market for dessert wines is just too small. Sleeping Giant opened with 11 dry fruit wines, including three — apricot, peach, and cherry — from the 8.5 hectares (21 acres) of orchard owned by Ted Atkinson's descendants.

This is the second time that Summerland Sweets has had a toe in the wine business. In the 1980s and 1990s the company canned a range of fruit purées for the home wine market. After a spike in sugar prices cooled demand from home wine-makers and big volumes of imported grape concentrate muscled in, Len wound up the business. He has never forgotten the messy process of making the fruit wine bases. "My head was covered with apricots because the fruit we used was so ripe and juicy, to maximize the flavour we wanted to get into the can," he says, laughing at the memory. "In a good season we would do about 30 tons of apricots, which is a lot of home winemaking." The experience seems to have discouraged him from making his own fruit wines. "My dad was a home winemaker but I am not interested in making wine," he says. "I am interested in wine and I am interested in a good product. That's why we have someone making it for us."

SONORAN ESTATE WINERY

OPENED: 2004

5716 Gartrell Road (corner of Happy Valley), Summerland, BC V0H 1Z7
250.494.9323
www.sonoranestate.com
When to visit: Open daily 10 am – 5:30 pm, 11 am – 5:30 pm Sundays. Licensed picnic
area

RECOMMENDED

ORANIENSTEINER DRY
RIESLING
13 MOONS CABERNET MERLOT
13 MOONS ORANIENSTEINER ICEWINE

THESE DAYS ADRIAN SMITS, A TALL, TANNED WINEMAKER, IS FULL OF PURPOSE
and confidence. Vineyard work has given him ruddy good health, and making wine
has opened a new career. His life took this turn for the better when his parents
liberated him from what he calls a "dead-end job" to help them launch Sonoran
Estate Winery in 2004.

"I was living in Chilliwack, doing computer tech support," he recalls, referring
to dealing with computer owners from a telephone call centre. "You can't make any
money doing it and you don't get outside. I like to be outside all the time. I found
working inside a building that my eyes were starting to go bad on me. Since I
have come out here, my eyes have gotten better. I guess I won't need glasses now
because they are fine."

Born in Holland in 1979, he was two when his parents, Arjan and Ada, immigrated to Canada. The pair are agriculturists who were landscapers and flower
growers, first in Ontario and then in British Columbia's Fraser Valley. In the West
they also had a hazelnut farm and, being a personable couple, opened a bed and

breakfast. In 2000 they moved to the Okanagan. On an apple orchard north of Summerland, they opened a second bed and breakfast with a highway-side windmill as its landmark.

Because apple growing had become so marginal, the trees were quickly replaced with 2.2 hectares (5½ acres) of vines — Merlot, Pinot Noir, Riesling, Gewürztraminer, and a few rows of Chardonnay. Syrah and Oraniensteiner were planted a few years later. The first harvest from these vines enabled the Smits family to open the winery in 2004 with estate-grown wines. The wines were made under the direction of a consultant while Adrian trained at Okanagan University College.

The Smits family also are something of real estate entrepreneurs. In 2005 they bought a second property in Summerland, another orchard that was immediately converted to vineyard. Their objective was to sell one property or the other, but they have been in no hurry. The original Sonoran winery, at the highway-side bed and breakfast, was attractively set on a slope with a dramatic view over vineyards and Okanagan Lake. The second location, on Summerland's Gartrell Road, does not have quite the same breathtaking view. However, Sonoran now is on the Summerland wine route, near Silkscarf, Thornhaven Estates, and Dirty Laundry.

The portfolio at Sonoran extends from table wine to icewine. If there is a signature varietal here, it is an obscure German white with a difficult name, Oraniensteiner, made in styles from dry to late-harvest to icewine. One of the many Riesling/Silvaner crosses created in the 1960s at the Geisenheim institute, it is another of those varieties named for a castle ruin on the Rhine — Schloss Oranienstein.

Oraniensteiner was one of the varieties that Geisenheim's Helmut Becker sent to the Okanagan in the late 1970s to evaluation in vineyards here. In 1984 Wolfgang Zeller planted some of the vines on his Naramata Road vineyard. When the vines produced, the Brights winery made some trial wines but then dropped the variety. Not only was the name judged too difficult for a wine label; this variety also tends to have high acidity even when mature. However, Wolfgang's son, Karl, was impressed with the wines, expanded his block of Oraniensteiner, then spent years searching for a winery to champion the variety. Sonoran is the first winery to feature the variety in its portfolio with some consistency.

In 2008 Adrian added a premium tier of wines under the 13 Moons label. Sarah Smits, Adrian's wife, explains that this refers to the lunar cycle and "pays homage to the natural rhythm at play in all aspects of winemaking." Inherent in this is a commitment to traditional organic or biodynamic practices in wine growing. "Centuries of experience have taught European winemakers that good soil management and careful vineyard maintenance produces high-quality grapes," Sarah adds. "And as anyone who has applied biodynamic techniques to home gardening can attest, there is truly something to planting and harvesting by the moons."

SOUTH ISLAND WINES

OPENED: 2008

4189 Judge Drive, RR3, Cobble Hill, BC V0R 1L3
250.929.7447
islandwines@shaw.ca
When to visit: No tasting room

RECOMMENDED

CURRENT RANGE NOT TASTED

PERHAPS GORDON GRAZIANO IS THE MOST COURAGEOUS MAN AMONG Vancouver Island's winemakers, and that is not just because he tries (and only occasionally succeeds) to ripen Cabernet Sauvignon in the Cowichan Valley. He turned his whole life around after a heart attack and stroke in 1998 by planting a profoundly therapeutic vineyard. It is a remarkable story.

A former packaging designer who was born in Toronto in 1946, Gordon began making wine at home about three decades ago in St. Albert, an Edmonton suburb. He had come to Alberta a few years earlier to study French at the Banff Centre, where he met Valerie and married her after a whirlwind three-week romance. She was completing law school in Edmonton, so he did not return to Toronto. Home winemaking with California grapes began as a shared project. Several families — most of them Italian like Gordon — made the wine together and took their share home.

The hobby mushroomed. When he was making more than home winemakers were permitted at the time (800 litres/175 gallons, later reduced to 400 litres/90 gallons), he applied for a winery licence. The regulators brushed him off repeatedly, telling him that he would not be licensed unless he was making 250,000 bottles a year. St. Albert was prepared to help him fight the regulators but Gordon declined.

"At the time I was 52 years old," he recalls. "All I wanted to do was make wine. I did not want to go to war with the liquor board."

Coincidentally, his wife's law firm was struggling to collect fees from delinquent clients during an economic slump. They decided they had had enough on a particularly nasty winter day; they sold their Alberta assets and moved to the Cowichan Valley in 1997, buying a house near Cobble Hill vineyards. Gordon intended to find a winery job but he suffered a vision-damaging stroke. The shock of it left him deeply depressed and unable to do much of anything. "I had worked as a designer," he says. "The worst thing that could happen to me was to lose my eyesight." As some sight returned, his family suggested he plant vines as a way of occupying his time.

The therapy worked. Gordon, who had never even been a gardener, sculpted his backyard perfectly. He planted three hundred vines in 17 short rows, with a different rose variety at either end of each row. "Once you get interested in growing grapes, it is a whole different world," he found. A red wine drinker by choice, he planted three of his favourite varieties — Cabernet Sauvignon, Cabernet Franc, and Merlot — although he knew these late ripeners are not really suitable for the Cowichan Valley. To his delight, the fruit got ripe in his first three harvests. In particular, his debut 2002 Cabernet Sauvignon, aged in used Robert Mondavi barrels, is full-bodied and tasty. "I am pleased with this [the 2002] because it shouldn't be possible," he says and smiles. Unfortunately, the next four harvests gave him unripe grapes, useful only when neighbours, his volunteer pickers, took part in his annual grape stomp party.

Gordon does not mind if his vineyard does not give him big reds. He prefers to make undemanding and affordable light reds for everyday drinking, even with ice on hot days. "That is my Holy Grail," he says, "to make a wine that everybody can afford."

Unlike Alberta a decade earlier, British Columbia gave Gordon a commercial licence, giving him scope to use purchased grapes and fruit, sometimes in combination. One of South Island's first releases was a carbonated blend of red wine, saskatoon berry wine, and almond essence. It is called Grandmother's Recipe because it is inspired by a historic home wine recipe. The berries are grown at the nearby Saskatoon Berry Farm, Vancouver Island's only commercial grower of saskatoons.

In late 2008, when Gordon discovered that South Island was too small to be viable under a commercial licence, he leased a portion of the berry farm, engaging its owners, Alwyn and Connie Dyrland, as partners in what has now become a land-based winery. This is, he's discovered, more viable because the liquor board scoops up far less of a land-based winery's revenues.

SOUTHEND FARM VINEYARDS

OPENED: 2009

319 Sutil Road, Box 484, Quathiaski Cove, Quadra Island, BC V0P 1N0
250.285.2257
www.southend.ca
When to visit: Open 10 am – 5 pm Friday through Monday May to early September
    and by appointment

RECOMMENDED

CURRENT RANGE NOT TASTED

YOUNG AND IDEALISTIC SUMS UP BEN MCGUFFIE AND JILL OGASAWARA, THE owners of SouthEnd Farm Vineyards. They are the youngest couple (he was born in 1977, she in 1976) to start a winery in British Columbia since the Gehringer Brothers did it in 1986, when Walter Gehringer was 31 and his brother, Gordon, was 27. They are idealistic, making wine only with grapes grown on Quadra Island. Ben describes that decision as philosophical. It is also practical to avoid ferrying grapes to their island winery.

Currently there are three vineyards on Quadra, and they are among the most northerly vineyards on the British Columbia coast. Since 2006 Ben and Jill have planted about 1.6 hectares (four acres) on the family farm where the winery is located. They have been buying grapes from the 2.4-hectare (six-acre) Terra Nova Vineyard nearby, developed by Bob Beck, who has long-term plans to build his own winery. As well, they are now buying the grapes from a similarly sized vineyard that formerly supported the Marshwood Estate Winery.

The first winery on Quadra, Marshwood opened in 2004. The winery closed two years later when the property was purchased by an owner more interested in preserving the 40-hectare (100-acre) marsh, often described as an ecological gem. However, the vineyard, which has Ortega, Agria, Pinot Gris, Pinot Noir, and Dornfelder, has continued to produce.

Ben grew up on Quadra, the son of a commercial fisherman and millwright. Ben's great-uncle, George Rose, who managed the island's roads, is believed to have homesteaded the five-hectare (12½-acre) farm in the 1940s. When Ben's parents took over the farm, they built the log cabin that has now been converted to the winery's tasting room. An engineering graduate from the University of British Columbia, Ben works as an engineer and foreman at a pulp mill in Campbell River, the Vancouver Island city that is just a 10-minute ferry ride from Quadra Island.

Jill was born in Vancouver and grew up in a logging community near Campbell River. After high school — where she and Ben met — she got a forestry degree and then qualified in landscape architecture. While she has never practised, her training has gone into the design of the vineyard and the buildings at SouthEnd Farm. With Ben still working at the pulp mill, she takes the lead role in viticulture and wine-making with consulting winemaker Todd Moore. "I supply the financing and the manual labour," Ben says and laughs. He looks forward to the time when the winery will support the island lifestyle that he and Jill chose when they bought the family farm from his parents in 2004.

They became interested in wine at an early age. "I think I can remember our first wine," Jill says. It was a domestic wine called Rotting Grape, an edgy label that one of the commercial wineries had created to draw in new consumers. In Ben and Jill's case, it was effective. Soon they began going to the Okanagan to visit wineries. "Maybe the romance of this started on those trips," Jill says.

Their estate vineyard has been planted primarily with Siegerrebe, Maréchal Foch, and Petit Millot; the latter is a red hybrid developed by Swiss plant breeder Valentin Blattner. Ben and Jill also planted some Bacchus and some Gewürztraminer, but when these varieties struggled to ripen, they replaced them with Siegerrebe. Bob Beck's vineyard also has Siegerrebe.

The exceptionally cool summers of 2007 and 2008 provided some brutal screening of which grape varieties will ripen on Quadra and which will struggle. Siegerrebe, a variety created in Germany and released for commercial cultivation in 1958, is a clear favourite for Quadra because it is usually ripe by the end of summer. The grape's varietal character — floral and spicy — expresses itself pleasantly even at a moderate level of ripeness. SouthEnd's Siegerrebe wine is aromatic but finished in a dry style.

SouthEnd is primarily a white wine producer, if only because white varieties like Siegerrebe and Ortega are better suited to Quadra's climate. Ben and Jill expect that Foch and the recently planted Petit Millot will succeed as Quadra Island reds. The Pinot Noir at the Marshwood vineyard is being tented to advance its maturity, but in cool years the variety is likely to be made into a blanc de noir (white) wine.

SPERLING VINEYARDS

OPENING PROPOSED FOR 2009

1405 Pioneer Road, Kelowna, BC V1W 4M6
250.762.2544

AT LONG LAST, THE CASORSO FAMILY, WHO PLANTED KELOWNA'S FIRST VINE-yard in 1925, has opened a winery. The winemakers are Ann Sperling and Peter Gamble. Ann's mother, Velma, is a Casorso.

Ann, who was born in Kelowna in 1962, started her illustrious winemaking career in 1984 with the Andrés winery in Port Moody, moved to CedarCreek in 1991, then moved to the Niagara Peninsula in 1995. She's also played a role in launching several wineries, including Malivoire and Southbrook. "It has always been in the back of my mind that I wanted to make wine here because I am so familiar with every foot and every slope and every grape on the property," she says about the family vineyard in East Kelowna operated by her parents, Bert and Velma Sperling. "Maybe it has taken a few years longer than I thought when I moved to Niagara, but the vines are still there and being well looked after." She has re-engaged with the Okanagan to make terroir-driven wines with her husband, Peter, adding another chapter in the remarkable Casorso legacy to Kelowna wine growing.

The family came to the valley when Italian immigrant Giovanni Casorso arrived in 1883 to work for the Oblate Mission's farm. Soon he had his own homestead near the mission. He brought his wife, Rosa, from Italy and industriously set out to pros-per. When tobacco was grown in the Okanagan, he was one of the largest tobacco growers. The family first got into the wine business when Rosa and Pete, one of their sons, invested in the consortium that in 1931 launched what became Calona Wines. When the Capozzi family gradually bought control of the winery in the 1950s, Pete (his full name was Napoleon Peter) refused for years to sell his shares. "His pastime for many years was to go to their board meetings and raise hell," Ann says.

A family history credits Charles Casorso with planting the first Kelowna vineyard near Rutland. His brothers Pete and Louis ordered vines in 1929 and planted grapes on Pioneer Ranch, as the family property was known. It appears, however, the major crops grown here were apples until Pete retired in 1960, turning the farm over to his daughter Velma and her husband, Bert Sperling. Bert switched the entire property to grapes. Initially he grew the same hybrid and labrusca varieties that everyone else had before switching to Riesling, along with four hectares (10 acres) of Sovereign Coronation table grapes. (He was the first grower to plant Sovereign Coronation after it was released from Summerland's grape breeding program.) Over the years he sold wine grapes to Calona, then to Growers in Victoria, and, in recent years, to Mission Hill.

The 19.4-hectare (48-acre) property today grows primarily Pinot Noir, Pinot Gris, Gewürztraminer, and Riesling, including a block of Riesling planted about 1978. Ann and Peter believe the vineyard, a comparatively cool site, is ideal for producing a classic Riesling, Pinot Noir, and sparkling wine. The vineyard also has a sunny south-facing slope with 45-year-old Maréchal Foch vines. In 2008, their first vintage for the Sperling label, Ann and Peter included some Old Vines Foch among the six hundred or so cases they made. When Ann helped launch the Malivoire winery in Ontario, she made an Old Vines Foch that quickly gained a cult following.

The first Sperling vintage was made at nearby Camelot Vineyards because the Sperling winery was not yet ready. In a remarkable coincidence of timing, the owners of Camelot had completed a winery in time for the 2008 vintage and were looking for a winemaker just as Ann and Peter showed up, looking for a winery. "It was serendipitous," Peter says.

The initial Sperling winery is located in Pioneer Market on busy Benvoulin Road. Not far from the historic Father Pandosy Mission, the market was established by Velma about 25 years ago. It sells local produce, specialty preserves, and baked goods, and serves elegant lunches at its licensed patio. The market's property includes a hectare (2½ acres) of Pinot Noir, enough to support the winery licence. The family's long-term plan is to build a winery in the vineyard, which is located fittingly on Casorso Road.

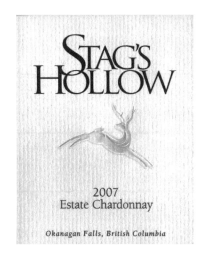

STAG'S HOLLOW WINERY

OPENED: 1996

2237 Sun Valley Way, RR1, Site 3, Comp 36, Okanagan Falls, BC V0H 1R0
250.497.6162 | 1.877.746.5569 (toll free)
www.stagshollowwinery.com
When to visit: Open daily 10 am – 5 pm May to October or by appointment

RECOMMENDED

RENAISSANCE CHARDONNAY
RENAISSANCE MERLOT
RENAISSANCE PINOT NOIR
SAUVIGNON BLANC
SIMPLY CHARDONNAY
TRAGICALLY VIDAL

DUE TO THE UNRAVELLING OF THE AMERICAN MORTGAGE AND CREDIT MARKETS
in 2008, Stag's Hollow founders Larry Gerelus and Linda Pruegger continued to run
this winery (at least as this book was being completed). They had decided the year
before that they were ready for a sabbatical from wine growing and advertised the
winery for sale.

Plenty of people kicked the tires. Stag's Hollow, after all, is among the greenest
wineries in the Okanagan, with a solid reputation for its wines. A would-be buyer
from the United States made an offer that Larry and Linda found acceptable. Then
the offer collapsed when the buyer's American bank backed out.

It is not that Larry is bored with what he is doing. "What I have found interesting since I left the ivory towers in Calgary is all the different things you do every
day," says Larry. "That's what makes it so fascinating." Born in Winnipeg in 1952,
Larry trained as an insurance actuary. He was an independent financial consultant
in Calgary while Linda worked in an oil company's marketing department. Long

wanting a winery, Larry in 1992 bought an Okanagan Falls vineyard planted entirely to Chasselas and Vidal. In 1994, when its grape sales contract expired, Larry grafted the Chasselas to Merlot and Pinot Noir, and most of the Vidal to Chardonnay. The vineyard was back in production in 1995, giving the couple wines to sell when Stag's Hollow opened the following year. The little bit of Vidal remaining attracted its own cult following after the winery released a tangy dry white called Tragically Vidal — because the formerly popular variety has almost vanished from the Okanagan.

Larry and Linda combined the original Stag's Hollow winery with their house, installing the first geothermal heating system in any Okanagan winery. It paid for itself in three years through energy savings. When they built a separate seven-thousand-case winery in 2006, they installed geothermal heating and cooling once again. The winery construction also enabled Larry to contour his three-hectare (7½-acre) vineyard and add Tempranillo.

The new winery's capacity was designed for more grapes than the Stag's Hollow vineyard grew. The intention was to buy additional vineyard land, but during the period in which the winery was designed and built, land prices in the Okanagan headed for the moon. That appears to have triggered the decision to find a buyer for Stag's Hollow. If that plan has been shelved for now, it is because Larry has been able to contract new growers to supply such varieties as Cabernet Sauvignon, Syrah, and Viognier. One of these growers already had been providing the winery the grapes for its award-winning Sauvignon Blanc.

As Stag's Hollow's winemaking evolved over the years (Larry employed several winemakers who later went on to stardom in other cellars), the red wines became increasingly bold and rich, with alcohols of 15 percent or higher. This reflects, of course, the warmer vintages the Okanagan has had this decade, with a general rise in wine alcohol levels. In common with some of his peers, Larry used technology a couple of times to reduce the alcohol. Then in 2005 he began shifting the style of his reds toward more Bordeaux-like elegance. "I just felt my wines were just too much like everybody else's," he explains. "I just started picking at an earlier time. We don't need to go that high in alcohol." When he found a source of Cabernet Sauvignon in 2006, the winery began producing blends of Bordeaux varieties.

The reserve tier at Stag's Hollow is called Renaissance and the wines are always made in limited volume. The best bet is to jump on the wines when they are offered at a discount (typically 15 percent) eighteen months to two years before release. This is the classic French practice, called "wine futures." Stag's Hollow was one of the first Okanagan wineries to offer futures. A remarkably good idea, it has, curiously, been adopted by only a few other wineries.

STARLING LANE WINERY

OPENED: 2005

5271 Old West Saanich Road, Victoria, BC V9E 2A9
250.881.7422
www.starlinglanewinery.com
When to visit: Open noon – 5 pm weekends May to September or by appointment

RECOMMENDED

PINOT BLANC
PINOT GRIS
ORTEGA
PINOT NOIR
MARÉCHAL FOCH
WILD BLACKBERRY DESSERT WINE
CÉLÉBRATION BRUT

THE SIX PARTNERS AT STARLING LANE INITIALLY CONSIDERED CALLING IT THE
Hanging Judge Winery because the winery is on a farm once owned by Sir Matthew
Baillie Begbie. British Columbia's first chief justice, he was unfairly dubbed the
"hanging judge" after his death in 1894, even though he did not hand out an unusual
number of death sentences for the times, and even commuted some. Starling
Lane's partners decided against using the judge's nickname, prudently perhaps.
"We started thinking that some of the victims may have relatives in the area," Jerry
Mussio quips.

The partners were among those pioneering Saanich Peninsula vineyards in the
early 1990s. Jerry, an educational consultant, and his California-born wife, Sherry,
bought their farm in 1993 and, in addition to raising sheep, planted a test plot of
Ortega. Jerry was born in Trail in 1944, the son of Italian immigrants, and he was a
home vintner. Planting vines on the farm's rugged soil expressed his Italian heritage.

Ultimately the couple expanded to just under a hectare (2½ acres) of Ortega, Pinot Gris, and Maréchal Foch. Sherry, a former teacher, is an artist and the designer of Starling Lane's folksy but smart labels.

The second couple in the partnership are John and Jacqueline Wrinch, whose Heritage Farm is the original Begbie property. John saw the Mussio vineyard while buying one of their lambs and soon began developing a similar-sized planting, with eight varieties dominated by Ortega, Foch, and Pinot Noir. A Victoria radiologist, John had begun making award-winning home wines while he practised in Kamloops. When Starling Lane was born, he was tapped as the winemaker because of his scientific training. Jacqueline, experienced as an event planner (the farm is a favourite wedding venue), became the tasting room manager.

The third couple, Sue and Ken Houston, met their partners at early meetings of the island's grape growers association. They also have just under a hectare of vines at their Hummingbird Vineyard, growing Foch, Pinot Noir, Pinot Gris, Pinot Blanc, and Gewürztraminer. They are both Victoria natives and former owners of a heating contracting business. Sue transferred her accounting skills to running the winery's books while Ken managed the renovations that turned the Heritage Farm barn into an attractive winery.

Many of the small vineyards that sprang up in the Saanich Peninsula in the 1990s intended to sell grapes to Victoria Estate Winery, which opened in 2002. However, the new winery's offering prices were less than the growers expected, and then that market evaporated as Victoria Estate slid toward receivership. The Starling Lane partners decided to pool their grapes, their talents, and their resources to create a boutique winery making between six and eight thousand bottles per year from their own vines and from a contracted two-hectare (five-acre) Cowichan Valley vineyard.

"Each of us was thinking about starting our own winery but we realized that, with two acres of grapes each, none of us would have much supply," Jerry says. "But if we got together, we would have six acres of grapes — a reasonable size to support a small winery. All of us have some sort of history in winemaking. The other thing is that we are similar in age. We were looking at the transition from professional careers and had a desire to spend a little more time growing grapes and drinking wine."

The winery works because the partners have talents that support each other and a shared passion for growing good grapes. That calls for unusual commitment, given the somewhat marginal growing conditions of the cool and sometimes rainy Saanich Peninsula. The most difficult grape to ripen among the varieties they grow is Pinot Noir (Jerry and Sherry pulled out the few vines they had). Yet, at the NorthWest Wine Summit in Oregon, the winery won a gold medal for its 2005 Pinot Noir and a bronze for the 2006 vintage.

The secret, they have found, is to carry only a small crop on the Pinot Noir vines so that the grapes ripen well. "And when we pick Pinot Noir, we selectively pick only the best bunches," Jerry says. "In a poor year like 2007, we pick the Pinot Noir early, combine it with Chardonnay, and produce a traditionally made sparkling wine." The winery wins awards with this wine as well. Like the Pinot Noir, all of the wines are handcrafted, starting with good vineyard management.

With limited production and brisk sales, Starling Lane opens its tasting room only on weekends in summer. Even when only one or two wines are available, the winery is worth the visit. The Wrinches have taken pains to retain features at Heritage Farm with a 19th-century feel. The spirit of Judge Begbie remains in residence.

STONEBOAT VINEYARDS

OPENED: 2007

7148 Orchard Grove Lane, Oliver, BC V0H 1T0
250.498.2226 | 1.888.598.2226 (toll free)
www.stoneboatvineyards.com
When to visit: Open daily 10 am – 5:30 pm May through mid-October or by
  appointment.

RECOMMENDED

PINOT GRIS
PINOT BLANC
NEBBIA (BLEND)
PINOT NOIR
PINOTAGE
VERGLAS DESSERT WINE

NOTHING ADDS TO A WINERY'S APPEAL LIKE FAMILY MEMBERS IN THE TASTING
room. There are five members in the Martiniuk family, the owners of Stoneboat:
parents Lanny and Julie and their three sons, Jay, Chris, and Tim. "I can't imagine
not having one of us in the wine shop," says Tim. Lanny notes that their personal
experience in the vineyards and the winery means that visitors are not getting
second-hand stories in the tasting room. Jay agrees: "We've been tying vines since
at least we were eight." He is Stoneboat's emerging winemaker, who helped to make
the 2007 wines when a heart ailment temporarily sidelined consultant Lawrence
Herder. "I feel very close to the 2007 vintage and I can't wait to talk about it in the
tasting room," Jay says. Chris, who is fulfilling a long-held desire to become a
commercial pilot, pitches in at crush.

The family has deep South Okanagan roots. Julie, a pharmacist, grew up on
an orchard beside the Okanagan River (now managed as a Martiniuk vineyard).

She and Lanny, whom she had met in Vancouver, moved to an orchard next door in 1979 and, within five years, began switching to grapes. Ultimately Lanny's nursery became a leading source of vines for new vineyards. In an average year Lanny propagates about 80,000 vines.

Lanny, who was born in 1949, grew up in the Vancouver suburb of Maple Ridge. He pursued an eclectic path before moving to the Okanagan, including claim staking, driving heavy equipment, landscaping, working as a stonemason, and crewing four years as a mate on a towboat. He was working as a nuclear medicine technician when he met Julie. Depressed from observing children desperately ill with cancer, he decided to switch to farming. After a quarter century of experience, he still describes farming as a humbling experience. "Every year I am taught something new," he says modestly. "I get more and more humble that it works out at all."

In the early 1980s, Brights Wines had Lanny plant about 1.6 hectares (four acres) of experimental varieties, including several Russian vines — Sereksia Chornaya, Rkatsiteli, and Matsvani. Brights wound up the project, even though the wines were good, because they believed, no doubt correctly, that it would be difficult to sell wines with such challenging names. "I have still got plants of every variety I have ever grown," Lanny says. He has propagated many of the varieties now found in the Okanagan, gaining a first-hand look at what succeeds and what does not. The Pinotage that grows well in several of his vineyards is a variety that he propagated originally for Lake Breeze, the winery that introduced this South African red into the Okanagan.

The Martiniuks began thinking of a winery in 1997 when they purchased a five-hectare (12-acre) orchard on Orchard Grove Lane and began converting it to vineyard. They now have a total of about 20 hectares (50 acres) of vineyard. This is just off Black Sage Road, a road that has emerged as a destination for wine touring. The impetus behind the winery was the Okanagan's rising land prices. Concerned about the economics of just growing grapes, the Martiniuks reasoned that they would wrest more value from their farms with a winery. The project was postponed while their sons were growing up. They revisited the idea in 2003 and engaged Similkameen winemaker Lawrence Herder to make Stoneboat's first vintage in 2005.

A consulting winemaker had always figured in Lanny's plans. "I was too busy doing the grapes," he recalls. In the 2007 vintage, Lanny and his three sons pitched in to help make the vintage after Lawrence was temporarily sidelined by health problems. They pulled off a successful vintage, at times calling in favours from their friends in the winemaking community. "Even after making the wine, I'll always be a farmer first," Lanny vows.

There is personal misfortune behind Jay's decision to become a winemaker. He was a scholarship student at Queen's, beginning an arts degree majoring in French, when a serious 2004 car accident sent him home for a long convalescence. He began doing the laboratory work for the family's nascent winery and got hooked. To gain more experience he did a vintage at the Herder winery and worked 18 months at Osoyoos Larose before returning to university for science and food technology courses. Jay plans to complete his winemaker training either at the University of California or at a French university.

Stoneboat (named for the sleds homesteaders used when hauling stones from their fields) has emerged as a Pinot house, with a tight varietal focus on Pinot Blanc, Pinot Gris, Pinot Noir, and Pinotage. And the experimental varieties that Lanny retains show up in proprietary wines. Nebbia — "mist" in Italian and inspired by the mists rising from the Okanagan River — is a tangy blend of Schönberger, Müller-Thurgau, and Kerner along with Pinot Blanc and Pinot Gris.

The tongue-twisting Oraniensteiner that he planted in 1984, a high-acid German white, is used for an excellent icewine-style dessert wine dubbed Verglas. "I have a really hard time pulling out old plants that have survived that long," Lanny says with a smile. "Maybe I have been growing too long and I get sentimental attachments."

SUMAC RIDGE ESTATE WINERY

OPENED: 1980

17403 Highway 97 North, PO Box 307, Summerland, BC V0H 1Z0
250.494.0451
www.sumacridge.com
When to visit: Open daily 9 am – 5 pm
Restaurant: Cellar Door Bistro open daily for lunch and dinner

RECOMMENDED

STELLER'S JAY
PINNACLE (RED, WHITE, AND SPARKLING)
WHITE MERITAGE
RED MERITAGE
MERLOT BLACK SAGE VINEYARD
CABERNET SAUVIGNON BLACK SAGE VINEYARD
SAUVIGNON BLANC PRIVATE RESERVE
CHARDONNAY PRIVATE RESERVE
GEWÜRZTRAMINER PRIVATE RESERVE
PIPE
PINOT BLANC ICEWINE

SUMAC RIDGE IS, AMONG ITS MANY ACCOMPLISHMENTS, THE LARGEST
producer of Gewürztraminer in Canada. The winery made its first vintage of this
spicy white in 1981, having committed itself to the grape because viticulturist
Lloyd Schmidt, Harry McWatters's original partner, believed it to be especially well
suited to the Okanagan. In addition to planting the variety at their vineyard near
Summerland, the partners quickly contracted at least half of all the Gewürztraminer
then being grown in the valley.

Today Gewürztraminer accounts for about a fifth of Sumac Ridge's annual
production, which totals about 100,000 cases. The popularity is perhaps surprising,

since consumers usually found it hard to pronounce. Harry theorized many consumers coped by remembering that the white wine with the uniquely appealing aroma and flavours was the one with the longest varietal name on the label. And as the variety became ubiquitous (and often misspelled) on wine lists, most adopted the same shorthand, Gewürz, used even by Mark Wendenburg, Sumac Ridge's winemaker. And he can speak German.

The flagship Gewürztraminer has helped make Sumac Ridge one of the most successful of the Okanagan's first estate wineries. The estate winery licence was created in 1978, modelled on the vineyard-based wineries that were then lifting the quality of California's wine. Ambitious young men, Harry (born in 1944) and Lloyd (born in 1940) worked together at the Casabello winery in Penticton while putting Sumac Ridge together. In 1980 they bought a nine-hole golf course at Summerland, installing a winery in the clubhouse. Shrewdly, they operated both the course and the club house, with the result that Sumac Ridge had the only winery restaurant in the Okanagan. It was not until 1995 that the government formally permitted winery restaurants.

A decade after the winery opened, the course was sold and the new owners built their own clubhouse. The original clubhouse, enlarged several times as wine production expanded, includes the winery's own Cellar Door Bistro restaurant, a year-round fine-dining establishment.

Sumac Ridge made room for its first three-hectare (7½-acre) vineyard by relocating a few fairways. As those vines (all white varieties) were maturing, the winery contracted fruit from vineyards in the Okanagan and elsewhere. The winery's first Chardonnay grapes came from an Ashcroft vineyard whose early promise was killed by a hard winter.

Then in 1992 Harry bought 46.5 hectares (115 acres) on Black Sage Road and put in what then was the single largest planting of Bordeaux varietals in Canada. His peers thought he was taking a big chance; one offered to provide Sumac Ridge with grapes when the Black Sage planting froze. Harry was vindicated when a Merlot wine from 1995, the vineyard's first harvest, was named Canadian red wine of the year in a national competition. The Black Sage fruit allowed senior winemaker Mark Wendenburg to establish Sumac Ridge as a top-quality producer. The flagship Pinnacle red wine, first made in 1997 with Black Sage grapes, was British Columbia's first $50 table wine and is now coveted by collectors.

The son of a German-born grape grower, Mark was born in Penticton in 1961. He became interested in wine as a teenager, visiting winemaking relatives in Germany. After graduating in 1987 from a German wine school, he packed in experience by doing four vintages back to back in two years — one each in New Zealand and Australia and two at the Brights winery (now Jackson-Triggs) in Oliver. He spent 1989–90 at a Swiss winery, returning to the Okanagan to work on a sparkling wine trial under the tutelage of Schramsberg Vineyards of California. When

Schramsberg decided against proceeding, he took his experience to Sumac Ridge and its emerging sparkling wine program.

Sumac Ridge pioneered sparkling wine in the Okanagan. "We did our first trials with sparkling wine in 1985," Harry recalls. This involved extensive work at the Summerland research station with different yeast strains and grape varieties before settling on Pinot Blanc as the backbone varietal. The first commercial vintage was made in 1987, the year in which the raucous Steller's jay was chosen as British Columbia's official bird, inspiring the name of the wine. It was released in July 1989. Today thousands of bottles mature in the stone cellars below the winery, still hand-riddled by Mark and Jason James, the winery's other winemaker.

Harry, an ebullient personality with the girth of Friar Tuck, has a particular passion for sparkling wine. "It is what I drink when I am deciding what to drink for dinner," he says with a laugh. He has mastered the art of "sabering" bottles, the technique of chilling the neck of the bottle and then striking it sharply with a knife. The neck cracks off in a foamy explosion. It is said that Napoleon's soldiers started the practice by opening Champagne with their sabers.

Since 2000 Sumac Ridge has been owned by Vincor, also the operator of Jackson-Triggs and several other Okanagan wineries. However, the public face of the winery has continued to be the McWatters family, either Harry or his daughter, Christa-Lee. She is the hospitality director, presiding over one of the Okanagan's most popular tasting rooms, including exceptional tutored tastings of Sumac Ridge's top wines. Harry retired from the winery in 2008 and established his own consulting firm.

SUMMERHILL PYRAMID WINERY

OPENED: 1992

4870 Chute Lake Road, Kelowna, BC V1W 4M3
250.764.8000 | 1.800.667.3538 (toll free)
www.summerhill.bc.ca
When to visit: Open daily 9 am – 7 pm mid-April to mid-October; 11 am – 5 pm
 October to April
Restaurant: Sunset Bistro open daily for lunch and dinner

RECOMMENDED

CIPES BRUT
CIPES ICE
CIPES PINOT NOIR BRUT
CIPES BLANC DE NOIR
PLATINUM GEWÜRZTRAMINER
EHRENFELSER
BACO NOIR
ZWEIGELT ICEWINE
CHALICE DESSERT WINE

SUMMERHILL PROPRIETOR STEPHEN CIPES REMEMBERS FISHING IN LONG
Island Sound when he was growing up in New York. "Today there is not a single fish
in the area because it is completely dead," he asserts. Once a successful developer,
he moved his family to an Okanagan vineyard near Kelowna in 1987 in search of a
cleaner environment.

What he discovered in the valley set him on an evangelical course of growing
grapes and producing wines organically. "I moved here with four children, to a
house in the middle of the vineyard. When I bought the place, people were suiting
up in these big white outfits with spaceman helmets and masks because they were
spraying Gramoxone [a contact herbicide that kills weeds by interfering with photo-

synthesis]. It's a very strong chemical. When you spray that nothing grows." He immediately stopped the spraying in Summerhill's vineyard and, in ensuing years, he converted most of Summerhill's growers to organic viticulture. He does not want to be responsible for chemicals that might seep into Okanagan Lake, fouling it both for drinking water and for fish.

This is just one of the several reasons why Summerhill demands organically grown grapes for most of its wines. Although the winery makes both table wines and icewines, it began as a sparkling wine specialist. "I only wanted to make sparkling wine," Steve says. "In sparkling wine, flaws and tastes of chemicals are more detectable than in table wines. So for that reason alone, I was very concerned that the grapes not be sprayed." In 2008 the winery also achieved organic certification for its production methods.

Born in New York in 1944, Steve established his family in a rambling house on a 26-hectare (64-acre) vineyard overlooking Okanagan Lake, near Kelowna. He opened a winery after taking part in the sparkling wine trial conducted in the Okanagan in 1990 and 1991 by Schramsberg Vineyards, a renowned California producer. The Californians thought the Okanagan had ideal conditions for making sparkling wine, just not enough Chardonnay and Pinot Noir grapes. Summerhill winemaker Eric von Krosigk, whose passion for bubble borders on obsession, had made Riesling sparkling wines while studying in Germany. The winery opened in 1992 with Cipes Brut, crafted from the Riesling in the Summerhill vineyard.

During the winery's initial years, production was done in the large garage beside the house. The tarpaulins covering the crush pad led local wits to refer to Summerhill as the "Blue Tarp" winery. The winery that Steve built in 1995 became the talk of the Okanagan. Unlike other wineries in the valley, Summerhill ages its wines in a scale model of the Great Pyramid of Egypt. Steve insists that pyramid aging makes good wines taste better. He recites three years of trials in which tasters compared wines from a pyramid to similar wines stored elsewhere. In most cases, he says, the pyramid wines were preferred. There is something to be said for his views. Many old wine cellars in Europe, with their Roman arches, share some of the geometry of pyramids. "There is a definite correlation between liquids and perfect geometry," Steve maintains.

A highlight of visiting Summerhill is a tour of the pyramid, especially if conducted by Steve himself. The elfin winery owner is a gently spiritual individual, given to quoting or keeping in touch with others who also have esoteric and spiritual ideas about the universe. Recently he was encouraged to sheath the pyramid in copper by a Swiss-born physicist named Nassim Haramein, who promotes his research through the Resonance Project Foundation, a non-profit group. Steve believes that the copper will intensify the resonance of the energy that he, and others, experience inside the pyramid.

Summerhill's winemaking, however, has always been in the hands of individuals with mainstream training. Geisenheim-schooled Von Krosigk, who was born in Vernon in 1962, is now in his second tour in the Summerhill cellar. After helping launch the winery, he left in 1994 and spent most of the next 11 years as the most active consulting winemaker in British Columbia. A succession of winemakers paraded through Summerhill until Eric returned in 2005.

While the winemaking focus occasionally wavered, Summerhill has built its reputation on sparkling wines and icewines, at times in combination. Cipes Ice is a sparkling Pinot Noir with a shot of icewine. It is an inspired pairing; the sweetness level of the sparkling wines is never excessive but the fruity aromas and flavours are enhanced. And when a red icewine is added — like Summerhill's rich-hued Zweigelt Icewine — the sparkling wines acquire a jewelled glow in the glass.

Among table wine varietals Summerhill's specialties include two aromatic whites, Ehrenfelser and Gewürztraminer, and perhaps the only Baco Noir still made in British Columbia. The grape is a French hybrid once grown widely in the Okanagan but now quite rare. The dark-hued wine with a touch of smokiness in the finish has acquired a cult following.

TANGLED VINES ESTATE WINERY

OPENED: 2006

2140 Sun Valley Way, Okanagan Falls, BC V0H 1R0
250.497.6416
www.tangledvineswinery.com
When to visit: 10 am – 5 pm daily during wine tour season

RECOMMENDED

GEWÜRZTRAMINER
RIESLING
PINOT BLANC
TICKLED PINK ROSÉ

THE POPULAR BRIDGES RESTAURANT ON GRANVILLE ISLAND IN VANCOUVER
is the common link among the four partners who now run Tangled Vines. Craig
McKenzie, the winery's managing partner, was formerly the operations manager
at the restaurant until the winery opened. The others — his brother Clark and the
husband-and-wife team of John and Maxine Hill — all worked there.

But it took an Okanagan weekend at the Quails' Gate guest house to propel
them into the wine business directly. Bridges is an important account routinely
wooed by wineries. The Stewart brothers, owners of Quails' Gate, offered Clark a
VIP summer weekend in the Okanagan in 2003 and he brought his friends along.
"We had an absolutely wonderful weekend," John remembers.

They were so taken with the wine country lifestyle that they picked up a
real estate newspaper, spending the drive back to Vancouver discussing vineyard
properties. "By the time we got back to Vancouver, we decided we had better put
together a business plan," John recounts. Persuaded that the venture was feasible,
they then devoted a frustrating year to trying to buy a property — frustrating

because they kept finding owners who were ready to sell but who had given the right of first refusal to someone else. Golden Mile Cellars, then a small winery and now called Road 13 Vineyards, was one property that slipped through their hands in that manner.

Finally, in 2005, they bought what was then called Black Widow Vineyard, directly across the road from Wild Goose Vineyards at Okanagan Falls. With just over a hectare of vines, it proved to be a good starter property for the youthful foursome. The vineyard, growing Pinot Noir and Pinot Blanc, had been planted in 1990 by Matt Leak, an Albertan who formerly owned an insurance brokerage, a golf resort, and an air charter company. When arthritis started to bother him, he and his wife retired to the dry Okanagan. Serial entrepreneurs, they developed a line of novelty T-shirts packaged for sale in wine bottles. Matt not only created the cartoon characters printed on the shirts but cut each wine bottle in half, folded the shirts inside and glued the bottles back together.

The vineyard had passed into other hands by the time the McKenzie brothers and the Hills bought it, but the original owner's infectious good humour is also the guiding principle here, as some wine labels show. For those who have trouble pronouncing Gewürztraminer, they released their first vintage as Premier Goo and the second as Gew II. "We are four young people," says Maxine Hill, who runs her own marketing company. "We want to do things that reflect our personality." Husband John's full-time job is with a family-owned office equipment company.

The foursome embarked on a steep learning curve after buying the vineyard. Craig is a graduate of Dalhousie law school who chose the restaurant business over law. His brother went on from restaurants to become an accountant. Craig, however, was in his second decade as a restaurateur in 2000 when he took time off to go to Australia, acquiring winemaking skills in the McLaren Vale. He has managed the vineyard since leaving the restaurant business for good in 2006.

In Australia Craig was impressed by the camaraderie within the wine business. He and his partners discovered a similar spirit in the Okanagan, where experienced neighbours bailed out the greenhorns a few times. Shortly after taking over the vineyard, they were alarmed that their irrigation water was not being delivered evenly through the field. Fortunately a neighbour also spotted the problem and pointed out that they had a plugged filter in the irrigation system.

In the winery's early years the priority has been planting the terraced vineyard below the winery. In no hurry to sink money into their own processing facility — the small winery was built only in 2008 — they started with a custom winemaking contract with Adora. And having few red grapes of their own, they have focused on white wines, supplemented with a rosé they called Tickled Pink. "The aspect of our land is more suited to whites," Craig believes. "And the style of our wines is suited to the foods we eat in British Columbia." Sparkling wines and possibly reds will be added in due course.

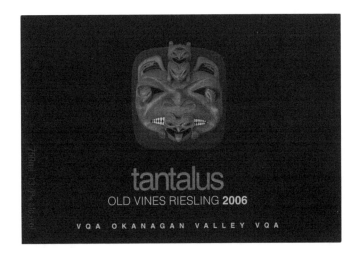

TANTALUS VINEYARDS

OPENED: 1997 (AS PINOT REACH CELLARS)

1670 Dehart Road, Kelowna, BC V1W 4N6
250.764.0078 | 1.877.764.0078 (toll free)
www.tantalus.ca
When to visit: 12 pm – 5 pm during summer weekends and by appointment

RECOMMENDED

OLD VINES RIESLING
RIESLING
PINOT NOIR
CHARDONNAY
PINOT NOIR ICEWINE

IN A QUAINT VINEYARD CEREMONY, THE RIESLING VINES PLANTED HERE IN 1978 had their roots christened with a splash of good German Riesling wine. The magic worked. Arguably the best Riesling in the Okanagan grows on the cool southwestern slope of the Tantalus vineyard.

This is a winery with one foot in history and, with its stunning new winery design, the other in the future. The vineyard looks over the valley were Father Pandosy, an Oblate missionary, is believed to have planted vines about 1860. This slope was planted about 1927 by J. W. Hughes, the Kelowna horticulturist who put vines on several of the area's best sites. In 1948 this vineyard was sold to Martin Dulik, a Hughes foreman. Den Dulik, his son, planted the Riesling (among other varieties), and in 1997 Susan, Den's daughter, opened Pinot Reach Cellars, so named because she expected to make her name with Pinot grape varieties. Her reputation, however, was earned with the full-flavoured wine she called Old Vines Riesling.

The Dulik family sold the vineyard and the winery in 2004 to Eric Savics, a Vancouver stockbroker with a passion for wine, although not for all the varieties that Dulik was growing. "The Duliks, as growers, were all things to all people, so they had 10, 12 different varieties," Eric says. His focus, as the owner of an estate winery depending entirely on its own fruit, has been on Riesling, Pinot Noir, and Chardonnay. These are well matched to the terroir and to the winery's premium objectives. Varieties such as Bacchus and Cabernet Sauvignon were removed and, beginning in 2005, the vineyard was renewed with more Riesling and multiple clones of Pinot Noir and Chardonnay. That precious 1978 block, however, continues to be nurtured for the singular Old Vines Riesling that it produces.

Eric also moved to replace cash-strapped Sue Dulik's modest winery, inviting Bing Thom, a leading Vancouver architect, to walk the vineyard in 2005 and sketch ideas for a new winery. It was three years before drawings were produced because Eric did not want to commit to a showpiece winery until the property produced showpiece wines. In the end, the downturn in the economy caused Tantalus to build a more practical and utilitarian winery in 2009.

To run the winery Eric brought in Jane Hatch as marketing manager and her husband, Warwick Shaw of Australia, as vineyard manager. It was a lucky hire. Warwick had previously worked for Quails' Gate. During that time a young wine-maker named Matt Holmes, taking time out from his studies in Australia, worked a crush at Quails' Gate. In the summer of 2005 Matt was back in Canada, driving across the country with a Canadian girlfriend. He contacted Warwick in the Okanagan just as Tantalus was looking for a new winemaker. Only 28 at the time, Holmes had an impressive resumé, including a degree from Charles Sturt University and wine-making experience with Bannockburn Vineyards, a small producer of premium Pinot Noir and Chardonnay. He was snapped up by Tantalus.

His winemaking style, he says, is "to allow the terroir to express itself. My winemaking philosophy is not about playing tricks. I just don't want to confuse the message in between the vine and the bottle." The mature Riesling vines produce intensely flavoured mineral-rich wine with a spine of bright acidity. With tangy cit-rus tastes, the sophisticated Rieslings that Matt began to make soon drew accolades from Europe's leading Riesling producers and aficionados. The Pinot Noir and the Chardonnay wines also showed the promise of what the vineyard will do when all of the recently planted clones are producing.

By the time Matt's third vintage was being released in the spring of 2008, the wines confirmed a premium quality that deserved a Bing Thom design. Founded in 1980, Bing Thom's architectural firm has created remarkable buildings all over the world. The Tantalus design raises the bar for winery design in the Okanagan. The building, to be under construction in 2010, takes advantage of a forested gulley that carves deeply across the northern edge of the vineyard, a contour ideal for a gravity-flow winery. The billowing roof of Thom's design rises majestically in a vast final three-storey wave curving over the tasting room. Visitors look out across the valley over Kelowna's Mission District, with the city and the lake in the distance. If the winery's daring design does not take a visitor's breath away, the view will.

VQA OKANAGAN VALLEY VQA
GEWÜRZTRAMINER 2005

THERAPY VINEYARDS

OPENED: 2005

940 Debeck Road, RR1, Site 2, Comp 47, Naramata, BC V0H 1N0
250.496.5217
www.therapyvineyards.com
When to visit: Open daily 10 am – 5 pm May through October (and to 6 pm
    on weekends)
Accommodation: Guest house

RECOMMENDED

CHARDONNAY
MERLOT
PINOT NOIR
SHIRAZ
PINK FREUD
FREUDIAN SIP
FREUD'S EGO
SUPER EGO

THIS IS THE WINERY THAT OFFERS FREUD'S EGO, FREUDIAN SIP, AND PINK
Freud, along with labels deliberately modelled after a controversial tool of
psychoanalysis, the Rorschach Inkblot Test. It is all in good psychological fun.
The winery's founders thought that the vineyard setting of both the winery and
the guest house was therapeutic. Their consultant, Bernie Hadley-Beauregard,
principal of Brandever Strategies in Vancouver, picked up on that idea to create the
name and the edgy labels.

In the fall of 2004 a group of Calgarians led by John McBean, then a director of the Opimian Society, purchased the buildings and the 3.4-hectare (8½-acre)
vineyard that was the original home of Red Rooster Winery, Red Rooster having
moved to a larger winery on Naramata Road. John raised financing for the winery

by selling investment units to about 120 partners in Alberta and British Columbia. He left the winery in 2008 during an acrimonious dispute among the investors and was succeeded by Rick Connors, a White Rock businessman who had been one of the original partners.

In November 2008 Marcus Ansems, the winery's general manager as well as its talented winemaker, also resigned after that tumultuous summer. The quarrel among the investors was so heated that a court-appointed receiver ran the business for a few weeks, posting security guards to keep an eye on the assets. This interrupted the construction of $2-million red wine processing facility and barrel cellar. Marcus had expected that he would be crushing and fermenting the 2008 grapes inside the new building. Instead he made do with a smaller existing winery (now the white wine cellar), placing the fermentation tanks on the driveway and the parking lot. His successor, Steve Latchford, took over in late November just as the new building was finally ready to accommodate the new wines.

In spite of the friction among the owners, Therapy has grown strongly since opening in 2005 with 2,500 cases of purchased wine. In that first vintage, Marcus made 4,500 cases of wine. In 2008 he handed 10,000 cases of wine over to Steve, as well as a business plan that projects Therapy will achieve a target of 15,000 cases per year by 2012.

Marcus left to run a club that imports exclusive wines for its members, a business that takes advantage of his exceptional connections. A graduate of the University of Adelaide, he comes from the highly regarded Australian wine family that once owned Mt. Langhi-Ghiran, a Victoria winery making a legendary Shiraz. "That wine inspired me to want to get involved with the industry," Marcus says.

Steve was 18 in 2001 when he enrolled in Niagara College's program for winemaking and viticulture, which gives its graduates hands-on experience in the college's vineyard and winery. From there Steve went to the new Jackson-Triggs winery at Niagara-on-the-Lake, further rounding out his experience by selling wine, working in vineyards, and helping to make wine through six vintages. In 2007 he moved to the Okanagan to work as an assistant winemaker for the Holman Lang group of wineries.

He says he came to the Okanagan because he believes in the region's potential for making top wines. Coincidentally, Marcus made a similar transition from Ontario, where he had done four vintages at the Creekside Winery. "It was a lot harder to make high-end premium wine in Ontario [than in the Okanagan]," he says. "You had to work a lot harder there as a winemaker and as a viticulturist. In Ontario you pick between rain events. Here you have a lot more choice of when you can pick."

Therapy's estate vineyard was planted in the early 1990s with Chardonnay, Merlot, Pinot Gris, and Gewürztraminer. A one-hectare (2½-acre) block nearby, planted in 2006, produces Pinot Noir and Sauvignon Blanc. The winery relies on contract growers elsewhere on the Naramata Bench and in the South Okanagan for other varieties, including Syrah and Viognier.

Some credit for Therapy's popularity also goes to provocative labels, somewhat resembling the inkblots that were developed in 1921 by Hermann Rorschach, a Swiss psychoanalyst who was a disciple of Sigmund Freud. Some psychologists use the inkblots as a tool to assess the emotional functioning of their patients. Needless to say, the Rorschach is a controversial tool. Authentic Rorschach blots (there are only 10) are guarded carefully by the professionals who use them. Consider yourself fortunate if the only therapy *you* need is a glass of Therapy.

THORNHAVEN ESTATES

OPENED: 2001

> 6816 Andrew Avenue (RR2, Site 68, Comp 15), Summerland, BC V0H 1Z7
> 250.494.7778
> www.thornhaven.com
> When to visit: Open daily 10 am – 5 pm May 1 to October 14 and by appointment
> Restaurant: Patio offers wine by the glass and deli food. Picnics welcome

RECOMMENDED

> SAUVIGNON BLANC
> GEWÜRZTRAMINER
> PINOT GRIS
> ROSÉ
> PINOT MEUNIER

ONCE DURING A VISIT TO THORNHAVEN, I NOTED A MAN SNOOZING ON A corner chair on the winery's patio, an empty wineglass by his side. An hour later he purchased a second glass of wine and continued to relax in the afternoon sun. On inquiring, I learned that he was a German tourist delighted to have discovered such an oasis of contentment in the Okanagan wine country.

Tucked away behind Giant's Head (Summerland's extinct volcano), Thornhaven is a special place. The 371-square-metre (4,000-square-foot) winery is a splendid Santa Fe–style building nestled harmoniously into a landscape of dry grass, pines, and cactus plants. It is set at the top of a long vine-covered slope. The patio, which relies on umbrellas for shade, offers such a picture-postcard view of vineyards and orchards that, like the German tourist, many visitors chose to linger.

Dennis Fraser, the winery's founder, intended to open Thornhaven's tasting room in his garage until his grand vision took over. "We went a little overboard," groused his son, Alex, who, after helping his father, went off to become an electrician. But Dennis was accustomed to thinking on a grand scale. Previously he had operated a 971-hectare (2,400-acre) grain farm near Dawson Creek, which he sold in 1989. When he planted vines on Thornhaven's 3.6-hectare (nine-acre) vineyard, a former apple orchard, he chuckled that his vineyard tractor ran all season on what would have been half a tankful for the giant Steiger tractor he once owned.

Sadly, cancer claimed Dennis's wife, Pamm. With Alex not interested in the wine business, Dennis sold Thornhaven in 2005 to relatives Jack and Jan Fraser, who had operated a vineyard down the road since 2000. Cousin Jack grew up on a farm in northern Alberta and went to work on oil rigs. He spent 24 years abroad, primarily in Libya, until he and his family had had enough of foreign adventures. They became grape growers in this peaceful oasis behind Giant's Head. Since the Frasers have taken over Thornhaven, Jan and daughter Cortney (trained as a lawyer) have managed the tasting room. Son Jason, who formerly owned a fruit juice franchise in Edmonton, moved into Thornhaven's cellar to mentor with Bordeaux-trained winemaker Christine Leroux, Thornhaven's long-time consultant.

The Thornhaven vineyard is planted with Gewürztraminer, Chardonnay, Sauvignon Blanc, Pinot Noir, and Pinot Meunier. Similar varieties from nearby vineyards support the winery's growing production. "Being sold out has always been a problem," Jack Fraser told me a few years ago. To begin with the winery produced about 1,500 cases per year. With new plantings coming into production — the winery now draws on 7.4 hectares (18¼ acres) in total — the new owners were able to reach five thousand cases by 2007, expanding the rather compact winery to handle all that production.

Obviously it takes more than a few German tourists to consume that volume. Thornhaven's wines have been selling out because the winery has earned a solid reputation for, in particular, Gewürztraminer, with a coveted Lieutenant Governor's Award of Excellence and gold medals at the national Canadian Wine Awards for recent vintages of this variety. The winery also has garnered awards for its Sauvignon Blanc, Chardonnay, and Pinot Noir. And it is one of the few wineries making a single varietal with Pinot Meunier, a cousin of Pinot Noir. In fact, the grape is in the Thornhaven vineyard only because a nursery added it in error to the winery's order of Pinot Noir vines.

TINHORN CREEK VINEYARDS

OPENED: 1995

32830 Tinhorn Creek Road, Box 2010, Oliver, BC V0H 1T0
250.498.3743 | 1.888.484.6467 (toll free)
www.tinhorn.com
When to visit: Open daily 10 am – 6 pm May through October, 10 am – 5 pm November
   through April
Restaurant: Scheduled to open in 2010

RECOMMENDED

OLDFIELD'S COLLECTION MERLOT
OLDFIELD'S COLLECTION SYRAH
OLDFIELD'S COLLECTION 2BENCH WHITE
CABERNET FRANC
MERLOT
CHARDONNAY
PINOT GRIS
GEWÜRZTRAMINER

TINHORN CREEK WAITED UNTIL ITS TENTH ANNIVERSARY IN 2004 TO INTRODUCE
its first reserve wine, a 2001 Merlot under the Oldfield's Collection label. In a daring
move to test consumer response, it used screw caps on 10 percent of the bottles in
that vintage. Screw caps then had such a blue-collar image that Vintners Quality
Alliance had once forbidden them on VQA wines.

To cushion the shock, Tinhorn Creek paired each screw-capped bottle with
a cork-finished bottle of the same wine in two-bottle packages. The twin packs
enabled comparison tastings to prove what Tinhorn Creek winemaker Sandra
Oldfield argued in *Tinhorn Tales*, the winery's newsletter: "From my perspective,
one of the biggest benefits of . . . the screw cap is that the true fruitiness of the wine
is so well captured. There is a vibrancy . . . that you just can't find in a wine that has

aged under cork." Screw caps also eliminate so-called corked wines, with unpleasant musty aromas and flavours originating from tainted corks. In the 1990s, before corks quality was improved, one bottle in twenty was liable to be tainted.

By 2006 Tinhorn Creek was bottling all of its wines under screw cap. "If this is the right closure for the quality of our wines, then how can we justify some of our wines still being in cork?" the winemaker asked. Some of Tinhorn Creek's peers — many of which have now switched to screw caps — worried about a backlash from traditionalists attached to the romantic dinner table folderol around corks. "If it's because of the romance of the cork," Sandra wrote, "then you may want to consider you are having dinner with the wrong person." Case closed!

Well, not quite. Unless winemaking is precise and clean, wines can also go skunky under screw caps. But Sandra is up for that challenge. She has a master's degree from the University of California's elite wine school at Davis, where she met Kenn Oldfield, who was also in the master's program, equipping himself to become Tinhorn Creek's general manager.

A chemical engineer from the University of Waterloo, Kenn was an Alberta oil industry consultant in 1992 when Bob Shaunessy, an oil company executive and also a Waterloo graduate, proposed a partnership to develop Tinhorn Creek. Beginning in 1994, they planted two South Okanagan properties, including the 12-hectare (30-acre) Fischer Vineyard where the winery is located and the 36-hectare (90-acre) Diamondback Vineyard, one of the early large-scale vinifera plantings on Black Sage Road.

From the start the partners planned that Tinhorn's production, just over 40,000 cases per year, would be two-thirds red and tightly focused. They planted Merlot, Cabernet Franc, and Pinot Noir. For whites they chose Chardonnay, Pinot Gris, and Gewürztraminer. The latter was Sandra's idea; she vetoed Pinot Blanc, arguing that it is too similar to the other two varieties. No Cabernet Sauvignon was planted (even though she was doing a thesis on the ripening of that variety) because the partners believed the vines needed a longer ripening period than the Okanagan offered. In 2005, with the Okanagan becoming perceptibly warmer, Tinhorn Creek planted a little Cabernet Sauvignon along with Syrah and Viognier, two other late ripeners. These varieties, plus a hectare each of Sémillon, Sauvignon Blanc, and Muscat, all support the growing Oldfield's Collection portfolio, including a Syrah and a complex dry white called, simply, 2Bench.

The winery remains primarily a red wine house, with Merlot accounting for about a quarter of total production and a good deal of Tinhorn Creek's reputation. In 1998, a great red vintage, the winery made a Merlot that was later acclaimed as Canada's red wine of the year. Most of the winery's Merlot is grown in the sandy soil of the sun-drenched Diamondback Vineyard, with a smaller quantity from a planting that was already on the Fischer Vineyard when the partners bought it. All the

Gewürztraminer is grown at Fischer, a cooler site that rises steeply to an elevation of 480 metres (1,575 feet) and is in shade by the late afternoon.

History and location add to Tinhorn Creek's charm. In both its name and its architecture, the winery echoes the 19th-century Tin Horn Quartz Mining Company. The ruins of a stamp mill that processed gold and silver ores are still visible along the hiking trail cutting through the mountain meadows west of the winery. It is an easy trail, with maps available at the winery.

The winery's four-square entrance is meant to mirror the stamp mill. Spectacularly perched at the tip of a plateau, the ochre-toned building, which opened in 1996, was designed by Calgary architect Richard Lindseth. The viewing deck adjoining the spacious tasting room is a breathtaking 100 metres (328 feet) above the floor of the valley. The same architect designed the eight-hundred-barrel cellar that was completed in 2002. Making the most of one of the Okanagan's most splendid winery locations, Tinhorn Creek also has a 350-seat amphitheatre for its popular summer concerts and is adding a restaurant to the top floor of the barrel cellar.

TOWNSHIP 7 VINEYARDS & WINERY

OPENED: 2001 (LANGLEY WINERY); 2004 (NARAMATA BENCH WINERY)

LANGLEY WINERY
21152 – 16th Avenue (at 212th Street), Langley, BC V2Z 1K3
604.532.1766
When to visit: Open daily 11 am – 6 pm except in winter

NARAMATA BENCH WINERY
1450 McMillan Avenue, Penticton, BC V2A 8T4
250.770.1743
www.township7.com
When to visit: Open daily 11 am – 5:30 pm, 11 am – 5 pm Friday to Sunday in winter,
    or by appointment

RECOMMENDED

SYRAH
SEVEN STARS
MERLOT
CHARDONNAY
SAUVIGNON BLANC/SÉMILLON

TOWNSHIP 7'S NARAMATA BENCH WINERY OFFERS THE TASTING ROOM FOR anyone who wants to get close and personal with a working winery. A wall of filled wine barrels stacked from floor to ceiling begins just an arm's length behind the tasting bar. Winery activity can be glimpsed and heard among the barrels. Except during vintage, when the aroma of fermenting wine causes a fruit fly explosion, this is a fascinating place to taste. "Who hasn't wanted a pit pass for a Formula One race?" winemaker Brad Cooper says with a laugh. "This is the same thing. You get right in there. It is a whole different experience."

A new tasting room is planned for a site nearby, with an interpretation centre designed to deliver the rich winery experience minus the fruit flies. For now, the most important improvement to the site happened in 2007, when the parking lot was paved after Mike Raffan had acquired the winery from founders Gwen and Corey Coleman in 2006. Brad says that he "wasn't completely sure of the formula that pavement equals customer visits" until he saw the triple-digit jump in visitors as soon as fresh blacktop beckoned.

The Colemans launched their first Township 7 winery near Langley, on a historic farm where they planted a 1.2-hectare (three-acre) vineyard in 2000. The winery name came from an old survey map identifying the district as Township 7. Copying the strategy of nearby Domaine de Chaberton, they opened in the Fraser Valley rather than the Okanagan, where most Township 7 wines are grown. They believed it would be easier to bring the winery to their Vancouver customers than to expect their customers to come to the Okanagan.

In 2003 Township 7's first winemaker, Michael Bartier, purchased a 2.8-hectare (seven-acre) orchard at the very beginning of Naramata Road. The Colemans financed the subsequent vineyard and winery. An aggressive and energetic couple, the Colemans had taken the lead in an association of Fraser Valley wineries. Now they also joined the Naramata Bench Wineries Association (ironically perhaps because, until the Naramata vineyard began producing in 2007, Township 7's wines were made primarily with south South Okanagan grapes). Running wineries located nearly 300 kilometres (185 miles) apart proved to be a burden. After Michael left for Golden Mile Cellars (now Road 13 Vineyards) in 2005, the Colemans decided to sell both Township 7 wineries.

Mike Raffan was among the many impressed by Township 7's wines, served to him whenever his visited the Langley home of his accountant brother, Alan, whose wife, Lynn, looked after Township 7's tasting room. The quality of the wine, notably the Merlot, convinced Mike that BC wines, once so mediocre, now were showing world-class quality.

Born in North Vancouver in 1954, Mike left university in his final year in commerce to invest in and manage a Keg restaurant franchise. That was the beginning of 30 years running restaurants, mostly Kegs, in British Columbia and Alberta. It was a wonderful vantage from which to nourish a passion for wine that began in his 20s. "I have been to a lot of [wine regions]," he says. "Burgundy, Tuscany, Piedmont, Champagne. I toured the caves. Being a restaurateur, the wine people treated you very, very well. I've been in Napa and Sonoma so many times, I can't even count."

As he turned 50 and decided to switch careers, he was comfortable buying a winery with as sound a track record as that of Township 7. "I am amazed at how many skill sets I have taken from one to the other," says Mike, who has retained the youthful appearance of the water polo player he was at college. "I am not at the age where risk is something I want to go find." He is at least as energetic as the

Colemans were. In the spring of 2006, while he was negotiating to buy Township 7, he and a partner simultaneously were opening their third Milestone's restaurant in Alberta. Mike sold his interest after buying Township 7 in partnership with his brother and with Kelowna restaurateur John Tietzen, another Keg alumnus.

To Mike, running two wineries is not much different from what he was doing. "I am used to running multiple restaurants, so I have no trouble delegating," he says. He is an easygoing boss. "When you are running three restaurants, you have to count on people and let them make mistakes. I can't look at mistakes as a negative. If you make mistakes and learn from it, that's good."

Township 7 had been producing about four thousand cases of wine per year and, to Mike's surprise, had been selling almost all of them from the Langley tasting room. He diagnosed the Naramata Bench winery's lack of "curb appeal" as a reason for its lagging sales. Mike is one of those optimists who always see the glass as half full, not half empty, so he tackled what needed to be done to get sales humming. Such as a spiffy new paint job, a paved parking lot, and partnership in an in-house marketing agency. He also took advantage of the Okanagan's big 2006 harvest to bump production to ten thousand cases that year.

The winery is likely to continue dealing with many independent growers, because its current vineyard base is too small to grow all the grapes it needs. The 2.2 hectares (5½ acres) on the Naramata Bench grow Chardonnay, Pinot Gris, Gewürztraminer, Merlot, and Malbec. Winemaker Brad Cooper, a Michael Bartier protegé and a former photojournalist, supplements this fruit with grapes from other terroirs so that he can build layered wines. A big Meritage red, blended from the best barrels in the tasting room, is the newest addition at Township 7. That should appeal to his boss, who once built his cellar on big California reds. "I'm a red wine drinker, but I do enjoy a glass of white," Mike says. But he also recognizes that Township 7 built its reputation with Chardonnay. "Why fight it?" he asks. "We have had two winemakers who do outstanding work with Chardonnay."

The 1.2-hectare (three-acre) Langley vineyard grows Pinot Noir, Merlot, and Chardonnay, primarily for the production of Seven Stars, Township 7's sparkling wine, and a rosé. Brad speculates that the Langley vineyard was planted "largely for eye appeal" but now produces some pleasant surprises. "The Pinot thrives down there," he says.

TUGWELL CREEK HONEY FARM & MEADERY

OPENED: 2003

> 8750 West Coast Road, Sooke, BC V9Z 1H2
> 250.642.1956
> www.tugwellcreekfarm.com
> When to visit: Open noon – 5 pm Wednesday through Sunday May 1 to October 31,
>   weekends the rest of the year. Closed in January

RECOMMENDED

> WASSAIL GOLD
> WASSAIL BLUSH
> VINTAGE MEAD
> SOLSTICE METHEGLIN
> MELOMEL

SIX SPICES FROM THE WEST INDIES ARE BLENDED INTO WASSAIL GOLD, TUGWELL Creek's delicately sensual dessert mead. The spice names are not disclosed. The exact recipe, locked safely in a vault, is known only to mead maker Robert Liptrot and his uncle, *whose name he keeps confidential*. Even Robert's wife, Dana LeComte, does not know the recipe.

Welcome to the arcane world of mead, the honey wine of antiquity that is enjoying a 21st-century revival while retaining its medieval vocabulary and the secrecy of tightly guarded family recipes. Tugwell Creek, located on the windblown west coast of Vancouver Island, was British Columbia's first meadery when it opened in 2003. It is entirely self-sufficient, using only its own honey and even breeding its own bees.

Technically mead is fermented honey wine, frequently flavoured subtly with spices, herbs, or fruit. Traditional or vintage mead is made by fermenting just honey to display the various flavours and aromas of the flowers from which the bees gathered nectar. When spices or herbs are added, the mead is called *metheglin*, said to be a transliteration of *meddyglyn*, a Welsh word meaning "medicine," presumably because medicinal herbs were made palatable by mixing them with mead.

When fruit or fruit juice is added, the mead is called *melomel*. There are abundant subcategories of this style. Mead made with rose petals is called rhodomel. When the fruit is apple or apple cider, the mead is called *cyser*. When grapes or wine are added, the mead is called *pyment*. All of these styles are made into beverages that either are dry or slightly off-dry. As Robert says, it is a myth that mead is necessarily sweet. However, those meads made to be rich and sweet are called sack.

Robert, who also gives beekeeping courses at Tugwell Creek, describes mead as the ultimate expression of beekeeping. "I have been keeping bees since I was seven years old," says Robert, who holds a master's degree in entomology. Born in 1956 and raised in East Vancouver, he juggled beekeeping with other jobs. He and Dana had been living in the Fraser Valley, keeping hives in forest clear-cuts each summer.

In 1996, seeking a pristine environment in which to produce pure honey, the couple found a five-hectare (12-acre) oceanside property north of Sooke, open to the cleansing ocean breezes. "We don't get a lot of pollution," says Robert, who can see the distant Olympic Mountains from Tugwell Creek's tasting room. The farm takes its name from a nearby creek which, in turn, was named for the Tugwell family that lived at this remote location in the 1850s.

In a quest for exceptionally pure honey, Robert places most of his hives (about a hundred) in the logged areas of the mountain forests beyond Sooke. "There is nobody driving around up in the clear-cuts," he notes. The bees gather nectar from plants flourishing there, including salal and fireweed. Depending on how generous nature is, Robert harvests between 1,800 and 2,700 kilograms (4,000 and 6,000 pounds) of honey each season. About two-thirds of the honey is used to make about 6,000 litres (1,350 gallons) of mead annually; the remainder is sold directly from the farm or from selected shops on Vancouver Island.

After a quarter century of dabbling in home mead making, Robert began to scale up about 1994, making four barrels of what he now calls vintage mead. His technique was modelled on flor sherry production, where the wine was left to age and oxidize in the barrels. "I walked on eggshells for about three years," he recalls. "We were not sure if we could pull it off, but we did. It produced a product very similar to sherry. It was very dry. It was an aperitif. It was exceedingly dry, with about 14.5 percent alcohol, and with really nice honey and blossom overtones to it." Initially, all the mead was for personal consumption or for gifts. When the meadery opened, however, a portion of this mead was bottled, selling out in a matter of months. Vintage mead now has a regular place in the Tugwell Creek range, along with spiced *metheglin* (called Solstice), fruity *melomel* (including Brazen Blackberry), and sweet sacks such as Wassail Gold.

"All of my meads are made in a wine style," says Robert, who uses standard wine yeasts. He ages most of the meads in French oak barrels; some also finish fermentation in the oak. The time in oak typically is shorter than would be the case with wine, to prevent the wood flavours from dominating the complex taste of mead. The fruit mead, or *melomel,* spends almost no time in oak. "*Melomels* are quite a delicate wine," he explains. "We are trying to bring forward the flavours of the fruit as well as the honey and marry them together in such a way that they won't be over-powering each other." The fruit comes from Tugwell Creek's own heritage bushes of marionberry, loganberry, and gooseberry. Blackberries grow in wild abundance all over Vancouver Island. The wine, slightly off-dry, has only 11 percent alcohol, enhancing its ability to be paired with foods. Robert recommends pairing this mead with salmon or serving it at picnics.

Robert acknowledges that mead is still a beverage that needs to be explained to consumers. "People show up at the farm every day and ask what is a meadery," he laments. To reach beyond its own shop, Tugwell Creek sells selectively through restaurants, such as the Sooke Harbour House, that have good wine lists and knowl-edgeable wine servers prepared to "spend some time with their clientele to explain mead," Robert says. "I don't think it does well unless someone sells it a little bit."

He and Dana welcomed the additional meaderies that have now opened — Middle Mountain Mead on Hornby Island and Campbell's Gold Honey Farm & Meadery in Abbotsford. "I'd like to see some more meaderies starting up," Robert says. "It will lend credibility to what we are trying to do."

TURTLE MOUNTAIN VINEYARDS

OPENED: 1994 (AS BELLA VISTA VINEYARDS). REOPENING PROPOSED FOR SPRING 2009

3111 Agnew Road, Vernon, BC V1H 1A1
250.540.1011

RECOMMENDED

CURRENT RANGE NOT TASTED

THE BELLA VISTA DISTRICT ON THE WEST SIDE OF VERNON IS APTLY NAMED FOR the lovely vista from these south-facing slopes. Sid Sidhu and his family have grown fruits and vegetables here since 1987, selling them directly through their successful Bella Vista Farm Market. The winery that was built higher up the slope in 1994 by a Vernon group of investors with no relationship to the Sidhu family also adopted the Bella Vista name. The winery was such an embarrassing failure that, after Sid bought the property in 2005 in a court-ordered bankruptcy sale, he decided to start afresh as Turtle Mountain (the name of a nearby peak) in order to shed negative baggage.

Sid bought the property with the intention of converting the vineyard to cherries and vegetables. By midsummer, however, the appeal of wine had ensnared him. "We'll get a grape crop off this fall," he said in an interview with the *Vernon Morning Star* in August 2005. Far from planting cherry trees, Sid disclosed that his priority after vintage would be "to fix the place up and get a marketable product." He began in 2006 by rejuvenating a vineyard so neglected that weeds were choking the vines. He replaced 3.5 hectares (nine acres) — the entire tangled planting except for a three-acre block of Maréchal Foch — with 11,400 vines, equally divided among Pinot Gris, Gewürztraminer, and Auxerrois. Sid made his way cautiously into the wine industry: the first crop from those varietals, picked in 2008, was sold to a Naramata Bench winery. However, the Foch, picked at superb ripeness, was retained for Turtle Mountain.

"I'm not in a rush," Sid says, with the long view of a farmer. "What I don't want to do is start sprinting before I know how to walk." His family has operated their Bella Vista farm since 1987. Born in England, Sid joined his family in 1991 after university, where he got a diploma in biotechnology and a degree in chemical engineering, with an expertise in fermentation that should be helpful in the winery.

Bella Vista Vineyards was launched in 1994 by a group headed by the self-described fun-loving Larry Passmore, the former owner of a home winemaking store. Personal problems and rustic winemaking led to the winery failing, in spite of Larry's best efforts to market the tasting room for weddings and other social functions. The site is superb. The colonial-style winery perches high above the vineyard, which is planted on a warm south-facing slope. Surprisingly, even though Vernon is at the north end of the Okanagan, this vineyard boasts one of the valley's longest frost-free growing seasons.

After getting the vineyard in shape, Sid turned his attention to the winery itself. The building, which had run down, has been renovated to recapture its original antebellum charm. Extensive landscaping was also required, for one of Larry's hobbies was moving a lot of earth around with his tractor.

Turtle Mountain has the potential to become a much larger winery than it ever was. Sid and his family own another 12 hectares (30 acres) nearby on which they grow apples and other tree fruits. Sid is open to switching to grapes as the winery's sales grow.

22 OAKS WINERY

OPENING PROPOSED FOR 2009

> 1 – 6380 Lakes Road, Duncan, BC V9L 5V6
> 250.701.0385
> When to visit: To be established

RECOMMENDED

CURRENT RANGE NOT TASTED

THE LUCKY NUMBER FOR SEVERAL PARTNERS BEHIND THIS COWICHAN VALLEY winery is 22. One partner had that number as a professional hockey player; one couple married on that day; one individual has a birthday on that date. And when the trees were cleared from Jeff MacLeod's property for a vineyard, 22 magnificent oaks remained. When the partners brainstormed winery names, nothing resonated quite like 22 Oaks.

Jeff and Lisa, his wife, are one of the four couples behind this winery. Jeff was born in New Westminster in 1963 and, after high school, followed his father into a career as a Safeway manager. He ended up in the Cowichan Valley when he was transferred to manage the Safeway store in Duncan in 1996. While he was subsequently promoted to run a larger store in Victoria, the vineyard and now the winery keep him rooted in the Cowichan Valley.

He came to winemaking through Lisa's Italian family, making many barrels of robust Zinfandel with Lisa's father and grandfather, both called Giovanni Cosco. "We used to drink it from mason jars right out of the barrel," Jeff recalls. "It was as Old World as it got. But I have always had a huge science interest, so the biology of it and the microchemistry intrigued me." About 2000 he was introduced to New World winemaking when a trip to Napa Valley provided opportunities to pick the brains of professional winemakers. He came back to Vancouver Island and started planning a winery with three other wine-loving couples who also live in the valley.

Greg and Judy Adams live in the other house on the winery property. The owner of several Tim Hortons franchises, Greg was born in Duncan in 1960. He played in the National Hockey League with seven different teams but spent most of his 10-year career with the Washington Capitals. When he retired from hockey in 1990, he returned to Duncan to establish a construction business as well as open restaurants.

The third couple is Doug and Tracey Bodger. Doug, who was born in Chemainus in 1966, played more than one thousand games in a 16-year career as a defenceman with six NHL teams. He finished his career with the Vancouver Canucks, retiring in December 1999. Returning to the Cowichan Valley, he operated a sporting goods shop in Duncan and coached the local hockey team. Described by Jeff as a "hands-on" operator, Doug often runs the vineyard tractor.

The final couple in this partnership is Jerry and Ronnie Doman. He is a member of the Cowichan Valley's most renowned forest products family (Herb Doman was his uncle). Jerry operates both Chemainus Forest Products, which has a planer mill, and Centurion Lumber, a lumber buyer and trucking company. Jerry owns the other vineyard behind the 22 Oaks project.

Planting began in both vineyards in 2007. Jerry has just over two hectares (five acres), with three clones of Pinot Noir on a sun-drenched knoll and a little room left over for white varieties, likely Ortega. Jeff's 1.4-hectare (3½-acre) vineyard is planted primarily with Cabernet Foch and Maréchal Foch, with small blocks of Merlot and Sauvignon Blanc. As well Jeff planted 120 Tempranillo vines, a variety in which he has taken a special interest.

Eager to get the winery open by mid-2009 even if their vineyards were not yet producing, the 22 Oaks partners turned to outside sources for grapes. They contracted the Adora winery in the Okanagan to produce Syrah and Pinot Gris. And because they did not have their own licence in time for crush, they arranged to have the nearby Deol winery make a vintage of Maréchal Foch. They expect to do the entire 2009 crush in their own winery, which has been built into Jeff and Lisa's home.

The tasting room and the winery's patio have views across the vineyard, which slopes toward Quamichan Lake, a shallow but picturesque lake just east of Duncan. The setting, Jeff believes, will help turn 22 Oaks into a destination winery that taps the Cowichan Valley's burgeoning wine tourism.

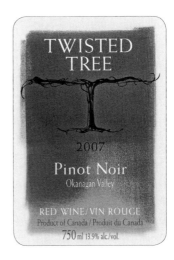

TWISTED TREE VINEYARDS & WINERY

OPENED: 2006

> 3628 Highway 3 East, Osoyoos, BC V0H 1V6
> 250.495.5161
> www.twistedtree.ca
> When to visit: Open daily 10 am – 5 pm May through October

RECOMMENDED

> SYRAH
> MERLOT
> PINOT NOIR
> SAUVIGNON BLANC
> RIESLING

THIS WINERY GETS ITS NAME FROM THE CHERRY TREES THAT ONCE STOOD where there is now a vineyard. Years of pruning had left the trees looking, as the winery owners put it, "haunted and twisted." The irony is that not a single tree remains. Chris and Beata Tolley wanted to keep one until they realized that it would just disrupt the disciplined vine rows in the 2.4-hectare (six-acre) vineyard.

Disciplined is an apt analogy for how the Tolleys, who met at university, went about developing Twisted Tree. Born in Montreal in 1966, Chris became a software engineer in Calgary. Beata, who was born in Poland and came to Canada with her family in her late teens, practised as a chartered accountant.

They were successful in their careers but not satisfied. "We were looking for something more, something better, and we decided to do a winery and vineyard," Chris says. Lacking a wine background, they went to New Zealand in 2003, where both took post-graduate degrees in oenology and viticulture at Lincoln University. "We thought a formal education had done fairly well in getting us started in our previous careers," Chris says, explaining that decision. "Both Chris and I are pretty risk averse," Beata adds. "We like to manage our affairs. It seemed like the sensible thing to do."

The career change initially was challenging. "The learning curve is so steep at the beginning that you can't even follow the conversations," Chris remembers. "It was occasionally like that when we were in New Zealand. A lot of fellow students had quite a bit of experience. When they would start talking, we had no idea what they were talking about. I just couldn't imagine being in that situation. So we thought we'd better have an idea of what's going on."

When the Tolleys were well prepared, and only then, did they start searching for a vineyard and winery property in the Okanagan. They found the old cherry orchard at the eastern edge of Osoyoos that was being sold after the previous owner's death. The highway frontage of what had also been a fruit stand attracted them, because the Tolleys intend to sell a considerable volume of wine directly from the tasting room.

They picked the property's last cherry crop in 2004 before converting it to vines the following spring. Meanwhile they made their first 327 cases of wine in 2004 with purchased fruit, establishing relations with growers that have continued. They rely on growers for mainstream varieties such as Pinot Noir, Merlot, and Riesling, because they have dedicated their own property to an eclectic selection of varieties seldom found elsewhere in the Okanagan. "We'd like to use fruit from our end of the valley if we can, because it is closer to home and it would be a nice representation of where we are," Beata says. The Riesling is the main exception, coming from vineyards in the central Okanagan better suited to Riesling than Twisted Tree's sun-baked west-facing slope at Osoyoos. "We make Riesling because we both love Riesling," Beata says.

"We decided to plant varieties that we could not readily find in the valley," Chris says. With budwood imported from California, they propagated Carmenère, Tempranillo, Tannat, Roussanne, Marsanne, and Viognier. "The one thing those varieties have in common is that they are seen to be capable of producing high-quality wines," Beata believes. "They are noble varieties." Subsequently they added five hundred vines of Corvina, an Italian red used in making Valpolicella wines. Theirs is the Okanagan's first planting of both Corvina and Tannat. The latter is a tannic red grown primarily in Uruguay and the south of France and almost nowhere else.

In choosing such varieties, the Tolleys have differentiated Twisted Tree from its peers in the Okanagan. In researching their entry into the wine business, the couple visited the tasting rooms of many Okanagan wineries. "When we were going winery to winery, we seemed to run into the same wines again and again," Chris recalls. "When somebody had a Viognier, we perked up a bit. We thought that is kind of fun." So they selected varieties that, if the vines succeed in the Okanagan, provide novelty for visitors to Twisted Tree.

Until completing a winery in 2007, the Tolleys made their wines in the buildings that formerly served the fruit stand. The cool, well-equipped winery, set slightly back from the highway, has the tasting room on the side away from the highway. The tasting room windows look out on the vineyard, with Osoyoos and the lake in the distance, a view that in itself is a reason for lingering while sipping Twisted Tree's well-made wines.

The refinement of the wines makes one forget that the Tolleys are recent to the wine industry — and that Beata is also the mother of two young children. She no longer practises as an accountant but, she adds, "I have retained my designation. It is a set of skills that is great to have and is put to good use in this business. This is nothing but problems. Half the battle is doing the right type of analysis. Accounting lets you make the best decision possible."

VAN WESTEN VINEYARDS

VAN WESTEN VINEYARDS

OPENED: 2005

2800B Aikens Loop, Naramata, BC V0H 1N0
250.496.0067
www.vanwestenvineyards.com
When to visit: Tuesdays and Saturdays by appointment

RECOMMENDED

VIOGNIER
VIVACIOUS
VOLUPTUOUS
VINO GRIGIO

IN LAUNCHING THIS WINERY, ROBERT VAN WESTEN FOUND A CLEVER WAY OF branding his wines — giving them all names that start with "V" and embossing that letter boldly onto each bottle. Worried that this could prove limiting, I checked the index of Jancis Robinson's classic book *Vines, Grapes and Wines* to discover more than a column of alphabetically suitable varieties. Valdepeñas, Valdiqué, Verdelho, Verdicchio, Vespaiolo — just for starters. Who knows? The Van Westen family still have substantial Naramata Bench cherry orchards to convert to vineyard.

Robert's father, Jake, a graduate of a Dutch agricultural school, set out to see the world in 1954, ending up working on Naramata orchards and then buying his own. Only in the late 1990s did he start converting some of his land to grapes. It was while he was helping plant vines that Robert found a passion for vineyards.

One of a family of four, he was born in 1966 — in the ambulance on the way to the hospital. School held him only to the tenth grade; he then went off to work in construction in Vancouver, ultimately becoming a superintendant. An industry slowdown coincided with his discovery that he enjoyed the vineyard. In 1999 Robert returned to Naramata to help his father and brother, Jake Jr., with the vines and the fruit trees.

He changed careers with ease. "We've grown tree fruits umpteen years and my dad passed his knowledge down to us," he says. "Grapes, we found out, are just a different weed out there to control." He took both the viticulture course and the assistant winemaker's course at Okanagan University College and was such an apt student that he took over teaching a course on operating tractors safely. He gets a little sheepish when he touches on that because, in 2006, his own tractor rolled over on him in a steep part of his vineyard. Between surgeries for a broken hip, the indomitable Robert managed his winery from his wheelchair.

Initially he sold his grapes to existing wineries. He decided to open his own winery after he thought he was not being paid as much for his grapes as their quality merited. "Before I started making wine, I toured Australia and New Zealand for three and a half months," Robert says, reciting at least six major wine regions in which he spent time. That included doing a practicum at an Australian winery. In making his first vintage — the Merlot and Cabernet Franc for his 2003 Voluptuous blend — he arranged to have Ross Mirko, then winemaker at Lang Vineyards, look over his shoulder.

The training wheels came off by the time Ross went to New Zealand in 2005. Robert arranged, as a precaution, to have Lake Breeze winemaker Garron Elmes on call. Judging from the taste of the Van Westen wines, especially the crisply clean whites, things hardly ever go wrong in the winery. That has a great deal to do with the family's meticulous grape growing. Robert is so detail-oriented that there are always two calendars in his desk, so that he can compare climate and other entries in this year's calendar with the previous year.

He eased his way into the wine business, operating for several years from the rural Naramata home that once had been his maternal grandfather's house. Robert and Tammy, his wife, delivered their wines directly to restaurants and other customers. The recovery from his accident delayed the construction of a tasting room. In 2008 he turned a fruit packing house into a winery, adding a tasting room in 2009.

"My vision of a tasting room at this time is just to be open on a Tuesday," he said a few years ago, not entirely in jest. "I enjoy working in the vineyard. I am in the vineyard all the time. Most of my winemaking is done in the evening."

His winemaking, however, is polished. The unoaked whites — the Viognier and the Vino Grigio (Pinot Gris) — are fresh and clean. While the red blend spends perhaps a year and a half in barrel, only a portion of the Vivacious blend (95 percent Pinot Blanc, 5 percent Pinot Gris) is aged in barrel, typically in older barrels to minimize the oak flavours. And that explains why he never expects to have a Chardonnay in his portfolio. That variety not only sits in the wrong part of the alphabet; it also typically carries a lot of oak, which he does not care for. "I have never been a Chardonnay drinker," Robert admits.

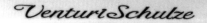

VENTURI-SCHULZE VINEYARDS

OPENED: 1993

> 4235 Vineyard Road (Trans-Canada Highway), Cobble Hill, BC V0R 1L5
> 250.743.5630
> www.venturischulze.com
> When to visit: 11 am – 4 pm during summer weekends; groups by appointment

RECOMMENDED

> BALSAMIC VINEGAR
> PRIMAVERA
> BRANDENBURG NO. 3
> BRUT NATUREL
> MILLEFIORI
> HARPER'S ROW
> PINOT NOIR
> INDIGO

THE ATTENTION TO DETAIL AT VENTURI-SCHULZE IS FANATICAL. WHEN WET weather during the 2007 vintage caused minor rot among the Ortega grapes, the winery's owners used nail scissors to snip away flawed individual berries before crush. It is all about the pursuit of winemaking perfection. "I think we are on the right track," Giordano Venturi said in one interview. "We've maintained our reputation. We are considered the best."

Giordano, his wife, Marilyn, and her daughter Michelle Schulze are self-described purists who use only the grapes grown on their own eight-hectare (20-acre) vineyard. "We do our viticulture without poisons," says Marilyn, meaning that pesticides and herbicides are never used in a vineyard where farming is virtually organic. Such discipline is necessary because the winery's most iconic products, a dessert wine called Brandenburg No. 3, and balsamic vinegar, both involve grape juice concentrated by simmering, which would magnify any impurities.

They also espouse the purist view that wines made on Vancouver Island should use only Vancouver Island grapes. At the very least, they have argued (with some success) that the labels should say so when an island winery uses Okanagan grapes. Giordano celebrates the uniqueness of island wines. "You can't get this wine anywhere else," he points out. "I would really like to develop this area as a destination. People would come here to get the wines they cannot get anywhere else." The winery makes fewer than two thousand cases per year, along with 2,400 miniature bottles of vinegar, and typically sells out in days, if not hours.

To understand the passion of Venturi-Schulze, one starts with the fact that Venturi was born into a poor bricklayer's family in Italy in 1941. "We knew our place and our dreams had to be constrained within these boundaries," Giordano wrote later in a short memoir explaining *Brandenburg No. 3*. One Sunday morning during his adolescence, a well-to-do friend whose family lived in a villa invited him to hear a new recording of that Bach concerto. He has never forgotten the music "leaping from wall to wall in an enchanting game," nor the taste of a liqueur served that morning. Years later he created a wine that he planned to call La Rocca until its taste recalled that Sunday morning. The amber wine, a silken medley of blackcurrant, caramel, and honey flavours, was renamed for the concerto.

The other luxury beyond Giordano's reach when he was growing up was balsamic vinegar, Modena's most famous product. Authentic Modena balsamic vinegar is made from wine grape juice that is first concentrated to half its volume through prolonged simmering; then inoculated with vinegar bacteria; and finally aged for many years in small barrels, achieving an intensity of flavour and aroma through evaporation. The real thing is very expensive. Before Giordano came to Canada in 1967, he had not tasted it. In 1970, as he was training to become an electronics teacher, he made his own small barrel of vinegar to experience what had eluded him.

When he and Marilyn began growing grapes on Vancouver Island in 1988, a portion of each year's vintage, beginning with 1990, was reserved for vinegar. Today the fragrant cellar of vinegar barrels (including the 1970 barrel) is slowly aging more than $1 million worth of balsamic vinegar. "It took me 30 years to reach this production," Giordano says. "By the time I am ready to leave either this earth or this vineyard, whichever comes first, the maximum [annual] production I see is about four thousand bottles." And in his first venture into a product not grown on the estate, he has begun trials making vinegar with maple syrup.

"There's no money in it," Marilyn says of her husband's vinegar. "There may be for the third generation. He's doing it to leave a legacy." She matches her husband when it comes to single-minded determination. Born in Australia in 1951, the daughter of a doctor who immigrated to Canada in 1970, she brings to the winery a highly useful degree in microbiology. She met Giordano when both were teachers, a stressful profession they left behind for the heritage farm (circa 1893) near Cobble Hill, where they initially planted 1.2 hectares (three acres) of vines.

They struggled with their vineyard. Their 1991 crop was consumed by birds. Deer, rabbits, and raccoons munched either on the vines or on the fruit. Periodically wasps sucked the juice from aromatic grapes. (In 1991 they tried to salvage some fruit by vacuuming the wasps from the grapes.) And when those challenges were overcome by the mid-1990s, weather patterns changed. "The first eight years here, we didn't get an April frost, let alone a May frost," Marilyn says. In recent years, bud-killing frosts have struck into early May.

In 1996 they were the first on Vancouver Island to begin tenting the late-ripening varieties such as Pinot Noir, Kerner, and Pinot Gris. Plastic tents deployed over the rows in the spring protected the vines from frost and created a greenhouse effect that accelerated growth by two or three weeks. "Everybody made fun of us," Michelle remembers. The laughing stopped when others, many now also tenting, saw that Venturi-Schulze Pinot Noirs were getting as ripe as those in the Okanagan. The winery's 2003 vintage topped out at 15.4 percent alcohol, a wine so robust that Marilyn recommended pairing it with buffalo.

The original vineyard was too small to support both wine and vinegar production. In 1999 they bought an adjoining pasture, making room for an additional 5.2 hectares (13 acres) of vineyard, part of a $2.5 million expansion that also included a new winery. With the exception of five clones of Pinot Noir and a test block with Swiss-developed red hybrids, both vineyards are dedicated to white vines, including Madeleine Angevine, Kerner, Schönburger, Siegerrebe, and Pinot Gris. "Vancouver Island is white wine country, with the exception of Pinot Noir, really," Marilyn believes.

Labels such as Brandenburg No. 3 illustrate the Venturi-Schulze strategy of creating proprietary labels, especially for wines made from varietals that grow well on the island but are not fashionable enough to fetch prices needed to cover the cost of growing grapes in the fanatical Venturi-Schulze style. Schönburger, thus, becomes Primavera; another fine dry white called Millefiori is made from Madeleine Angevine, Siegerrebe, and Ortega. "We decided to create our own identity around our proprietary names," Marilyn says. The identity extends even to the packaging. Except for the No. 3, the wines all go into heavy Champagne bottles that have been closed with crown caps since 1996. That liberates the winery from quality concerns, such as bottle variation and taint from faulty corks. "I would not want to go back to anything else," Giordano says.

THE VIEW WINERY & VINEYARD

OPENED: 2008

2287 Ward Road, Kelowna, BC V1N 4R5
250.215.1331
theviewwinery@shaw.ca
When to visit: No tasting room

RECOMMENDED

RED SHOE GEWÜRZTRAMINER
RED SHOE PINOTAGE

THE FARMHOUSE ON WARD ROAD, NEXT TO THE HULKING GREY PACKING HOUSE, has been a home to members of Chris Turton's family ever since his grandfather, George Ward, settled on this slope overlooking Kelowna and the Okanagan Valley. For most of those years the slope has been covered with apple and cherry trees. Chris Turton and his forebears have been among the major apple growers in the area.

A decade or so ago, apple prices softened so much that Chris needed another way to create value. He took out some of his trees to plant grapes in 1994. And he teamed up with Jeff Harder (now one of the owners of the Ex Nihilo winery) and Calona Vineyards to crush some of his apples for cider. A brand called Ward's Apple Cider was exported to the United States. As well the partners enlisted Calgary's Big Rock Brewery to develop Rock Creek Premium Dry Cider, which is sold in western Canada both in cans and as pub draft.

In 2006 Calona, running short of space in its winery, ended its agreement to ferment the apple juice that Chris was producing. Moving quickly, he installed his own tanks at the Ward Road warehouse so that his company, Canada West Tree Fruits Ltd., could take over fermenting and producing Rock Creek. And that decision was also the spark that led to the creation of the View Winery.

Chris's daughter, Jennifer, and her husband, television journalist Kent Molgat, had spoken to her father about starting a small winery of their own one day. When Calona decided to stop fermenting cider, Chris turned to his daughter and, as she remembers it, said: "If you want to own a winery, get me a licence."

Born in Kelowna in 1969, Jennifer is a teacher. She happened to be on maternity leave when her father asked her to get a winery licence. She took another year off from teaching, giving her time to work on the winery project and to decide whether to change careers. "My dad sort of roped me in because he knew I had the time," she says with a smile. "But I am glad he did. I am enjoying this and I am excited about the future." However, she still keeps a foot in teaching; a skilled equestrian, she teaches children how to ride.

Chris expanded the vineyard to 14 hectares (35 acres). To the Ehrenfelser, Optima, and Pinotage already in the ground, he added Gewürztraminer, Riesling, and Baco Noir, all of them varieties believed well-suited to the View's comparatively cool site. The two hectares (five acres) of Baco Noir, a full-bodied and dark-hued red, is believed to be the first significant planting of this variety in the Okanagan in 20 years. The Pinotage, with vines that Chris sourced in South Africa, is the most northerly planting of this red variety. The View also has a South African vineyard manager, Willem Semmelink, with experience growing Pinotage.

Needing help to ferment both the cider and the new grape wines, Jennifer and Chris first tapped the consulting expertise of Soaring Eagle's German-born winemaker Bernhard Schirrmeister (see Holman Lang Wineries, page 186). They were impressed by the winemaker's knowledge of grape growing and asked if he could recommend a similarly trained German winemaker. He suggested Markus Haken, who was born in the Pfalz wine region in 1966, trained at Weinsberg, and gained experience at family wineries after apprenticing at Dr. Bürkin-Wolf; after vacationing in the Okanagan several times, he wanted to move here. However, he spent only the 2007 vintage here before deciding to return to Germany.

Jennifer replaced him with Marie-Thérese Duarte, a 33-year-old French-trained winemaker. She came to the Okanagan from California, working initially at Rollingdale Winery. "She is excited about working with apple wine," Jennifer marvels. "It is hard work because it involves big volumes." No apologies need be made for the cider business, which provides needed cash while the winery becomes established. The cider is so successful that Chris, who even has a grove of select European cider trees, has regretted removing some of his apple trees.

Jennifer credits her father for naming the winery. The name suggests itself to anyone standing at the upper edge of the vineyard, looking over the valley with, at night, the lights of the city twinkling across the horizon. When it proved impractical to open the tasting room in the old packing house, Jennifer delayed opening one until the View has a winery on the vineyard slope.

VIGNETI ZANATTA WINERY & VINEYARDS

OPENED: 1992

5039 Marshall Road, RR3, Duncan, BC V9L 6S3
250.748.2338
www.zanatta.ca
When to visit: Call for seasonal hours
Restaurant: Vinoteca on the Vineyard (250.709.2279) open noon – 2:30 pm
    Wednesday to Friday, noon – 4 pm Saturday and Sunday

RECOMMENDED

GLENORA FANTASIA BRUT
FATIMA BRUT
ALLEGRIA BRUT ROSÉ
TAGLIO ROSSO BRUT
DAMASCO
PINOT NERO
ORTEGA
PINOT GRIGIO

IT IS NOT SURPRISING THAT A THIRD OF THIS WINERY'S PRODUCTION SHOULD be sparkling wine, since winemaster Loretta Zanatta did post-graduate work in Italy, making spumante at a relative's winery. But according to Jim Moody, her husband and the winery's vineyard manager, the sparkling tradition began with his father-in-law's home winemaking.

Dennis Zanatta, who grew up in northern Italy but settled on this Cowichan Valley farm in 1958, had been making wines in a rustic style from vines planted in the early 1970s. "Dennis made the wine according to the phases of the moon," Jim explains. Wines would be racked and later bottled during the full moon. "Sometimes the wine hadn't finished fermenting because it was out in the barn during the wintertime. Then it would re-ferment in the bottle. It turned out quite well. So when

Loretta went to Italy, she perfected it." She put her stamp on the winery's sparklers beginning with the 1990 Glenora Fantasia, now the flagship wine among the sparkling wines (including a red one) made at Vigneti Zanatta.

Dennis Zanatta's contribution to wine growing on Vancouver Island until his death in 2008 went well beyond sparkling wines. In 1983 he provided a corner of his property, along with farm labour and equipment, for a grape-growing trial begun that year by the provincial government. This so-called Duncan Project tested at least 50 varieties before government funding ran out in 1990 — the same year that Loretta completed her professional training in Italy. Dennis had learned enough from the Duncan Project that he planted six hectares (15 acres) of vines in 1989 and later doubled that. In 1992 the Zanatta family opened the first new winery on Vancouver Island in about 70 years.

From the very beginning, Vigneti Zanatta has made wine only from its own grapes, never purchasing Okanagan grapes. The winery's owners are determined that the wines should express the island terroir, even if the climate on Vancouver Island is so capricious that the winery's production can swing between 1,500 and 2,500 cases per year.

Jim argues that the style of Vancouver Island wine "is a little more aromatic and the flavours are a little more subtle" than Okanagan wines. The Ortega grape, which can yield a dry fruity white with a hint of spice, is a Vancouver Island specialty. A German-created cross, Ortega matures reliably in cool climates to yield no more than 12 percent alcohol. But in those seasons that are warmer than average, Ortega ripens exuberantly. "One year we got 13 percent," Jim recalls. "It was kind of embarrassing really for a white wine."

In most vintages, Zanatta sells grapes to other wineries on the island, because its vines yield more fruit than the winery needs to support its sales. The Zanatta vineyard is one of the island's largest, growing not only the most successful Duncan Project varieties (such as Ortega, Auxerrois, and Pinot Gris) but also Cabernet Sauvignon, Merlot, and Cabernet Franc, the big reds of the Okanagan. The winemaking at Zanatta needs to be more flexible to deal with the lower ripeness of those varieties on the island. The Cabernet Sauvignon has been turned into Taglio Rosso, one of British Columbia's first red sparkling wines. Some of the reds are blended artfully with, if needed, a touch of the vineyard's blood-red Castel grape, a French hybrid that came through the Duncan Project well.

Loretta's answer to what she calls "the incredible variability" of Vancouver Island's season is demonstrated by Damasco, a fruity white wine incorporating at least four grapes, including Auxerrois. The Damasco is not vintage-dated because the winery prefers to make a more consistent wine by blending several vintages. On Vancouver Island a fully ripe vintage can be followed by a cool, high-acid vintage. Consistent quality has made Damasco the best-selling of Zanatta's wines.

As one of the largest plantings in the Zanatta vineyard, Auxerrois shows up in several wines. It goes into the cuvée with Pinot Noir to make another of the winery's four bubblies, the Allegria Brut Rosé. As production has grown, Zanatta has been able to age all of its sparkling wines for four years on the lees before the final bottling, in a quest for complexity.

The winery's flagship sparkler gets the Glenora half of its name from the local district. Fantasia, the second half, is pronounced *Fant-a-ZEE-ah*. It is British Columbia's only wine made with Cayuga grapes. This is an aromatic grape developed in New York State in 1945 by plant scientists looking for a winter-hardy, productive white. Cayuga was included in the Duncan Project because the government's grape expert saw the reliable variety as "a mortgage maker." Zanatta maintains enough vines to produce about three hundred cases per year of Glenora Fantasia.

The best place to taste the Zanatta wines is the winery's Vinoteca restaurant, which opened in 1996. The restaurant is in a fully restored farmhouse built in 1903, with views from its veranda over the vineyards. Indeed, some Zanatta wines are made in small volumes, to be served only in the Vinoteca.

VISTA D'ORO FARMS & WINERY

OPENED: 2008

20856 4th Avenue, Langley, BC V2Z 1T6
604.514.3539
www.vistadoro.com
When to visit: Open 10 am – 4 pm Thursday through Saturday and by appointment

RECOMMENDED

D'ORO
PINOT NOIR

THE FLAGSHIP WINE HERE IS D'ORO, A WALNUT WINE DELICIOUSLY RECALLING an Oloroso sherry. However, when Patrick and Lee Murphy applied for a winery licence, the regulators said there is no such thing as a walnut wine. They finally received a licence after a strenuous submission by one of their former partners in the winery, lawyer Wade Nesmith, a former regulator himself (with the British Columbia Securities Commission).

In fact, D'oro is based on an old French recipe from the late 18th century handed down through the family of Jerome Dudicourt, a friend of Patrick and Lee and a former Vancouver pastry chef. Several years ago he was invited to the Murphy farm to coach Lee on culinary matters. During a relaxing stroll through the orchards on this four-hectare (10-acre) Fraser Valley property, he asked what they intended to do with their walnuts. "Walnut oil," Patrick replied. Jerome paused and then shared the family recipe for walnut wine.

The technique seems to have been perfected by Jerome's grandfather, Jean-Baptiste, a farmer in northern France who lived to 98, which in itself is an endorsement of walnut wine. Generally he harvested his walnuts on Bastille Day, July 14, when the nuts are still green fruit. Following this practice Patrick, for his initial barrel of D'oro, made his first harvest on Bastille Day in 2001. The nuts, still green and soft, are macerated in brandy. When sufficient flavour has been extracted, the liquid is racked, blended with a full-bodied red wine, and aged in barrels (primarily American oak). The result is a rich, amber liquid with a warming 18.5 percent alcohol. Because no fermentation is involved, Patrick is not permitted to put wine on the front label. The story of the recipe is on the back label, however.

Patrick has family recipes of his own. A skilled home winemaker, he started learning the art from his Lithuanian-born maternal grandfather, Ciprijonas Grencas, who fermented almost everything, including plums. The Italian plum trees were planted along the driveway at Vista D'oro for plum wines. "I have always made my wine," Patrick says. "I started with California Merlot and Zinfandel. Then in the early 1990s I met some growers in the Okanagan. I got hooked and started picking my own grapes up there."

There was also a life before wine. Born in New Westminster in 1962 and trained in management at the British Columbia Institute of Technology, Patrick spent 16 years, until 1996, at Ritchie Brothers, a Vancouver heavy equipment auction house that now operates across the globe. Lee, his wife, worked in the accounting department there until leaving to have their first child. After they bought their Fraser Valley property in 1997, Patrick, a talented carpenter and woodworker, began making custom-designed furniture while Lee, after studying at the Northwest Culinary Academy in Vancouver, created an ever-expanding range of preserves, using the produce from their farm and elsewhere in the valley. The produce includes heritage tomatoes that Patrick starts as plants in his greenhouse.

"I had a passion for tomatoes," Patrick says. "When we first started marketing Vista D'oro [in 2002], we would go down to farmers' markets in Vancouver and sell our tomatoes and whatever else we had. That's where Lee first started selling her preserves. People came back looking for more. That gave us the endorsement and confidence to build this facility." When chefs and restaurateurs began visiting the farm for Lee's preserves, Patrick often invited them to sample his wines. "The restaurateurs loved my Meritage and said, 'Go get your licence,' " Patrick recalls. It was the encouragement he needed.

In the spring of 2008 he planted about 1.4 hectares (3½ acres) of vines on his Langley property, carefully choosing varieties — Maréchal Foch, Ortega, Siegerrebe, Schönburger, and Pinot Gris — that are likely to ripen here. For his other wines, including Pinot Noir and reds from Bordeaux varieties, he is contracting grapes from growers in the Okanagan. For the time being the winery has taken over what was his woodworking room. Eventually he plans to build a gravity-flow winery with a tasting room — along with Lee's retail shop — in the farm's character-rich heritage dairy barn.

WELLBROOK WINERY

OPENED: 2004

4626 – 88th Street, Delta, BC V4K 3N3
604.946.1868
www.wellbrookwinery.com
When to visit: Open daily 11 am – 6 pm

RECOMMENDED

BLUEBERRY
CRANBERRY
WHITE CRANAPPLE
FORTIFIED BLUEBERRY DESSERT WINE

TERRY BREMNER'S DEDICATION TO PRESERVING HERITAGE SHOWS AT THIS winery, where everything glows with the patina of age except for the wines and the fruit juices. The Old Grainery Store, as the wine shop is called, is one of the original buildings on the hundred-year-old Delta farm. Formerly used for grain storage, it has been restored meticulously: there is a new roof on the exterior but the underside of the original roof is visible in the interior, soaring four metres (13 feet) above a tasting bar crafted from century-old barn boards. The two-wheeled wooden cart in the corner, now filled with wines and other products, was salvaged from the nearby barn, another original building so dangerously near to collapse when Terry acquired it that some tradesman refused to work inside it. He restored it, with the help of a gutsy carpenter. "I love heritage," he says.

Terry and his mother, Caroline, bought the farm in 2001, becoming only its third owners. It was developed by Seymour Huff, a pioneering Delta farmer who operated it for 50 years before turning it over to his grandson, Gordon, who ran it for another 50 years. As an adolescent, Terry, who was born in Delta in 1959, delivered newspapers to the Huff home. Later Terry was a member of the volunteer fire department when Gordon Huff was the chief.

Seeking a farm on which to develop the winery, Terry was close to buying elsewhere in Delta when he discovered that the Huff farm was available. "This just had so much character," he says. "It was a perfect match." In the two years that Terry spent renovating the buildings, including the house with its wraparound veranda, Gordon provided details of the design and the farm's history. One of those details inspired the winery's name: the property was once called Wellbrook Farms because it had one of the few wells in the area. "I have a picture of the old windmill and the water tower," Terry says.

Terry's vision of Wellbrook is that of a working farm enriched not only by the wines in the Grainery but also by a petting zoo, a pumpkin patch, an antique store, and a display of farming practices. The 22-hectare (55-acre) property, just west of exit 20 on busy Highway 99, grows cranberries, blueberries, and one day a small vineyard. Terry and a brother, Alan, also operate a 33-hectare (82-acre) blueberry farm nearby.

Terry inherited his taste for agriculture from his late father. A long-time assessor for the Corporation of Delta, Stan Bremner changed careers in the 1970s to farm. He once had a flock of three hundred to four hundred sheep whose lambs were so prized that the customer list developed entirely by word of mouth. The Bremner family farm switched to blueberries in the early 1980s and again, the Bremner trademark became known for quality fruit.

When he graduated from high school, Terry managed to see the world by becoming a diamond driller. Warm and gregarious, Terry prefers hands-on experience with cultures when he travels. He worked in North and South America as well as Asia, coming back with colourful stories about the people of the jungles of Indonesia and about living for a month in a Mongolian *ger* (as the country's traditional round tents are called). Those eclectic tastes inform his effort to turn Wellbrook into a memorable destination.

The idea of a winery evolved from the fresh juice business that Terry started in 2000 to offer ultra-premium blueberry and cranberry juices. "I had tried another juice," he recalls. "It did not taste like blueberries. I found they make juice from juice-grade fruit, which is the lowest-grade fruit there is." The juice business was a sheer gamble. "I did all this with no contracts, nothing," he says. "I put away 30,000 pounds of fruit with no idea where it was going." He had a product by Christmas, entered a trade show in January, and just plugged away. He now distributes throughout Canada and into the United States, having built a market even though the juices are almost the same price as fruit wine and — reflecting the raw material cost — often double the cost of competing products.

When the Fort Wine Company opened in 2001, it bought Bremner blueberries and the winemaker praised the berry quality. This inspired Terry, a home fruit wine maker for years, to contract the Fort's winemakers to make wines for Wellbrook as well. "You want to make a good end product," Terry explains. "In my mind the ingredients are the most important item and that's what we do. We grow the best ingredients. Then we found someone who is knowledgeable and good at making the wine." Terry finally took over his own winemaking in 2008 when the Fort stopped providing its services.

With nine varieties of blueberries on his farms, Terry wonders whether there might be a place in the future for named varietals from the four now blended in the Wellbrook wines: Bluecrop, Hardyblue, Olympia, and Spartan. It might be an uphill battle. "With wines, you can say specific varieties of grapes because people have been educated for one thousand years about them," Terry says. "With blueberries, most people don't even know there is more than one variety."

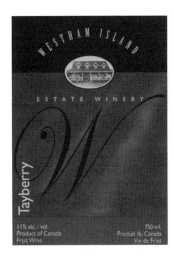

WESTHAM ISLAND ESTATE WINERY

OPENED: 2003

2170 Westham Island Road, RR1, Delta, BC V4K 3N2
604.940.9755
www.westhamislandwinery.com
When to visit: Open 11 am – 5 pm Monday through Friday, 10:30 am – 6 pm weekends
and holidays

RECOMMENDED

STRAWBERRY
RASPBERRY
TAYBERRY
PEACH
BLACK CURRANT
FRAMBOISE
WESTHAM WHITE TABLE WINE
JUST DUCKY

WHEN ANDY BISSETT APPLIED FOR THE FIRST WINERY LICENCE IN DELTA, HE
did not have an easy time breaking the ice with the city. By the time Westham Island
Estate Winery actually opened in the summer of 2003, three other fruit wineries in
the Fraser Valley had opened and two were under development. Sadly, Andy had
died the year before. His feisty widow, Lorraine, took his dream to completion,
breaking a zoning logjam by telephoning the mayor directly. (It may have helped
that she works for the city of Richmond and understands bureaucracy.)

Perhaps Andy Bissett had been a bit of a rough diamond who got under
the skin of the bureaucrats at city hall. "If you piss them off, you suffer," suggests
Lorraine. The oil painting in the winery's antique-rich tasting room shows another
side of Andy Bissett: an amiable figure in hunting gear with his bird-hunting friends
gathered around him.

Besides being a good hunter, Andy was a successful farmer. His 16-hectare (40-acre) property at Agassiz is one of the valley's larger blackcurrant and rhubarb farms. The rich, 14-hectare (35-acre) Westham Island farm, owned by the Bissett family for a quarter century, grows a profusion of berries and even a few rows of Concord, Maréchal Foch, and Madeleine Sylvaner grapes. The cultured blackberries are menu items on cruise ships. The farm's jams, syrups, and produce, which are sold at its fruit stand during the season, have a strong following.

Andy began laying winery plans about the same time that a farmer friend, John Stuyt, opened the Fraser Valley's first fruit winery, Columbia Valley Classics, in 1998 near Cultus Lake. Andy engaged Ron Taylor as the winemaker after meeting him at Columbia Valley, where Ron was consulting. Fruit wines opened a second career for Ron. "Never made fruit wine in my whole life until the last eight or nine years," he says. "It's been a journey!" Born in Vancouver in 1942, he went to work in 1970 at the Andrés winery in Port Moody after graduating in microbiology from the University of British Columbia. In his 22 years there, the avuncular Ron mentored many younger winemakers in his laboratory. After leaving Andrés to work with a bottled water company, Ron returned to wine, this time with fruit wines. He consulted to Columbia Valley and has since helped at least half a dozen fruit wineries, including Westham Island.

Its location on Westham Island, the home of the George C. Reifel Migratory Bird Sanctuary, is an advantage for the winery. "We get an awful lot of traffic," Lorraine observes. Many of the 80,000 visitors to the sanctuary also stop at the winery or the nearby fruit stand. This is the year-round traffic that wineries need. Birdwatchers come from afar in November, for example, to see the thousands of snow geese that return to the island annually. Never missing an opportunity, the winery produces a gooseberry wine called SnoGoos.

Flat and fertile, Westham Island, 648 hectares (1,600 acres) in size, is in the mouth of the south arm of the Fraser River and has been farmed at least since 1870. In the 1920s, George C. Reifel, a successful distiller, bought land on the island for, according to local legend, shipping spirits to the United States during Prohibition. Later he developed a significant farm that, during World War II, produced sugar beets. Ultimately his family leased, sold, and donated the parcels that comprise the bird sanctuary today. Only about five percent of the island is cultivated now, growing berries, fruits, and vegetables.

At the Westham Island winery, most of this profusion — even including pumpkins — has been made into wine by the indefatigable Ron Taylor. One of the winemakers famously involved in the creation of Andrés's Baby Duck, Ron revisited the idea at Westham with a summertime rosé from the Concord and Maréchal Foch grapes. "It is called Just Ducky," he says and chuckles. It is one of the most popular wines in the tasting room.

Westham Island's tayberry wine, with an exotic spicy perfume and taste, is unique, since the Bissett farm is one of the few places in North America growing this fruit. Tayberry is a cross of blackberry, raspberry, and loganberry, so named because the berry was first grown in a Scottish region called Tayside. Ron has also made wines from red, black, and white currants, blueberries, raspberries, peaches, rhubarb, blackberries, and cranberries. His personal favourite is a luscious strawberry dessert wine that he calls a milkshake for adults.

Generally the wines are off-dry to sweet. "I think it's required," Ron explains. "There are some fruits that make interesting dry wines." Indeed, Ron has made commendable dry fruit wines both for Westham Island and for his other clients. "But historically, if you look at fruit wines, people made them for social wines. Sweeter wines can go very well with spicy foods." Although his dessert wines might have about 16 percent alcohol, Ron keeps the table wines at a "gentle" 11 percent to ensure the fruit flavours come through cleanly. "The wines have been very well received," Ron says. "People have been coming back."

WILD GOOSE VINEYARDS

OPENED: 1990

2145 Sun Valley Way, Okanagan Falls, BC V0H 1R0
250.497.8919
www.wildgoosewinery.com
When to visit: Open daily 10 am – 5 pm April 1 to October 31, by appointment
    November through March. Licensed picnic area
Accommodation: Mystic River guest cottage

RECOMMENDED

RIESLING
GEWÜRZTRAMINER
PINOT GRIS
PINOT BLANC
AUTUMN GOLD
MARÉCHAL FOCH
BLACK BRANT (PORT-STYLE)

HERE'S AN ILLUSTRATION THAT TELLS YOU JUST HOW GOOD A WINERY WILD Goose really is. Mission Hill, a major producer with almost unlimited resources, was the winery of the year at the 2007 Canadian Wine Awards. Tiny Wild Goose was a runner-up. Both wineries scored with just about every wine entered — Wild Goose just didn't have as many wines to enter. As it happens, the two wineries have a shared history. A grape purchase contract from Mission Hill, which ended in 1996, enabled Wild Goose founder Adolf Kruger to get into the wine business.

Born in Germany in 1931, Adolf made a career in engineering after arriving in Canada at the age of 20. "Sometimes I think that our success, that we got where we are, is because I worked at engineering and it was fairly disciplined," Adolf says. When an engineering industry downturn threatened his job, he changed careers. A friend made a comfortable living with an Okanagan vineyard. Adolf, who was making wine as an amateur, purchased a rugged four hectares (10 acres) of raw land southeast of Okanagan Falls in 1983. When first inspecting the land, he spooked a flock of geese into flight, the experience that later inspired the winery's name.

Adolf initially aspired only to be a good grower. Then the 1989 free trade agreement created uncertainty for Okanagan vineyards. Adolf joined with other owners of tiny vineyards to press for a farm gate licence so that they could still make a living if the big wineries stopped buying their grapes. The bureaucrats in Victoria were skeptical. One asked Adolf how much wine he expected to sell in a year. "I had a vision of a little wine shop and doing the vineyard and selling wine on the side," Adolf remembers. "I said, 'I'm looking at least at selling two thousand to three thousand bottles a year.' And he looked at me and said, 'I don't think you can sell two thousand bottles.' The vision just wasn't there." Wild Goose now sells close to 100,000 bottles per year.

When Adolf planned his vineyard, the industry consultants warned him that his chosen European varieties would not grow in the Okanagan. Relying on German technical literature, he ignored that warning and planted Gewürztraminer and Riesling, with just a few rows of Maréchal Foch. "One major consideration at the time was the frost," Adolf says. Thus he chose varieties known for their ability to survive moderately cold winters — and that were in tune with his German palate. Wild Goose specialized in white wines long after reds had become the flavour of the decade. In 1999 the winery planted its second vineyard, call Mystic River, just north of Oliver, putting in Pinot Gris, Pinot Blanc, and Gewürztraminer. It was only when the winery's third vineyard, called Kruger's Claim, was developed near Okanagan Falls in 2005 that Wild Goose planted not only more Riesling and Gewürztraminer but also, for the first time, Merlot and Malbec. In 2008, when the family planted a 4.5-hectare (11-acre) vineyard northwest of Oliver, more Merlot was planted but also Riesling and Gewürztraminer, varieties that Wild Goose is comfortable with.

The original vineyard stretching up the hill behind the winery was called Stoney Slope for good reason. Naturally occurring rocks are so numerous between the vine rows that visitors often ask if they have been placed there deliberately. Adolf and his sons, Hagen and Roland, struggled to prepare the site for vines. The Krugers wrestled with a high-pressure water gun to drill holes for the vineyard posts. "Hagen worked this water gun all weekend," Adolf remembers. "On Monday morning, he was eating a bowl of cornflakes and the spoon fell out of his hand . . . he couldn't hold onto it." And Hagen is a sturdy, big-boned man. The vines now are more than 25 years old and, fortunately, not showing any decline. "They'll be ready for replanting when our kids are old enough to do it," Hagen says and laughs. "Because I sure don't want to replant those myself, that's for sure!"

Hagen took over as winemaker from his father in the late 1990s. He seems one of those individuals with an effortless talent. On the strength of the family's superb viticulture, he has made an astonishing number of award-winning wines, which have won several Awards of Excellence in the rigorous lieutenant-governor's competition.

The winning wines have included Riesling, a varietal that once was very out of fashion. Wild Goose even dropped Riesling from its portfolio for five vintages after 1995, bringing it back in the 2001 vintage when the Riesling renaissance began. It is now close to a third of Wild Goose's annual production and rivals Gewürztraminer as the winery's flagship wine. "We've been very successful with our whites," Hagen observes. "For me personally, improving the reds is kind of a challenge. I don't feel complete."

These days Roland, who looks after the winery's marketing, struggles to keep enough for the tasting room, one of the friendliest tasting rooms in the Okanagan because it is almost always staffed by a member of the Kruger family. This is very much a family winery, with the third generation interested in what Adolf started. To the family's delight, Hagen's sons have joined the business. Alexander has developed an interest in viticulture. Brother Nikolas has wanted to make wine since he was a teen. Nik has trained at Okanagan University College and spent time in the cellars at both Tinhorn Creek and Hester Creek. In 2008 he worked the vintage at an Australian winery called Bremerton Wines at Langhorne Creek, also family-owned for several generations. He went there because Langhorne Creek is known for producing big reds. "I want to make better reds," Nik says.

WILLOW HILL VINEYARDS

OPENED: 2005

12315 – 326th Avenue, Box 597, Oliver, BC V0H 1T0
250.498.6198
www.willowhillwines.com
When to visit: No wine shop

RECOMMENDED

MERLOT ICEWINE

AT WILLOW HILL, LANNY SWANKY AND JOY VENABLES ARE PURSUING ONE OF the most challenging business plans of any winery. They make icewine exclusively — and late-harvest wines in those rare years when winter is not cold enough for icewine.

The challenge is not making the wine — Willow Hill's Merlot icewines are first-rate. "I had no idea it would be that difficult to sell the little bit of wine we make every year," Lanny says, a note of surprise in his rumbling drawl. "It is a tough sell. People may drink a case of red wine every month, but they don't drink [even] one bottle of icewine every month." That may explain why only two other of Canada's four hundred wineries make dessert wines exclusively. Lanny has been making about 2,500 bottles of icewine each vintage, with the objective of doubling that as he unlocks the markets that he knows are out there. He has had more time to sell since retiring in April 2008 from being a Vincor vineyard manager.

Making and selling icewine is just the latest venture in Lanny's colourful history. He was born in Prince George in 1947, the son of a sawmill owner. On a scholarship, he began studying engineering at Montreal's Concordia University but decided to return to Prince George and work in the lumber industry. He spent about two decades running his own lumber company or working as a contract logger. After winding up that business, he took over one of the city's roughest hotels and ran it until moving to the Okanagan in 1990 to develop a mobile home park near Oliver. He thought that might be a good "retirement project" until, six years later, he sold his interest to his partners. He became interested in viticulture after meeting Joy Venables in 1997. The daughter of a packing house manager, she had grown up in the Okanagan and has worked many years with the government's crop insurance agency. Together Lanny and Joy took the viticulture course at Okanagan University College, primarily to learn how to plant vines on the two-hectare (five-acre) property on the Golden Mile south of Oliver where her family had once grown peaches.

Lanny put his new skills to work first with Richard Cleave's vineyard management crew. He next became the vineyard manager at Hawthorne Mountain Vineyards in 1999 and, after Vincor took over that winery, he was placed in charge of some of Vincor's new plantings.

Meanwhile he and Joy planted primarily Merlot on their Golden Mile property and set about creating Willow Hill. The strategy has been to sell most of the grapes to other wineries. In 2001 they set aside a block of vines just for icewine and engaged Michael Bartier (now Road 13's winemaker) to make the wine. Encouraged by the result, they sold it through Fairview Cellars until Willow Hill had a licence of its own.

The first hiccup was the 2002 vintage, when the freezing conditions needed for icewine (the grapes must be picked at –8°C/18°F) did not occur until the end of February. "We had a holiday planned for Mexico for the end of January," Lanny recalls. They picked the grapes for late-harvest wine before leaving on vacation, having concluded there was little chance of getting the icewine freeze that late in the winter. It was a decision that other Okanagan wineries also made, and not a bad one commercially. Lanny and Joy discovered that late-harvest wine, perhaps because it is half the price of icewine, is easier to sell. It might also be a future strategy for Willow Hill, although Lanny is determined to be an icewine specialist first.

What also distinguishes Willow Hill is that Merlot is seldom used for icewine because the grapes do not cling to the vines as tenaciously and late into the season as, for example, Cabernet Franc or Riesling. Yet Lanny not only succeeds, he has also been refining his style to produce icewines notable for their dark colour and varietal character. "My aim," he says, "is to make a Merlot icewine that you can recognize as Merlot."

Since 2003, after taking a winemaking course, Lanny has been his own winemaker. He has mastered the art with considerable success, winning awards in several wine competitions. He admits some frustration with competitions because wineries seldom get to see the comments of the judges. "I really want to know what the judges think of our wine, good or bad," Lanny says. "It is very difficult to objectively evaluate my own wine. I always think, 'It sure tastes good to me.' But is that accurate or not?" His peers would say he worries too much.

2003
PINOT NOIR
SHARP ROCK VINEYARD

WINCHESTER CELLARS

OPENED: 2004

> 6170 Old West Saanich Road, Victoria, BC V9E 2G8
> 250.544.8217
> www.winchestercellars.com | www.victoriaspirits.com
> When to visit: Open 11 am – 5 pm Saturdays, Sundays, and holidays

RECOMMENDED

> VICTORIA GIN
> EAU DE VIE SPIRITS
> PINOT GRIS
> ORTEGA/BACCHUS

WHAT LIES AHEAD FOR THE WINES OF WINCHESTER CELLARS IS UNCERTAIN after a dispute among partners late in 2008 led to the departure of Ken Winchester, one of the founders and the winemaker. Consequently, Winchester Cellars skipped the 2008 vintage. Under the new managing partners, Bryan Murray and Valerie, his wife, the current focus is on the production of spirits, including the wildly successful Victoria Gin that was launched early in 2008. Both the winery and the distillery tasting room remain at the Barking Dog Vineyard, the organic vineyard operated by John and Lana Popham. Perhaps the winemaking might be picked up by Lana, who worked in the cellar with Ken. The Barking Dog Vineyard — named for the Pophams' clamorous vineyard dogs — grows Bacchus, Ortega, Dornfelder, and four clones of Pinot Noir on 1.5 hectares (3¾ acres).

Before the split it was Ken who learned distilling, purchased a German still, and began developing gin and the other spirits. The Victoria Spirits website lists 10 of the botanical products that flavour the gin, adding that there is an 11th secret ingredient. One can always ask Ken what it is, as if it were that easy to blend a superior gin.

Born in New York in 1952, Ken learned home winemaking with a group of amateurs in 1980 while he was a *Reader's Digest* editor in Montreal. Eventually he pursued a growing love of wine to California, working in magazines while taking winemaking courses at the University of California at Davis. "It carried my wine-making to another level," he recalled. He set up his own winery in 1996 in Paso Robles, specializing in Syrah until selling it in 2002 to move to Victoria. The second Winchester Cellars winery opened here two years later, making wine both with Okanagan grapes and with fruit from Barking Dog. In the 2007 vintage, when Ken decided Okanagan grapes had become too costly, the winery made wine only with island fruit.

"I've distilled just about as long as I made wine," Ken says. "It's a logical exten-sion of the process." In 2006 he invested $50,000 to import a German-built still. He also took relevant courses at Michigan State University, then did a practicum at the famous Bruichladdich distillery on the Isle of Islay in Scotland. "I originally set out to make the first great Canadian single malt whisky," he says. "That being a three- to five-year project, I turned to gin to help pay the bills in the meantime. In the two years I studied and tested gin, I fell in love with its history and complexity, and with the fact that every botanical has a story as well as a flavour." A case in point is angelica, one of the botanicals: it was once used to protect against witches!

Bryan teamed up with Ken in 2006 on the distillery project. A man with a keen palate, he can claim to have tasted every batch of gin made here. When Ken left the partnership, his understudy, Peter Hunt, took over as the distiller. Perhaps the gin eclipsed the wine because of its high-profile launch in May 2008, at the Bombay Room of Victoria's Empress Hotel. The patronage served to validate Ken's gin, and the beverage has been selling out faster than Winchester Cellars can make it.

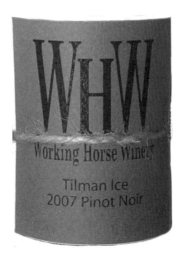

WORKING HORSE WINERY

OPENED: 2009

> 5266 Coldham Road, Peachland, BC V0H 1X2
> 250.448.5007
> www.workinghorsewinery.com
> When to visit: By appointment

RECOMMENDED

> TILMAN ICE
> PINOT NOIR
> ROSÉ

THIS WINERY'S CURIOUS NAME DESCRIBES WHAT ACTUALLY HAPPENS HERE: in 2008 Tilman Hainle and Sara Norman used two Percheron draft horses to work the 2.4-hectare (six-acre) vineyard. It has probably been half a century since anyone in the Okanagan has seriously farmed with horses. Tilman and Sara, two of the most idealistic people in wine country, are deliberately going back to create a future of sustainable wine growing. They acquired a team of Suffolk Punch horses, named Meagen and Greta, the oldest breed (16th-century) of English draft horses, now rarely seen due to farm mechanization. Tilman and Sara regard the breed as something of an endangered species.

Tilman has been at the environmental leading edge before. He converted the Hainle (rhymes with "finely") family vineyards on the slopes above Peachland to organic grape growing in 1993, making him Canada's first producer of certified organic wine. Working Horse, a boutique winery (three thousand cases at most), is being taken well beyond that, a demonstration of how to make fine organic wines with the least possible impact on the fragile Okanagan. Ultimately a small sustainable community is planned on parts of the nine-hectare (22¼-acre) property not used as vineyard.

The property, forested with Ponderosa pine, was a settler's homestead in the 1920s. It had fallen into disuse by the time Walter and Regina Hainle, Tilman's parents, camped there and then bought it in 1972. Walter was a German textile salesman with ulcers who retired to Canada with his family when his doctor told him to change his stressful lifestyle. By 1974 he began planting grapes. "It was going to be just a hobby," Tilman says, "but Dad was always hatching big ideas."

One idea was icewine, a German specialty then not being made anywhere in North America. After making a few experimental lots, Walter, with Tilman helping him press juice from the frozen grapes, made several trial vintages and then North America's first commercial icewine in 1978 — commercial in that it was sold in their wine shop when the Hainle Vineyards winery opened in 1988. An icewine interpretation centre planned for Working Horse will relate the story, exhibiting historic photographs and the basket press used for the early vintages. In his personal cellar Tilman still has one small bottle of the 1974 wine, the first icewine his father made. He recalls taking the bottle to an aunt in Germany who never opened it and then gave it back to him years later.

Tilman, who was born in Stuttgart in 1958, spent two years studying computer science and one year as a customs officer at the Osoyoos border crossing before his father's dabbling with icewine led to the decision to open a winery. Tilman was sent to Weinsberg, a leading German wine school, from which he graduated with honours in 1982. While the family winery was under development, he made four or five vintages for Uniacke Wines, which later became CedarCreek. And with Walter (who died in 1995), he made vintage after vintage of icewine so that the family winery could open with an enviable selection.

He and Sara have done the same at Working Horse, thanks to a bit of luck. In the winter of 2007 the cold weather needed for icewine did not occur until late January 2008. Tilman, losing hope that he would have an icewine to sell when the new winery opened, went on vacation. Two days after returning home, on a bracingly cold full-moon night, Westbank organic grower Alex Lubchynski offered five tons of frozen Pinot Noir if they were able to accept the grapes by dawn. Tilman and Sara jumped at the chance to make Working Horse's debut icewine. The winery also has a very limited release of 2006 Riesling icewine, called the 30th Anniversary edition of a Hainle icewine.

After selling the family winery in 2002, Tilman became a consulting winemaker. Recently he and Sara, a marketing whiz, set up Estate Vineyards Consulting. He also polished his art by working two crushes abroad, one in Australia and a second one at a South African winery called Vilafonté. There he worked with Zelma Long, a legendary Californian who was the first female winemaker graduate from the University of California and one of Robert Mondavi's first winemakers. "For me it was not just enlightening but formative in that it refocused my mind on what was important in winemaking," Tilman says. "Zelma is such an exacting woman."

To turn Working Horse into a showcase of sustainability, Tilman and Sara have hired a Seattle architect specializing in designing green wineries. The design of the proposed winery includes geothermal heating, a "green" roof, and complex systems to recover waste water and grey water for irrigating the organic vines. Many of the varieties grown here are vines originally planted by Tilman's father three decades ago, including White Chasselas and Red Chasselas.

Perhaps no variety is closer to Tilman's heart than the one his father called Queen of the Vineyard, because that was the only name given it by the original vine supplier. "We figured out that it is a clone of Muscat Ottonel," Tilman says.

AQUAHERBS WINERY HOUSE

Box 2099, Station R, Kelowna, BC V1X 3K5
250.491.9576

THERE MAY NEVER BE A WINE SHOP FOR AQUAHERBS. IT HAS A COMMERCIAL winery licence just so that the owner, chemist Stan Maciaszek, can add ginseng wine (and echinacea wine) to all of the other ginseng products that have emerged from his other company, Okanagan Ginseng Laboratory Ltd. in Kelowna. Stan would actually prefer to sell the wine business if he can find a buyer — probably someone from Asia — who appreciates these curious wines.

Born in Poland in 1940, Stan first came to Canada in 1979 on a two-year post-doctoral program. He returned to Canada in 1982 when Poland's military regime asked him to leave because of his anti-regime views. He taught at Lakehead University until, for family reasons, he moved to the Okanagan in 1990. "I had to look at what I could do in the Okanagan as a chemist," he says. "At that time ginseng was doing phenomenally." So he established his company to develop value-added products, selling the concepts to appropriate manufacturers. He was doing well until a serious car accident in 1996 sidelined him for three years. By then ginseng's boom times had ended. Subsequently Stan applied his skills to the development of other products based on herbs and plants.

"Maybe I was consuming more than the average quantity of wine with my friends here," he says with a laugh. "Someone asked, 'How about trying to make ginseng wine?' " And he took the challenge. The wine is made with both the root, which has medicinal uses, and with the plant's brilliantly red berries, resulting in a vivid garnet-hued wine with the typically earthy flavour of ginseng. From that start Stan moved on to develop a ginseng-flavoured Cabernet, a pomelo liqueur, and a seductively delicious wine with echinacea flowers and honey. More recently he has made trial lots of wine with elderberries and with rosehips. "I like what I do," he says, relaxing in his modest quarters in a Kelowna industrial park. "If I would be younger, I would be fascinated to have a winery."

BACCATA RIDGE WINERY

OPENING PROPOSED FOR 2010–12

66–68 McManus Road, Grindrod, BC V0E 1Y0
250.838.0512

A FORMER TECHNOLOGY MARKETER, SHELDON MOORE SPENT MORE THAN 15 years in Southeast Asia and Australia before returning to his native British Columbia. An interest in grapes developed in Australia. In 2001, he bought a 64.7-hectare (160-acre) farm not far from the Shuswap River. Here in one of British Columbia's more northerly wine-growing areas, his organic vineyard includes Ortega, Gewürztraminer, Siegerrebe, Zweigelt, Gamay, Maréchal Foch, and Vidal (for icewine). He is somewhat ambivalent about opening a winery, having tried to sell the property in 2008 to go to New Zealand. The sale did not go through; he sold his grapes and has put off opening until 2010 at the earliest.

CANYON VIEW VINEYARD

OPENING PROPOSED FOR 2010–12

7315 Canyon View Road, Summerland, BC V0H 1Z7
250.404.8681

KRIMO SOUILAH, WHO HANDLES WEST COAST SALES FOR TONNELLERIE Mercier S.A. of France, discovered the Okanagan during a barrel-selling trip in 2003. "It took me a couple of visits to realize that this is going to be another Napa North, with time," he says. But when he reached that conclusion, he planted Pinot Noir in a quiet Summerland neighbourhood, on a terraced plateau overlooking a canyon, the source of the vineyard name. The winery, which may open as early as 2010, will have a different name but the wine shop will be on the vineyard. There may be a little Chardonnay offered as well, but if Krimo achieves his objectives, he will be making Pinot Noir primarily, not only from his vineyard but with grapes from other selected Summerland vineyards. And only Summerland. "Pinot Noir in this area is perfect," he believes.

Born in Algeria in 1948, Krimo completed his winemaking studies in Montpellier's renowned university and then spent several years working in wineries in southern France and Bordeaux. After wedding an American in France, Krimo moved with his wife to California in 1978. He joined fellow Montpellier classmate Bernard Portet at the Clos du Val winery in Napa and worked there as a winemaker until 1997, when he left to consult and then to run Mercier's barrel sales on the west coast of North America.

Barrel salesmen get to taste a lot of wines. Krimo liked the Okanagan Pinot Noirs he was tasting with his winemaker clients. Since there were far fewer Pinot Noirs than Merlots, he figured that he was more likely to succeed by opening a winery in the less crowded field. He found a four-hectare (10-acre) orchard almost within view of Summerland's Trout Creek railway trestle and planted three clones of Pinot Noir. One was the so-called Scherzinger clone, with cuttings from the vineyard nearby that Edgar Scherzinger planted in the 1970s. (It is now part of Dirty Laundry's holdings.) During one of his early sales trips to the Okanagan, Krimo had taken early morning walks in the vineyard and was impressed with the flavours of the grapes.

In 2008, when his Canyon Road vineyard was reaching full production, Krimo struck a deal to sell the grapes to and have the wines made at the new Hijas Bonitas winery for several years. Technically, Krimo's immigration status prevented him from making the wine; he supervises its production as a consultant, however. Hijas Bonitas is selling these as vineyard-designated wines. It is an arrangement that gives Krimo time to assess his vineyard and the wines and then to order his business affairs so that he can open a winery. "I don't have an ego to make a wine better than the neighbour's," he says. "My point is to make a good wine, to make whatever the dirt here gives me."

EMERALD COAST VINEYARDS

OPENING PROPOSED FOR 2009

2787 Alberni Highway, Port Alberni, BC V9Y 8R2
250.724.2300

A FEW YEARS AFTER PORT ALBERNI'S FIRST VINEYARD WAS STARTED IN 1996 by Vaughan Chase, Evan McLellan decided he would prefer vines on his farm rather than the livestock he had. "Plants just seemed a little quieter," he says. Born in Port Alberni in 1955, Evan operates West Van Isle Contracting Ltd., a company specializing in marine construction. Farming has been an avocation. His property is on the same slope of the Beaufort Range as Vaughan's Chase & Warren Vineyard.

To get started Evan turned for advice to Domaine de Chaberton founder Claude Violet, the first person with a successful commercial vineyard in the Fraser Valley. In

2001 Claude supplied cuttings of Madeleine Angevine from his vineyard. Gradually Evan added to the vineyard until he now has almost five hectares (12 acres). All are early-ripening varieties, including Schönburger, Siegerrebe, Reichensteiner, Pinot Gris, Pinot Noir, and Maréchal Foch.

Because the Alberni Valley gets summer temperatures above 30°C (86°F), ripening usually is not a problem. The bigger challenge is keeping birds, deer, bears, and raccoons from getting to the grapes first. Helped by his son, Adam, and consultant George Phiniotis, Evan began making Emerald Coast's initial wines in 2008, with the planned opening in 2009. The wine shop is strategically located on the heavily travelled highway to Tofino and Ucluelet on the Pacific coast. "There's about a million and a half people a year go by there," Evan says. "And then they turn around and come back."

ENRICO WINERY

3280 Telegraph Road, Mill Bay, BC V0R 2P3

HARRY SMITH, THE OWNER OF THIS WINERY, IS A HARD-DRIVING VANCOUVER Island businessman who honed his competitive skills in hockey. Born in Trail, he played defence with the world champion 1961 Trail Smoke Eaters, and later with the Detroit Red Wings and with numerous editions of Team Canada. In the early 1980s he coached the Swiss national hockey team, during which time he lived with a winery owner near Lausanne and picked grapes during one vintage. That was the start of his interest in wine.

Harry pursued business rather than hockey because, in his day, there was not enough money in hockey. He walked out of a Red Wings camp in the early 1960s because he thought an offer of $30,000 a year was inadequate. A generation later Harry's son, Jim, got a $1.5-million signing bonus from the Red Wings. However, after a couple of years in the American Hockey League, he joined his father in running Columbia Fuels Inc., the largest petroleum products distributor on Vancouver Island.

Success in business has allowed Harry to invest in real estate (including a coffee plantation in Hawaii). In the 1990s he bought a Cowichan Valley farm and raised beef until he decided one day there might be a better return from grapes and winemaking. Late in 2006 he engaged a consultant and a vineyard manager to switch the 20-hectare (50-acre) farm to vines. Within two years the Telegraph Road side of the property was growing seven hectares (17 acres) of vines. Gravel was being removed from the rear of the property, making room to contour a good exposure and eventually plant more vines. The varieties in the initial planting include Pinot Gris, Pinot Noir, Ortega, and two Blattner varieties, Cabernet Foch and Cabernet Libre.

The tentative plan calls for opening a winery no earlier than 2010 and perhaps later. During a cycling holiday in Tuscany a few years ago, Harry was impressed by stills and by grappa. As a result he also plans to include a still at Enrico Winery. The winery name is the Spanish equivalent of Henry, his given name. It seems it was suggested by his Mexican-born wife, Maru. She is a realtor and a marketer, and Harry hopes that she will look after marketing the wines. "It's a business, if you are going to do it right, not a hobby," Harry says of the wine business. "You have to devote a lot of time to it. And I don't have much time to devote to it."

HEAVEN'S DOOR VINEYARD WINERY

64455 Ainslie Road North, Boston Bar, BC V0K 1C0
604.867.9721

HEAVEN'S DOOR VINEYARD IS A JOINT VENTURE NEAR BOSTON BAR IN THE Fraser Canyon launched by friends Gina Davidson and Sandra Clark. About one hectare (2½ acres) of vines, primarily Pinot Noir and Chardonnay, has been planted since 2003 on a property owned by Sandra, a banker, and her husband. The impetus for vines appears to have come from Ron Davidson, Gina's husband, a former chef and now a millwright who has become a keen home winemaker. He grows 27 vines at the Davidson's Boston Bar home, an eclectic assortment of varieties purchased or scrounged from a variety of sources. These budding vintners are still discovering the challenges of pioneering a new wine region. Their first significant production was 123 litres (22 gallons) of Chardonnay from the 2008 vintage. However, the birds beat them to the Pinot Noir.

Grape growing in the Fraser Canyon began in the 1960s at Riverland Irrigated Farm near Lillooet, an experimental farm operated by BC Electric. After the power company was taken over by the province to become BC Hydro, the farm was sold in 1972. Farm manager Robert Roshard moved some of the vines, primarily Maréchal Foch, to his farm beside the Fraser south of Lillooet. That small plot, about two hundred vines, has produced reliably since 1974.

In 2004 a group of Fraser Canyon landowners, including Robert's daughter, Christ'l, and her husband, Doug Robson, decided to make trial plantings of other wine grapes. Christ'l, a former community newspaper editor and a municipal councillor and mayor in Lillooet, wanted to explore new economic development in the community to replace the collapsing ginseng farms and the struggling forest industry. The group secured vine cuttings from several Oliver vineyards. In the spring of 2005 and again in the spring of 2006, four plots totalling 1.6 hectares (four acres), were planted between Lillooet and Lytton to test 18 varieties. With provincial funding, almost one hundred remote weather data recorders were also deployed. There is certainly enough sunlight in the Lytton-Lillooet corridor to ripen wine grapes.

(A mayor of Lillooet once fried an egg on the main street.) However, there is some question about what grape varieties can survive the severely cold early winters that occur from time to time.

Doug and Christ'l, who also planted Petit Verdot and Viognier, began picking modest harvests from their one acre (0.4 hectare) in 2007 and making wine for personal consumption. Pinot Gris and Gewürztraminer show early promise. Cabernet Sauvignon seems winter tender. Several more years of experience will be needed to determine the best varieties of wine grapes and then to attract a winery investor. "The whole intent of the project is to entice somebody already established in the wine industry to move some of their business to this area," Christ'l says. "If there is going to be a winery here, it is likely not my husband and myself who will be doing it."

KOOTENAY RIDGE WINERY

OPENING PROPOSED FOR 2009

> 1140 – 27th Avenue South, Creston, BC V0B 1G1
> 250.428.8768.

WITH THE INTENTION OF RETIRING IN CRESTON, CALGARY PETROLEUM engineer Bob Johnson and Petra Flaa, his wife, bought a cherry orchard there in 2001. Then Al and Marleen Hoag planted a vineyard in Creston to support their Skimmerhorn Winery. In 2006, just as that winery was being developed, an apple orchard across the road from Skimmerhorn came on the market. Bob and Petra sold their cherry orchard, bought this property, and quickly replaced the apple trees with 5.9 hectares (14½ acres) of grapes. Forty percent of the vineyard grows three clones of Pinot Noir. The remainder of the property is split among Chardonnay, Pinot Gris, Sauvignon Blanc, and a little bit of Schönburger (for blending purposes). The winery's first vintage is expected to be 2009, with wines made from the estate vineyard and from grapes purchased from a nearby grower.

Bob was born in Red Deer in 1958 and has had a long career as an oil industry consultant. Petra, who was born in Brandon, formerly managed the staff at a computer industry help desk but, with courses from the University of Washington, has become the full-time manager of their Creston vineyard. The couple are long-time wine enthusiasts; Bob once made wine at home before becoming a collector with a good cellar. In recent years they have spent a lot of time touring wine regions, tasting and seeing how others have designed their wineries. Their objective is to produce up to five thousand cases per year at Kootenay Ridge, employing a professional winemaker. "Eventually I do want to retire and move there and be part of it," Bob says. "I think my forte will be more in marketing."

KOOTENAY RIVER WINES & SPIRITS

Creston, BC

WHEN KOOTENAY RIVER WINES AND SPIRITS (KRWS) BEGINS MARKETING ITS products in late 2009 or early 2010, it expects to offer not just wine but British Columbia's first potato vodka. KRWS is owned and operated by a local Creston family, who took note of the substantial potato production in the area. KRWS plans to source potatoes from a local potato farm and from other BC producers and turn the surplus potatoes into potable spirits, using a still that is imported from Germany. For wines, KRWS will get grapes from a one-hectare (2½-acre) vineyard on a hillside overlooking Creston where two clones of Pinot Gris, three clones of Pinot Noir, and two clones of Chardonnay were planted in 2007. They are also going to grow Rotberger and Pinot Meunier in a vineyard at nearby Erickson. By operating under a commercial licence, KRWS has given itself the option to produce other wines with purchased local and Okanagan grapes as well as with imported bulk wine.

MAAN FARMS FRUIT WINERY

790 McKenzie Road, Abbotsford, BC V2S 7N4

DEVINDER MAAN AND HUSBAND KRIS ARE PLANNING THIS WINERY AS A LOGICAL value-added extension of their Abbotsford-area farms and farm markets. Kris's family emigrated from the Punjab in the early 1970s and began growing vegetables a few years later. In the 1980s they switched to more lucrative raspberries, strawberries, and blueberries and began selling them at farm markets after Devinder joined the family through marriage. Also born in India, she is a teacher by profession but runs their two farm markets while Kris is a technical manager at a fruit processing plant.

The decision to add a winery at one of the farm markets is driven by the volatility of berry prices. "You have to be diversified," Devinder maintains. More than two years of planning has gone into this project, including visits to most of the other wineries already operating in the Fraser Valley. Their own winery plans call for erecting a building with the personality of a large country store, serving both as a market and as the wine shop, strategically located near the intersection of two busy highways.

MISCONDUCT WINE COMPANY

Penticton, BC

AS THIS BOOK WAS BEING COMPLETED, MISCONDUCT WAS STILL A "VIRTUAL" winery — that is, the wines (the first vintage was 2006) have been made in a custom crush winery and are sold directly to clients in a database maintained by the partners. A storefront Penticton wine shop is planned, giving Misconduct more visibility than it has now. The winery is the creation of Richard Silva and what he calls a "clandestine syndicate" of silent partners. The marketing strategy here is the mystery, creating curiosity about the wines by deliberate non-disclosure of the partners and the vineyard sources.

"Our clandestine syndicate, the Uncrushables, will not reveal its vineyard sources or what truck those grapes may have fallen off of," Richard says, reading from a back label. "Many secret meetings, late night sit-downs and back road handshakes [assures you] that you are drinking wines from the best grapes of the south Okanagan." Some of the labels are built around 1920s gangster themes. "The St. Valentine's Massacre Rosé is a play on the story behind the St. Valentine's Day massacre," Richard says. "The wine is the bleed from seven of our varietals, representing the seven guys that Al Capone whacked."

A lot of this whimsy represents Richard's irrepressible personality. An Oliver grower and vineyard manager born in 1971, he confesses that he was a rebellious youth. "In my early 20s, I was a nightmare to society," he says. That's why the winery is called Misconduct, even though he has turned his life around now.

MONTAGU CELLARS WINERY

OPENED 2005

#29 1350 West 6th Avenue, Vancouver BC V6H 1A7
604.837.0086
www.montagucellars.com
When to visit: no tastings

THIS IS MORE A PROFESSIONAL HOBBY THAN A WINERY. OWNER TOM DOUGHTY, a Vancouver restaurant owner, makes about one hundred cases of wine a year, most of it red. Currently, he uses the facilities of Blackwood Lane winery in Langley, selling through that winery's licence to clients. "I love to make wine," Tom says. "When I am on the crush pad, I am just giddy. I would love to make more, but I would have to ask somebody for money. I always like to use my own money—and I am not rich." Most of his own capital has gone to developing restaurants.

Tom was born in Calgary in 1975, the son of a former Royal Air Force pilot who christened him Thomas Scott Montagu Doughty IV and had him educated in Victoria's elite St. Michael's University School. To his father's exasperation, Tom never used his haughty moniker. Thus, when he launched his wine label, he called it Montagu Cellars as an homage to his father. When Tom finished college (a humanities degree with a major in European history), he planned to study law but became a sommelier instead. Two years after acquiring that diploma, he also graduated at the top of his class in a professional cooking course on French cuisine — a course he took just to improve his knowledge of food and wine pairing. Winemaking was the next logical step in rounding out his skills. In 2004, he talked Poplar Grove winemaker Ian Sutherland into coaching Tom through his first professional vintage. With a start like that, he has not set a foot wrong.

MT. LEHMAN WINERY

OPENING PROPOSED FOR 2009

> 5094 Mt. Lehman Road, Abbotsford, BC V4X 1Y3
> 604.854.5406
> www.mtlehmanwinery.com

DEVELOPER VERN SIEMENS BEGAN GRAPE GROWING TRIALS WITH A 1.2-HECTARE (three-acre) vineyard he planted here in 1989, soon after he and his wife, Charleen, acquired this 32-hectare (80-acre) property where her parents once ran a dairy farm. He estimates that he tested perhaps 60 different varieties. Once he narrowed his selections down, he planted another 3.2 hectares (eight acres), mostly Pinot Noir and Pinot Gris, and converted a machine shed to a modest winery. The tasting room was scheduled to open in 2009.

Vern was born in 1956 in Paraguay, where his parents helped establish a Mennonite colony. He grew up in Abbotsford, where his parents moved soon after he was born. Armed with a college business diploma, Vern succeeded as a builder of condominiums and commercial buildings. "That's why I can pay for my hobby," he says. "I have a passion for wine." That began when he was still in the eighth grade and made raspberry wine. He progressed through most of the other country wines before moving to grapes. His self-taught winemaking is informed by a deep knowledge of international wines. He and Charleen travel extensively to taste wines, and they keep their personal cellar stocked with Burgundies and other Pinot Noirs. "We drink Pinot Noir virtually every day," he says.

It goes without saying that Pinot Noir will be the signature wine at Mt. Lehman, although the winery debuts with a selection including blends made both from Okanagan grapes and from his own vineyard. Vern has set a high bar for himself. "I drink every kind of wine, so I have a fair idea of the kind of flavours I really want," he says. "Eventually, if I can't pull it off, I'll shut it down." He seems not to expect that outcome, since he has already picked out the site on the farm for Mt. Lehman's showpiece winery.

ORCHARD HILL ESTATE CIDERY

OPENED: 2006

> 23404 Highway 97, Oliver, BC V0H 1T0
> 250.495.4325
> www.orchardhillcidery.com

THIS CIDERY WAS OPENED IN 2006 BY GIAN DHALIWAL AND HIS SON, RAVI. Grape growers and orchardists, they have also been selling fruit and vegetables at the Sunshine Valley Fruit Market. The market's highly visible location beside Highway 97, midway between Oliver and Osoyoos, serves admirably for the cidery's outlet as well.

PLATINUM HILLS WINERY

OPENING PROPOSED FOR 2010

> 9756 – 382nd Avenue, Oliver, BC V0H 1T0

SET TO OPEN IN 2010, PLATINUM HILLS GREW FROM LANNY KINRADE'S decision to develop a vineyard after running a turf farm and then growing vegetables. "I got tired of managing the farm," he says. "Most of my friends in Oliver have vineyards and wineries." Lanny was born in Kimberly, where both his father and grandfather worked in the famous Sullivan lead-zinc mine. Perhaps because the mine was nearing the end of production, Lanny's father advised him to find different employment. He became a telephone lineman in Vancouver until he moved to the Okanagan in 1988. He ran his own organic vegetable farm near Oliver for 10 years before selling it in 2006.

"I do renovations on the side," he says. "But I wanted to keep my hands in the dirt." He planted 1.2 hectares (three acres) of Cabernet Sauvignon on a property where the previous owner had had a wedding chapel. When it came time to apply for a winery licence, Lanny considered Hidden Chapel before settling on Platinum Hills, a reference to the precious-metal mines that once flourished in the South Okanagan.

Even though some friends suggested he plant Merlot, Lanny decided to chance Cabernet Sauvignon, a favourite variety of his. He is considering Malbec to complete his plantings, and he expects to buy other Bordeaux varieties and Syrah from neighbours. He is one of three growers occupying this warm microclimate on a slope above the highway, about five minutes north of Oliver. Although confident in his own winemaking, he shrewdly has retained Charles Herrold, the owner and winemaker at Blackwood Lane, as his mentor through the initial vintages.

SEOUL RICEWINE

OPENED: 2003

> 208 – 20167 96th Avenue, Langley, BC V1M 3C5
> 604.513.3605

SINCE OPENING THIS WINERY IN 2003, SUP YOO KEEPS A LOW PROFILE, selling his traditional rice wines almost entirely within the Korean community in Vancouver. Born in Seoul in 1950, he came to Canada in 1996. In Korea he had been a dealer in Canadian lumber used in constructing timber frame houses. The decision to open a winery grew from the wines he was making at home. "Some friends asked why I don't make it and sell it?" he says. "The Korean community wanted to see this kind of product, so that is the main reason I started this."

Using California rice he produces two basic wines that are similar to Japanese sake: one has eight percent alcohol and the other has 14 percent. The most likely place to find these wines is in a Korean restaurant. "It is impossible to sell it through the liquor stores," he explains. "Our rice wine is slightly fermenting. It is kind of alive. So it should be stored in a walk-in cooler at 6 degrees Celsius."

THADD SPRINGS ESTATE WINERY

OPENING PROPOSED FOR 2012

> 2761 Shuswap Road, Kamloops, BC V2H 1S9

IN WHAT MANY SEE AS THE PIONEERING OF A NEW WINE REGION, BUSINESSMEN Ed and Jeff Collett started in 2008 to plant what should ultimately be a 22.3-hectare (55-acre) vineyard just 16 kilometres (10 miles) east of Kamloops. They are planning to open Thadd Springs Estate Winery about 2012, the first major vineyard and winery in an area that has only had hobby vineyards until now. The Collett brothers, advised by consultants Richard Cleave and Harry McWatters, have contoured and planted a choice, sloping southern exposure above the banks of the South Thompson River. The varietals chosen include Pinot Gris, Riesling, Chardonnay, and Gewürztraminer for whites and Merlot, Cabernet Franc, Pinot Noir, and perhaps Zweigelt for reds. The planting has been stretched over several years, in part to assess the site and what will thrive.

This is a controversial planting because the Kamloops area on occasion has severely cold winters with dry, desiccating winds. "Winter is one of the issues we have to deal with," Jeff acknowledges. "That's the way it goes." Some of the experts he and his brother consulted initially told them to forget about planting vinifera here. They are gambling that the obvious trend to warmer winters will allow the vineyard to succeed, along with some precautionary practices. To mitigate the winds they have placed windbreaks made from ginseng shade cloth on both the eastern and western borders of the vineyard. They thought of planting trees until they realized that trees would provide habitat to grape-eating birds.

Both brothers were born in the Fraser Valley — Ed in 1958 and Jeff in 1961 — and grew up in Kamloops. In 1987 Ed set up a company that sells and services mining equipment. Jeff is a cabinetmaker by trade who once taught at Thompson Rivers University before setting up a construction company with his brother. Jeff is a wine lover who introduced his brother to the passion. Thadd Springs was conceived when Jeff organized a wine weekend in the Okanagan in 2006 that included a lunch in the vineyard-view restaurant at Quails' Gate.

"Ed and Vicki were pretty impressed with the whole thing," Jeff says of his brother and sister-in-law. "Ed basically said, 'I want one of these. Find me one.' " After cold-calling at the door of a farmhouse on the bank of the South Thompson, Jeff found the property, which the brothers bought in 2007 for their vineyard. Ultimately they expect to build an attractive winery there with a restaurant. Local history buffs, they will name the winery after a creek on the property. The creek in turn is named for Thaddeus Harper, the 19th-century American-born rancher who founded the legendary Gang Ranch, once one of the largest ranches in the British Empire.

TWO REDWOODS ESTATE WINERY

27907 Township Line Road, Abbotsford, BC V4X 1P8
604.607.0323

ABBOTSFORD LAWYER PATRICK SELINGER AND HIS WIFE, JANET, WILL HAVE sparkling wines in mind when they launch their Two Redwoods Estate Winery sometime in the next several years. Their 1.5-hectare (3½-acre) vineyard, planted gradually since 2000 on a slightly rolling property, a former daffodil farm just north of the Trans-Canada Highway, grows Chardonnay, Pinot Noir, Pinot Meunier, and Gamay. "We live in an area where weather is always a factor," Janet says. Her intuitive skills for vineyard management were developed during a 15-year career as a florist, followed later by four years in quality control with a Fraser Valley greenhouse. "We just never knew if our conditions would ripen grapes. We planted varieties so that, in a marginal year, we would be able to make sparkling wine. Hopefully that will be our little niche."

The winery, however, is driven by Patrick's passion. "For many years I always wanted to do it," he says. "I really enjoy wine and I like different wines. I like the fact that different varieties from different areas taste different from year to year. It is one of those mysteries of life that you can look at." Born in 1960 in New Westminster, he spent 10 years as a BC Parks ranger before enrolling in law school. A baseball fan, he chose Osgoode Hall in Toronto in 1987 so that he could also take in big-league ball games. He and Janet began touring Niagara wineries, becoming so immersed in the business that Patrick did a law school thesis on the free trade agreement and its impact on wineries. Today the demands of a busy law practice have delayed the winery indefinitely, but it remains in their plans.

WINDRIFT ESTATE WINERY

OPENING PROPOSED FOR 2010

2400 Anderton Road, Comox, BC V9M 4E5
250.339.9274

BILL MONTGOMERY NURTURED THE DREAM OF A WINERY FOR ABOUT 10 YEARS before moving ahead on one in 2007 in a big way. Over two years he planted 23,000 vines on his Comox farm within sight of the military jets that thunder overhead from the nearby airport. Born in Prince Rupert in 1949, Bill formerly owned Burrard Towing Company, a Vancouver tugboat firm. (His father had owned one in Prince Rupert as well.) After selling the business, he and his wife moved in 1996 to the farm near Comox, where they kept some livestock. Bill hesitated to plant vines because, as his wife put it, he thought one needed to be born into the wine business — until he decided otherwise. "I wish I had done it 10 years ago because I would have been 10 years younger," he reflects now.

On the advice of an Okanagan consultant, Bill planted mostly the Pinot family, including 8,500 Pinot Noir vines, along with Gamay and little bit of Merlot. The farm's capacious barn, built in 1990 when this was a dairy farm, is gradually being converted for use as a winery. There is room on the barn's mezzanine floor for a generous tasting room with a view over the vineyard. At the earliest Bill's winery would open in 2010, although he is inclined to take his time and stretch the timetable a few years. His enthusiasm for the dream is undiminished, even if it is tempered by the scale of the project he launched. "I have friends who have a blueberry farm," he says. "I thought this has to be kind of similar to what they are doing. Well, they have 10 rows, I have 250 rows. I have to bring pruners in from the Okanagan to help me."

INDEX

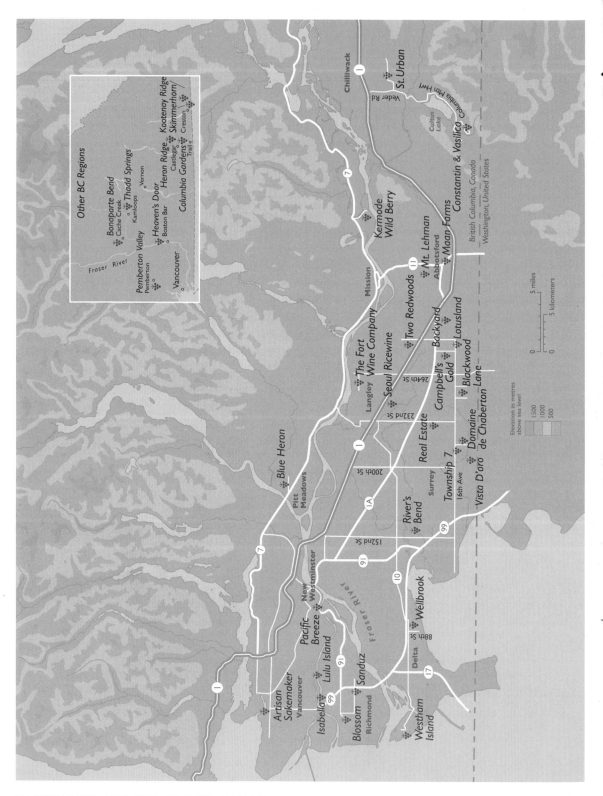

VANCOUVER AND THE FRASER VALLEY